Airpistols

3rd Edition

Revised and enlarged by

Dennis E. Hiller

ISBN 0 9507046 6 0

Published by Dennis E. Hiller

Acknowledgements

My sincere thanks go to all the numerous people who have helped in ways known and unknown that have led to the publication of "Airpistols" Third Edition.

In particular I would like to thank Basil Sykes of Swindon for his regular Christmas food parcels of cigars, booze and food that go down and up very well. My deep appreciation goes to Bob and Jackie Gulliford of Cardiff for their excellent coastal rescue service. Chris Young, of Southampton, for the bottomless pit of bottomless humour. S. J. Roche, who always had faith in me, even though I never realised it. Paul Mattic, my missing link with the past. Fred Liady of America for many favours yet to be given. Jim Cunningham of Bellfield, Kilmarnock, for teaching me Scottish. My son, Jonathan Euxton, what can I say about him — one day my son, all this will be yours!! Errol Calvert of Joplin, U.S.A. for his Welsh jokes. My mother, who started the whole thing off by giving in to my father. To Archie Morgan who died, and to Kane Thorn.

DENNIS E. HILLER
56 Princess Way, Euxton, Chorley,
Lancs PR7 6PJ, England

Previous Editions and Publications

1978 "Air Rifles" First Edition
1979 "Air Pistols" First Edition
1980 "Air Rifles" Second Edition (Revised & enlarged)
1982 "Air Pistols" Second Edition (Revised & enlarged)
1984 "Air Rifles" Third Edition (Revised & enlarged)
1984 "Complete Airgunner" (1907), R. B. Townshend B.A.
1992 "Complete Airgunner"

1993 "Airpistols" Third Edition

HILLER, DENNIS E.
Airpistols — 3rd Edition
1. Air guns — Collectors and collecting
1. Title
Library Reference No.

ISBN 0 9507046 6 0

Typeset and printed by
T. Snape & Co. Ltd.,
Boltons Court, Preston, Lancs.
Tel: (0772) 254553

Introduction

The time is now right for the Third Edition "Airpistols" as since the last publication a lot of new information has been collected and researched. As this information comes to light it is added to the original text of "Airpistols" Second Edition and will gradually build itself into a publication that meets the needs of collectors, dealers and dabblers in the now expanding field of collecting airguns. At the moment the collecting of airguns is open to anyone over seventeen and is without the useless red-tape of licences etc.

Airpistols appear in alphabetical order by manufacturer where possible, unless the manufacturer is not known: then it will appear under its selling name, i.e. "Limit Gat" will appear under "L" as actual manufacturer is not known. Within the maker's name, where more than one model exists, I have tried to place them in chronological order and follow the particular model through as information will allow. The airpistols are listed with a text made up of the following: MODEL, MAKER, DATE, VALUATION, DETAILS.

MODEL: Usually the model name appears somewhere on the airgun and this is used. Sometimes the one model can last for years with variations, as with the Webley airpistols, so I have treated these as a set and continued their progress until cessation, then back peddled to any parallel models. Some airguns are produced overseas, and may appear under the importer's name, as is the Milbro G10 repeating airpistol which appears to be made in America.

MAKER: Again, this usually appears on the airgun and is entered as such. Some makers are not known so the importer may be entered in their place.

DATE: Usually approximate and only more research of catalogues and advertisements will produce a more clearer picture. Dates can even be established by talking to the older generation. If any readers have information that they feel would be useful, please don't hesitate to contact the Author through one of his adverts in "Airgun World" or "Airgunner".

VALUATION: The Author cannot accept any responsibility for monies lost or gained in any deals made based on the valuations and other price guides given. They are only a guide and should be used as such. Airgun prices depend on condition, how badly you need to sell, or how badly someone wishes to purchase from you, even area, as little interest creates low prices and vice versa. Secondhand airgun values have remained very stable over the last few years and only the very rare and minty specimens have gone up in value. The run-of-the-mill airgun has in some cases even taken a small fall in value, but so has almost everything else. It also takes about nine months to prepare this publication so even now prices should be used as a guide only, as even these vary from the recommended retail price down to the quick turn-over discount price airgun merchant. Three price guides are shown, the first followed by "n" is the approximate new price and will of course only apply to current airguns. This new price will try to be its recommended retail price, but you should be able to purchase below this figure if you shop around, unless the discount shops do not stock the particular model required. The second price will be two figures and represent the average values you would expect to pay for a secondhand example from average to very good condition, i.e. £20-£30. For rough or minty specimens the asking prices could be lower or higher respectively. Bargains are always to be found and when they appear they make collecting even more interesting. The last two figures will have "a" after them and stand for auction: this represents the average limits of what to expect if you place the airgun into auction. Obviously a gun auction and not a general household auction. Again a guide only, as sometimes the prices realised can be very low or even the sky is the limit! These auction prices can also represent the reserve price placed on the airgun and it could be that bidding may not have reached this figure whereupon the airgun is withdrawn from sale and returned to the owner. Where no auction price is stated then the airpistol has not been recorded in auctions.

MUZZLE VELOCITY: These have been discontinued as they were very time consuming and of very little value.

WEEKLY MAGAZINES:

"Exchange and Mart", available Thursdays
"Shooting Times", available Thursdays

MONTHLY MAGAZINES:

"Guns Review", Ravenhill Publishing Co. Ltd.
"Airgun World", Burlington Publishing Co. Ltd.
"Airgunner", Romsey Publishing

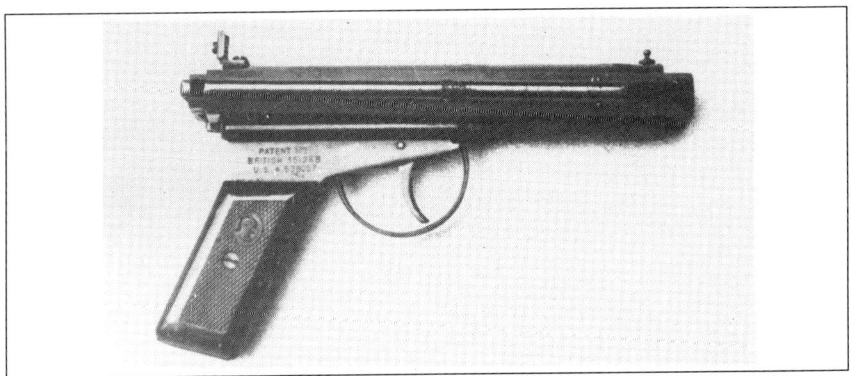

The "Warrior" R.H.S. (early model).

Warrior airpistol, later design. Note no rounding off of front of cocking lever, and "turn-back" of trigger guard.

The "Warrior" L.H.S. (early pattern).

"Warrior" box lid. Union Jack forms background.

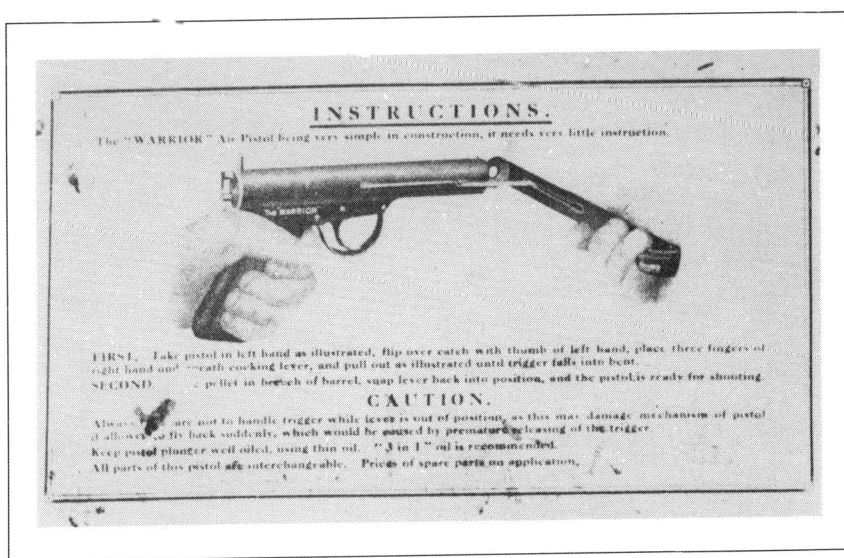

Inside of Warrior lid.

Model: **THE "WARRIOR"**

Maker: **Accles & Shelvoke Ltd.,**
Talford Street Engineering Works,
Aston, Birmingham 6, England.

Date: Between 1931 and around 1939.

Valuation: £50 - £125, £40a - £70a, although have seen prices as high as £105 gained in auction. Boxed mint examples have been sold as high as £225.

Details: Above example is boxed. Measures 7½ inches long. Blue finish with Vulcanite grips. ·177 rifled barrel running down the centre of the piston. Cocked by side lever pivoted at front. On L.H.S. of frame is stamped "THE "WARRIOR" MADE IN ENGLAND" just above the grip, and on the other side is stamped "PATENT NOS. BRITISH 351268 U.S.A. 538057". Serial number is not visible although this usually appears on the front metal strap of the grip. Grips are black, chequered with a warrior's plumed helmet set in an oval. Weight 29½ ozs.

Other "Warrior"'s differed from the above in that stamped on the L.H.S. of the action above the butt grip appeared "THE WARRIOR" — ACCLES & SHELVOKE LTD — BIRMINGHAM", whilst on the other side appeared "F. Clarke's PATENT Nos. — BRIT. 351268 — U.S.A. 538057". It would appear that the above model without serial number could be a very early variation. The Patent 351268 was taken out during 1930/31 and covered the side lever cocking action. Further details of the above patent may be seen in *"Guns Review"*, April, 1980. In the end of the cocking lever is a breech seal for the rear of action, should this ever need replacing, it has been suggested that the barrel breech washer from the Feinwerkbau 124/127 sporting air rifle should fit. The Webley Junior mainspring should fit the action.

Appears to have been available nickel plated in small numbers. Interesting to note that James George Accles was born in Bendigo, Australia, 1850. Educated in the U.S.A. and later became an apprentice to Colt. He later came to England and became the senior partner of Accles & Shelvoke.

The Warrior altered very little during its production run, but some minor alterations were made as follows:

First models were produced without serial numbers, which is unusual as many airgun manufacturers started off using serial numbers, then stopped in order to cut production costs, as did Webley's. These without serial numbers were stamped "THE WARRIOR MADE IN ENGLAND" on one side of the body and "PAT NOS. BRITISH 351268. U.S.A. 538057" on the other side. Soon after the start of production the inscriptions were altered to "THE WARRIOR, MADE BY ACCLES & SHELVOKE LTD., BIRMINGHAM" and "F. CLARKE'S PATENT NOS. BRIT. 351268. U.S.A. 538057". This second model also had the serial number stamped on the front butt strap and earliest serial number encountered is 1176 to the highest, 57707. The first models also had the front part of the side cocking lever shaved off, whereas on the later types this was omitted and the front was almost square with the front of the barrel. Another give-away to age is that on the early models the barrel protruded about half an inch out from the front whereas on the later models the barrel was encased in a square projection and did not protrude when the cocking lever was closed. Finally, towards the end of production, about serial number 4777, the trigger guard was altered from the circular shape to one in which the rear was bent out instead of inwards in order to give a more comfortable grip.

For further details see *"Airgun World"*, September, 1981. Nearly all Warriors encountered have been in ·177, but the Author has seen three ·22 Warriors with serial numbers, 2768, 3202 and 3310, all were rifled.

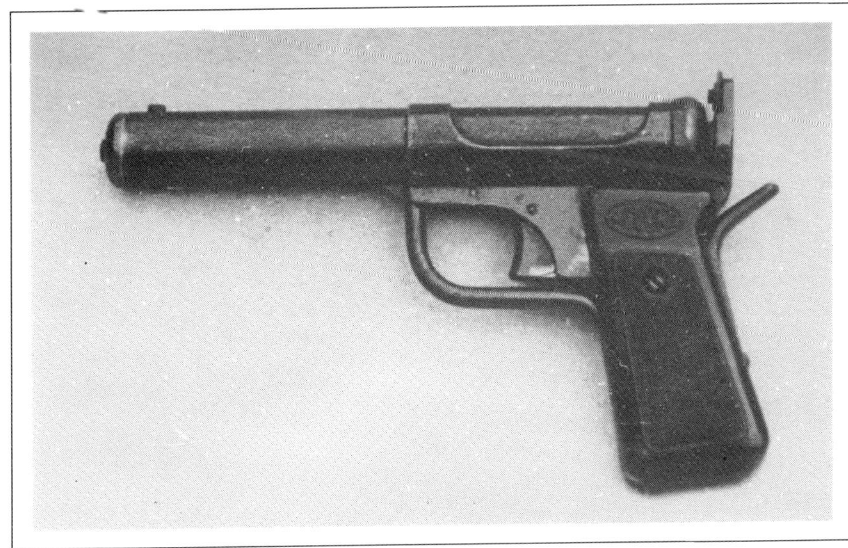

Acvoke airpistol.

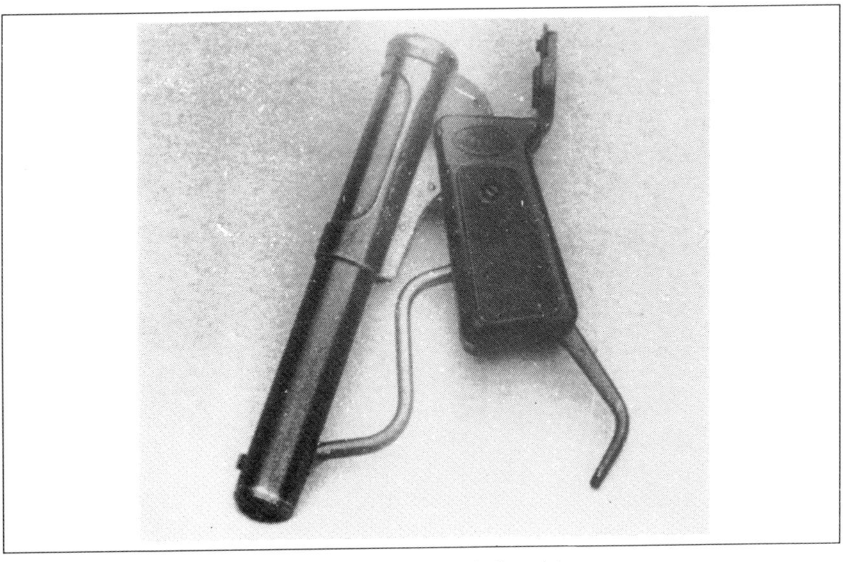

Acvoke airpistol in cocked position.

Boxed Acvoke airpistol

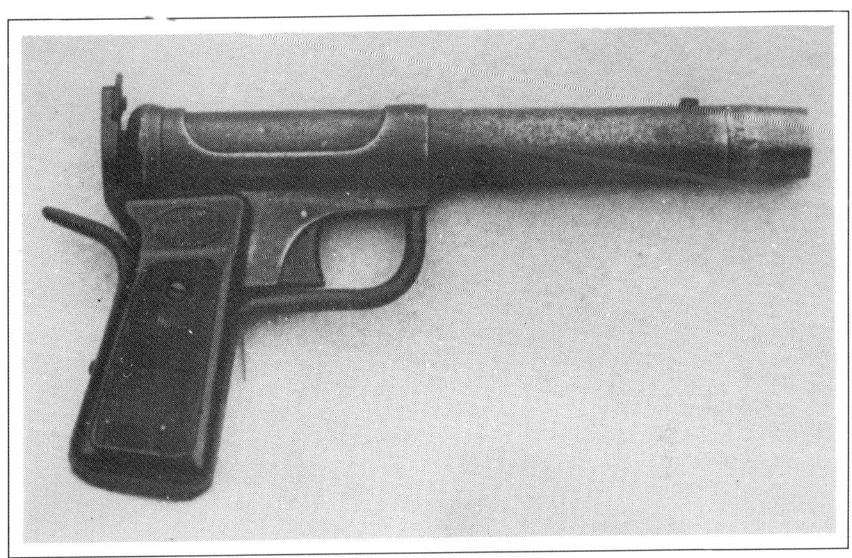

Acvoke with cork firing adaptor.

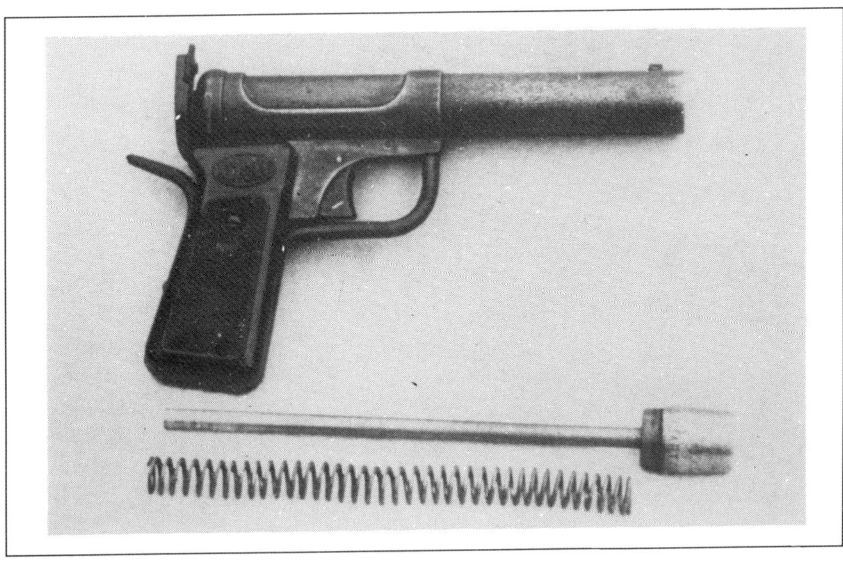

Cork firing adaptor stripped.

Model: **"ACVOKE"**

Maker: **Accles & Shelvoke Ltd.,**
Talford Street Works,
Talford Street, Aston, Birmingham 6.
Address at time of manufacture.

Date: From around 1946 to 1956.

Valuation: £50 - £125, boxed examples have fetched between £150 and £200. £50a - £90a.

Details: Unusual cocking action and recoil. Blued metal with black plastic grips. Cocking lever has pellet gauge and a serial number stamped on side. "ACVOKE" on top of each grip. At back of air cylinder above cocking lever is a circular print of maker's name, address, and "Patent Applied For". Photo also shows a cork firing adaptor that screws into the front of the air cylinder. The copper air pipe is smaller than ·177 so the air pistol can only be used for corks. The head of the cork adaptor is marked "ADAPTOR FOR CORK SHOOTING". Numbers are 13858 & 13227 with adaptor. Advertised as having no leather washers.

It would appear that towards the end of production the stamping of serial numbers ceased as I have seen a boxed example bearing no serial number. Available in ·177 only. The above was designed by a John Arrowsmith in 1946. Patent number 619108 of 1946 with provisional number 34486/46 was finally accepted on the 3rd March, 1949. For further details see *"Guns Review",* October, 1980. The cocking lever back strap often had a small hole acting as a pellet guide or sizer, the serial number was also stamped on the back strap. Unusual airpistol in that the rifling is anti-clockwise.

Over zealous cocking will cause the slender trigger guard to bend into itself and thus shortening the actual length in the travel of the cocking arm along the chamber slot. This will eventually lead to even more strenuous effort in trying to get the action to engage until finally no engagement can be made at all. Although this gives the impression that the sear has failed, try removing the trigger guard and gently bending it into the more correct "S" shape — in other words, open out the shape a little and see if this is successful before attacking the sear arrangement.

Serial numbers seen range from 10076 to 13111, which begs the question "Did they start from 10000?". Number 13227 was fitted with the cork firing adaption.

The "Firefly" by E. Anson.

Model: **"FIREFLY"**

Maker: **E. Anson,**
Steelhouse Lane, Birmingham, England.

Date: Advertised 1932/1933.

Valuation: Due to its rarity, boxed specimens have changed hands for as much as £200. Usually £50 - £100. None have appeared in Auctions.

Details: Quite a rare model of the Gat style air pistol. The butt and trigger block is one casting with "THE FIREFLY" on the L.H.S., whilst on the other side appears "FIREFLY". The casting is painted black and gives most of the weight to the airpistol. Outer airchamber is nickel plated with simple rearsight cut and bent up from body of chamber tube. At the rear is a small hole for a spring that joined with the removeable breech plug thus preventing any chance of loosing it. On the above the spring is missing. The air chamber is of wide measurement, being one inch across on the inside.

The outer casing of the barrel appears to be WOOD with a black enamelled finish. As with all gats the barrel is ·177 smoothbore. Barrel travel when fired is 1⅜ inches. Foresight is a simple pillar. The metal trigger is blued with cut out for body screw and nut, stamped on the L.H.S. "O.K." and on the other side "ANSON". Seen advertised in 1933 costing 8/6 and price inclosed in box for above being 13/6, so allowing for slow rate of inflation, the period of availability could have been quite long, say up to the outbreak of W.W.2.

Note label in box is bordered by a swastika design, which would have been very popular if produced during the War. The barrel breech screw has a floating wire loop for the other end of the captive spring to prevent loss of the pellet pusher. The travel of the pistol/barrel is short, but to make up for this there are two mainsprings, one inside the other as with the Walther LP53 airpistol. For an exploded diagram see *"Airgun World"*, 1978.

Abas Major, Serial number 26.

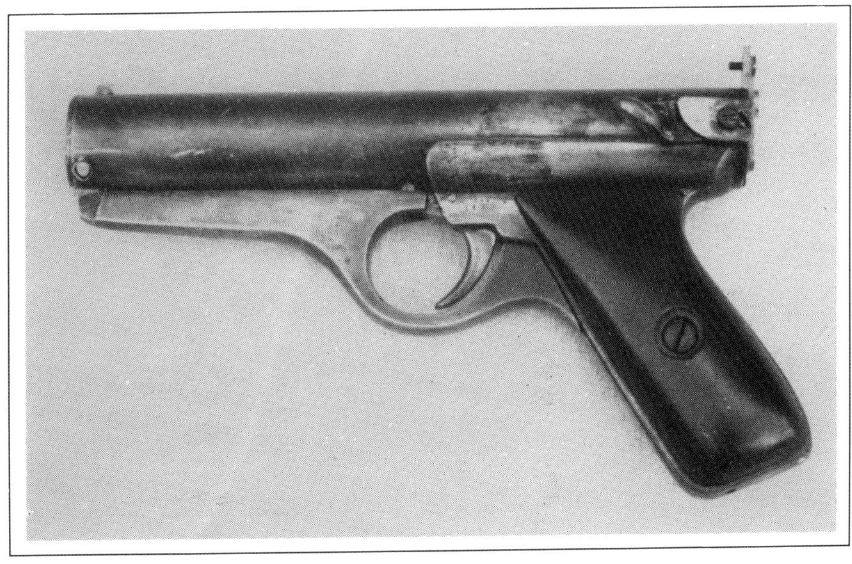

Abas Major, left hand side.

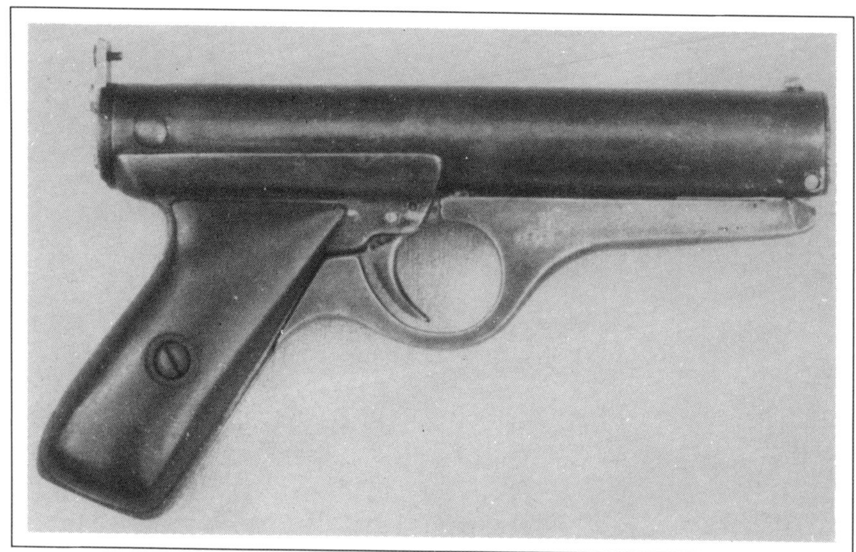

Abas Major, right hand side.

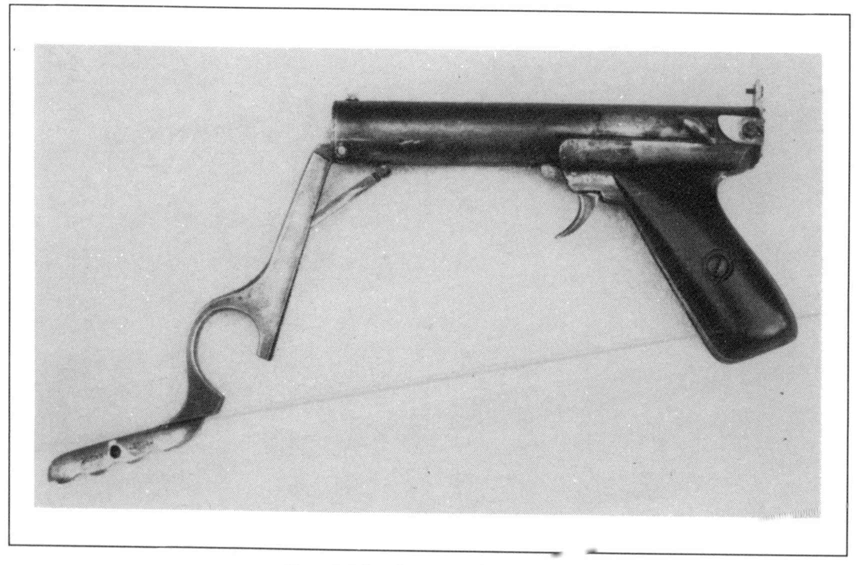

Abas Major in cocked position.

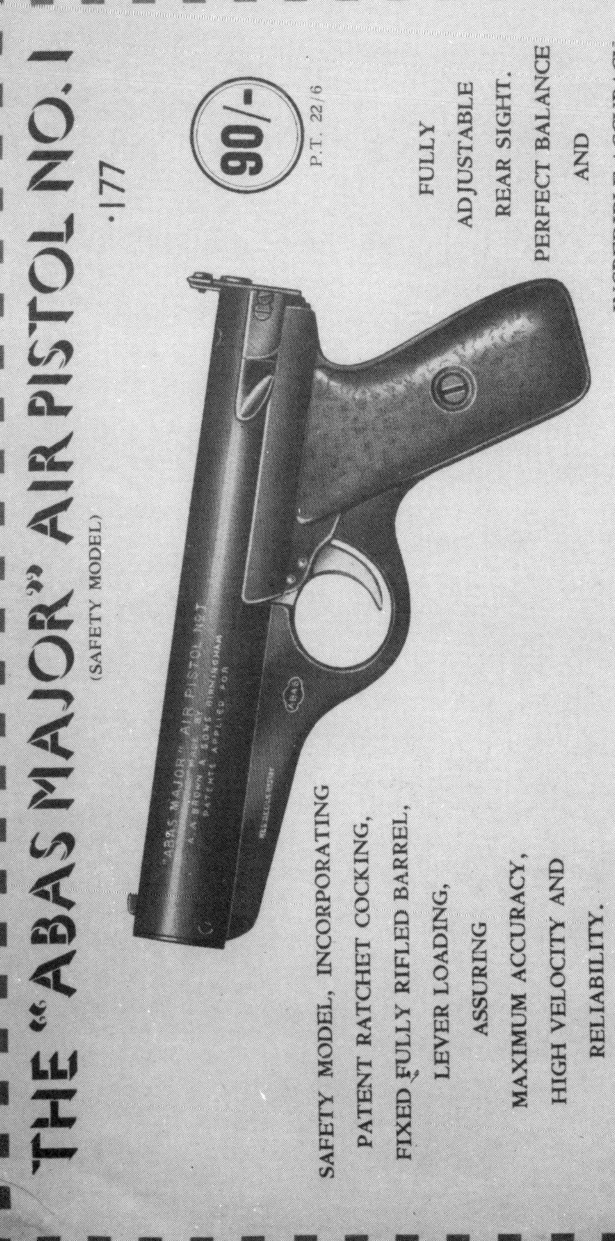

THE "ABAS MAJOR" AIR PISTOL NO. 1
(SAFETY MODEL)
·177
90/-
P.T. 22/6
SAFETY MODEL, INCORPORATING
PATENT RATCHET COCKING,
FIXED FULLY RIFLED BARREL,
LEVER LOADING,
ASSURING
MAXIMUM ACCURACY,
HIGH VELOCITY AND
RELIABILITY.
FULLY
ADJUSTABLE
REAR SIGHT.
PERFECT BALANCE
AND
INCREDIBLE ACCURACY.
A PRODUCT OF THE SPORTING GUN TRADE
Made by A. A. Brown & Sons, Sand St., Birmingham 4, Eng.
BRITISH MADE THROUGHOUT

Box label for 'Abas Major'.

ADVANCED DESIGN AND
MODERN FEATURES
of the

'ABAS MAJOR' AIR PISTOL NO. 1

FIXED FULLY RIFLED BARREL.
LEVER TYPE LOADING.
PATENT RATCHET COCKING.
ADJUSTABLE REAR SIGHT.
PERFECT BALANCE AND MODERN DESIGN COMBINING TO GIVE MAXIMUM ACCURACY, HIGH VELOCITY AND RELIABILITY.

MADE BY

A. A. BROWN & SONS
Sporting Gun and Air Pistol Makers
SAND STREET, BIRMINGHAM 4

A MODERN AIR PISTOL DESIGNED
TO GIVE
HIGH VELOCITY AND ACCURACY
AT LONG RANGES

THE

"ABAS MAJOR" AIR PISTOL No. 1

(SAFETY MODEL)

SECURITY AND POWER
ACCURACY AND
RELIABILITY

Instruction leaflet

METHOD OF COCKING YOUR
"ABAS" MAJOR No. 1

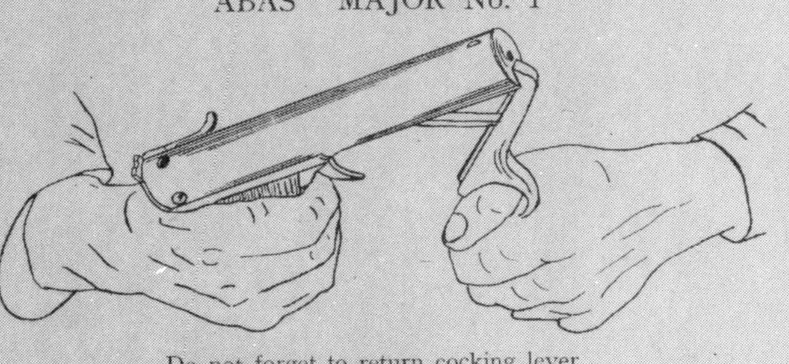

Do not forget to return cocking lever.

METHOD OF COCKING, No. 2

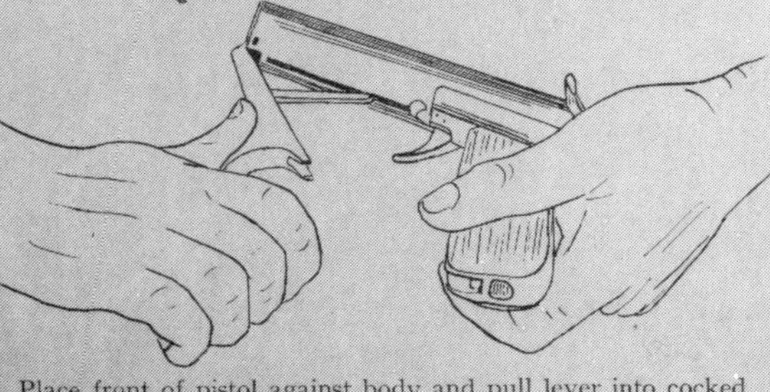

Place front of pistol against body and pull lever into cocked position.

HOW TO USE YOUR
'ABAS MAJOR' AIR PISTOL No. 1

1. To cock spring : Pull cocking lever out of grip, hold cocking lever by grips provided and pull apart until sear engages in main bent.
2. **It is most important** to return cocking lever to closed position.
3. Turn loading lever down into loading position, insert pellet (round nose first), return loading lever to firing position. Pistol is now ready for firing.

—:—

It is most important to fully cock pistol, otherwise sear will remain in safety ratchet and you will be unable to fire pistol.

—:—

ALWAYS USE "ABAS" PELLETS FOR BEST RESULTS. SUPPLIED IN BOXES OF 500 AND 1,000 FROM ALL GUN DEALERS.

Also

CLEANING BRUSHES TO SUIT YOUR "ABAS MAJOR." Price **8d.** each.

SPARES LIST ON APPLICATION, **1d.**

Instruction leaflet.

SPARES LIST.

No.		s.	d.
1.	Body (including Bungs) (not sold separately)	—	
2.	Cocking Lever (complete)	15	0
3.	,, ,, Axis Pin		4
4.	,, ,, Set Pin		3
5.	,, ,, Catch		10
6.	,, ,, Plunger		4
7.	,, ,, Plunger Spring		2
8.	,, ,, Plunger Set Pin		3
9.	Set Pin Key		3
10.	Piston	5	0
11.	Piston Plate		6
12.	Piston Washer		6
13.	Piston Pins		2
14.	Main Spring	1	3
15.	Barrel	5	0
16.	Front Bung	—	
17.	Long Link		9
18.	Short Link		9
19.	Long Link Pin		2
20.	Short Link Pin		2
21.	Fore Sight		6
22.	Loading Lever	4	6
23.	,, ,, Catch	2	0
24.	,, ,, Catch Pin		2
25.	,, ,, Catch Pin Locking		2
26.	,, ,, Plunger		3
27.	,, ,, Plunger Spring		2
28.	Sear	1	0
29.	,, Spring		2
30.	,, Axis Pin		2
31.	Intercepting Sear	1	6
32.	,, ,, Spring		3
33.	Trigger		9
34.	,, Axis Pin		2
35.	,, Spring		2
36.	Rear Light Body	1	6
37.	,, ,, Disc	1	0
38.	,, ,, Disc Pin		2
39.	,, ,, Body Pin		2
40.	Stock Sides (Pair) pr.	3	0
41.	,, ,, Pin each		4
42.	Washer Distance Studs		2

All prices plus postage.

ALWAYS USE "ABAS" PELLETS FOR BEST RESULTS.

Box of 500, 2/3; 1,000, 4/6.

Exploded Diagram and Parts List.

Model: **ABAS MAJOR**

Maker: **A. A. Brown & Sons,**
1 Snake Lane,
Alvechurch, Birmingham B48 7NT

Date: Early 1945 to late 1946.

Valuation: £100 - £300.

Details: A rare air pistol. Period of manufacture speaks for itself. Unusual cooking action, the cocking lever forms the trigger guard and folds under the air chamber and into the butt, also contains a pellet gauge for a ·177 pellet. L.H.S. of cocking lever stamped "REG. DESIGN 845425" and near the trigger guard part "A. A. BROWN & SON — B'HAM". The serial number is stamped on the inside of the lever near the rear of the trigger guard. On the R.H.S. appears "ABAS" in a triple circular surround and near the pivot "PROV. PAT". The piston is grooved so as to form a simple but very effective safety ratchet when action is being cocked. The action is stripped from the front. The barrel is central through the piston. Front of air chamber stamped ".177" just above barrel opening. L.H.S. of air chamber stamped "ABAS MAJOR" and on top near loading orifice "LOAD".

Serial number also stamped on rear metal butt strap. Number of above 1189. To load the tap lever is pulled down and pellet inserted, then pushed up so that it is parallel to the barrel. The two brown plastic grips are smooth but have seen chequered grips very similar to the Webley Senior. See *"Shooting Times",* December, 14-20, 1978. If memory serves me correctly the above is the only air pistol that loads by way of a tap similar to air rifles.

Advertised weight 2 lbs. Length 7½ inches. Available in ·177 only. First models had plain walnut grips. There was also three types of finishes, blued, black crackled enamel, and an aluminium finish, could be "anodised". Barrel was rifled. Only about 1800 were produced. See *"Airgun World",* October and November, 1978. There were also available "ABAS" pellets for the above. These came in boxes of either 500 or 1000. The Patent for the above design is covered by D. H. Commins in *"Guns Review",* October, 1980. It would appear that the patent was finally granted after cessation of production.

On the earlier models the cocking lever was held in place by a small sliding button, as can be seen in the illustration, they were also fitted with plain walnut grips. The trigger mechanism also differed in that there was a separate safety sear that operated on the grooved rings cut around the piston. On later models this safety sear was removed and the actual trigger sear acted as the safety.

Serial numbers seen range from 26 to 1870 and this last one was reported to be unfinished. See *"Airgun World",* April, 1982.

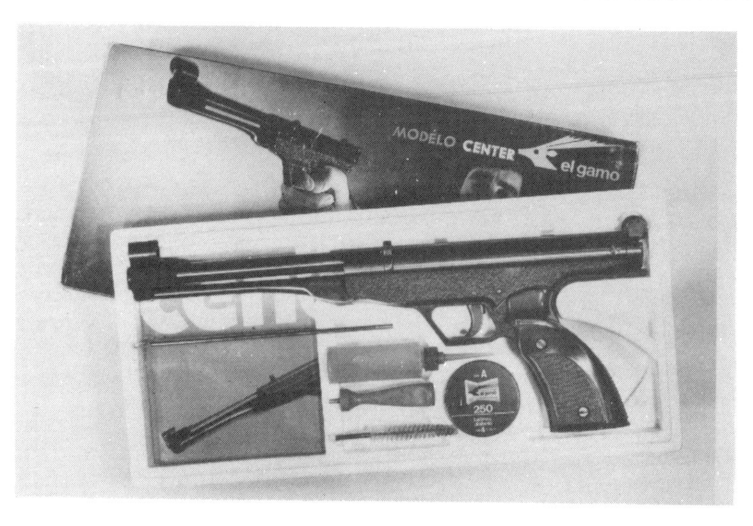

A.S.I. Center.

Model: **THE CENTER**

Maker: **El Gamo,** Spain.
Imported by A.S.I.,
Alliance House,
Saxmunden, Suffolk.

Date: Current model, introduced sometime in 1975.

Valuation: £50n, £15 - £30, around £25a.

Details: Supplied with fitted polystyrene packing case. Compartments contain cleaning rods, pellets, oil bottle, and instruction booklet. Underlever cocking with pull out loading gate for pellet. Has a sliding breech on air chamber side as air seal. Loading gate cannot be opened unless action is cocked. Sighting plane of 14 inches. Tunnel foresight and fully adjustable rearsight. Top of air chamber has oiling hole and is also stamped "ELGAMO" with the deer's head trade mark.

L.H.S. of breech stamped "CAL 4.5 (.177) "F" — MADE IN SPAIN", then serial number, for the above H47424. Advertised weight 2¾ lbs. Angle of grip to body can be altered by loosening the top grip screw and the screw from under the butt. Trigger adjustment is by way of small screw at rear of trigger guard. The larger screw of the two could be a locking screw. For a review of the above see *"Airgun World"*, April, 1978. Advertised as also being available for left hand shooting. The piston is fitted with a leather washer.

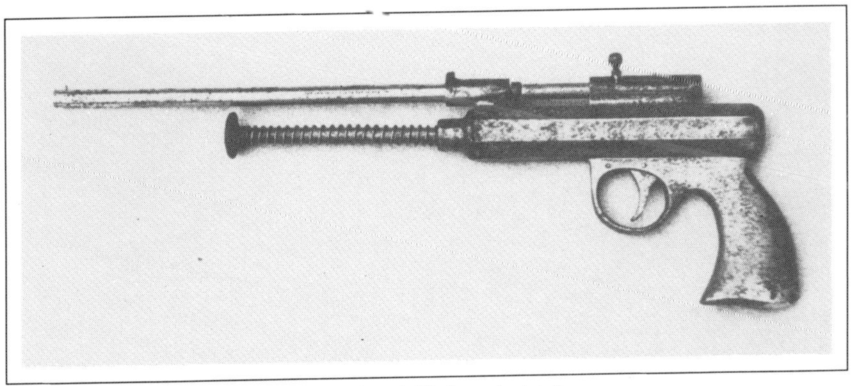

Bedford and Walker airpistol.

Model: Could be "**EUREKA**" target air pistol

Maker: Could be **Quackenbush** under licence from **Pope,** or **Bedford,** or **Walker,** or any combination of the above.
See pages 74/75 of *"Airguns"* by Eldon Wolff.

Date: Around the 1880's.

Valuation: £60 - £150, £50a - £100a.

Details: All metal with nickel plated brass barrel. Above design and improvements are on the original Pope 1874 patent air pistol. George Walker patented the bolt action breech that is still used today in pump action air pistols. Cocked by pressing downward on the plunger under the barrel. Butt is drilled for a wire shoulder stock. Trigger sear is adjustable. Smoothbore barrel and appears to have a seam running full length. L.H.S. of barrel stamped "PAT. JAN. 18, JULY, 18, '76. PAT. IN ENG". Measures 14¼ inches from barrel to base of butt. All examples seen have been nickel plated. Made in ·200.

Advertised in 1880 as being sold in a neat box with wire stock, six darts, six targets, 100 slugs, a push rod, "claw" and a wrench. Last item assume to be a spanner for undoing air chamber plug. Sold either blued or fully plated, assume nickel plated. Was also available with a self-adjusting bell target.

Patent dated 18th January, 1876 was by Bedford and covered the design of moving the barrel forward and using the bolt action breech with cam sealing. The spring and piston moved backwards to cock. The piston in the patent drawing was shown to be in two parts with a middle leather washer. Number of above patent 172376.

Patent dated the 18th July, 1876, number 179984 was by George Walker of Boston and covered the rear loading bolt with cam. This was an improvement on the above patent. It also used a leather washer on the bolt head and an extended rod to push the pellet into the barrel passed the small air hole. Similar action to the present day Gat airpistols. For further details see *"Airgun World"*, October, 1980.

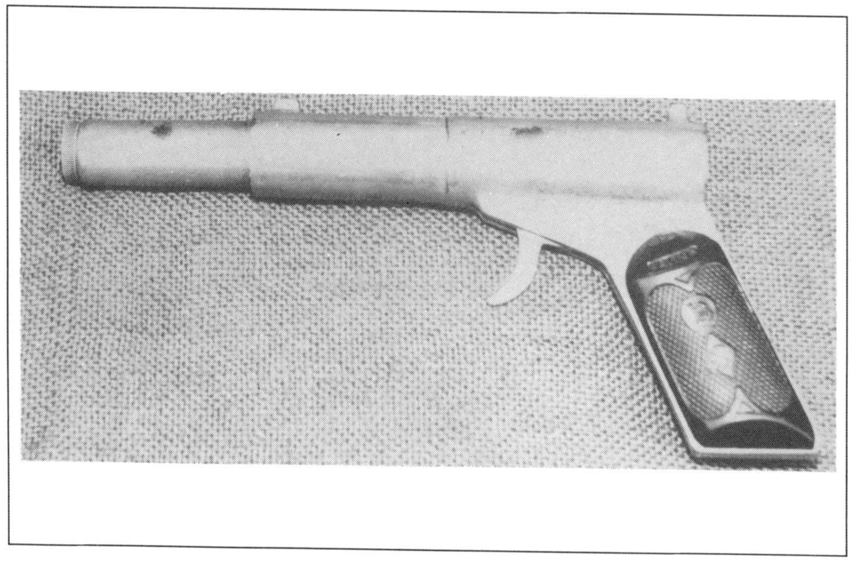

The Briton Gat (for the purists)

Model:	**The "BRITON" Airpistol.** May have been the "**Super-Briton**" sold in the 1930's when the cheaper tinplate "**Briton**" appeared.
Maker:	"Made in England". From the style of grips either: **Edwin G. Anson,** of 126a, Steelhouse Lane, Birmingham, or by: **Frank Clarke,** 39-41 Lower Loveday Street, Bormingham, . . . or both.
Date:	From the early 1920's to middle 1930's.
Valuation:	£50 - £90.

Details: Unusual in that as like the Scout Gat airpistol it was sold without any trigger guard. Rather wider in the body than the Dolla and other gats except for the Fire-Fly. Available either nickel plated or blued finish. ·177 smoothbore barrel. No trigger adjustment or serial number, but cast into the frame under the grip was a figure three. Fixed sights as is normal with these type of airpistols. The grips are valcanite with "B" in a circular logo.

Now, on the subject of grips in *"Guns Review"*, April, 1980, page 261, there is an illustration of Edwin George Anson's patent for the Warrior airpistol and the grips are almost identical, in fact too much so to be coincidental. So I would hazard at a guess and suggest that either the grips came from a common source for both the Warrior and the Briton airpistols, or the Briton was made by Anson, as was the Fire-Fly and Warrior. He could have also made the Scout gat style airpistol.

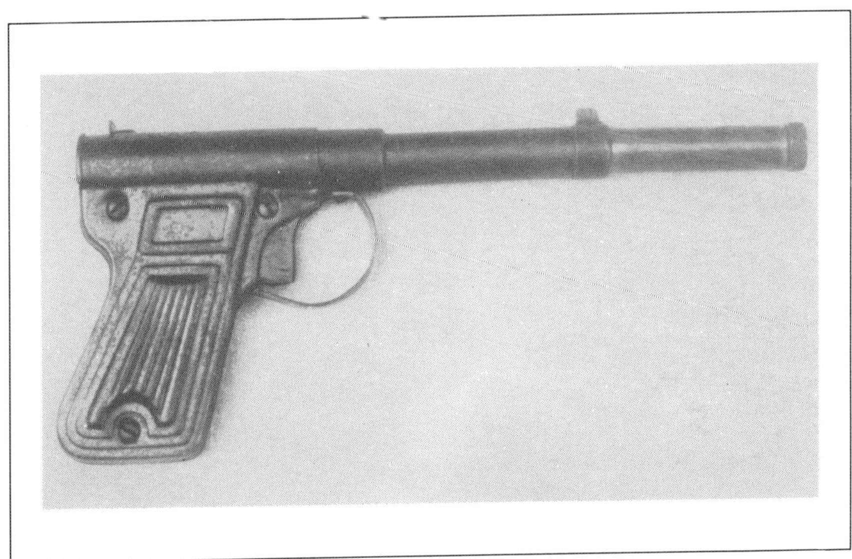

The "Briton" Gat.

Box lid for the Briton airpistol.

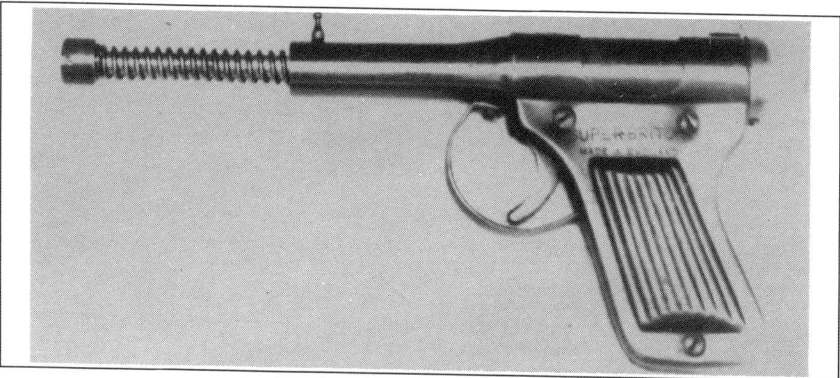

The Super Briton Push-in barrel Airpistol.

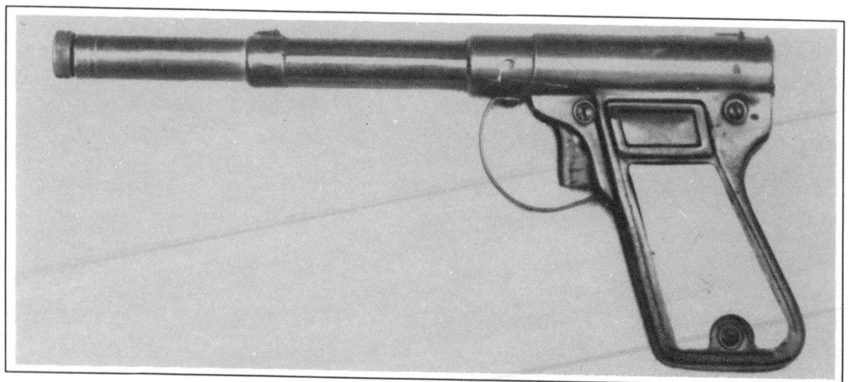

The "Briton" De Luxe with white plastic chequered grips.

Model: **TINPLATE GAT. "THE BRITON". SUPER-BRITON**

Maker: Could be sub-contracted to **Diana,** see below, although advertised as "BRITISH MADE"

Date: Advertised around 1928. Seen advertised in 1939 as "British Made". Sold in "Attractive box", also advertised a "SUPER-BRITON", much stronger and heavier.

Valuation: £15 - £35, boxed examples £40 - £60.

Details: Tin plate. Identical to Diana Mod2 as advertised around 1930. On top of air cyclinder has stamped "THE BRITON" with a funny looking dog between "THE" and "BRITON", then beneath that "MADE IN ENGLAND". Following from above also, appeared advertised in 1956 as the "STANDARD" model only. They were advertised as "air pistols" and not as "GAT's". The word gat appears to have been first used by T. J. Harrington & Son. Another variation has "MADE IN ENGLAND" stamped on one side of the grips instead of on top of the air chamber. See also Smith's book, page 12, identical gat listed as The Limit.

The Super Briton was smaller than the tinplate Briton but more strongly made. It had a solid steel airchamber and barrel housing with tinplate plate trigger guard and grips. The grips were pressed from one piece that wrapped around and over the air chamber, and held in place by three screws on each side. One side is stamped "SUPER BRITON, MADE IN ENGLAND" and on top of the wrap over stamped "THE BRITON" with the ugliest dog you have ever seen. Screw-in piller foresight and a fixed thin metal rearsight that is screw mounted to the chamber and wrap over metal of the grips. The box cover describes this as the "All steel British air pistol". The barrel is as usual a ·177 smoothbore.

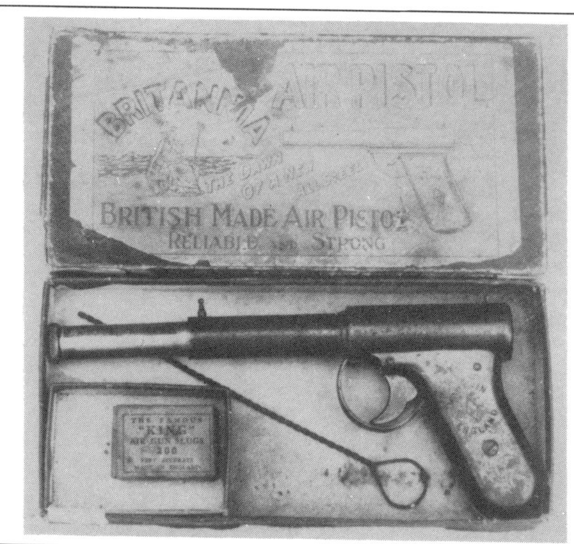

The Britannia airpistol.

Model:	**BRITANNIA AIRPISTOL**
Maker:	Not known, but advertised as being British.
Date:	1930's.
Valuation:	Above example is boxed and had no hesitation in paying the asking price of £30. Often is the case that any box has greater collecting value than the airpistol. £50 - £75.
Details:	All metal gat style airpistol. Sights non-adjustable. Piller foresight and rearsight formed from raised cut out section of the outer metal skin. Left hand grip stamped "MADE IN ENGLAND" with a diamond shape in the centre of the circular stamping. On the right hand grip appears "THE BRITANNIA" with the Britannia style figure. 8¼ inches long and just over 6 inches when cocked. Box contains wire push rod for easing pellets down the barrel and what appears a compartment for pellets. Box did contain a packet of "KING" airgun slugs. Available blued or nickel plated.

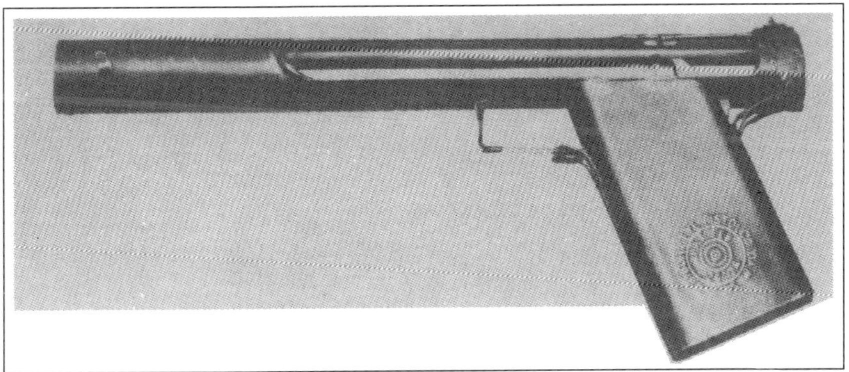

The Fly Dreaded Bull's Eye (American Rifleman).

The Bull's Eye's Box (American Rifleman).

Sharpshooter with spare shot, elastic bands and rubber target stamp (American Rifleman).

Model: **BULLS EYE and SHARPSHOOTER CATAPULT AIRPISTOL**

Maker: **Bull's Eye Pistol Co.,**
Rawlins, Wyoming, U.S.A.
In 1948, the address became:
Bulls-Eye Mfg.,
7533 Fay Ave., La Jolla, California and by the 1960's it was:
Bull's Eye Mfg. Co.,
Division of Golden Key Enterprises,
Sherman Oaks, California 91413, U.S.A.

Date: The Bull's Eye was patented in 1924 and 1926 and from advertisements production started in 1928. The Sharpshooter was patented in 1937 and production began in 1938 and but for a gap in the 1940's, due to W.W.2, they were offered to the public right up to the middle 1970's.

Valuation: Around £50 for complete set.

Details: These catapult airguns were "Guaranteed accurate enough to kill a house fly at ten paces". Such were the joys of hunting in America! The Bull's Eye airpistol was patented February 6th, 1924 and again on January 12th, 1926. One of the inventors was a machinist for the Union Pacific Railway while another could have been a doctor from Wyoming. The original Bull's Eye was about 9 inches long and was sold in repeater form firing number 6 shot with a capacity of around 58 shots. Blued metal finish with black catalan grips and basically a tinplate construction.

Power could be varied by the choice of elastic bands. They were sold boxed with three celluloid bird shaped targets and a tube of shot, about 100. Believe it or not the Bull's Eye was quite powerful and deadly in the right hands and this lead to the less powerful Sharpshooter in 1938. It was advertised that the Bull's Eye was capable of penetrating light cardboard at 20 feet. From descriptions in American magazines it would appear that they are not true airpistols, but in fact the ball is fired by a push rod similar to the Daisy Model 179 Colt "Peacemaker" airpistol. The Bull's Eye and Sharpshooter were both available in the late 1930's to early 1940's. By 1948 the Bull's Eye was sold with fold down spinning target on a wire frame that could be collapsed into the box.

The original box for the Bull's Eye had a very homely scene on the top showing father and son firing the airgun in a very spacious lounge, with daughter looking on. The lid proudly proclaimed that the airpistol was for "Men and Women, Boys and Girls" which just about covers every living human being on earth.

The Sharpshooter was patented on September 7th, 1937 and production began in 1938 at Rawlins. It was heavier and stronger than the Bull's Eye but was shorter, measuring only 7¼ inches and this led to less power due to the shorter stroke from the elastic band. It was sold in a plainer cardboard box complete with a loading funnel, a target rubber stamp and ink pad, a tube of shot and a variety of power bands of varying thickness for varying the power. It also had separate grips. It was advertised as being capable of de-lifing a fly at 20 paces. This being borne out by the fitting of adjustable sights. Three grades of finish were offered; de luxe model with nickel plating and ivory grips, a blued finish with black grips, the poor man's model with tinplate grips.

Apart from shooting flies, another favourite pastime was placing matches against a wall and firing to ignite the heads. By the 1960's it was sold in a plain white box with extra elastic bands, a tube of round shot, a sheet of 2⅛ inch paper targets and an instruction sheet. The pistol was marked "BULL'S EYE MFG., CO., LA JOLLA, CAL.". For the technical minded the Sharpshooter formed 2·35 inch group at 15 feet with ten shots and with an average muzzle velocity of 165 f.p.s., this being ·117 foot lbs energy.

During the 1950's the Sharpshooter was sold in a box that doubled as a shooting gallery: this had targets printed at the rear and wire frames in the front on which birds could be sat, then knocked off, then put back again, then knocked off again, and so on. The catalan grips would appear to be imitation white ivory or pearl, and the basic junior model with tinplate grips were slightly smaller in size, this being for the junior hand size. By 1954 the Sharpshooter was up against the Daisy Targeteer and appeared for the last time in Steegers during the middle 1950's. The Sharpshooter was a 48 shoot repeater using number 6 shot. For further details see the *"American Rifleman",* October, 1980.

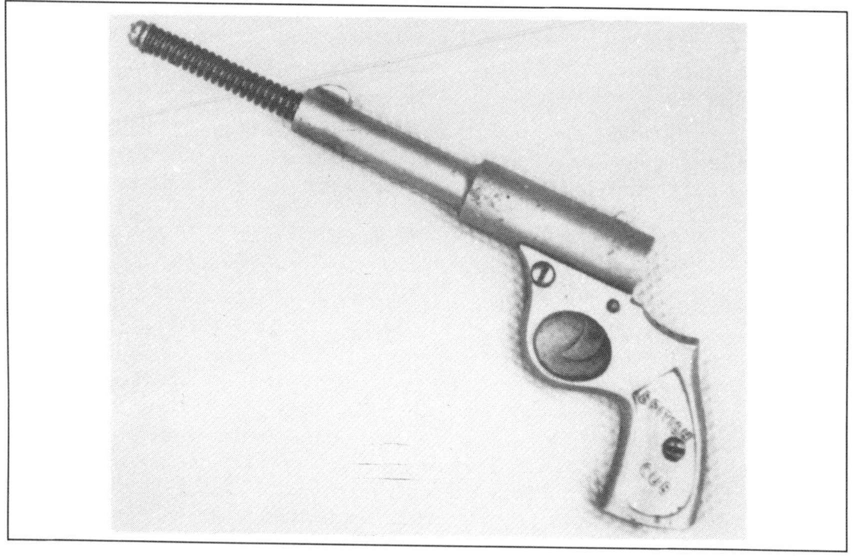

The "British Cub" Push-in barrel airpistol.

Model: **THE "BRITISH CUB"**

Maker: Originally by
F. R. Langenham,
Zella Mehlis, Germany,
but the above could be postwar. The design might have brought over to England along with the Diana airgun factory and production started using scrap Spitfires, Hurricanes, etc.

Date: Would assume just postwar.

Valuation: £20 - £50.

Details: Another "Dolla" Gat, but this time the body is cast aluminium. The variation in the humble Dolla gat now fails to amaze me. Cast aluminium frame is unusual and I can only assume that just after the War there were quite a few scrap aeroplanes lying about, so someone thought of using them to make airpistols. Can this be the last of the Dolla type airpistol? The previous model to this was steel and stamped "CUB" and marked made in Germany. Comparing this with the previous model you can see that once again the barrel housing is identical, but the grip and trigger action has altered. One wonders if the next model in this range would have been in plastic, made by the Japanese?

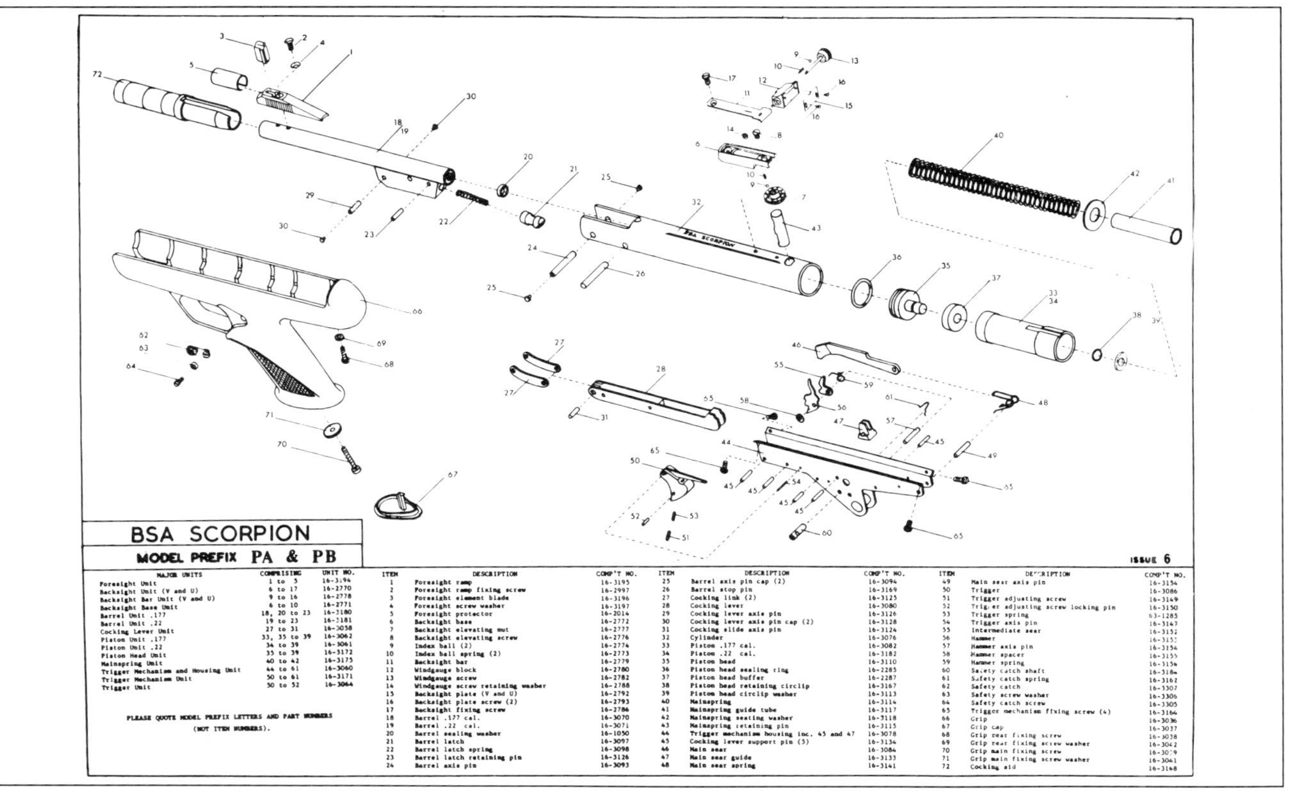

MAJOR UNITS	COMPRISING	UNIT NO.
Foresight Unit	1 to 5	16-3194
Backsight Unit (V and U)	6 to 17	16-2770
Backsight Bar Unit (V and U)	9 to 16	16-2778
Backsight Base Unit	6 to 10	16-2771
Barrel Unit .177	18, 20 to 23	16-3180
Barrel Unit .22	19 to 23	16-3181
Cocking Lever Unit	27 to 31	16-3058
Piston Unit .177	33, 35 to 39	16-3062
Piston Unit .22	34 to 39	16-3061
Piston Head Unit	35 to 39	16-3172
Mainspring Unit	40 to 42	16-3175
Trigger Mechanism and Housing Unit	44 to 61	16-3060
Trigger Mechanism Unit	50 to 61	16-3171
Trigger Unit	50 to 52	16-3064

PLEASE QUOTE MODEL PREFIX LETTERS AND PART NUMBERS (NOT ITEM NUMBERS).

ITEM	DESCRIPTION	COMP'T NO.
1	Foresight ramp	16-3195
2	Foresight ramp fixing screw	16-2997
3	Foresight element blade	16-3196
4	Foresight screw washer	16-3197
5	Foresight protector	16-2014
6	Backsight base	16-2772
7	Backsight elevating nut	16-2777
8	Backsight elevating screw	16-2776
9	Index ball (2)	16-2774
10	Index ball spring (2)	16-2773
11	Backsight bar	16-2779
12	Windgauge block	16-2780
13	Windgauge screw	16-2782
14	Windgauge screw retaining washer	16-2788
15	Backsight plate (V and U)	16-2792
16	Backsight plate screw (2)	16-2793
17	Backsight fixing screw	16-2786
18	Barrel .177 cal.	16-3070
19	Barrel .22 cal.	16-3071
20	Barrel sealing washer	16-1050
21	Barrel latch	16-3097
22	Barrel latch spring	16-3098
23	Barrel latch retaining pin	16-3126
24	Barrel axis pin	16-3093
25	Barrel axis pin cap (2)	16-3094
26	Barrel stop pin	16-3169
27	Cocking link (2)	16-3125
28	Cocking lever	16-3080
29	Cocking lever axis pin	16-3126
30	Cocking lever axis pin cap (2)	16-3128
31	Cocking slide axis pin	16-3124
32	Cylinder	16-3076
33	Piston .177 cal.	16-3082
34	Piston .22 cal.	16-3182
35	Piston head	16-3110
36	Piston head sealing ring	16-2285
37	Piston head buffer	16-2287
38	Piston head retaining circlip	16-3167
39	Piston head circlip washer	16-3113
40	Mainspring	16-3114
41	Mainspring guide tube	16-3117
42	Mainspring seating washer	16-3118
43	Mainspring retaining pin	16-3115
44	Trigger mechanism housing inc. 45 and 47	16-3078
45	Cocking lever support pin (5)	16-3134
46	Main sear	16-3084
47	Main sear guide	16-3133
48	Main sear spring	16-3141
49	Main sear axis pin	16-3154
50	Trigger	16-3086
51	Trigger adjusting screw	16-3149
52	Trigger adjusting screw locking pin	16-3150
53	Trigger spring	63-1285
54	Trigger axis pin	16-3147
55	Intermediate sear	16-3152
56	Hammer	16-3153
57	Hammer axis pin	16-3154
58	Hammer spacer	16-3155
59	Hammer spring	16-3156
60	Safety catch shaft	16-3184
61	Safety catch spring	16-3162
62	Safety catch	16-3307
63	Safety screw washer	16-3306
64	Safety catch screw	16-3305
65	Trigger mechanism fixing screw (4)	16-3164
66	Grip	16-3036
67	Grip cap	16-3037
68	Grip rear fixing screw	16-3038
69	Grip rear fixing screw washer	16-3042
70	Grip main fixing screw	16-3039
71	Grip main fixing screw washer	16-3041
72	Cocking aid	16-3148

BSA Scorpion — Exploded Diagram and Instructions

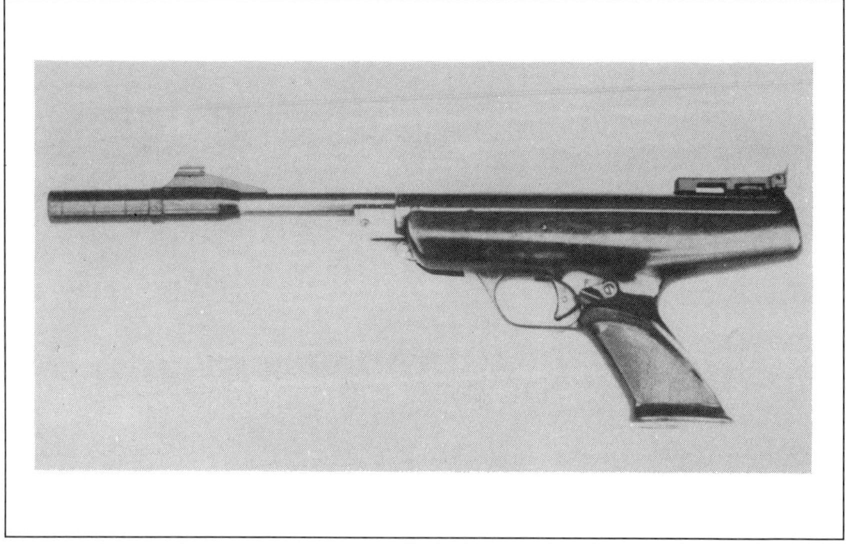

The B.S.A. Scorpion.

Model: **SCORPION**

Maker: **B.S.A. Guns Ltd.,**
Birmingham, England.

Date: Current model. Introduced early 1974.

Valuation: £30 - £60.

Details: Grooved for telescopic sight, but earlier models were not. Powerful and well made, but would recommend double handed use. Has plastic tube as cocking aid that fits on end of barrel. Looks good with this left on. Have seen some with home-made shoulder stocks that push into two holes drilled in rear of plastic grip, another good idea. Automatic safety. Measures 18 inches long with cocking aid fitted.

For a review of the above air pistol, see *"Guns Review"*, February, 1974. Advertised weight 3·6 lbs. Advertised muzzle velocities: ·177 — 510 f.p.s., and for ·22 — 380 f.p.s. Hints on stripping and basic tuning may be obtained from *"Airgun World"*, July, 1980. Smoothbore barrels were available when it first appeared.

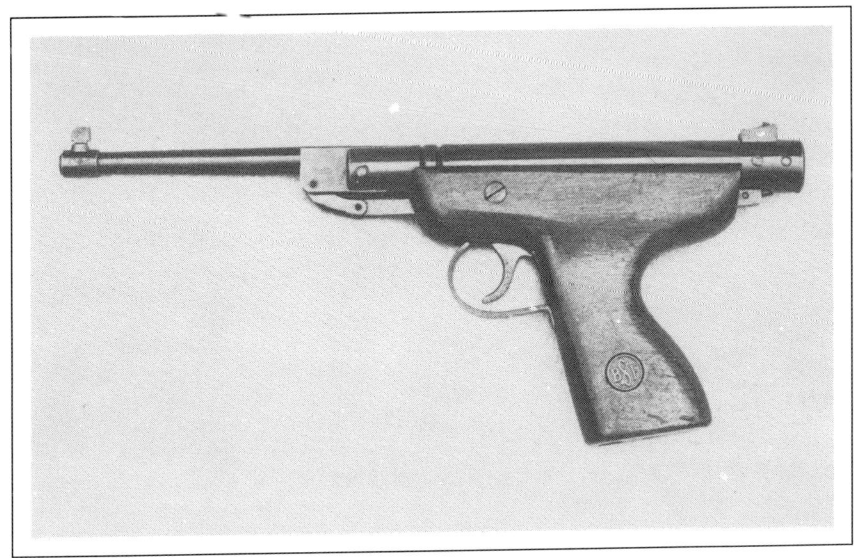

B.S.F. Model S20.

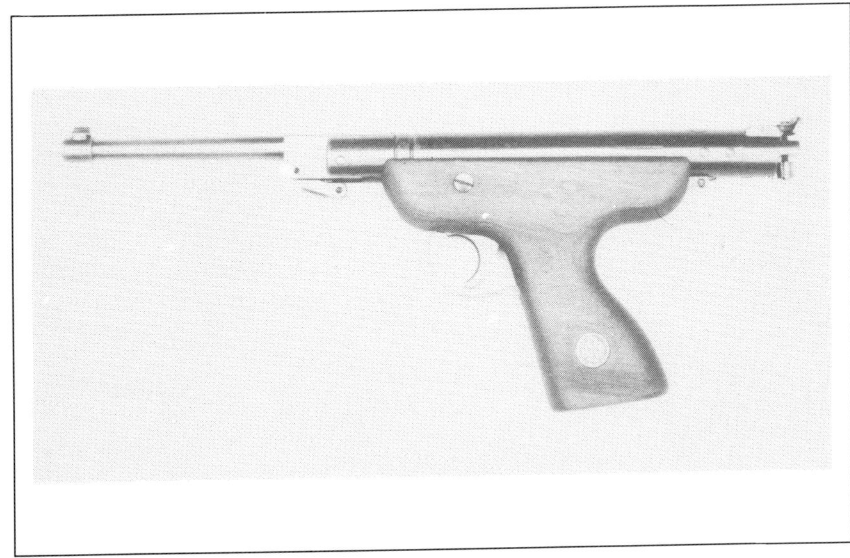

B.S.F. S20 Target Model.

Model: **S20**

Maker: **Bayer Sportswaffen-Fabrik, G.m.b.H.,** Erlangen, West Germany.

Date: Introduced sometime after 1930 and still a current model, although have not seen it advertised for some time.

Valuation: £40 - £80.

Details: 14½ inches along the barrel line with a 6¾ inch rifled barrel. One piece wooden butt with a very wide grip. Set in each side is a "BSF" green enamelled medallion. Air chamber has the two distinctive grooves at the breech end. Above example had a very long trigger pull. Stamped on L.H.S. of barrel "ModS20", serial number appears on the underside of the barrel breech, for the above A1947. On R.H.S. of barrel breech appears "MADE IN GERMANY". The circular BSF trademark is stamped on the top of the air chamber, the middle "S" has an arrow through it. At the rear of the air chanber is the trigger adjustment. Advertised weight 2 lb. 6 ozs. Appears to have been sold in ·177 only. The "S20 EXPORT" was as above but was wrapped in an "attractive gift box with one box of Diabolo pellets". There was also the "MATCH" and "MATCH EXPORT". These had a micrometer rear sight and adjustable trigger pull by screw "on lower side of flange end" ??? The "Export" came in the box with pellets. The match models were ½ inch longer than the standard, this accounts for the micrometer sight. Appears to be sold in the U.S.A. under the B.S.F./WISCHO trade name. The match version appears to have been introduced in the middle 1950's.

Distributed by the Hyscore Company in the U.S.A. as their Model 817M. Available in ·177 only and advertised as having a muzzle velocity of 472 f.p.s. with Hyscore No. 215 wadcutter pellets. On some examples it would appear that the serial number is also stamped on the underside of the air chamber near the cocking link, these should be identical. Advertised weight 2½ lbs. The Wischo model sold in America is identical to the above but for the lettering on the air chamber, which reads "WISCHO — KG, ERLANGEN, GERMANY" and on the side of the air chamber "MADE IN GERMANY WEST". The Medallions set in each side of the grip are brass with a "W" logo with an arrow through the "W".

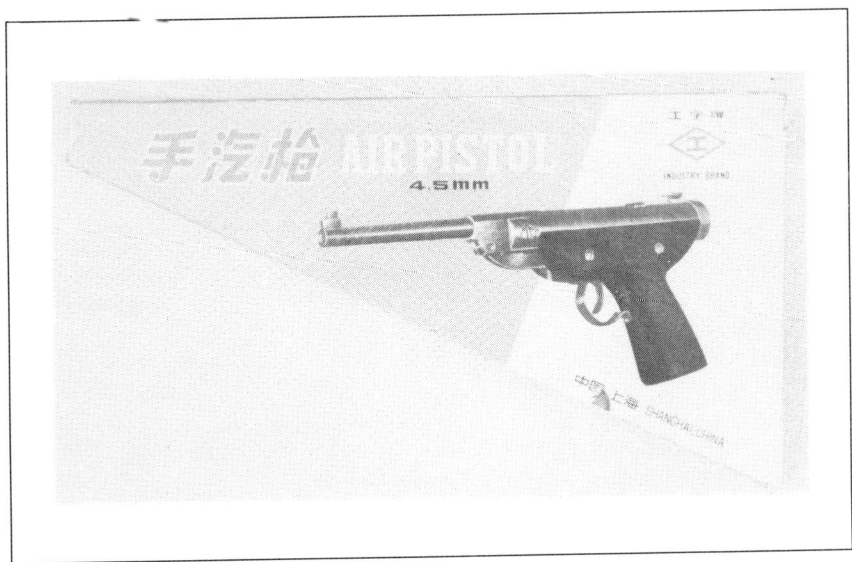

Box lid for Chinese airpistol.

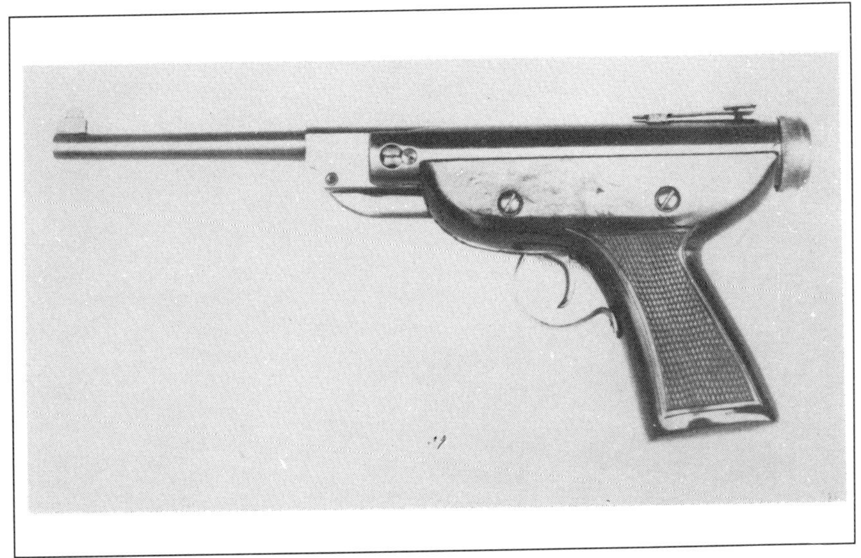

Chinese airpistol.

Model: **CHINESE AIRPISTOL,** retailed by Nickerson, who called it: **THE "MARK I"**

Maker: Shanghai, China.

Date: Imported from the late 1970's to middle 1980's.

Valuation: £5 - £20. £22n.

Details: Very similar to the Slavia ZVP, pre-war German Diana Model 5, and the Slavia Tex. Sold in ·177 only and with either a brown or black one piece thick plastic stock. Very strongly made, but lacking in power. Appears to originate from the same factory that produces the "Arrow" and "Lion" air rifles. Almost 13 inches long. Fixed foresight and dovetail mounted rearsight, adjustable for windage only. Top of air chamber stamped with Chinese writing and "MADE IN SHANGHAI, CHINA". Box is marked "ART. No. G6235".

Trigger action has anti-bear safety device and lacks adjustment. On other models of the above the trigger could be released after action had been cocked, so it would appear that the anti-bear device could vary from airgun to airgun.

Model 1300 Assemblies and Parts List

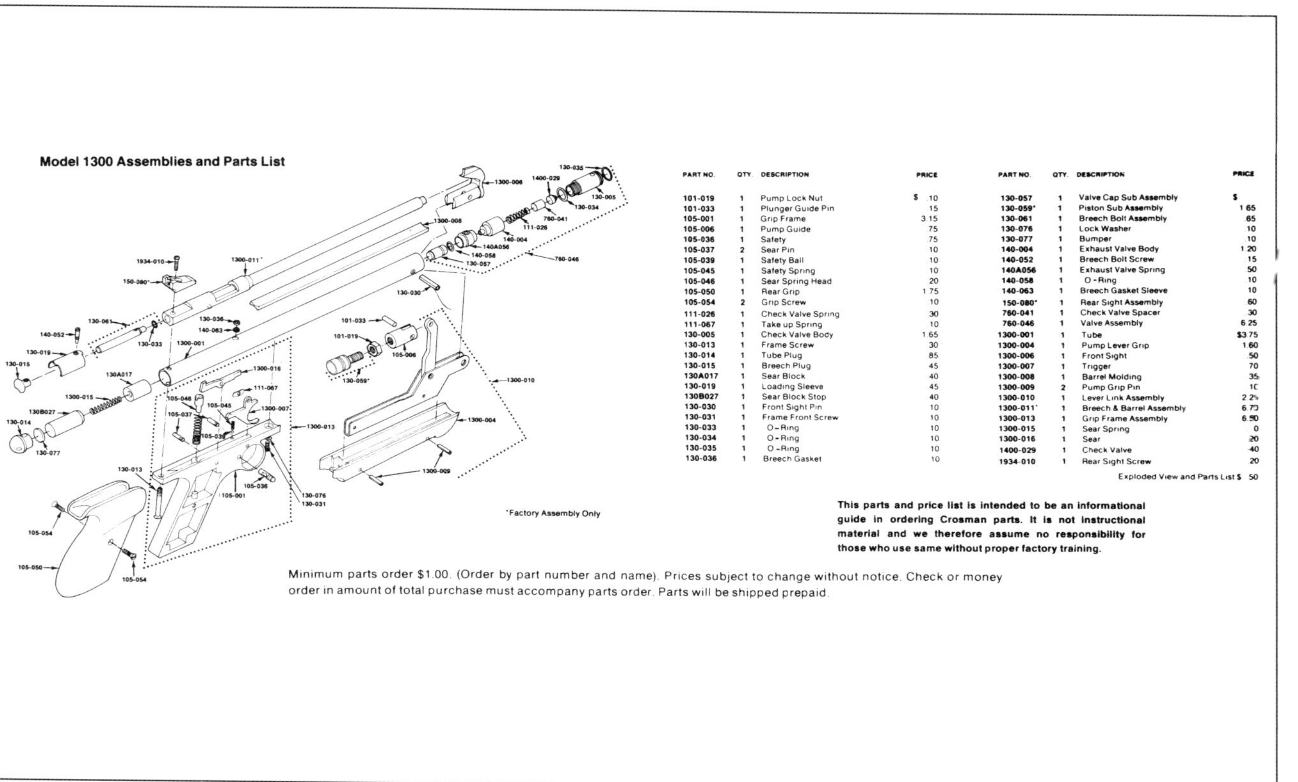

PART NO.	QTY.	DESCRIPTION	PRICE
101-019	1	Pump Lock Nut	$ .10
101-033	1	Plunger Guide Pin	.15
105-001	1	Grip Frame	3.15
105-006	1	Pump Guide	.75
105-036	1	Safety	.75
105-037	2	Sear Pin	.10
105-039	1	Safety Ball	.10
105-045	1	Safety Spring	.10
105-046	1	Sear Spring Head	.20
105-050	1	Rear Grip	1.75
105-054	2	Grip Screw	.10
111-026	1	Check Valve Spring	.30
111-067	1	Take up Spring	.10
130-005	1	Check Valve Body	1.65
130-013	1	Frame Screw	.30
130-014	1	Tube Plug	.85
130-015	1	Breech Plug	.45
130A017	1	Sear Block	.40
130-019	1	Loading Sleeve	.45
130B027	1	Sear Block Stop	.40
130-030	1	Front Sight Pin	.10
130-031	1	Frame Front Screw	.10
130-033	1	O-Ring	.10
130-034	1	O-Ring	.10
130-035	1	O-Ring	.10
130-036	1	Breech Gasket	.10
130-057	1	Valve Cap Sub Assembly	$
130-059*	1	Piston Sub Assembly	1.65
130-061	1	Breech Bolt Assembly	.65
130-076	1	Lock Washer	.10
130-077	1	Bumper	.10
140-004	1	Exhaust Valve Body	1.20
140-052	1	Breech Bolt Screw	.15
140A056	1	Exhaust Valve Spring	.50
140-058	1	O-Ring	.10
140-063	1	Breech Gasket Sleeve	.10
150-080*	1	Rear Sight Assembly	.60
760-041	1	Check Valve Spacer	.30
760-046	1	Valve Assembly	6.25
1300-001	1	Tube	$3.75
1300-004	1	Pump Lever Grip	1.60
1300-006	1	Front Sight	.50
1300-007	1	Trigger	.70
1300-008	1	Barrel Molding	.35
1300-009	2	Pump Grip Pin	.1[illegible]
1300-010	1	Lever Link Assembly	2.2[illegible]
1300-011*	1	Breech & Barrel Assembly	6.7[illegible]
1300-013	1	Grip Frame Assembly	6.50
1300-015	1	Sear Spring	[illegible]0
1300-016	1	Sear	.20
1400-029	1	Check Valve	.40
1934-010	1	Rear Sight Screw	.20
		Exploded View and Parts List	$ .50

This parts and price list is intended to be an informational guide in ordering Crosman parts. It is not instructional material and we therefore assume no responsibility for those who use same without proper factory training.

Minimum parts order $1.00. (Order by part number and name). Prices subject to change without notice. Check or money order in amount of total purchase must accompany parts order. Parts will be shipped prepaid.

Model 1300 Assemblies and Parts List.

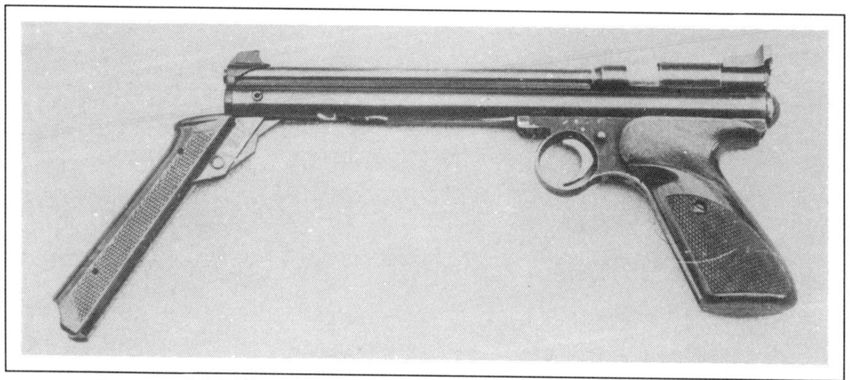

Crossman Medallist — pump handle down and breech plate drawn back.

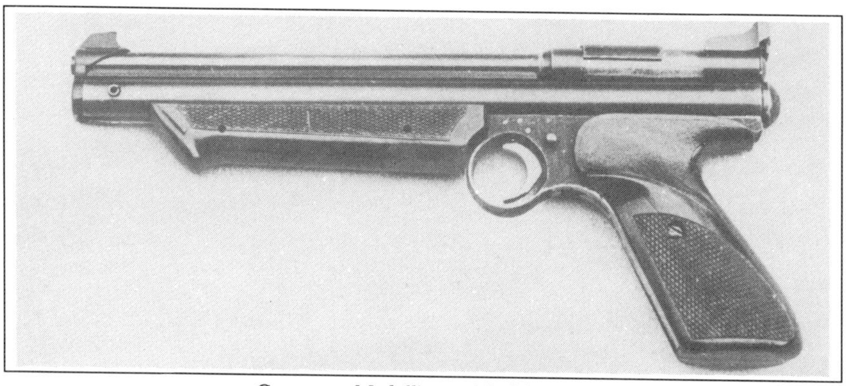

Crossman Medallist — Model 1300.

Model: **"MEDALLIST II" MODEL 1300**

Maker: **Crosman Arms Co.,**
Fairport, New York, U.S.A.

Date: 1970 to 1978.

Valuation: £20 - £40.

Details: Main advantage is the recoiless action. Single shot. Instruction leaflet is excellent. Serial number can be either stamped on the breech slide or on side of trigger block above safety catch. The above has a serial number 9 digits long. Can be strenuous work if firing in rapid succession. The shoulder stock was made available in the latter half of 1975. Have seen some of the above with a "D" bar handle fitted to the pump handle. These appear to have been available from early January, 1976. Advertised weight 2 lb.

Advertised muzzle velocities: 3 pumps .... 130 f.p.s.
6 pumps .... 290 f.p.s.
10 pumps .... 340 f.p.s.

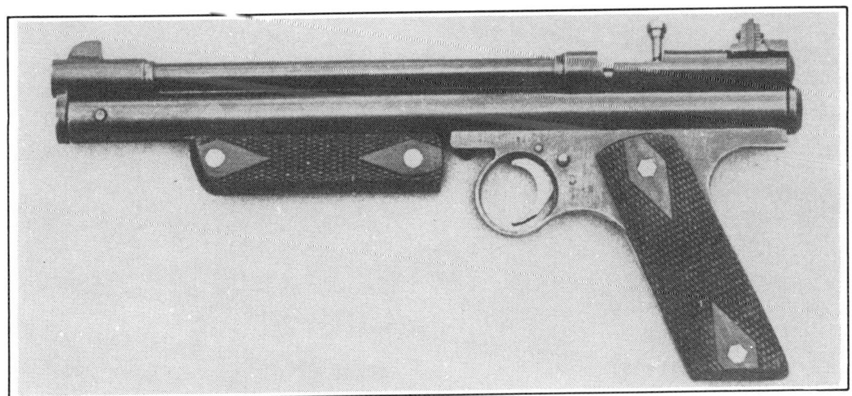

Customised Crosman "Medallist".

Model: CUSTOMISED "MEDALLIST II" Model 1300

Maker: **Crosman Arms Co.,**
Fairport, New York, U.S.A.

Date: Original model current, 1970 to 1978.

Valuation: £30 - £50.

Details: Altered and improved so that it has no plastic parts. The grips are walnut, hand chequered and fitted. The breech plate has been removed and a bolt fitted in its place. The rear sight has been removed, a flat single surface filed and a Webley Mk. III rear sight fitted in its place. The blade was filed open to accommodate the rather wide Crosman foresight. The front cylinder plug and barrel support has been remade in metal and the plastic insert between barrel and air chamber has also been removed. No alteration has been made to the pumping arrangement or seals.

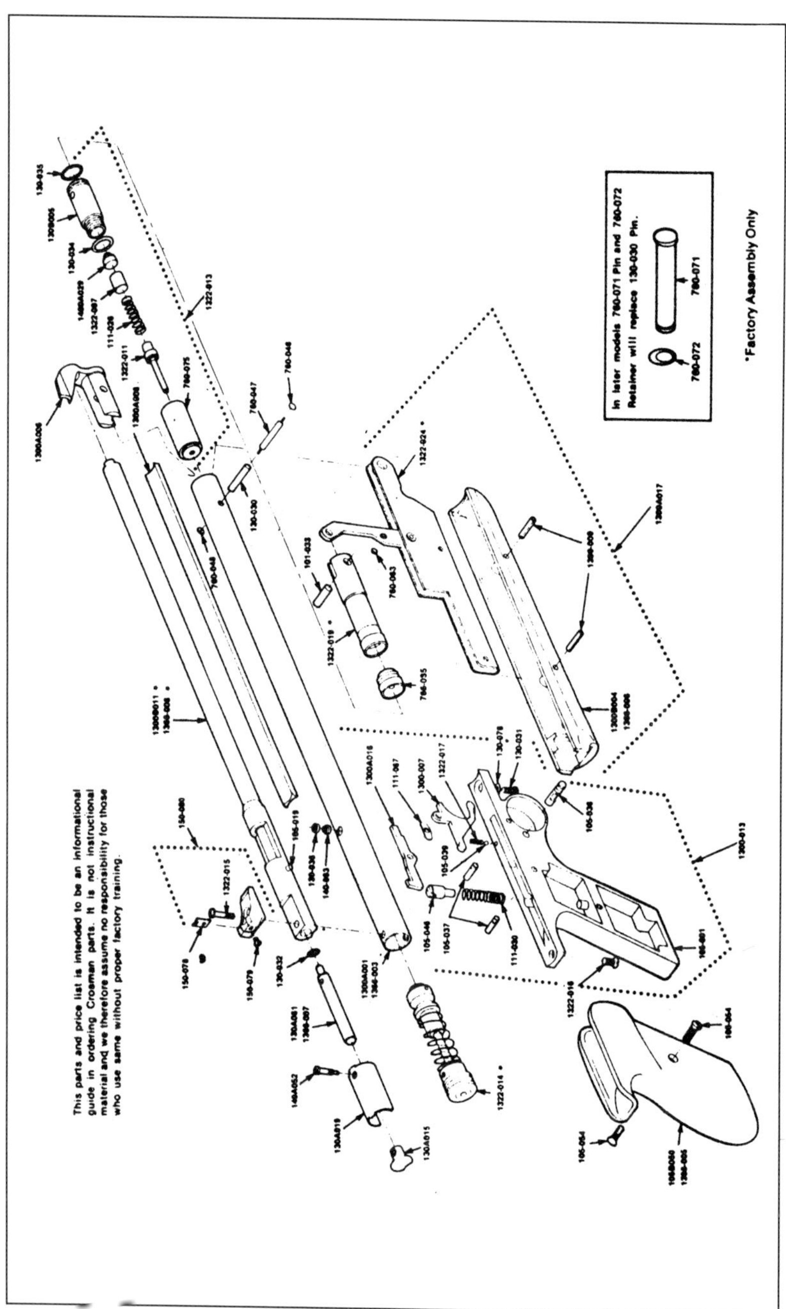

Model 1322 & 1377 Assemblies.

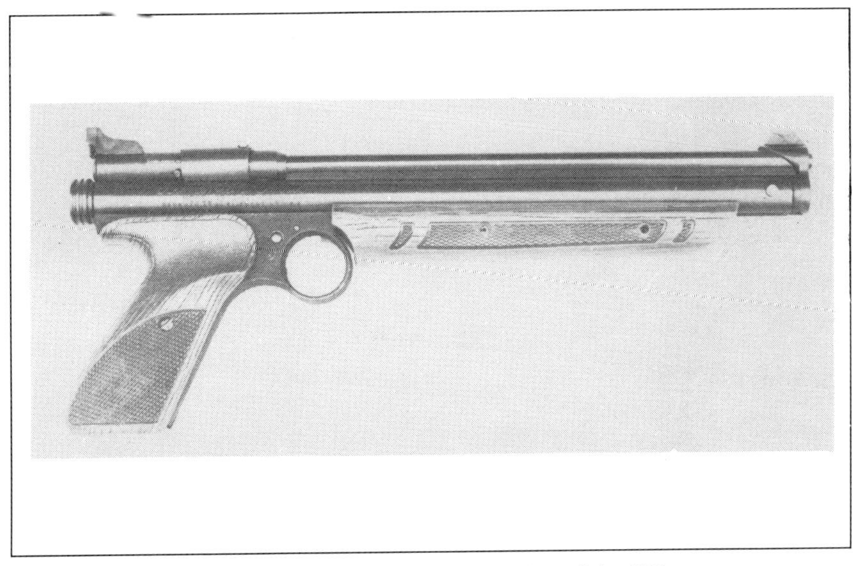

Crosman Model 1377. The ·177 version of the 1322.

Model: **1322/1377**

Maker: **Crosman Arms Company,**
980 Turk Hill Road,
Fairport, New York, 14450, U.S.A.
Imported into Britain by:
Sussex Armoury, 34 North Street, Hailsham, Sussex.
(Who have now gone into liquidation).

Date: Introduced in 1978 to take the place of the Model 1300, The "Medallist II".

Valuation: £25 - £50.

Details: A large airpistol that packs power enough for small vermin shooting. Matt black finish with brown plastic grips. Strong pump action with a long leverage. The above is ·22 whilst the Model 1377 is in ·177. L.H.S. of air chamber stamped with serial number and L.H.S. stamped with "CROSMAN MEDALLIST MODEL 1322 ·22 CAL CROSMAN ARMS FAIRPORT N.Y., U.S.A." It is recommended never to fire the airgun with less than two pumps. After pumping the trigger is set by pulling out the plunger at the rear of the air chamber and releasing. Rearsight fully adjustable.

Advertised muzzle velocities: 3 pumps .... 220 f.p.s.
6 pumps .... 315 f.p.s.
10 pumps .... 370 f.p.s.

The maximum pumps possible is ten, with a distance of 25 feet recommended for vermin shooting. Advertised weight 2 lbs 7 ozs. Length 13⅝ inches with a 10 inch rifled barrel. Crosman supply a holster for the above, catalogue number 26. A review appears in *"Airgun World"*, November, 1979.

It is recommended that the maximum velocity is reached with eighteen pumps and never to exceed twenty. The model 1377 could be used with either BB's or pellets and the following table illustrates the average performance:

Pumps	*Muzzle Vel.*	*Pellet/BB*	*Pellet/BB WT*
3	350 f.p.s.	·177 BB	5.42 grains
6	460 f.p.s.	·177 BB	5.42 grains
10	530 f.p.s.	·177 BB	5.42 grains
3	330 f.p.s.	·177 pellet	8.2 grains
6	430 f.p.s.	·177 pellet	8.2 grains
10	490 f.p.s.	·177 pellet	8.2 grains

The air chamber of the Model 1377 is stamped "AMERICAN CLASSIC MODEL 1377 ·177 CAL" followed by the address.

During the early part of 1977 some models of the 1322 Medallist and the 1377 were produced with a weak tightening screw that could cause the action to malfunction after continual use. This screw held the grip frame to the pump tube and when it loosened, three things could happen:

a) Pistol can't be locked and will not fire unless action is held together by hand.

b) Action can be locked but may go off with the safety on.

c) Action can be cocked and then may fire without trigger being pulled.

Apparently all guns returned to the Crosman Company in Texas will be repaired at no cost. It would appear that all is needed is retightening the locking screw or even applying a little lock-tight when screwing down.

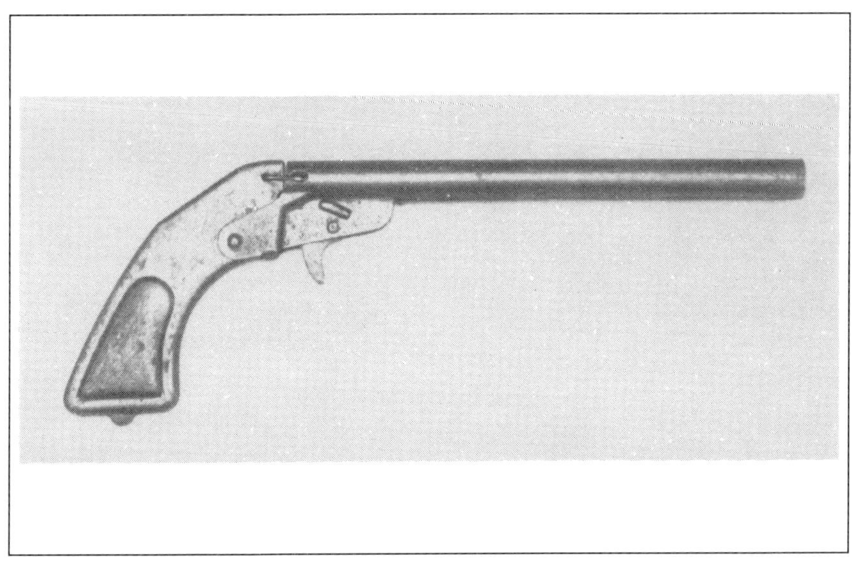

The Daisy "Safe Shot Target" Cork Pistol, Model No. 41.

Model: **No. 41 "SAFE SHOT TARGET" CORK PISTOL**

Maker: **Daisy Mfg. Co.,**
Plymouth, Michigan, U.S.A.

Date: The barrel is stamped with the Patent number 1,830,291 which appears to date from the 1930's.

Valuation: Swopped the above for a Webley Mk. 3 mainspring!! So value the mainspring. Would assume £1 - £5. Now worth about £10 - £20.

Details: Well, it is an airgun!!! A neat little tinplate airpistol that fires corks only. 11¾ inches long. Similar cocking action to the Model 1 tinplate air rifle. One of the wire cocking levers has a kink in it so that it engages with a hole in the side of the action in order to lock the barrel in the firing position. Blued finish all over with "DAISY MFG. CO. PLYMOUTH, MICH., U.S.A., PAT. 1,830,291".

A very neat airgun, that could give many days of pleasure. Barrel has a ½ inch bore. Original retail price was 1/6, 7½ new pence. Was sold with five corks, and a special target that when fired at retained the corks where they struck. Advertised as Daisy Model number 41.

Daisy "Targeteer" micro-bore airpistol.

Action pulled back into cocked position. Barrel/air chamber is then pushed forward into original position for firing.

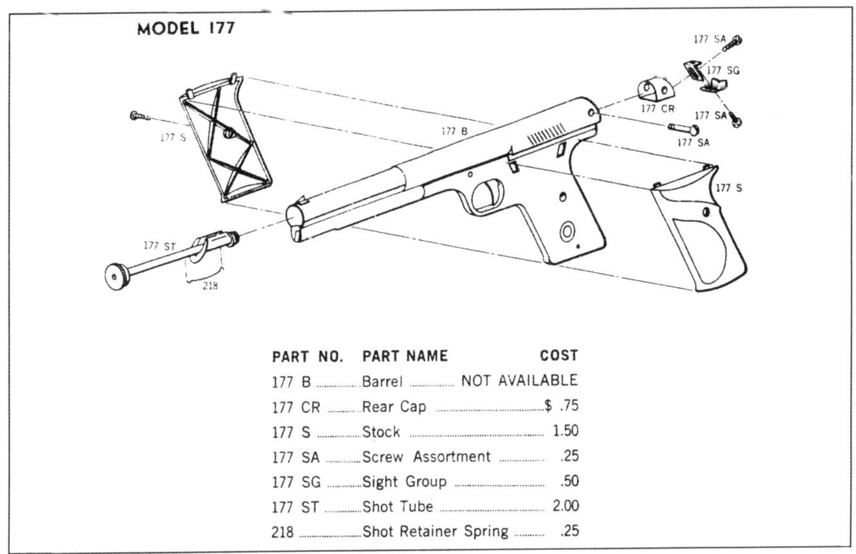

PART NO.	PART NAME	COST
177 B	Barrel	NOT AVAILABLE
177 CR	Rear Cap	$ .75
177 S	Stock	1.50
177 SA	Screw Assortment	.25
177 SG	Sight Group	.50
177 ST	Shot Tube	2.00
218	Shot Retainer Spring	.25

Parts Diagram for the Model 177 Target Special.

Model: **No. 118 "TARGETEER"**

Maker: **Daisy Manufacturing Co.,**
Plymouth, Michigan, U.S.A.

Date: 1937 to 1952, with break in manufacture from 1940 to 1946. First model had fixed rearsight. So pre-war examples had non-adjustable sights. There was also a pre-war nickel plated model. On re-introduction in 1946, models were fitted with adjustable rearsight. Production ceased 1950. From above, pre-war are scarce, whilst post-war are common. Re-introduced 1958 in BB calibre and called the Model 177. This model had a dummy barrel weight and plastic target grips.

Valuation: £15 - £40.

Details: All tinplate construction. A slide repeater that works on the same system as the slide action air rifles with screw-in barrel and BB magazine. Airpistol uses sub miniature "BB" of calibre ·118. The blued pre-war model was sold with a box that converted to a back stop with small spinning targets. The pre-war nickel plated model was boxed in a more elaborate design that converted to a back stop with three spinning targets. The post-war model was boxed that doubled as a target back-stop. The airpistol was designed by Charles Lefever and appears to have been his last patented design. This was patent number 2,131,173. Now for the confusion, because stamped on the postwar model is the patent number 2,132,173. The airpistol was designed in 1936 and patent granted in 1938.

The Targeteer was modelled from the Colt Woodsman fire-arm pistol. Advertised length 10 inches. 500 repeater magazine. To load, turn airpistol upside down and on the underside of the barrel is a small cut-away, turn knurled barrel face clockwise and a small hole will align itself with the cut away. You now pour the small BB's into the magazine. Turn knurled barrel fact anti-clockwise to close and form air seal. To fire just pull back the slide action until it cocks and then push slide forward. Should fire when trigger is pulled.

Stamped on top of the air chamber for the pre-war airpistol:

DAISY NO. 118 TARGET SPECIAL
CALIBRE ·118 PATENTS PENDING.
DAISY MFG. CO. PLYMOUTH, MICH., U.S.A.

and on the post-war airpistol:

DAISY NO. 118 TARGETEER
CALIBRE ·118 PATENT 2,132,173 OTHERS PENDING.
DAISY MFG. CO. PLYMOUTH. MICH. U.S.A.

The above have a 4¼ inch smoothbore barrel. Advertised weight 1½ lb. Appears to have been chrome plated during the middle 1950's and sold as the "Targette Model 320". Same micro-calibre and sold with a plastic shooting gallery. Although production had now long since ceased, the Targeteer was advertised well into the late 1950's. Number 4 shotgun cartridge shot will fit the above and a few pounds should last a lifetime.

By the late 1970's the lettering on the air chamber had changed to:

"DAISY NO. 177 TARGET SPECIAL — CALIBRE ·177
PATENTS 2,758,586 - 2,724,897 —
DAISY MFG. ROGERS, ARK., U.S.A."

It helps the action to function if the airgun is held in the vertical position as you pull back the slider to cock the action. On the latest models the grips are held on by one screw, whilst the left hand grip has a dummy plastic screw head.

The above model with the changed lettering was also available with a gold/grey glossy lacquered finish with amber plastic grips. This variation is quite rare. A true fun shooter.

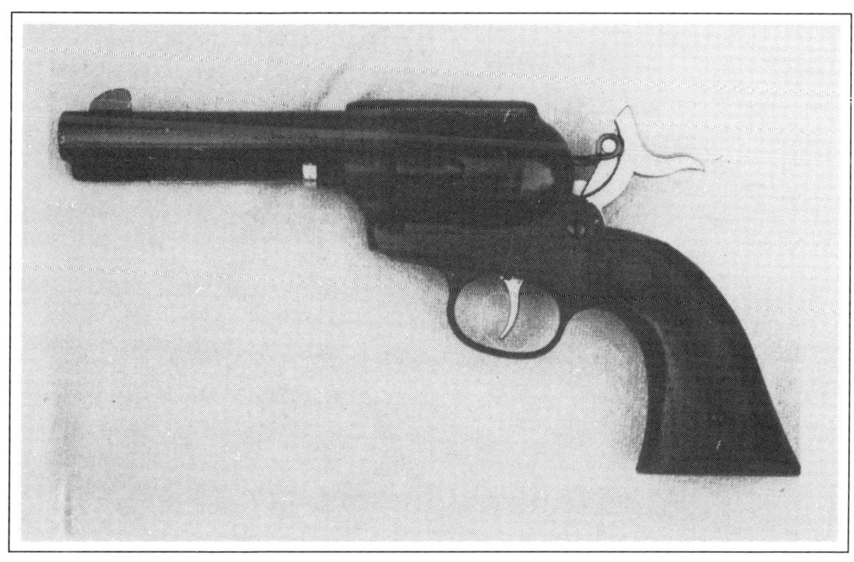

Daisy Model 179 in cocked position.

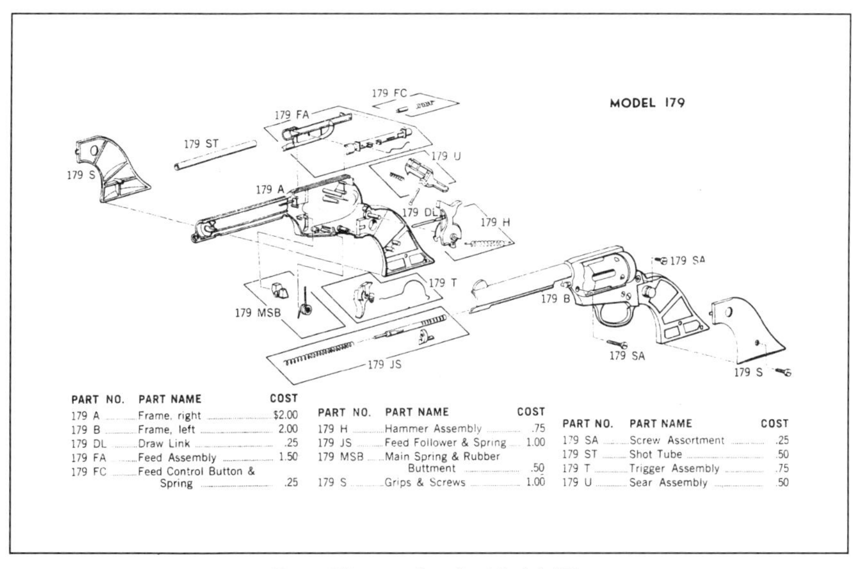

PART NO.	PART NAME	COST
179 A	Frame, right	$2.00
179 B	Frame, left	2.00
179 DL	Draw Link	.25
179 FA	Feed Assembly	1.50
179 FC	Feed Control Button & Spring	.25
179 H	Hammer Assembly	.75
179 JS	Feed Follower & Spring	1.00
179 MSB	Main Spring & Rubber Buttment	.50
179 S	Grips & Screws	1.00
179 SA	Screw Assortment	.25
179 ST	Shot Tube	.50
179 T	Trigger Assembly	.75
179 U	Sear Assembly	.50

Parts Diagram for the Model 179.

Model: **DAISY MODEL 179**

Maker: **Daisy MFG. Co.,**
Rogers, Ark., U.S.A.
Imported by Milbro Sports, Scotland.

Date: Introduced 1961 and still current model.

Valuation: £10 - £25.

Details: A copy of the Colt "Peacemaker" revolver. A superb "fun-gun" if using lead BB's. Can be used in the lounge by a seven year old as long as Mother is out. Low muzzle velocity and ease of operation makes it a perfect introduction to pistol shooting. Brown plastic grips with grey enamel finish to metal parts. Hammer and trigger plated. BB's are dropped into force fed magazine under the barrel. Advertised as a twelve shot repeater. To fire, pull hammer back as far as possible and then fire, if held in downward position. BB's can roll down barrel. 11½ inches in length.

A supply of lead BB's can be obtained by ordering BB size lead shot for loading shotgun cartridges. Above example often fed two BB's into breech and one occasionally ran down the barrel if it was held in a downward position, but would still fire the remaining BB pellet. Prior to distribution, about one hundred of the above were made from brass as commercial salesmen's samples.

The above operates on spring power only and not on air pressure. During the middle 1960's a fast draw holster was available for the above. This was in solid hide leather and was sold as a complete kit with the airgun. Advertised muzzle velocity 140 f.p.s.

During 1974 a commemorative set of two matching airpistols were advertised complete with a fitted box. This honoured the Texas Lawmen or Rangers as they were often called. The grips were imbedded with miniatures of the commemorative seal and the Ranger badge of office. The barrels were stamped "1823-Texas Rangers-1973". The sets also contained a 48 page history of the Texan Rangers.

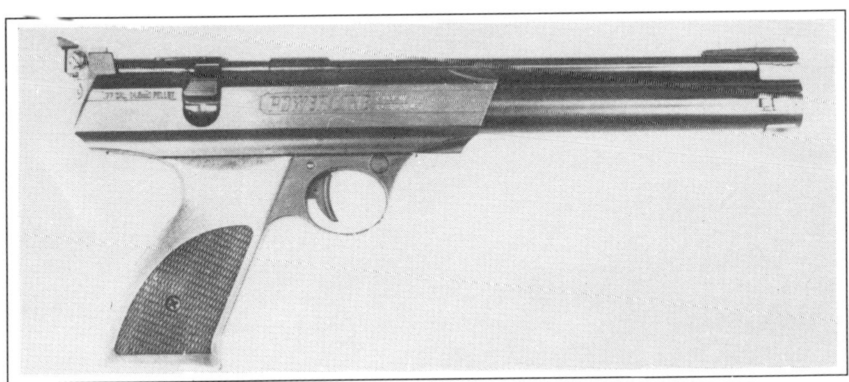

Daisy Powerline 717/722 Single Stroke Pump-up Recoiless airpistol.

Model: 717 (·177) and 722 (·22)

Maker: **Daisy Manufacturing Company, Power Line Products,** Rogers, Arkansas 72756, U.S.A.

Date: Appeared in England during 1980 although may have been available in small numbers before this date as 1978 is referred to as the date of production in the States.

Valuation: £20 - £40.

Details: A single pump action, single shot recoiless airpistol. Very well made and of surprising simple construction. Only one pump will compress the air, there is only one valve, that connected to the trigger. Deep blued, lacquered with brown grips. Rearsight fully adjustable with the foresight blade being rather broad. Trigger has safety just in front of it and is non-adjustable. The system of loading and pumping is very important and must be followed if the airgun is to function properly:

a) Pull back the breech.

b) Pump side lever once to compress air.

c) Place pellet into breech and push home the bolt.

d) FIRE!

If the above is not followed, the pump will either not work or air will slowly hiss passed the one valve seal. In the field of moderate power recoiless airpistols, they represent excellent value for the price. All major parts are from diecast metal, except for the air chamber which is brass. Overall length is 13½ inches with a weight of 2 lbs. 13 ozs. The ·177 muzzle velocity was measured at 360 f.p.s., whilst for ·22 it was 290 f.p.s. For reviews of the above see *"Airgun World"*, May, 1980. The above should become quite rare because the Model 777 was introduced in 1982 as an improved model of the above. Left hand grips are available for the above. Even more rare is the rosewood fitted case for the Model 777 target version with moulded compartments for the airpistol, pellets and oil, cleaning rod, patches and adjuster tool. As advertised in *"American Rifleman"*, May, 1982.

Pre-war Diana Model 1 airpistol.

Model: **FIRST MODEL TINPLATE AIRPISTOL**

Maker: **"Diana", Mayer & Grammelspacher,** Rasttat, Germany.

Date: Middle 1920's to middle 1930's.

Valuation: £30 - £90.

Details: Diana's first tinplate airpistol. Unusual design with a tip down barrel and airchamber in the butt. Action is cocked with a separate tool that clips onto a projecting nipple on the base of the butt, it is then pulled down until action is cocked. Spring held barrel is pulled forward about a quarter of an inch and tipped down for loading. Both sides of the body pressing have "DIANA" and the huntress trademark, whilst near trigger guard "MADE IN GERMANY". There is also a small hole through which trigger adjustment can be made with a screwdriver. Appears to have been available in ·177 only. Barrel 5¾ inches long. Non-adjustable sights. Sold with a blued finish only. From the example seen the barrel is rifled, although could have also been available in smoothbore. Interesting to note that the next model to follow was the Model 2 gat style airpistol so was the above Model number 1? Advertised weight 1 lb 3oz.

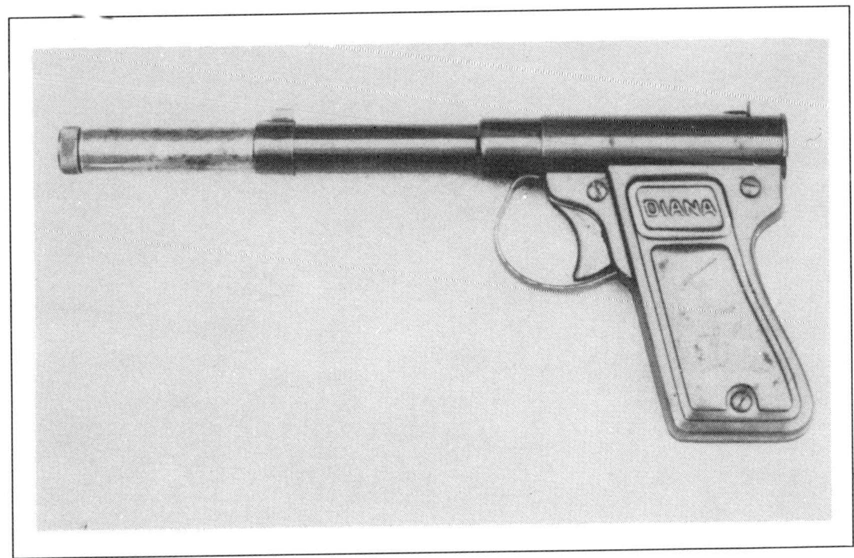

German Diana Model 2.

Model: **2**

Maker: **"Diana", Mayer & Grammelspacher,** Rastatt, Germany.

Date: Early 1930's to 1945.

Valuation: £5 - £20.

Details: All metal tinplate gat airpistol. Available in either blued or nickel plated finish. Produced after W.W.2 in Scotland by Millard Bros., with the "original" presses as brought over from Germany after they lost the War. Other maker's name appear on these gats, see Briton Gat etc. Push-in action and load from rear as expected. ·177 smoothbore brass barrel. Both grips have the Diana Huntress trademark and stamped just in front of butt "MADE IN GERMANY". Plain non-adjustable sights. Length 9⅜ inches. The butt is a wraparound fit to the air chamber. During 1939 the above style was also sold under the names "Garanta" and "Briton" and as being British Made. Weight 11 oz. At a later date the trademark was stamped on top of the air chamber. The production figures for the Model 2 must have been enormous as during the early 1940's, they were turning out 100,000 per year!

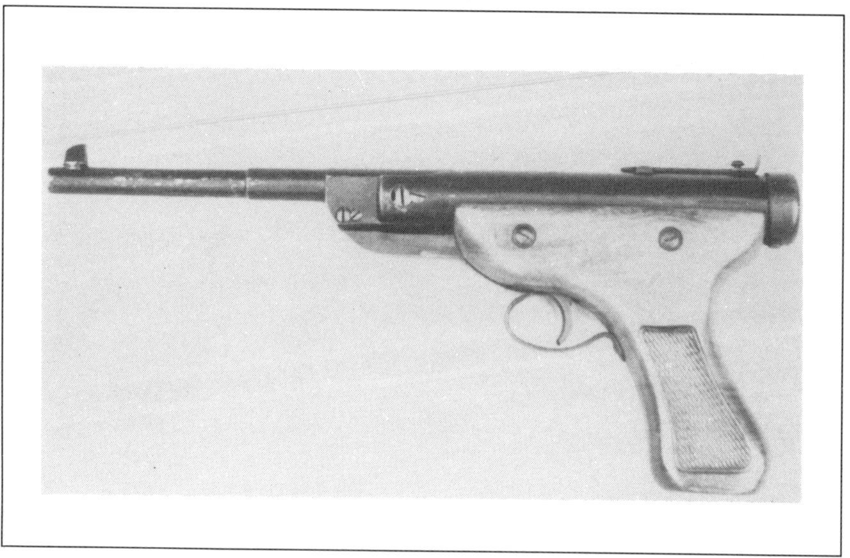

German Diana No. 5 Target airpistol.

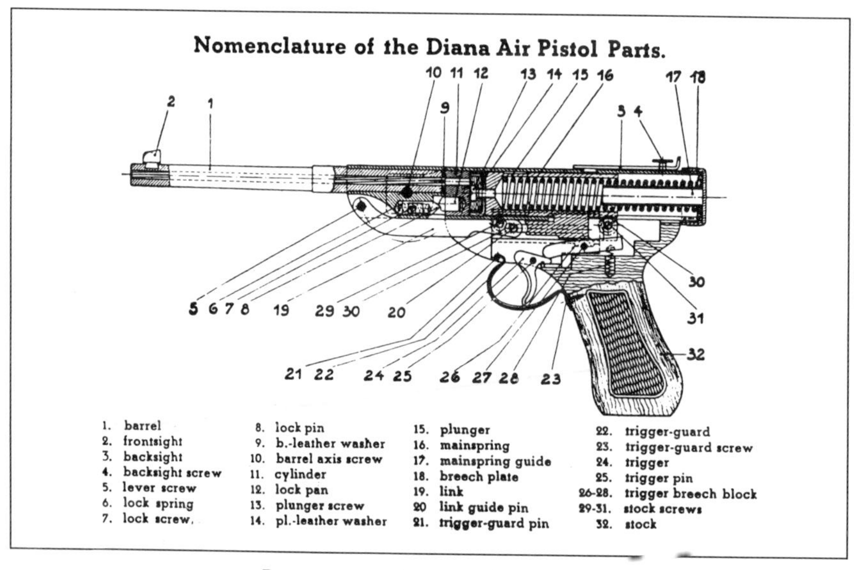

Pre-war Diana Model 5 Spares List.

Model: **No. 5 TARGET AIRPISTOL**

Maker: **German "Diana" by Mayer & Grammelspacher,** Rastatt, Germany.

Date: 1933 - 1945. See issues 1 to 5 of *"Airgun World"* for articles on the German Diana airpistols.

Valuation: £20 - £50.

Details: See Slavia "ZVP" for similarity in design to the above model. 13¼ inches long with 7¼ inch barrel. Wooden hand chequered stock. Stamped on top of air chamber "DIANA" with a "D" circular trademark with arrow pointing along the chamber towards the barrel. Serial number not visible. Stamped on the underside of the barrel "CAL. 4.5 m/m". Was advertised as ·177 and could be obtained with either a smoothbore or rifled barrel. It appears that this is the only Diana airgun that bears the "D" circular trademark. Have seen other models with a smoothbore barrel.

Patent 416560 dated 1932 was placed for the above design in that it was made in such a way as to improve the balance of a break action airpistol. The patent was not accepted. See *"Guns Review"*, May, 1980. "MADE IN GERMANY" may appear stamped on the side of the air chamber just above the grip. Some models may also have "MODELL 5 D.R.P." as well.

The survival rate for the Model 5 is pretty poor as according to War Records, Mayer & Grammelspacher were producing about 50,000 per year in the early 1940's.

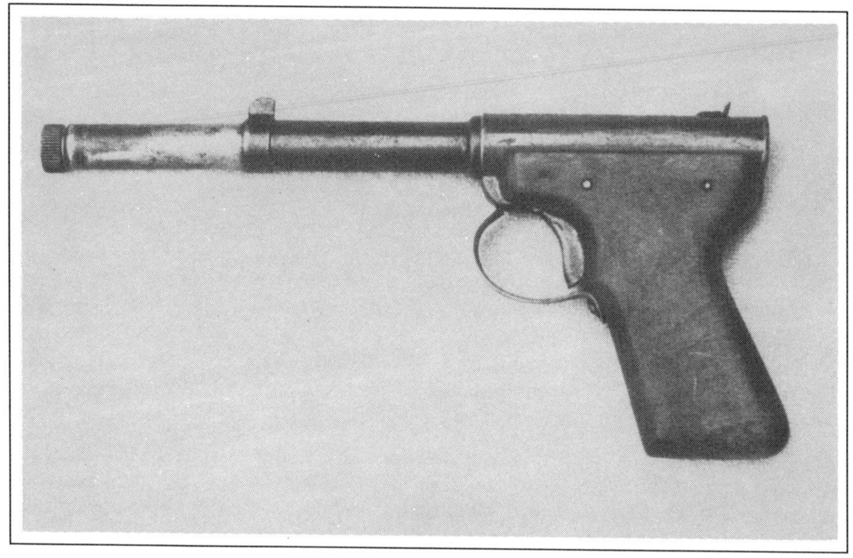

British Diana gat.

Model:	**MODEL 2 "GAT"**
Maker:	**"Diana", Millard Bros.,** Motherwell, Lanarkshire, Scotland.
Date:	Identical to pre-war German Diana Mod2, but is post-war. Seen advertised in 1956, and 1963.
Valuation:	£5 - £15.
Details:	Identical to the Model 2 gat sold by Diana in Germany in the 1930's, but the above is marked "MADE IN GREAT BRITAIN" so has been made post-war. Top of cylinder stamped with "Huntress" trademark and "DIANA MOD2 MADE IN GREAT BRITAIN". Has a wooden stock fixed to the action by two brass pins. Advertised in 1956 as the "Diana" Airpistol. The Webley Junior mainspring will fit the above should a replacement be necessary.

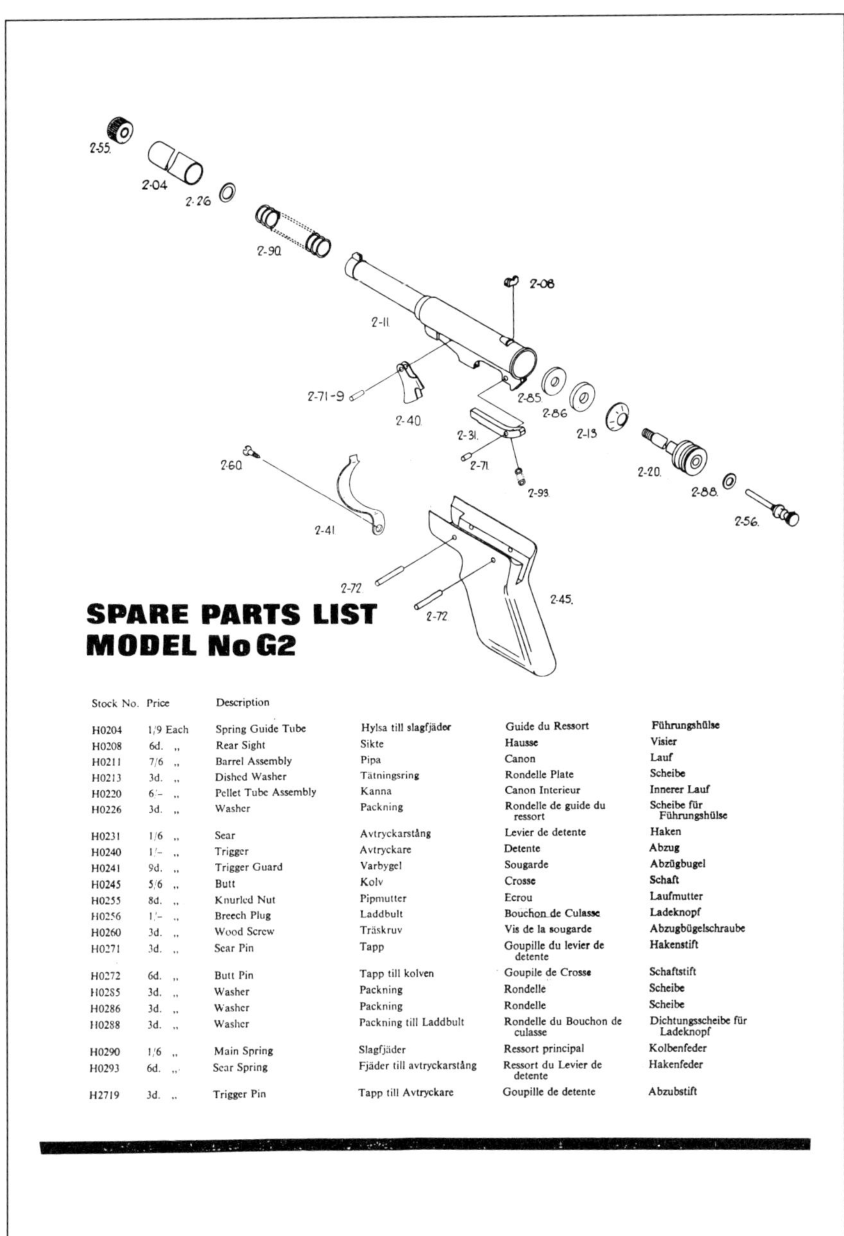

SPARE PARTS LIST
MODEL No G2

Stock No.	Price	Description			
H0204	1/9 Each	Spring Guide Tube	Hylsa till slagfjäder	Guide du Ressort	Führungshülse
H0208	6d. ,,	Rear Sight	Sikte	Hausse	Visier
H0211	7/6 ,,	Barrel Assembly	Pipa	Canon	Lauf
H0213	3d. ,,	Dished Washer	Tätningsring	Rondelle Plate	Scheibe
H0220	6/- ,,	Pellet Tube Assembly	Kanna	Canon Interieur	Innerer Lauf
H0226	3d. ,,	Washer	Packning	Rondelle de guide du ressort	Scheibe für Führungshülse
H0231	1/6 ,,	Sear	Avtryckarstång	Levier de detente	Haken
H0240	1/- ,,	Trigger	Avtryckare	Detente	Abzug
H0241	9d. ,,	Trigger Guard	Varbygel	Sougarde	Abzügbugel
H0245	5/6 ,,	Butt	Kolv	Crosse	Schaft
H0255	8d. ,,	Knurled Nut	Pipmutter	Ecrou	Laufmutter
H0256	1/- ,,	Breech Plug	Laddbult	Bouchon de Culasse	Ladeknopf
H0260	3d. ,,	Wood Screw	Träskruv	Vis de la sougarde	Abzugbügelschraube
H0271	3d. ,,	Sear Pin	Tapp	Goupille du levier de detente	Hakenstift
H0272	6d. ,,	Butt Pin	Tapp till kolven	Goupile de Crosse	Schaftstift
H0285	3d. ,,	Washer	Packning	Rondelle	Scheibe
H0286	3d. ,,	Washer	Packning	Rondelle	Scheibe
H0288	3d. ,,	Washer	Packning till Laddbult	Rondelle du Bouchon de culasse	Dichtungsscheibe für Ladeknopf
H0290	1/6 ,,	Main Spring	Slagfjäder	Ressort principal	Kolbenfeder
H0293	6d. ,,	Sear Spring	Fjäder till avtryckarstång	Ressort du Levier de detente	Hakenfeder
H2719	3d. ,,	Trigger Pin	Tapp till Avtryckare	Goupille de detente	Abzubstift

Spare Parts Lits Model No. G2.

Box lid for the Diana G2.

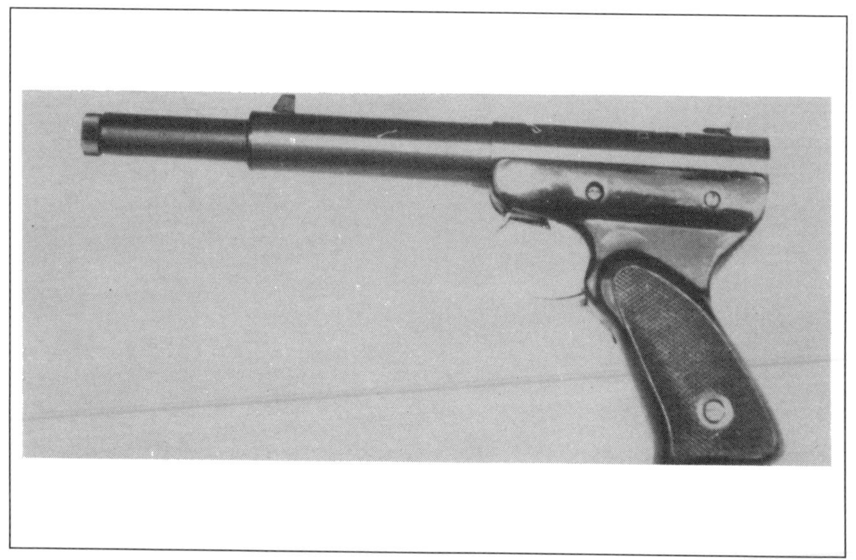

The Diana G2 airpistol.

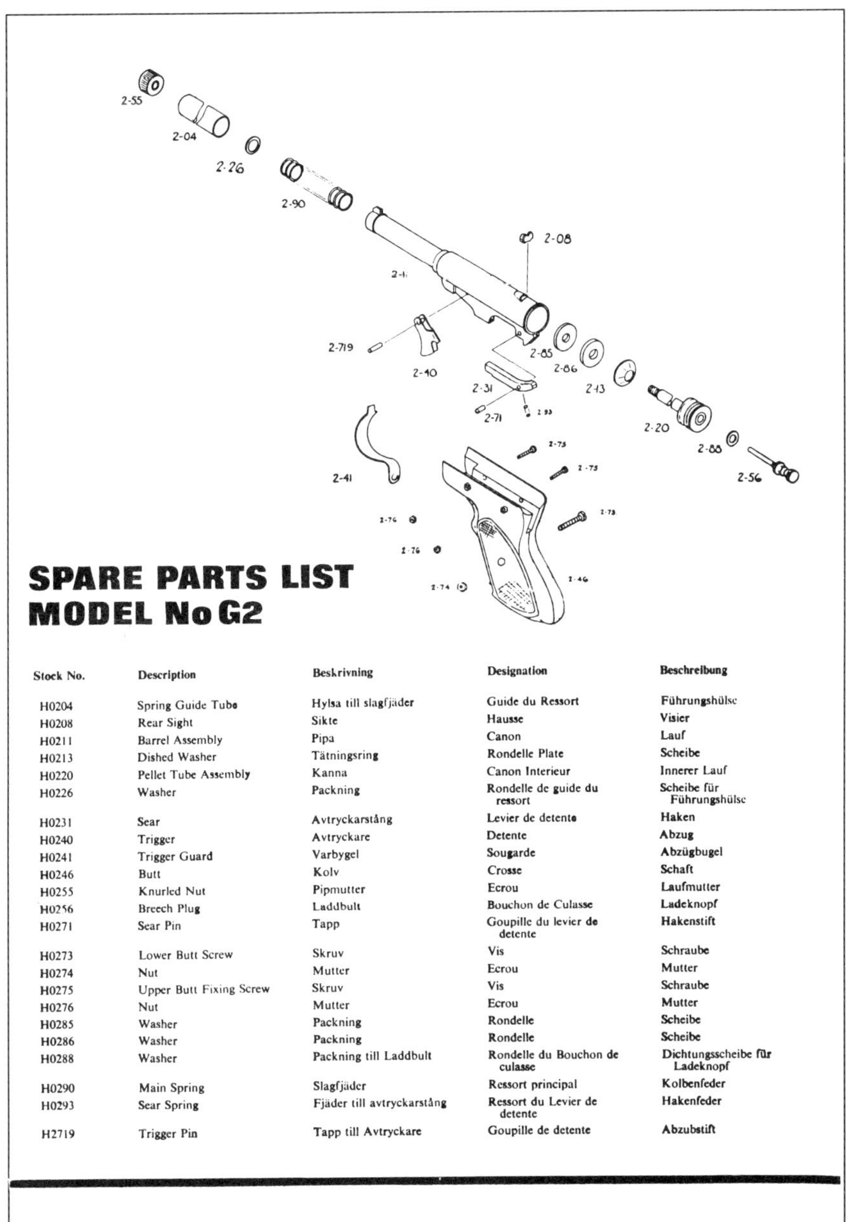

SPARE PARTS LIST
MODEL No G2

Stock No.	Description	Beskrivning	Designation	Beschreibung
H0204	Spring Guide Tube	Hylsa till slagfjäder	Guide du Ressort	Führungshülse
H0208	Rear Sight	Sikte	Hausse	Visier
H0211	Barrel Assembly	Pipa	Canon	Lauf
H0213	Dished Washer	Tätningsring	Rondelle Plate	Scheibe
H0220	Pellet Tube Assembly	Kanna	Canon Interieur	Innerer Lauf
H0226	Washer	Packning	Rondelle de guide du ressort	Scheibe für Führungshülse
H0231	Sear	Avtryckarstång	Levier de detente	Haken
H0240	Trigger	Avtryckare	Detente	Abzug
H0241	Trigger Guard	Varbygel	Sougarde	Abzügbugel
H0246	Butt	Kolv	Crosse	Schaft
H0255	Knurled Nut	Pipmutter	Ecrou	Laufmutter
H0256	Breech Plug	Laddbult	Bouchon de Culasse	Ladeknopf
H0271	Sear Pin	Tapp	Goupille du levier de detente	Hakenstift
H0273	Lower Butt Screw	Skruv	Vis	Schraube
H0274	Nut	Mutter	Ecrou	Mutter
H0275	Upper Butt Fixing Screw	Skruv	Vis	Schraube
H0276	Nut	Mutter	Ecrou	Mutter
H0285	Washer	Packning	Rondelle	Scheibe
H0286	Washer	Packning	Rondelle	Scheibe
H0288	Washer	Packning till Laddbult	Rondelle du Bouchon de culasse	Dichtungsscheibe für Ladeknopf
H0290	Main Spring	Slagfjäder	Ressort principal	Kolbenfeder
H0293	Sear Spring	Fjäder till avtryckarstång	Ressort du Levier de detente	Hakenfeder
H2719	Trigger Pin	Tapp till Avtryckare	Goupille de detente	Abzubstift

Spare Parts Lits Model No. G2.

Model: **MODEL 2**

Maker: **"Diana", Millard Bros.,**
Motherwell, Lanarkshire, Scotland.

Date: Appeared sometime after 1963.

Valuation: £5 - £15.

Details: Appears to be an improved model of the previous Model 2. Extensive use of plastic and alloy components. Standard "Gat" design with 7 inch brass smoothbore barrel in blued metal liner. Pistol can be dismantled from the front by carefully unscrewing the serrated nut at the end of the barrel. Outer barrel and air chamber are blued metal with a plastic inner foresleeve and foresight. The rearsight is a simple blade with "V" notch. Trigger guard again blued metal with an alloy non-adjustable trigger. The butt is black plastic, two piece, held by nuts and bolts to the action. Top of air chamber stamped with the "Huntress" trade mark and "DIANA — MOD 2 — MADE IN GREAT BRITAIN". The Gat system works on the principle of the barrel being fixed to the piston, thus the barrel travels down the air chamber with the piston when fired. One, maybe two small holes in the breech end of the barrel allow air to travel from the outer air chamber into the barrel. The above is not very accurate, but has certainly stood the test of time.

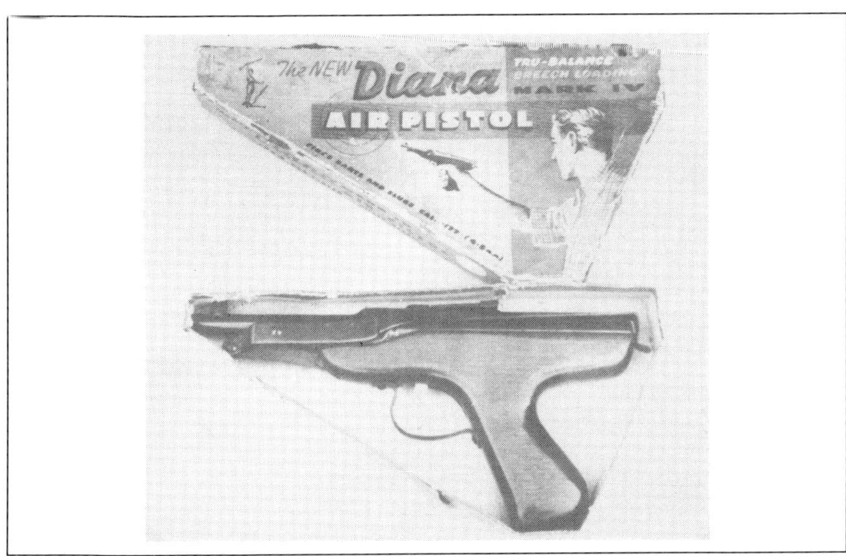

Diana Mk. IV in six-sided box (A packer's nightmare!).

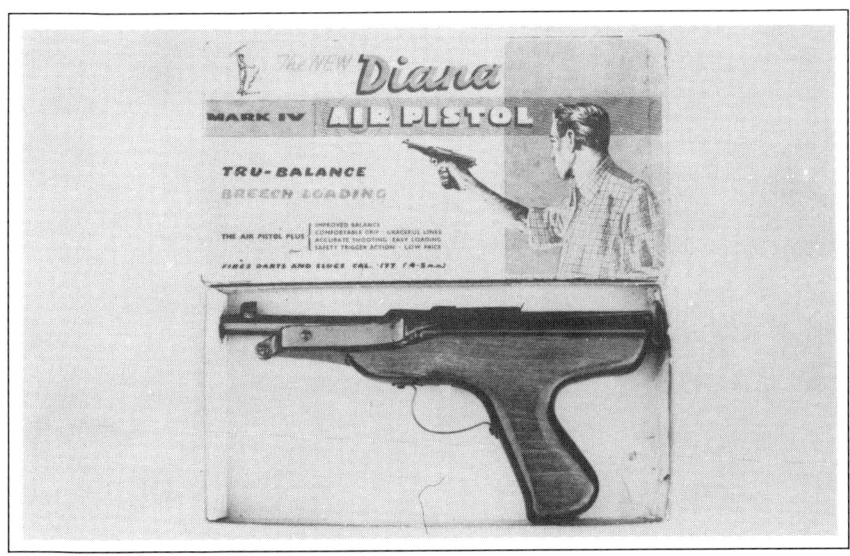

Diana Mk. IV Airpistol and box.

Diana Mark IV brochure (cover and back page).

Diana Mark IV brochure (inside pages).

Model: **MARK IV**

Maker: **Millard Bros. Ltd.,**
Carfin, Motherwell, Scotland.
(Address at time of manufacture).

Date: Above variation from the late 1950's to the middle 1960's.

Valuation: £15 - £45.

Details: Appears to be the first model Mk IV airpistol. Fixed foresight and rearsight, note similarity of foresight to pre-war Diana/Haenel foresights. Single pull trigger as opposed to double pull on later models. Available in rifled or smoothbore barrels. Top of cocking lever stamped "MILBRO — MARK IV — MADE IN GT. BRITAIN". Base of butt has what appears to be a date stamp "7 62 A". This type of stamp also appears on other Milbro products, i.e. see Diana Model 25 in companion book *"Air Rifles"*. Advertised length 11 inches and weight 1½ lbs. Price in 1960 for rifled model £4/19/6 and for smoothbore £4/18/6. Available in ·177 only. Trigger has intersecting sear so cannot be fired when being cocked. Length of barrel 4⅝ inches. Serial number not visible.

The above design was patented in 1937 and made in Germany by "Em-Ge" and called the "Zenit". They also produced a repeater model. Production ceased on outbreak of W.W.2, but some may have been produced just after, these would have appeared from the Russian Zone of Germany. For further details of the original patent see *"Guns Review"*, July, 1980. On airpistol with date stamp "2 64 R" the top of the cocking lever is stamped "DIANA MK IV MADE IN GT. BRITAIN". An even earlier model dated September, 1957 was sold in an odd shaped box with six sides that roughly followed the outline of the airpistol, it also had an adjustable rearsight with a slider and ramp.

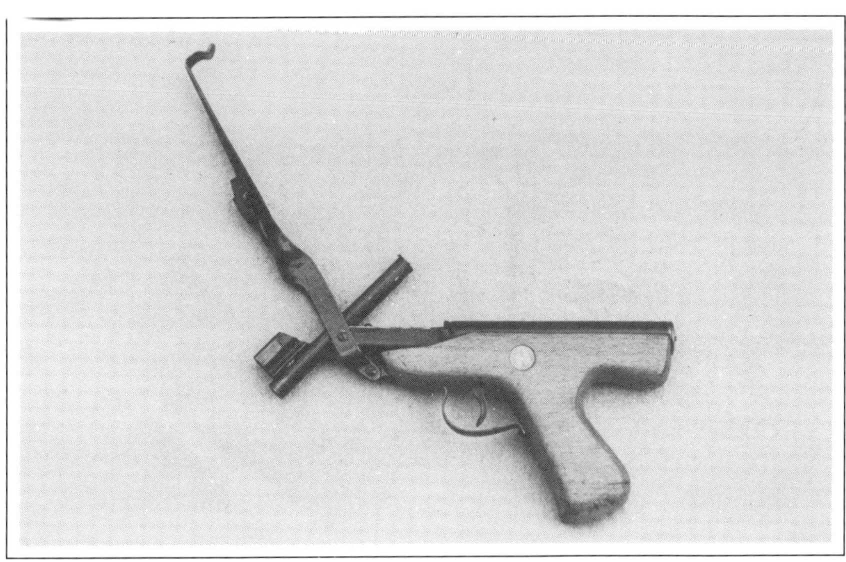

Diana Mk. IV in cocked position.

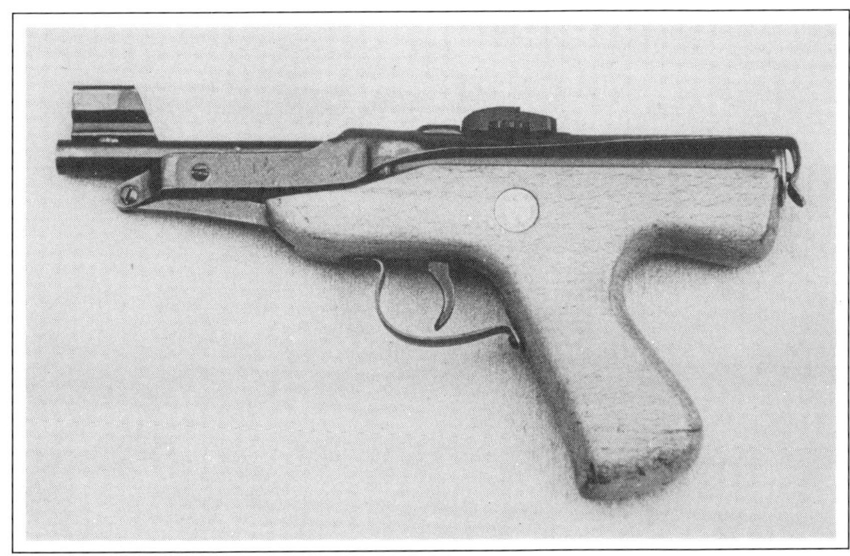

Diana Mk. IV.

SPARE PARTS LIST

PART NO.	DESCRIPTION	PART NO.	DESCRIPTION
4–04	Piston	4–29	Butt
4–05	Cup washer	4–30	Spring
4–06	Washer	4–31	Gimped Washer
4–07	Washer	4–32	Trigger Guard
4–08	Screw	4–33	Screw
4–09	Main Spring	4–34	Screw
4–14	Leaf Spring	4–35	Screw
4–15	Screw	4–38	Pin
4–16	Cocking Lever	4–41	Spring
4–17	Barrel	4–45	Sight Body
4–18	Breech Washer	4–46	Sight
4–19	Pivot Bearing	4–51	Front Sight
4–20	Pivot	4–52	Cylinder
4–21	Screw	4–60	End Plug
4–22	Link	27–141	Diana Motif
4–23	Link Pin	27–142	Milbro Motif
4–24	Slide	30–04	Nut
4–25	Sear	30–06	Spring
4–26	Sear Pin	30–07	Screw
4–27	Hinge Pin	30–08	Ball
4–28	Trigger	36–37	Sight Shield

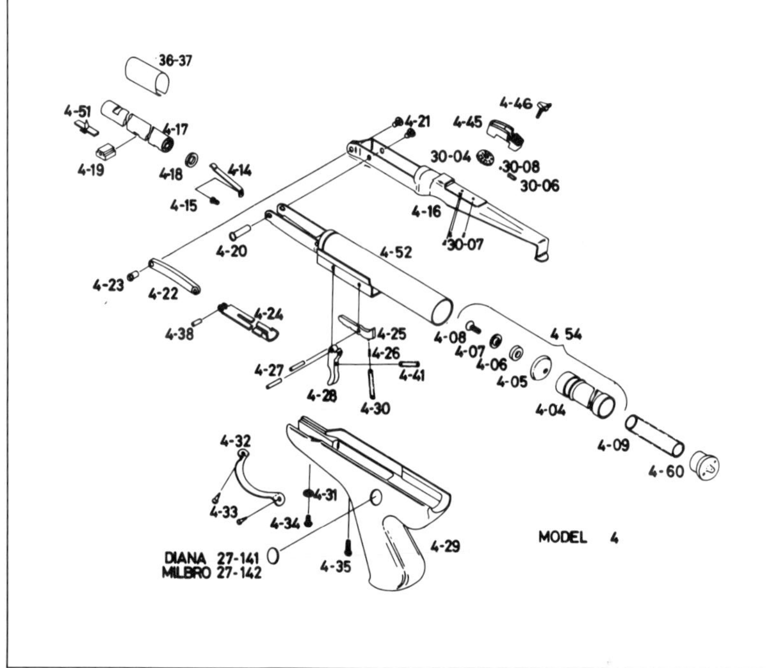

Model G-4 Spare Parts List.

Model: **MK. IV. Also referred to as the Model "G4"**

Maker: **"Diana", by Millard Bros.,**
Lanarkshire, Scotland.

Date: Seen advertised in 1960 as "new deluxe model". Appeared in the late 1950's and phased out in the 1980's.

Valuation: £20 - £35.

Details: Similar in design to German "Zenit" airpistol by EM-GE. Unusual design and very novel to use. Non-adjustable double pull trigger. On side of stock set in is the Diana trademark and "DIANA SERIES 70" and stamped on the cocking lever is "MARK IV, MADE IN GT. BRITAIN". Plastic adjustable rear sight. Originally sold with choice of rifled or smoothbore ·177 barrel. Overall length 11 inches. Advertised weight 1½ lbs.

Variation may occur as to the style of foresight protector, have seen a rounded shape other than the square style, also type of medallion set in stock, this can be either for Diana, either huntress trademark or just name with laurel leaves, which could be for Milbro, see parts diagram.

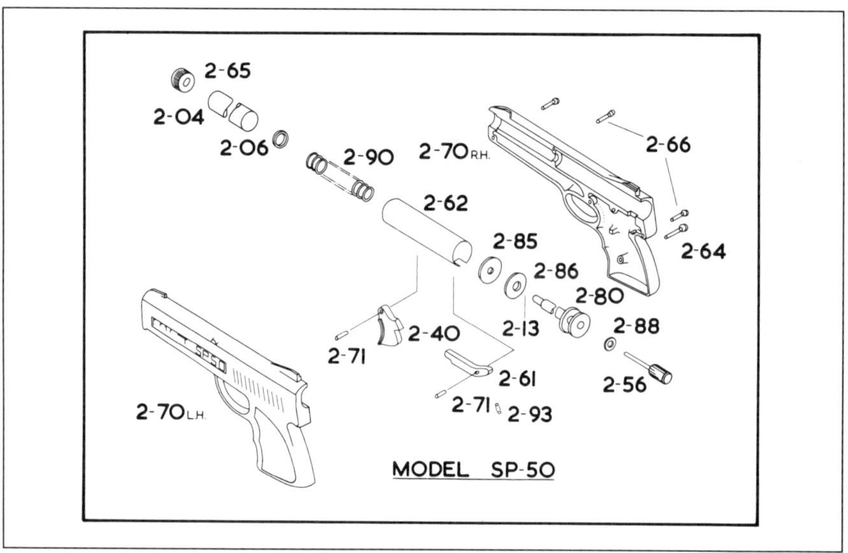

Model SP-50 diagram.

SPARE PARTS LIST

PART NO.	DESCRIPTION	PART NO.	DESCRIPTION
2-4	Guide Tube	2-70*	L.H. Body Casting
2-6	Washer	2-70*	R.H. Body Casting
2-13	Washer	2-71	Hinge Pin
2-40	Trigger	2-80	Barrel Assembly
2-56	Breech Plug	2-85	Washer
2-61	Sear	2-86	Washer
2-62	Liner Tube	2-88	Plug Washer
2-64	Butt Screw	2-90	Main Spring
2-65	Knurled Nut	2-93	Sear Spring
2-66	Stock Screw		

* Please state L.H. or R.H. when ordering 2-70

Model SP-50 Spare Parts List.

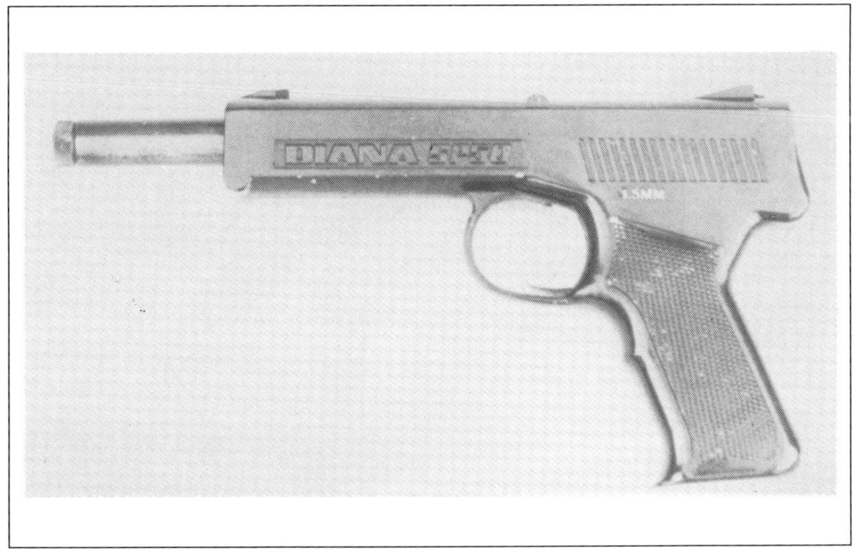

The Diana SP50.

Model: **SP50**

Maker: **Milbro Sports Ltd.,**
P.O. Box 24,
Motherwell,
Lanarkshire ML1 4UP, Scotland
(Address at time of manufacture).

Date: From the middle 1970's to 1982.

Valuation: £5 - £20.

Details: The ultimate gat. Die-cast metal with matt black stove enamel finish. ·177 smoothbore barrel and advertised for darts and pellets. Each was sold with 100 Milbro pellets and 12 darts. Styled to look like a Colt automatic pistol. Advertised weight 25 oz. (700 gms). What more can you say about one of the longest running designs of airgun manufacture.

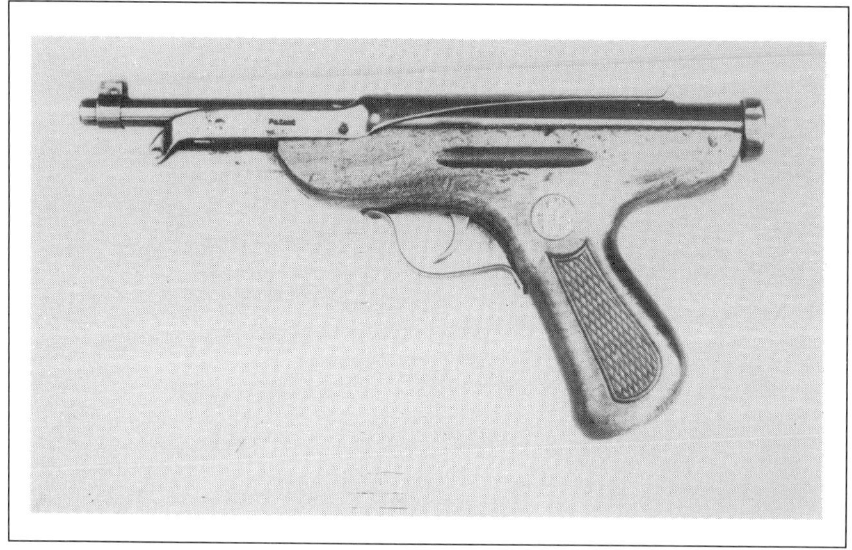

The Zenit Airpistol.

Model: **ZENIT SINGLE SHOT AIRPISTOL**

Maker: **Em-Ge, trade name of Moritz & Gerstenberger,**
Zella-Mehlis,
Thuringia, Germany.
(Formerly Eastern Germany).

Date: Design patented in 1937 and outbreak of War in 1939 means a very short period of production. Many writers give the impression that the Zenit is common, but in my experience it is not. Would suggest that the production was very short, only about three years. Some of these may have appeared after the War from the Russian sector of Germany, but this seems most unlikely.

Valuation: £40 - £70.

Details: The predecessor of the Diana Model 4. Top strap lifts up and is raised over the end of the airpistol in order to cock the action. Fitted with an intercepting sear so that action must be fired when cocked. Top strap is stamped "PATENT" on side and on one example seen was stamped with a silhouette of a twin funnelled ship with "GERMANY" inside. Top of strap marked <ZENIT> and <EM-GE> ZELLA-MEHLIS (THUR.). From tip of barrel in ·177 only, rifled or smooth bore. Steel barrel had a brassliner. Barrel stamped "CAL. 4.5m/m (·177)".

Some barrels had "gcz" after the calibre, this indicates a rifled bore. The foresight was adjustable for both windage and elevation, this is accomplished by unscrewing the only one on the sight. It can then be either turned to the right or left for windage or the foresight blade can be highered or lowered for elevation. There are graduation marks on the barrel and blade to mark degree of adjustment. The barrel is spring tensioned so that as soon as the top catch is raised the barrel immediately tips down for loading. The rear chamber plug is a bayonet fit and can easily be removed by pushing in and turning.

The cocking linkages are pivoted by pins whereas on the post-war British models screws were wisely used. One-piece hardwood butt with EM-GE medallions on each side. The rearsight is formed by upturned metal of the top loading catch, and has a "U" cut into it. The Patent for the above design was number 472021, dated 1937 so manufacture could have started in the same year.

Would assume that it was only made for about three years at the most so contrary to what other books state the above is quite a rare airpistol. It was also made in a repeater version, but this is rarely encountered. The butt has pressed chequering. The patent was made by Franz Moller of 10 Rathaus Strasse, Zella-Mehlis, Thuringia, Germany and his British agent for the patent was A. P. Thurston, 329 High Holborn, London.

The Patent was for the novel design of the above and the top cocking lever. The end cap can have the annoying habit of flying off and hitting the user full in the face; the Author, when using the above, kept his thumb over the end cap as the thought of the pellet coming from the front and the mainspring, guide and cap proceeding from the rear was just too much to bear.

Apart from the above ship-like trademark, another type of marking seen is "PATENT ANG-GERMANY".

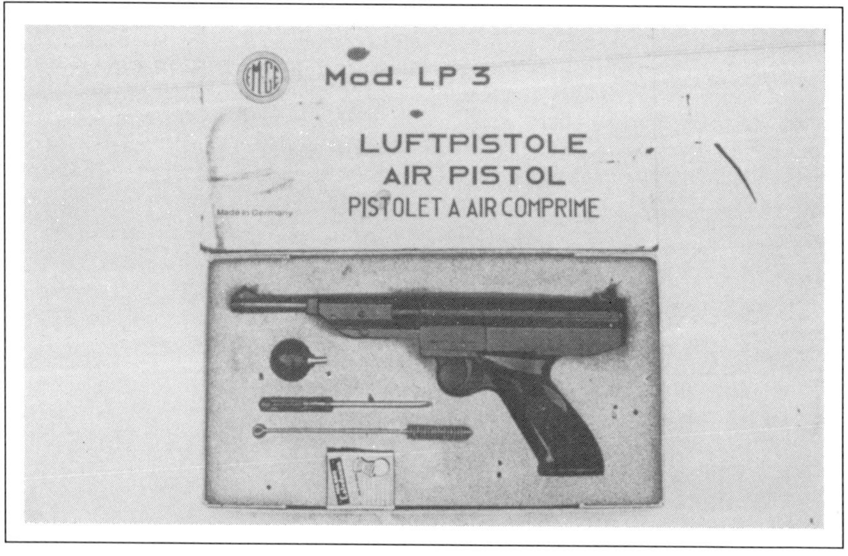

LP 3 in original box with accessories. Pellet box and cut away recess are not original.

Model: **LP 3**

Maker: **Gerstenterger,**
Eberwein, Western Germany.

Date: Not listed in Smith's, but is a current model, so assume manufacture from around the late 1950's to introduction of LP 3a.

Valuation: £20 - £60.

Details: Sold in cardboard box with cocking aid for end of barrel, screwdriver and barrel bore cleaning brush. Very deep blued finish with brown plastic grips. Stamped on L.H.S. of trigger block "EM-GE, GERSTENTERGERU, EBERWEIN" and further to the back of the action "MOD.LP3 MADE IN WESTERN GERMANY". Stamped on the same side of the barrel "CAL.4¼mm", whilst on the other side of the barrel is stamped the Germany muzzle velocity level pass sign, the "F" in a pentagon with the serial number in front. Serial number of above 24246. Rear sight is adjustable for windage only and the foresight for elevation. Trigger pull is adjustable by way of the hole drilled in the frame at the rear of the trigger guard, turning the screw to the left sets the trigger to a heavier pull. For stripping instructions for the LP 3a, see *"Guns Review"*, August, 1976. For the LP 3 see *"Guns Review"*, December, 1974. The slender B.S.A. foresight blade as fitted to early Airsporters will act as a substitute foresight element for the above. In 1974 it was advertised as the Hy-score Model 822T in the U.S.A. and available in either ·22 or ·177 calibre. Advertised weight 2 lb. 11 oz. It has been suggested that the "blued finish" is in fact anodised, i.e., a black zinc chromatic film.

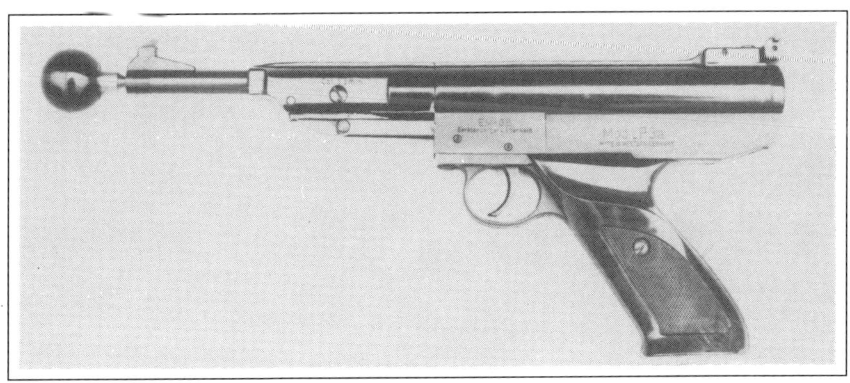

EM-GE Model LP 3a.

Model: **LP 3a**

Maker: **"EM-GE", Gerstenbergeru,** Eberwein, Germany.

Date: Seen advertised in 1976, *"Guns Review",* April. Also in 1978, see *"Airgun World",* September. Appears to be a follow-on from the LP 3. Would assume the letters "LP" to stand for "LUFTPISTOLE". Production ceased in 1980 on introduction of Model 100. See "Airgun World", June, 1980.

Valuation: £20 - £60.

Details: Deep smooth blueing with brown plastic grips. Cast foresight and rearsight. The rearsight is now fully adjustable for windage and elevation. Trigger adjustment appears to be by way of small hole at rear of trigger guard. Top of barrel and air chamber is ribbed. L.H.S. of barrel stamped with the calibre whilst on other side appears the serial number and the "F" in pentagon denoting lower level of muzzle energy required for European Countries. Stamped on L.H.S. of trigger block "EM-GE GERSTENBERGERU, EBERWEIN" followed by "MOD. LP 3a" and finally "EM-GE GERSTENBERGERU, EBERWEIN, MADE IN WESTERN GERMANY". Serial number of above 39934, also has "F" stamped on the underside of the barrel. Sold in polystyrene fitted box with cocking palm aid, screwdriver and barrel bore cleaning rod. Outside of case is identical to the printing on the older cardboard box for the LP 3. Cast into the polystyrene on the inside of each piece appears "WALTHER KUNSTOFF — VERPACKUNGSWERK, D - 7923 KÖNIGSBRONN, TEL. 07328 - 5051". Could Walther have made the box, or airpistol, or both? Advertised weight 2 lb. 6 oz. Imported by A.S.I. For details of stripping the LP 3a see *"Guns Review",* August, 1976. With a little persuasion the barrel will unscrew from the outer casing. Imported by Milbro, Millard Bros. Ltd., P.O. Box 24, Motherwell, Lanarkshire, Scotland, ML1 4UP. The rather very deep blued finish could be a black zinc chromatic film as it has been suggested that the frame, air chamber, outer barrel sleeve and even the piston are all made from zinc alloy.

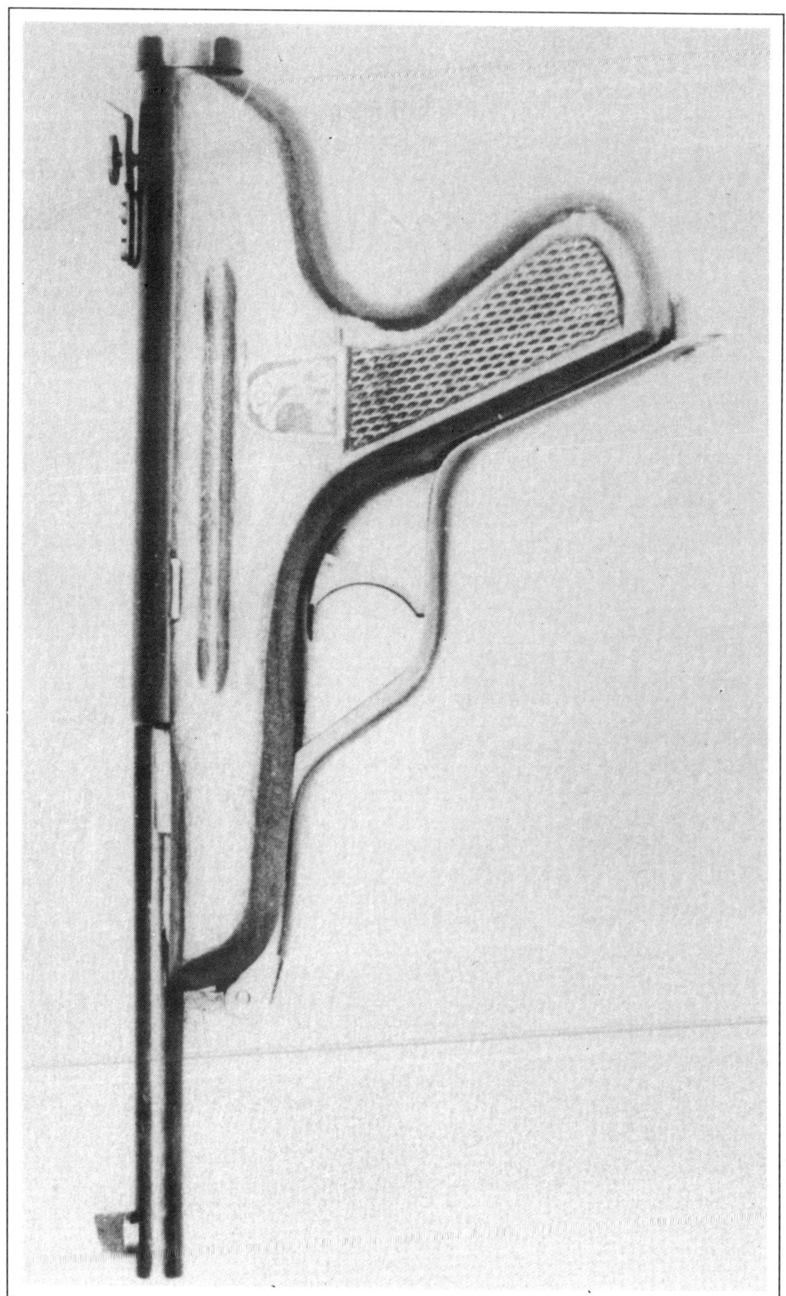

Falke Model 33.

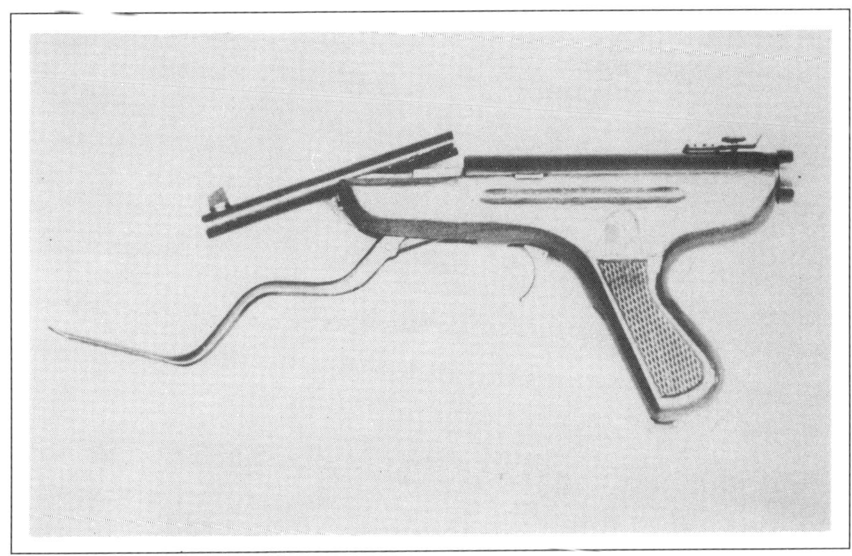

Falke Model 33 in cocked position.

Model: **33**

Maker: **Falke, Albert Fohrenbach, G.m.b.H.,**
Bennisgsen, Hanover, Germany.

Date: Available in small numbers from the early 1950's to the late 1960's.

Valuation: £40 - £90.

Details: Similar in operation to the Diana (Milbro) Mark 4 airpistol, in that the barrel tips down for loading. Almost one foot in length along the barrel line. 5¼ inch rifled barrel, although a smooth bore was available. Foresight set in dovetail and barrel stamped "KAL 4·5m/m gez." and on the underside "MADE IN GERMANY". Top of air chamber stamped "FALKE MOD 33 DBP". End chamber plug can be removed by pushing in and rotating in clockwise direction. Rearsight adjustable for windage and elevation. Trigger guard forms cocking lever and is held in place by catch at base of butt.

Although in theory it cannot be fired in the cocked position, in practice the action could often be fired in this position. One piece wooden butt with pressed chequering and alloy "Falke" medallions set in each side. Serial number not visible. The rearsight has two screws, the back screw is for rotation and locking whilst the fore screw is for adjustment for windage. Both must be loosened for adjustment to take place.

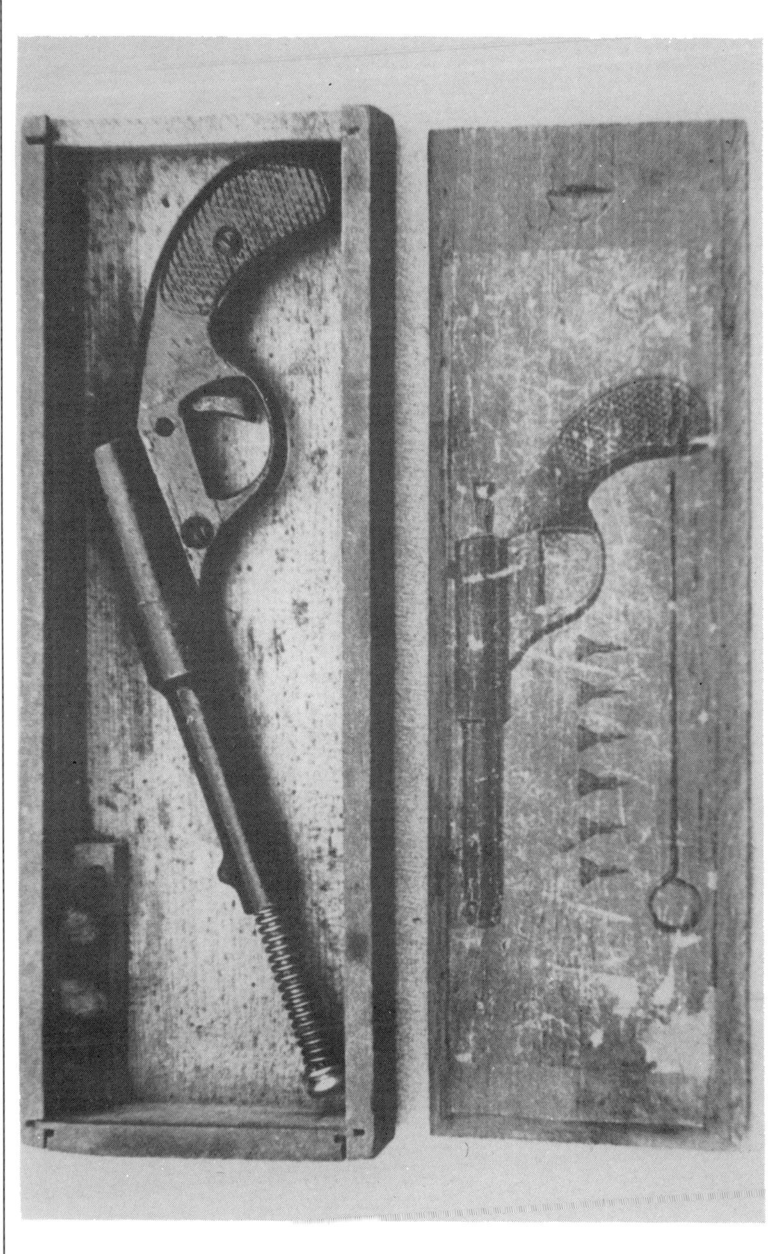

The "Spring Air Pistol", 1890 to 1933 model.

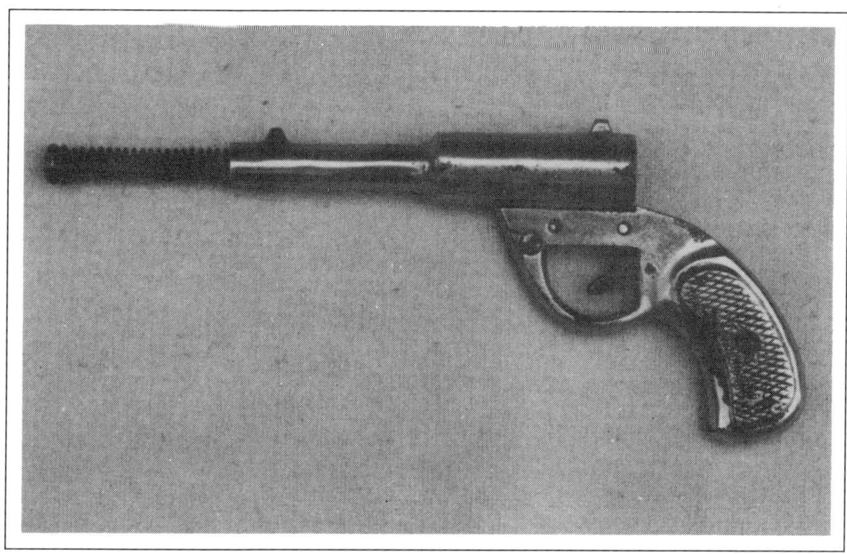

The nickel plated Mk. II "Dolla". (May also have been called "No. 2". The above pattern of "Dolla" air pistol, seen advertised in 1927 Catalogue of G. C. Bell & Sons, 19 Thistle Street, Glasgow C3, who appears to have marketed many a product under the "Clyde" name. The Clyde airpistol is in fact the break barrel action by F.L.Z., Friedrich Langenham. Advertised at 5/6 post-free in neat box with darts and slugs.

Nickel plated "Dolla" airpistol marked "No. 2" on box and lid. The flat sided to round trigger hole was advertised from 1890 to 1933, when the hole was changed to an oval shaped pattern.

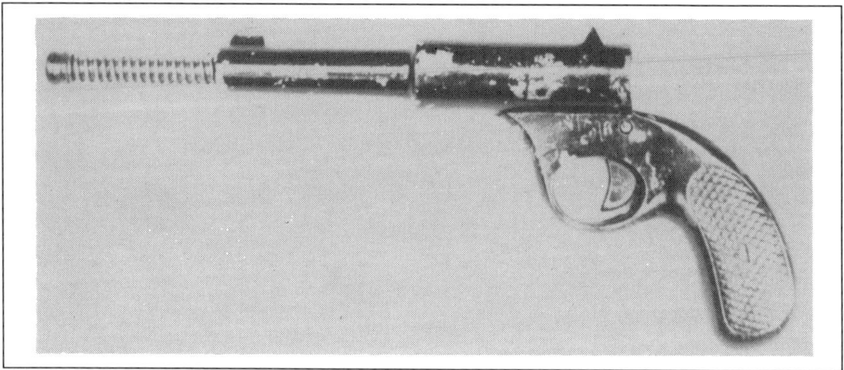

1933 and up to 1939 model Dolla with oval shaped trigger hole.

Model: **A "SPRING AIR PISTOL".** So placed under GAT!!

Maker: Listed in 1933 German catalogue as being made by **JGA (IGA), the initials being for J. G. Anschütz.** Earlier they may have been made by **F. R. Langenham,** Zella-Mehlis, Germany.

Date: Advertised from 1890 to around 1939, have seen 1930's catalogue with same air pistol, but with updated box. Seen advertised 1939 in box with round tin of pellets and three darts.

Valuation: £20 - £35, boxed examples appear to sell between £40 and £60.

Details: Illustration on lid used in catalogues. Cast metal on a brass liner tube. The above airpistol has suffered a split all the way around the air cylinder just in front of the trigger, so if fired, the barrel slowly creeps away from the air cylinder. Could be bought nickeled or painted black. Length of airpistol is 10 inches.

Footnote: Seen advertised 1932 - 1933 as the "DOLLA" with (FOREIGN) added. Sold as two models. The Mark I, all nickel in box with pellets and darts. "Dolla" Mark II, all steel body, unbreakable and sold in box. Prices 5/- and 8/- respectively. Have seen an identical model as above, but nickel plated and has "No. 2" stamped on box lid and side of box. As above, has one pin trigger action, whilst later model has two pin trigger action.

The dismantling of the "Dolla" Mk. II or "No. 2" model airpistol is shown in Harvey's Collectors' Page, *"Airgun World",* December, 1979. Has been suggested that the name "DOLLA" came from the fact that the airpistol cost 5/- in the 1920's and 1930's and as there were four dollars to the pound and one dollar equalled 5/- hence the name "DOLLA". During the late 1800's to early 1900's, Lane Brothers sold the above as the "William Tell" in two finishes, nickel plated and japanned for 3/- and 2/6 respectively.

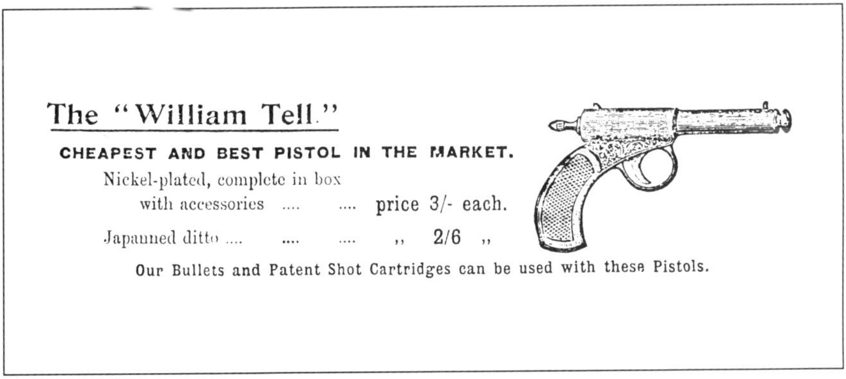

The "William Tell."

CHEAPEST AND BEST PISTOL IN THE MARKET.

Nickel-plated, complete in box with accessories .... price 3/- each.

Japanned ditto .... „ 2/6 „

Our Bullets and Patent Shot Cartridges can be used with these Pistols.

A 1900 advert for the German "William Tell".

The "William Tell" Dolla airpistol.

Model: **THE "WILLIAM TELL"**

Maker: Retailed by Lane Brothers, 45a New Church Street, Bermondsey, London S.E., although the airpistol has obvious German "Dolla" characteristics. The Dolla trademark is the barrel and airchamber with varying trigger mechanisms. One such airpistol was found boxed with the maker's name **"E.G."** This could be from **Bergmann, Eisenwerk,** Gaggenau, Germany. See *"Guns Review",* September, 1979.
By the middle 1930's the above was advertised as being made by **J. G. Anschutz.**

Date: Around 1900.

Valuation: Boxed examples £40 - £80.

Details: A cut above the normal "Dolla" gat in that it has a serial number stamped on the underside of the barrel housing, trigger, trigger guard and rear barrel block. Number stamped is 116. Action is one casting unlike other models which have half of the grip removable. Trigger guard is mounted with two pins whilst trigger and sear pivot of the other two. Trigger has small adjuster screw. Available either nickel plated or japanned finish, black paint. Sold in a black covered box with a small circular tin of cat slugs and six darts. Box is felt lined and has recesses for the airgun and pellet tin. The name "William Tell" was also used by the retailer G. C. Bell & Son, 19 Thistle Street, Glasgow during the 1920's for the German Militia air rifle.

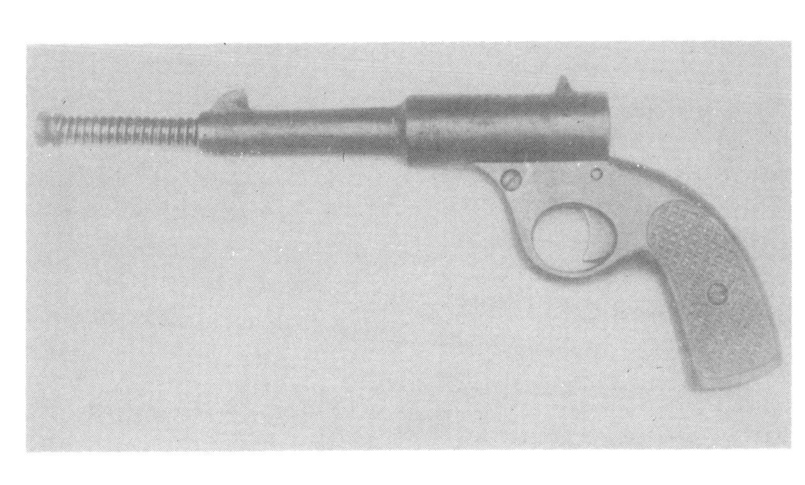

The Dolla-Cub airpistol.

Model: **"CUB"**

Maker: **F. R. Langenham,**
Zella-Mehlis, Germany.
At a later date, it might have been made by **Anschutz** under the J.G.A. trade name.

Date: Would assume the above variation of the "Dolla" style gat to date from the 1930's to the middle 1940's. Note change in trigger guard design as compared to the "Dolla".

Valuation: £15 - £25, £5a - £32a.

Details: Another "Dolla" type gat. Identical air chamber and barrel design, but the trigger and butt vary from the more common style of "Dolla" gat. The manufacturers appear to be able to produce the air chamber as standard and then vary the trigger mechanism and butt at will. Notice the differences in the butt, chequering and shape of trigger guard compared to the "Dolla" gats featured elsewhere. The above bears traces of nickel plating. Air chamber stamped "CUB" and on other side "MADE IN GERMANY". For details on how to dismantle see *"Airgun World"*, December, 1979.

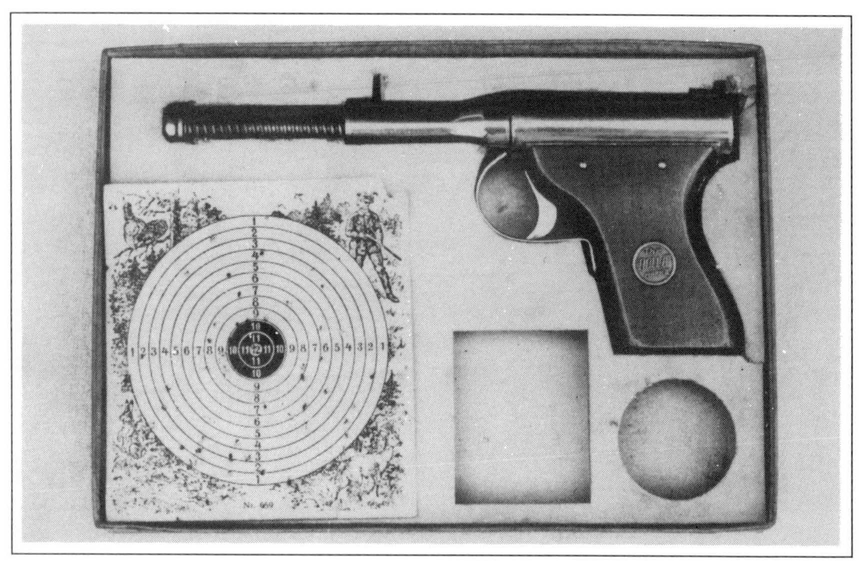

Dolla Mk. II with box and lid. Note odd shaped pellets and darts.

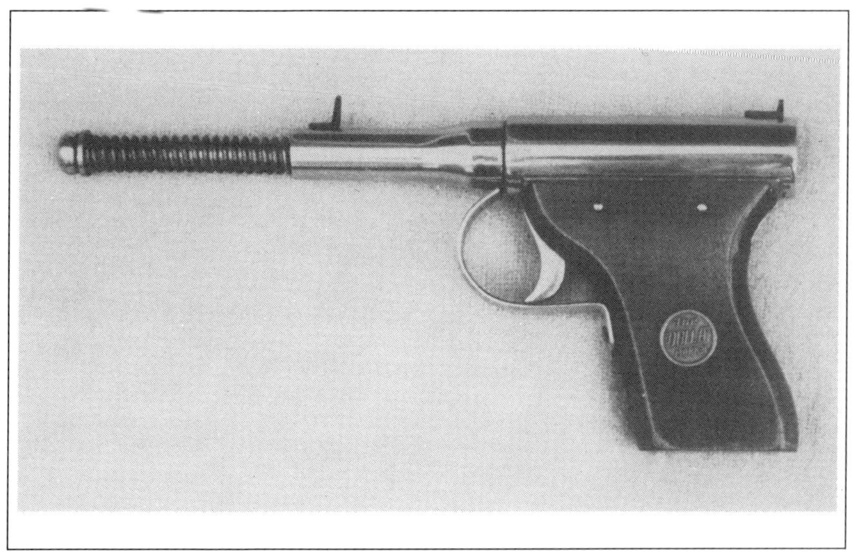

Dolla Mk. II airpistol.

Model: **THE "DOLLA" MARK II**

Maker: **J. G. Anschütz, G.m.b.H. Jagd-und Sportwaffenfabrik,** 79 Ulm/Donau, West Germany.

Date: The first metal die cast gat appears in the 1890's and was priced at 8/9. The all metal version appears to be the Mark I whilst the Mark II is as above. First seen advertised 1932-33 and cost 8/- complete in box. The Mark II model also appears in a catalogue dated 1939 as all metal with a blued finish, boxed with darts, pellets and targets, priced 7/6. The price appears to be steadily decreasing since 1890! In 1954 a new model J.G.A. gat style airpistol was introduced similar to the above, but with a black butt and more modern styled sights. From the above, would assume the date of this particular model to be between 1946 and 1953.

Valuation: £20 - £50.

Details: The box lid is deep blue with gold printing. The letters and other illustrations are either depressed or embossed. Bottom L.H.S. of lid states "REG. U.S. PATENTS OFFICE" whilst on the R.H.S. under the remains of a three leafed clover or shamrock price of trade label appears the word "GERMANY". The airpistol is shown in the cocked position firing strange looking pellets and darts into the bull of a target. The pellets and darts are snub nosed with a smaller blunt protrusion for sticking into the target. The airpistol is identical to the one enclosed except that the medallion set in the wooden butt does not bear the "JGA" label. On the base of the box is the price 10/6, inflation at last! Box measures 9⅝ x 6⅞ x 1 inches. The inside has a raised platform with compartments for the airpistol, two boxes for darts and pellets, finally a small clip for holding a selection of paper targets, whether the target shown is original I would not like to say.

Finally, the little airpistol, chrome plated body, trigger guard and trigger with blued metal rear and foresight spot welded on. The body is held to the butt by two metal pins. The wooden butt has brass medallions on both sides bearing the message "THE "DOLLA" MARK II" and stamped under one of the medallions "FOREIGN". As with all gats the above has a ·177 smoothbore barrel. Measures 8⅛ inches uncocked and 6 inches when cocked.

The paper target featured appears to be original as I have seen another boxed Dolla Mk. II with similar contents. The small round cut-away held a tin of 100 pellets with a pale blue label with the following message: "for J.G.A. — Diana ot Haenel AIR PISTOLS" then "GERMANY". The blue label was stuck over an enamel label with the following printed in the centre: "100 ZUNDHUTCHEN 6,45 mit Amboss" and around the edge in the lid top "SCHONEBECK a,ELBE * ZUNDHUTCHEN-UND PATRONENFABRIK VORMALS SELLIER & BELLOT". The last part rings a bell as manufacturers of shotgun cartridges. There is a striking resemblance between the butt of the Dolla Mk. II and the Haenel Model 100 airpistol, see *"Airgun World"*, June, 1980. It would appear that there could be some connection. The "Shamrock" trademark was used by Frank Dyke & Co., 10 Union Street, London Bridge, London SE 1 during the 1920's and 1930's. Address dates from that period. German catalogues also list the above as being made by "IGA".

Haenel Model 26.

Haenel Model 26 airpistol in cocked position.

Model: **26**

Maker: **C. G. Haenel,**
Thuringer Wald, Germany.
Present day address:
Suler Jagwaffen G.m.b.H.,
60 Suhl, Strasse der Freundsschaft 10, Postfach 161, East Germany.

Date: From the late 1920's to the late 1930's.

Valuation: £40 - £90. Boxed examples have fetched as much as £150. £40 - £90.

Details: The cheapest model of the pre-war Haenel airpistols. Same action to load and cock. 10 inches from tip of barrel to base of butt. 4 inch smoothbore brass liner barrel in outer alloy body. Side of barrel stamped "HAENEL MOD 26 — BRIT. PAT. No. 277265 — D.R.P.". On R.H.S. of chamber at rear stamped "MADE IN GERMANY". Main spring can be removed by unscrewing the knurled plug at rear of air chamber. Foresight set in dovetail groove and could be adjusted for windage only, whilst rearsight was adjustable for elevation. Deeply grooved grips. The serial number is stamped on the base of the grip. Advertised weight 1½ lbs.

Available in ·177, rifled and smoothbore, only. Serial number of above 1032. The standard finish appears to be a black paint. Further details see *"Airgun World"*, April, 1978 to September 1978. For further details of the Patent 277265 see *"Guns Review"*, March, 1980. The patent covers the tilting air chamber action.

Haenel Model 28.

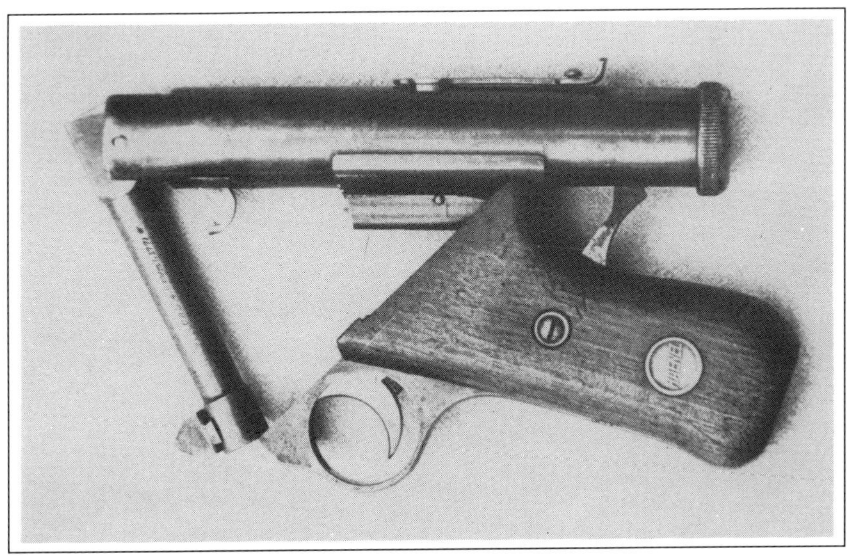

Haenel Model 28 in cocked and loading position.

Model: **MODEL 28**

Maker: **C. G. Haenel**

Date: 1927 - 1936 approx.

Valuation: £40 - £90.

Details: All metal with wooden grips. Brass medallions set in either side of grips. Serial number of above 9395, stamped on base of butt. 10½ inches long. ·177 rifled barrel. Stamped on top of air chamber "HAENEL MOD 28 — BRIT. PAT. No. 277265 D.R.P." R.H.S. of barrel stamped "MADE IN GERMANY". Calibre is stamped on the other side. For further details see *"Airgun World"*, April, May, June, July, August and September, 1978. During the early 1930's the Model 28 was available with either smoothbore or rifled barrels in ·177 only. The asterisk following the calibre denotes a rifled barrel. Smoothbore barrels do not have this asterisk mark stamped on the barrel.

Early models were stamped with the British Patent only. Somewhere between serial numbers 9395 and 13729 the U.S.A. Patent marking was added to the air chamber. Highest number seen is 21990. One example seen doesn't quite fit into the above picture. It bore no serial number, had plain circular brass medallions with "HAENEL" in capital letters only and no other decoration, the action catch under the air chamber was not like the usual horn or tusk shape but was very much like that fitted to the Webley Mark 3 air rifle, a piller with a notch cut into it, the calibre was stamped on the side of the barrel whilst under the barrel "MADE IN GERMANY". The greatest difference lies on the top of the air chamber which is stamped: "HAENEL AIR PISTOL, BRIT. PAT. 277625" and makes no mention of Model 28! This model is the first production airpistol from Haenel. It later became the Model 28 somewhere between serial numbers 9680 and 10,430.

Haenel Model 28 Repeater with action released. Note downward position of spring fed loading gate.

Haenel Model 28 Repeater and box lid.

Model: **28 REPEATER**

Maker: **C. G. Haenel, SuhlerJagdwaffen G.m.b.H.**
60 Suhl, Strasse der Freundsschaft 10,
Postfach 161,
East Germany.
(This address appears to be their latest.)

Date: From 1930 to 1939 or thereabouts.

Valuation: A rare model, £100 - £250.

Details: A very solid well made airpistol. Same dimensions as Model 28. Can only be used with repeating action as barrel does not break down for single pellet insertion. Has very tall foresight and usual long rearsight with adjuster screw. Repeating action is very similar to that used on the A.S.I. air rifles and on the RELUM style repeating air rifle. See Hiller's "Air Rifles", First Edition. Whereas the above air rifles have an external magazine tube, the Heanel repeating airpistol has an internal magazine tube that runs down the centre through the piston.

As the action is broken for cocking, a loading gate falls down and a pellet is fed into the gate; on closing the action, this pushes the gate up and positions the pellet in line with the barrel. So much for the theory, in practice it should appear on "Shut That Door". The pellets cannot be loaded in the magazine as there is no way that the tension spring can be held back and have found that pellets can be fed one by one into the hole for the magazine and when twenty for ·177 or 15 for ·22 have been introduced, the magazine tube is then introduced into the action and screwed home. The previous owner enjoyed many a happy hour filling the magazine tube first, then seeing the pellets spray about the room when he tried to introduce the loaded tube back into the airpistol.

Side of barrel stamped "CAL. 4·5m/m (·177)+" and top of air chamber stamped "HAENEL MOD 28-R" and "BRIT. PAT. No. 277265". Serial number is stamped on R.H.S. of trigger guard. Wooden grips have brass Haenel medallion set on both sides. End of air chamber cap stamped "·177-CAL CAL 4.5". Underside of barrel stamped "MADE IN GERMANY". Safety catch fitted on L.H.S. of trigger guard and acts on trigger only. Serial number of above, 473.

Advertised as having been tested for accuracy at 12 yards and "If used from rest then the aim should be taken three inches above the centre of the target in order to obtain central striking." The box of the above example has a price of 22/6 written inside. Seen advertised in 1930 as being available in ·177 only. Advertised weight 2½ lbs. Length 10½ inches.

For further details of the repeating Haenel see *"Airgun World"*, August, 1978. It has been suggested that the repeater action works better with either "cat-slugs" or round ball because present day waisted pellets are too long for the sliding breech block and tend to be cut off at either end as the breech is pushed back up into the firing position. Steel BB's should **never** be used.

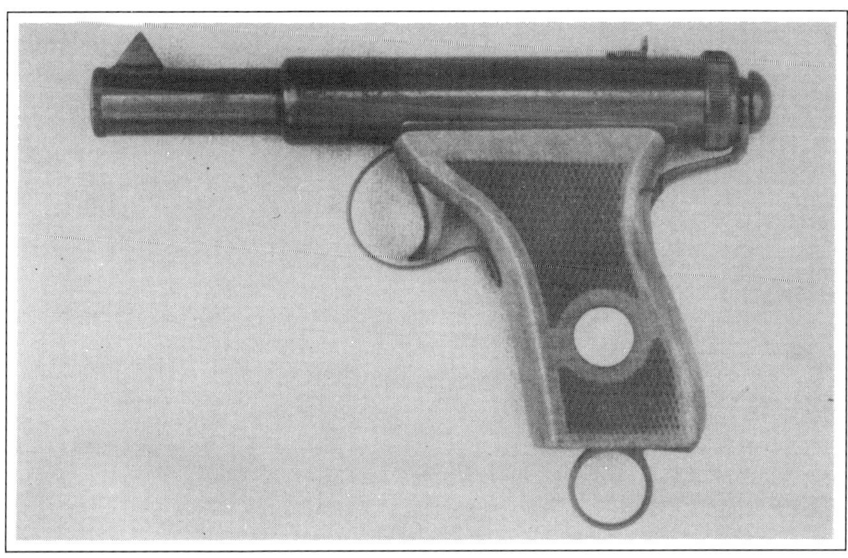

Haenel Model 100.

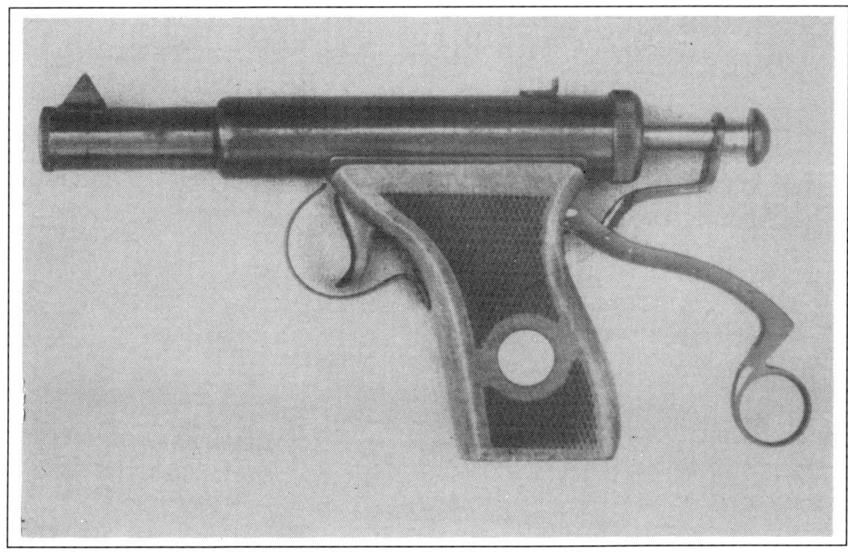

Haenel Model 100 in cocked position.

Model: **100**

Maker: **C. G. Haenel,**
Suhl, Thuringer Wald, Germany.

Date: Very short period of production as two examples seen were date stamped 1935 and 1937. Outbreak of W.W.2 would mean a cessation of production, so would assume production from 1934 to 1938.

Valuation: £75 - £125.

Details: A rare Haenel airpistol. One design fault is that the butt is a slide-on fit onto the action and if used as a bracing point when cocking is very liable to slide off. The only way to cock the action is to grip the barrel and pull the cocking ring with the other hand with the airpistol held in a vertical position. All metal parts blued. Top of air chamber stamped "HAENEL MOD. 100 D.R.P." Folded sheet metal foresight formed into a pyramid and braised on as is the simple rearsight. Barrel can be screwed out, but 4·5mm lead ball can be poured into the reservoir through a hole in the top of the outer barrel casing. Smoothbore barrel 3⅜ inches long.

To load, barrel is rotated to reveal loading hole in true Daisy fashion. Airpistol quite powerful for its size. Slide on stock held in place by spring steel trigger guard slotting into underside of air chamber. Pressed chequering and "Haenel" medallions set in both sides. Stamped on the bottom of the grip "MADE IN GERMANY" and a date stamp "11 6 35". Overall length along barrel 7⅝ inches. The action has an anti-bear trade device so that it cannot be fired until the cocking lever has been returned into the butt.

A review appears in *"Airgun World",* June, 1980. The piston works on very much like the gat system. The barrel has an inner air tube that is fixed to the head of the piston. As the action is cocked the air tube is drawn back down the barrel until it passes the hole in the barrel to allow a lead BB to fall into the barrel, this is prevented from rolling down the barrel by a small wire spring. When the action is fired the piston and air tube rush forward, passing the loading hole, thus forming an air seal and pushing the lead ball further down the barrel until air pressure begins to take over. The magazine holds about 50 lead BB's. Action works well when cocking in the vertical position.

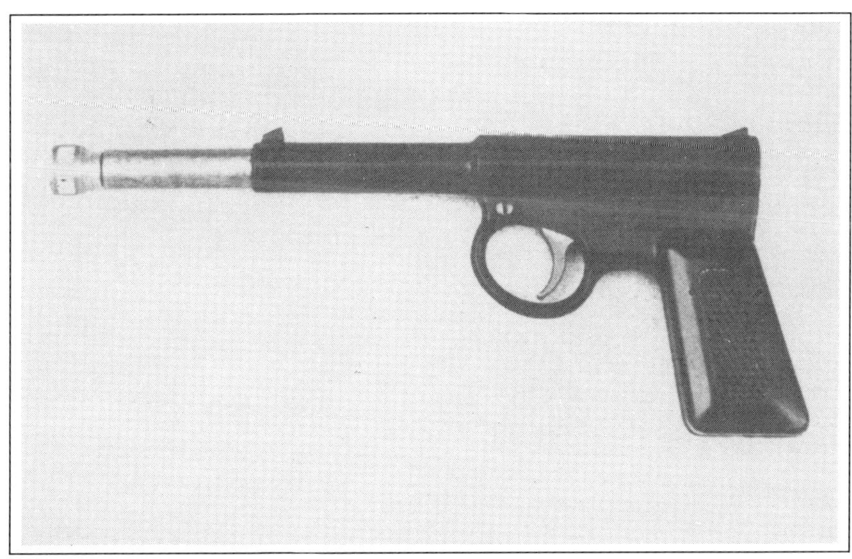

Harrington Gat.

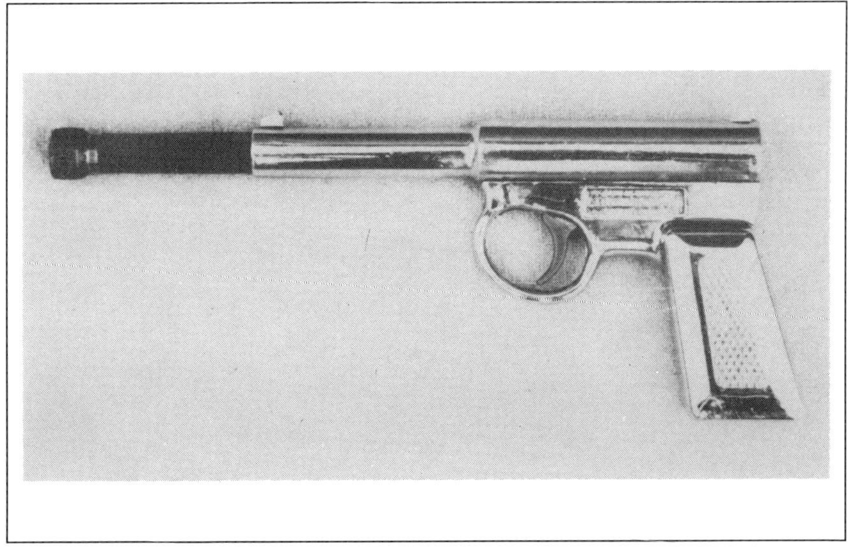

Chrome plated Gat by Harrington with thin black plastic spring cover.

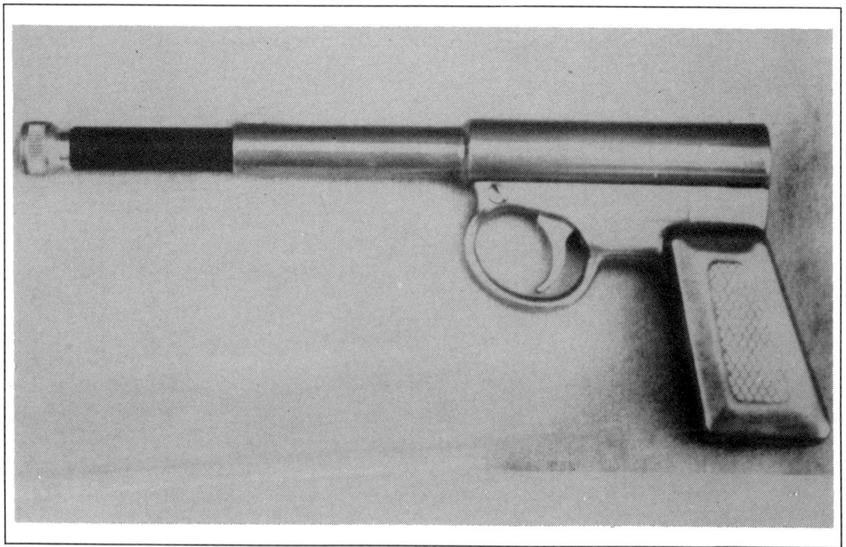

Polished finish Gat airpistol and packet cover.

Model.	**THE GAT**
Maker:	**T. J. Harrington & Son,** Walton, Surrey.
Date:	Current model. Above make appeared just before W.W.2 and then re-appeared in 1948.
Valuation:	£10 - £20.

Details: Sold in three finishes, chrome plated, black enamel, and during the 1960's, a polished alloy finish, and described as the export model. The gat pattern must be the longest type of airgun design running. My first airgun was a gat, I used it to shoot flies in my bedsitter days and could hit a matchbox at thirty feet, but had to aim about two inches low and to the right of the target. The above can be found in many secondhand shops and usually give years of service. Measures 9¾ inches along barrel line. Die cast frame and barrel. Cast on L.H.S. is "MADE IN ENGLAND T. J. Harrington & Son, Walton, Surrey" and on the other side "THE GAT". See *"Guns Review",* December, 1978.

The above firm appear to be the first to advertise this type of air pistol as the "G.A.T." as seen in an advert dated 1956. This could be an abbreviation of "GARANTA", a tinplate gat advertised in 1939 as being an "entirely new 100 per cent all-British product". Later the initials became the word "GAT". The extra wide extension to the barrel front served as a protector when the barrel was pushed against rough ground and a muzzle loader for corks. Can remember being hit by a cork fired from one of these when a small boy, it left a neat round red mark on my face.

Has also been suggested that the word "GAT" came from the American slang word for "GUN". Full address: T. J. Harrington & Son Ltd., Magda Works, Trading Estate, Molesey Road, Walton on Thames, Surrey. The first models were marked "MADE IN ENGLAND T. J. H. & SON PAT. APP'D FOR" instead of the above body markings. In 1982 they were sold fitted with a safety catch.

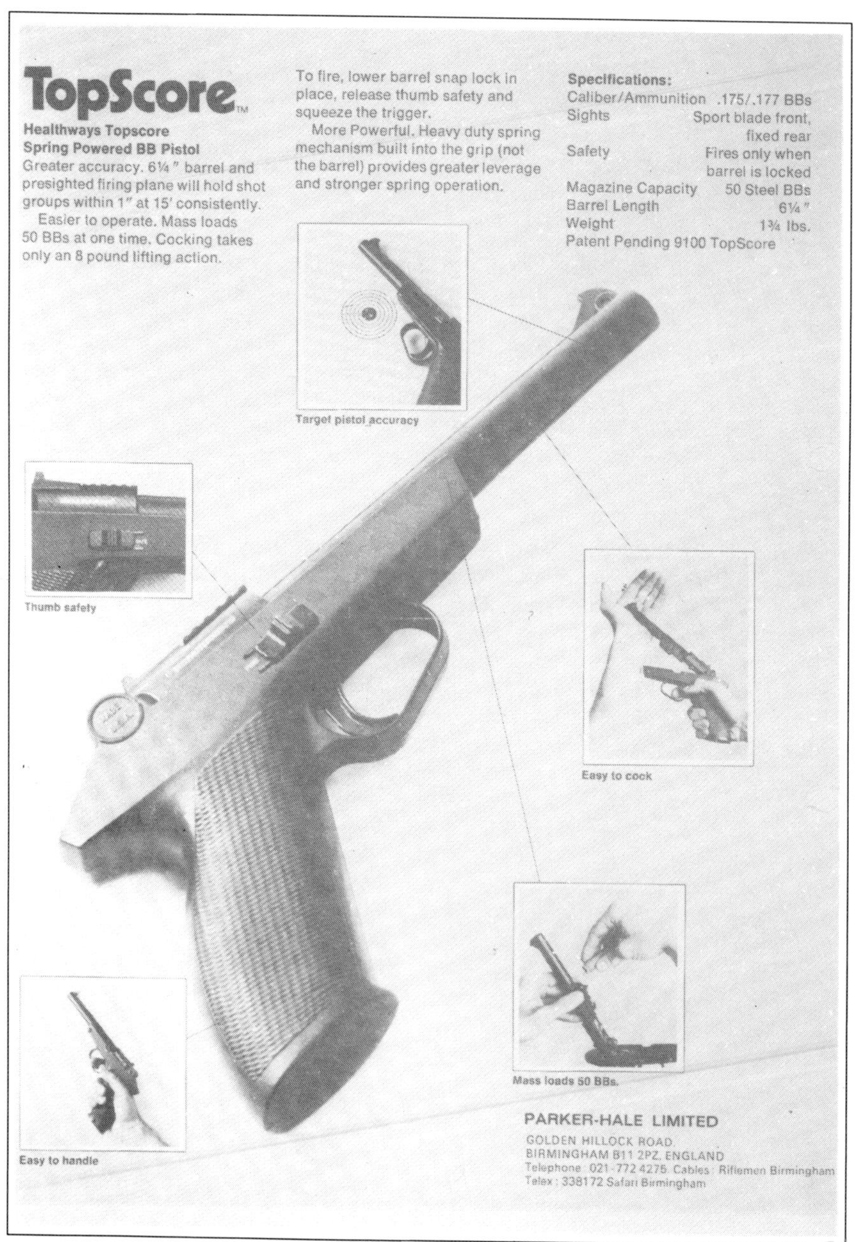

TopScore™
Healthways Topscore
Spring Powered BB Pistol
Greater accuracy. 6¼" barrel and presighted firing plane will hold shot groups within 1" at 15' consistently.
Easier to operate. Mass loads 50 BBs at one time. Cocking takes only an 8 pound lifting action.
To fire, lower barrel snap lock in place, release thumb safety and squeeze the trigger.
More Powerful. Heavy duty spring mechanism built into the grip (not the barrel) provides greater leverage and stronger spring operation.
Specifications:
Caliber/Ammunition .175/.177 BBs
Sights Sport blade front, fixed rear
Safety Fires only when barrel is locked
Magazine Capacity 50 Steel BBs
Barrel Length 6¼"
Weight 1¾ lbs.
Patent Pending 9100 TopScore
Target pistol accuracy
Thumb safety
Easy to cock
Mass loads 50 BBs.
Easy to handle
PARKER-HALE LIMITED
GOLDEN HILLOCK ROAD
BIRMINGHAM B11 2PZ. ENGLAND
Telephone: 021-772 4275. Cables: Riflemen Birmingham
Telex: 338172 Safari Birmingham

Topscore Spring Powered BB Pistol instructions

Model: **"TOPSCORE 175"**, also known as **"Sharpshooter 175"**. On side of box called **"Model 9100"**

Maker: **Healthways Gun Division,**
Los Angeles, California 90045.
Imported by Parker-Hale Ltd., Golden Hillock Road, Birmingham B11 2PZ.

Date: Available from early 1974 to late 1970's.

Valuation: £5 - £15.

Details: All metal diecast design giving very good value for money. All black matt finish with trade lettering "whited-in". A full size repeating "fun-gun". Non-adjustable sights. To cock, lift lever on L.H.S. of barrel and lift up until action cocks. In this position the magazine can be loaded with about 50 BB's. On the underside of the barrel, just in front of the barrel latch is a small lid that can be raised. This reveals a reservoir for the BB's. The barrel can now be lowered and the latch returned to lock the barrel. The airgun should not be ready for firing until the latch is in locking position. Serial number stamped on L.H.S. of action.

"Whited-in" on L.H.S. of barrel is "TOPSCORE 175", but in *"Guns Review"*, December, 1974, the airgun is called "SHARPSHOOTER". On the R.H.S. appears "HEALTHWAYS", and on the cover of the barrel pivot is cast "MADE U.S.A.". On the R.H.S. of the action is a safety catch. Advertised accuracy of one inch groups at fifteen feet. The air cylinder is housed in the butt, similar to the Walther LP 53, and action cocking is similar to the Improved Model Britannia Air Rifle. The repeating action has the novelty of gravity and magnetic feeding in that the breech bolt has a small magnet at its head to retain the BB, so would not recommend the use of lead BB's. A small point of weakness is the trigger, this is pivoted on one side only and being made of die-cast metal is prone to shear if too much pressure is applied to the trigger. Advertised weight 1¾ lbs.

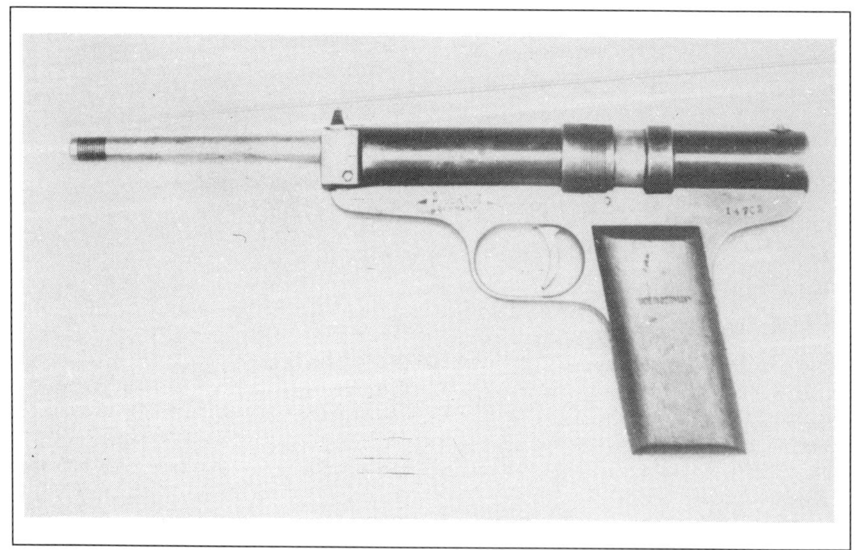

Hubertus airpistol.

Hubertus in cocked and loading position.

Model: **HUBERTUS**

Maker: **Hubertus Metal Works,**
Molln, Germany;
but other addresses appear to crop up: Waffenfabrik Imman, Meffert, Suhl, Germany.
The first address was also the home of the "Jung Roland" airguns. The Hubertus airpistol was retailed in Britain by the Midland Gun Company.

Date: Late 1920's to middle 1930's.

Valuation: £75 - £150.

Details: Unusual and rare airpistol. Very similar cocking action to the gat style airpistol. All metal with walnut grips. Barrel is used to cock the action by pushing it in as far as it will go. Originally available rifled or smoothbore in ·177 and ·22, but later it would appear that the smoothbore option was dropped. End of barrel had small rings cut into it to aid drawing the barrel out after loading. Non-adjustable sights. Foresight set in dovetail whilst rearsight screwed into rear of air chamber. The chamber splits into two where the sliding ring is: the rear houses the piston and spring, whilst the front part is the air chamber. L.H.S. of body stamped "D.R.G.M. HUBERTUS GERMANY" and the serial number nearer the butt. Nothing appears on the R.H.S. Both sides of the pistol grip stamped "MADE IN GERMANY".

They were sold boxed with 100 slugs. It could be that the earlier model was also slightly smaller and fitted with a shorter smoothbore barrel. The rifled model measures 10½ inches long, whilst the earlier smoothbore was 8½ inches. See *"Guns Review"*, December, 1975 and May, 1973. The sliding partition between the two parts of the air chamber also acts as a safety when it has been pulled back to allow the barrel to tip forwards for loading. The letters "D.R.G.M." is the German equivalent of a patented design and stands for "Reichsgebrauchsmuster" and Hubertus means "St. Hubert". Advertised weight 1 lb. 6 oz.

According to an advertisement, the following procedure should be followed in order to load and fire the Hubertus:

1. Push barrel back into action until it remains firm.
2. Slide ring on top of action back so that the barrel may fly open.
3. Insert pellet or dart into chamber (barrel) which is visible.
4. Draw out barrel into its original position.
5. Close ring over barrel again.
6. FIRE!

Could be the start of a new party game — "PASS THE HUBERTUS". The winner is the team that can load and fire before anyone else.

Hyscore airpistol.

Hyscore in cocked position.

Model: **800 TARGET AIR PISTOL**

Maker: **Hy Score Arms Corporation,**
Brooklyn, New York, U.S.A., also:
Hy-Score Arms Corporation,
25 Lafayette Street, Brooklyn 1, New York.

Date: Development began in 1938 and the design was patented during 1947. Both single and repeater models appeared in 1948. Actual production ceased very late 1960's or very early 1970's, but were still being advertised and sold up to the late 1970's.

Valuation: £40 - £80.

Details: Tinplate construction, but made to last a lifetime. 10½ inches long along barrel line. Single shot, although a repeater was available. Could be "dry" fired for practice. Brown plastic (tenite) grips for right hand use. L.H.S. of air chamber stamped "HY-SCORE. TARGET AIR PISTOL, HY-SCORE ARMS CO. NEW YORK, N.Y. PATENT PENDING, MADE IN U.S.A.". Was also produced as a chromed model. 10¼ inch button rifled barrel. Advertised weight 30½ ozs. (855 gm). Advertised accuracy is 7/16 inch group from machine rest at a distance of 33 feet (10 m.). Barrel has six micro-groove rifling.

The 802 is the repeater available in either ·22, ·177, or smoothbore for BB's, and could also be chrome plated. It appears that the Model 800 was also available in the above combination of calibres and finish. During the early 1950's, a snub barreled model was available with screw in barrels. Barrels were 7¾ inches in length. A boxed kit was sold called the "SPORTSTER", this included the airpistol body with three interchangeable barrels and a box of pellets. Again, available in either blued or chrome plated finishes. These short barreled models were 803 single shot and 804 repeater. The very first models were available with the following choice of stock finishes: walnut, petrified wood, ivory or onyx. See *"Guns Review",* November, 1980 for details of Patents for the above. Besides a brown butt there was also a whitish mottled pattern plastic stock available. The ·177 calibre is quite rare.

In a 1954 catalogue, the following models were listed; all based on the Model 800:

Blue finish	*Chrome finish*
Model 800B in ·177	Model 800C in ·177
Model 800B in ·22	Model 800C in ·22
Model 800BB for BB's	Chrome models cost $5 extra.

When it first appeared in 1948, it was called the "Target Model" as the repeater version was not yet available. These early models had a screw through the upper portion of the grip and it would appear from the adverts that the barrel was screwed and pegged into the wider air chamber, and the pivot for cocking was enclosed and not exposed as in later models. The foresight and barrel collar may also be longer. The rearsight was adjustable for both windage and elevation and may have been screw mounted and not dovetail mounted as on later models. Velocities given in 1948 were 400 f.p.s. for ·177 and 300 f.p.s. for ·22.

For a short time in the 1970's B.S.A. Guns Ltd., of Redditch, Worcestershire, were the British agents for the Hyscore single shot airpistol.

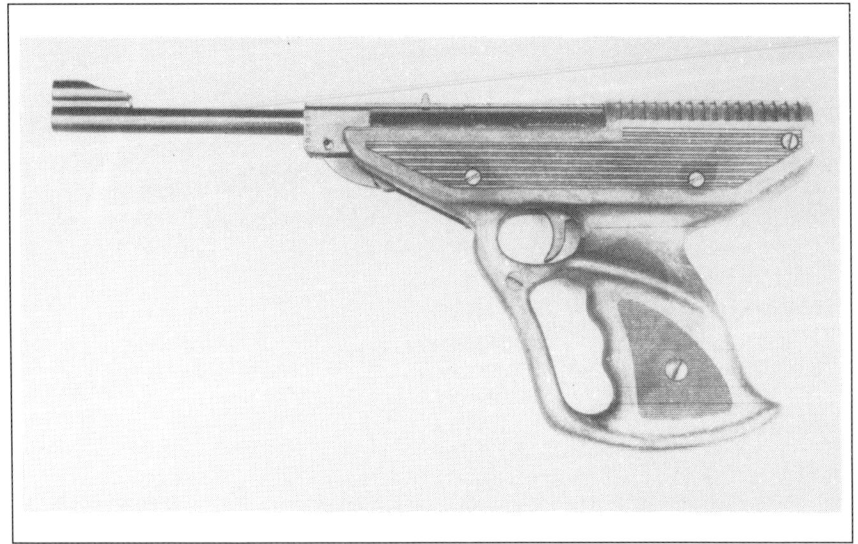

IGI Domino Model 207.

Model: **207**

Maker: **Igi Domino,**
Italy.
During 1980, an announcement was made to the affect that Igi Domino airguns will now be sold under the FAS trade name. FAS is Fabbrica Armi Sportive SRI, Milan, Italy.

Date: Around 1979 to late 1980's.

Valuation: £10 - £30.

Details: Futuristic airpistol. Could even be sold as a Dan Dare Ray Gun. Die cast construction with wrap-around plastic grip. ·177 smoothbore barrel with black lacquer finish to metalwork. 13 inches along barrel line with a 7 inch barrel. Fixed sights, unless you wish to bend the barrel!! Serial number stamped on side of barrel and cast into the air chamber "igi DOMINO" and "MOD 207, CAL., 4·5 - ·177, MADE IN ITALY" on the other side. The plastic two piece stock wraps around the rear of the air chamber. Non-adjustable single pull trigger.

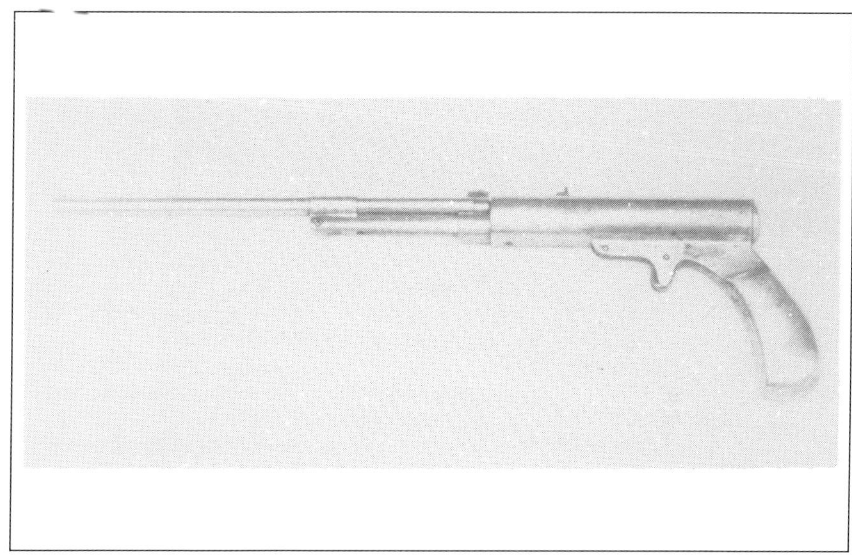

The Champion Airpistol.

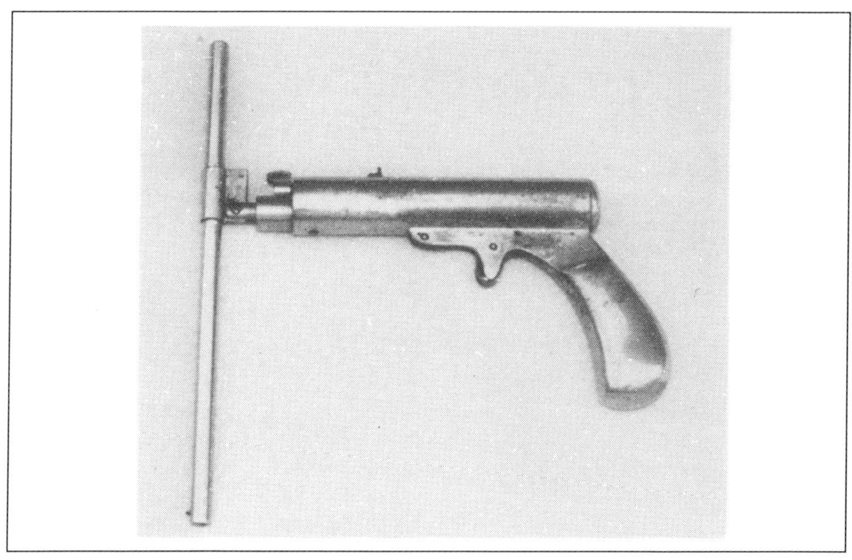

Champion Airpistol in cocked position.

Model: **"THE CHAMPION"**

Maker: **Iver Johnson Arms & Cycle Works,**
Worcester, Massachusetts, U.S.A.
The main retailer appears to have been Pope Mfg. Co., 45 High Street, Boston, Massachusetts, U.S.A.

Date: From around 1875, late 1880's.

Valuation: £75 - £150.

Details: Another example of the introduction of cheaper, mass produced target gallery airpistols that brought indoor shooting to many Americans. 15½ inches long with an 8⅜ inch smoothbore barrel of either ·20 or ·21 calibre. Example seen is all metal with nickel plated finish to all parts except to the rearsight, trigger and sear. Serial number not visible. Various patents are stamped on top of the barrel but were indistinct on the example seen. To cock the action rotate the breech bolt anti-clockwise, this releases the barrel. The barrel will fall into the vertical position as it pivots on the cocking rod. It now forms a type of "T" handle and is pushed in until the action cocks. Pellet is inserted into the barrel after it has been drawn out of the action. The airgun is ready to fire when the barrel is returned to horizontal position and breech bolt tightened clockwise. Advertised weight 1 lb. 10 oz.

There were three models available: black lacquer, nickel plated, and nickel plated with rosewood handle. Each airpistol was sold boxed complete with wire stock, 6 darts, 100 pellets, 6 targets, ramrod and a claw and wrench tool. The hole drilled into the lower back of the grip is for the wire shoulder stock. The above design was patented by Iver Johnson and Martin Bye.

For further details of the patent see *"Guns Review"*, September, 1977. The patent also introduced a groove around the piston for engaging the sear instead of the usual practice of allowing the sear to engage on the front of the piston. Although all the patent dates mentioned refer to 1876 the above airpistol bears a date "July 1 '75".

It is strange to note that in the appendix to *"Airguns"* by E. Wolff the Champion airpistol is listed as being produced by Quackenbush and from the factory records, they listed 69 as having been manufactured, sold, or produced in 1884. One wonders if Quackenbush produced everything in airguns during this early era of American airgun history.

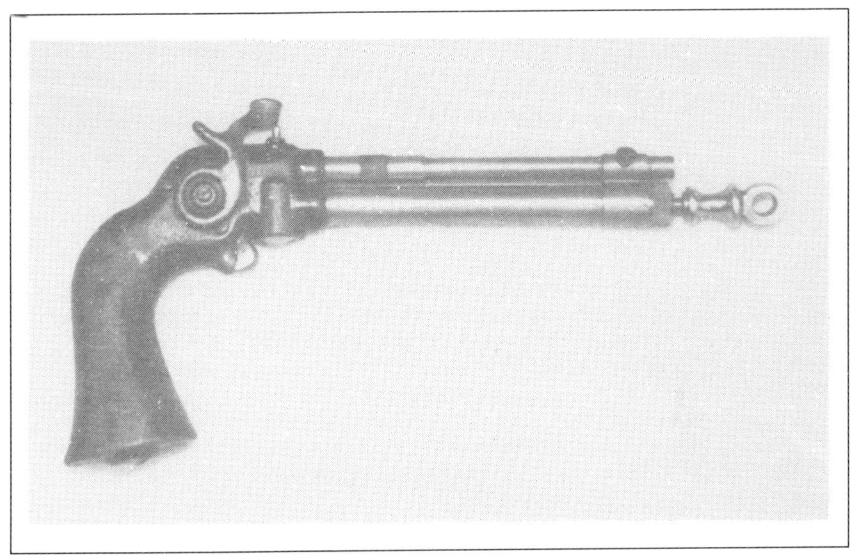

The "Kalamazoo" Pump-up airpistol.

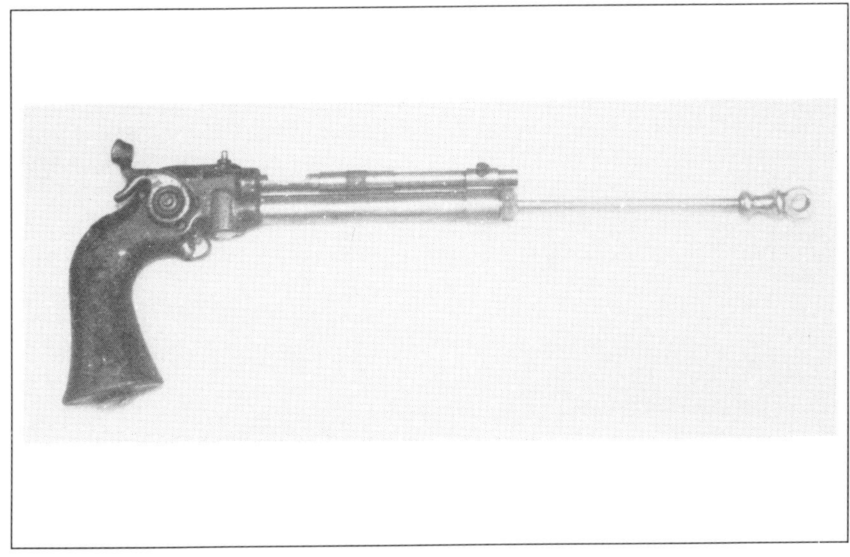

The "Kalamazoo" with cocked action.

Model: **"KALAMAZOO" PUMP UP AIRPISTOL**

Maker: **Snow & Cowe,**
New Haven, Conn., U.S.A.
Patented by E. H. Hawley.

Date: Patented 1st June, 1869, and production started in the same year. Would assume period of production to be very short so cessation of production very early 1870's.

Valuation: £150 - £350.

Details: Brass and cast iron construction. Pump-up action. ·25 smoothbore barrel with sliding breech cover tube that is pulled forward for loading either pellet or dart. Barrel stamped "PAT. JUNE, 1st, 1869". Pump lies under the barrel and could have separate handle that fits through the hole in the pump handle to ease pumping. The fixed sights are offset to the right so as to by-pass the hammer when it is cocked. The cast iron grip also acts as the air reservoir and houses the valve that when struck by the hammer releases all the air. The grip has three brass screw-in plugs, although these could be lead on other models. The plug in front of the trigger houses the simple valve mechanism. This must be quite a rare airpistol.

The patent granted for the above was number 90,249, and since E. H. Hawley lived in Kalamazoo, Michigan, U.S.A., it must have seemed very appropriate to name the airpistol after his home town. An advert in the "Scientific American" dated 1870 states that "Superman" killed seven squirrels with eight shots, whether the squirrels were hand held at close range it didn't say. It would appear that some models could be fitted with a skeleton stock, although on the above example this is not evident.

There are two valves in the air chamber/butt, the inlet and outlet valve, the inlet valve works by air pressure alone whilst the outlet is released by the percussion type hammer. Another point of interest is that the hammer pivot screw is the only thing holding the hammer, hammer spring, trigger pivot, spring and trigger together. A review of the above appears in *"Airgun World",* November, 1979. According to Eldon G. Wolff in *"Airgun Batteries"* the Kalamazoo was patented in 1871, 12th September, patent number 118,886.

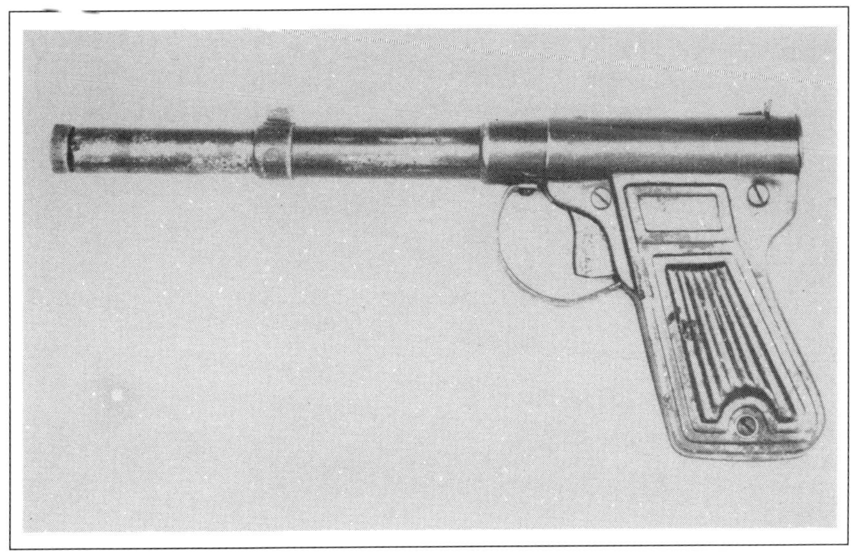

The "Limit" Gat airpistol.

Model: **"LIMIT"**

Maker: **"Made in England".** Either from machinery brought over from Germany after W.W.2 or made under contract by **Dianawerk, Mayer & Grammelspacher,** Rastatt, West Germany, as the above is identical to the Diana Model 2.

Date: 1930's to 1940's.

Valuation: £10 - £20.

Details: All metal construction. ·177 smoothbore. Usual gat airpistol. Top of air chamber stamped with "LIMIT" in an oval and "MADE IN ENGLAND" on the top. Shown in Smith's *"Gas spring airguns of the World"* as a German airpistol. The Diana Model 2 with the wooden stock was also advertised as the Limit in 1939.

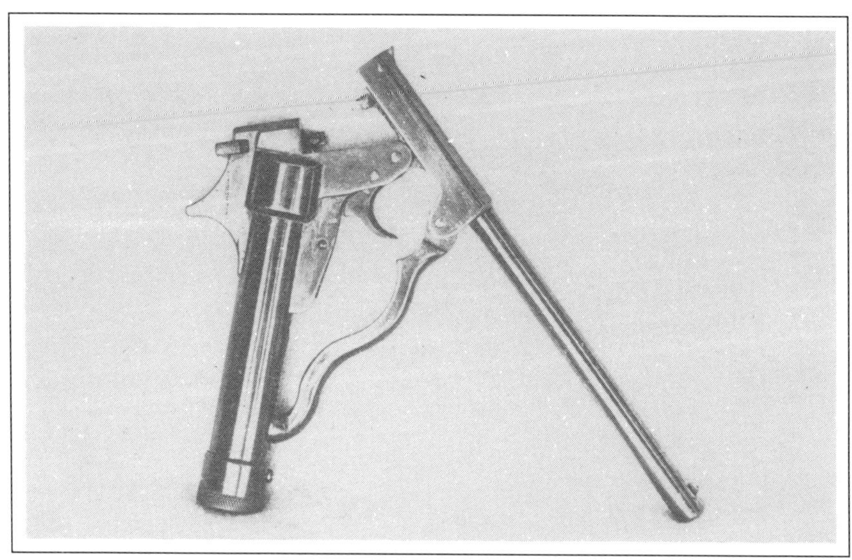

Lincoln airpistol, R.H.S. in cocked position.

Lincoln airpistol, L.H.S. in cocked position.

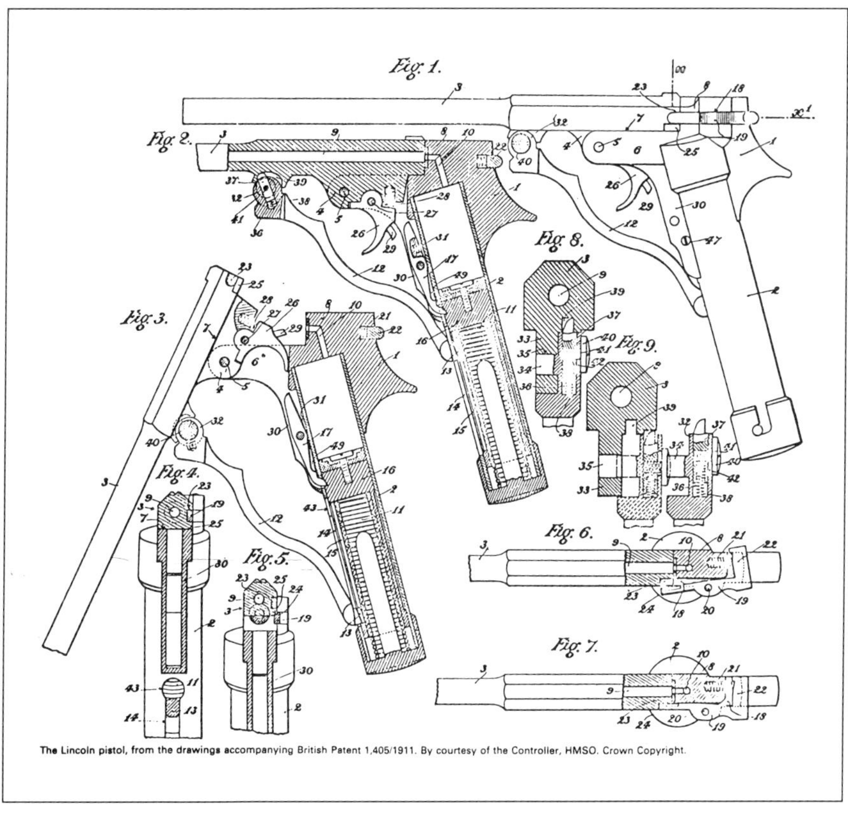

The Lincoln pistol, from the drawings accompanying British Patent 1,405/1911. By courtesy of the Controller, HMSO. Crown Copyright.

The Lincoln pistol, from the drawings accompanying British Patent 1,405/1911. By courtesy of the Controller, HMSO, Crown Copyright.

Model: **THE "LINCOLN" AIR PISTOL**

Maker: **Lincoln Jefferies**

Date: From around 1921 and seen advertised as late as 1930.

Valuation: A rare airpistol. £75 - £200. Even more for mint examples. £160a.

Details: Serial number of above, 541, and appears stamped on all parts, although the last two digits appear on minor parts. All metal construction with no non-metal fixtures. Nine inch rifled barrel with 5¾ inch air cylinder in butt. Similar cocking action to the Walther LP 53 and has a similar "feel" when held for firing. Rear sight non-adjustable but foresight can be drifted laterally for windage. No pins or rivets appear to be used in the construction. Screw heads all face out on the L.H.S. of the airpistol. Stamped on top flat of the barrel breech "THE "LINCOLN" AIR PISTOL", whilst on the R.H.S. of barrel breech appears "BEST ENGLISH MAKE". Stamped on the R.H.S. of the top grip extension "PAT. No. 181277". See Smith's "AIRGUNS OF THE WORLD" pages 50 & 51. The above appears to be only available in ·177 and cost 39/6 in 1926. Was also advertised with the Parker crank airpistol and the "Titan". See *"Shooting Times"*, October 13-19, 1977. For details of earlier patents, see *"Guns Review"*, April, 1979. For details of the patent for the "Lincoln" Airpistol, see *"Guns Review"*, September, 1979. Weight 2 lb. 1 oz.

With the later style with the extended air chamber, the B.S.A. Merlin mainspring will fit without cutting down. The highest serial number recorded for the standard model is 1213, but a modified example exists with a serial number just over 2000. This modification had a slightly longer barrel, although still in ·177, and the butt air chamber is three inches longer than normal and is also larger in diameter. Body stampings are the same as the standard models. Dovetail mounted foresight and windage adjustable rearsight. The airpistol is fitted with walnut chequered grips that wrap around the upper half of the air chamber. Apparently various models were produced with varying air chamber sizes for experimentation and customer requirements. For further details, see *"Guns Review"*, June, 1981.

The Argentinian "Mahely" airpistol.

Model: **"MAHELY"**

Maker: **Mahely Ind. Y Com., S.R.L.,** Buenos Aires, Argentina.

Date: The 1950's.

Valuation: £40 - £80.

Details: A very rare airpistol in Britain because it was never intended for sale in this country. Very similar in design to the homely Webley airpistol. Steel air chamber and barrel with aluminium grip and trigger guard. Wooden grips, although the example featured in *"Guns Review"*, September, 1978, was fitted with black bakelite grips bearing the trade name "Mahely". It could be that this is a later model. Available in ·177 only. Serial number stamped on base of butt "129", then the last two digits were stamped all over the place, even written on the underside of each grip. 8⅛ inch rifled barrel that overlaps the end of the air chamber by one inch. Last two digits of serial number stamped on the underside. Other end of barrel spiral grooved for gripping in order to cock the action. Simple blade foresight set in dovetail. Barrel latch is a sliding thin lever pivoted and spring loaded. Rearsight adjustable for elevation only. Side of action stamped with serial number and "MAHELY CAL. 4·5 INDUSTRIA ARGENTINA". Air chamber can be stripped from either end, but a small grub screw must be removed from the underside of the air chamber before the rear plug can be unscrewed. The overall size is larger than the Webley Premier. The trigger block is cast aluminium and has a non-adjustable trigger. Weight 2 lb. 1½ oz.

Cub airpistol and box lid.

Cub with detachable rearsight.

Model: **"CUB"**

Maker: Would assume **Millard Bros.,** P.O. Box 24, Motherwell, Lanarkshire, Scotland, ML1 4UP.

Date: After 1946, but cessation of production not known.

Valuation: £20 - £50.

Details: The smaller BB pellet size is most unusual and the only other airgun known to me using smaller BB's is the Daisy "Targeteer", see *"Guns Review",* December, 1978. The airpistol appears to be made from a single casting of alloy with no moving parts. The body of the airpistol has a deep uniform purple anodised finish. Measures 6 inches along barrel and 7 inches from tip of barrel to base of butt. Stamped on the L.H.S. of the body above the grip appears "MILBRO CUB — CALIBRE 2 m/m 55". This is repeated on the R.H.S. in the same location. Stamped on the R.H.S. just behind the artificial air slits is the word "VALVES" and something else but can't make it out.

At each end of the barrel there is a plastic screw. The front acts as a support for the barrel whilst the rear is removed to pour in the micro BB's. These fall down into the butt and when required for firing, the airpistol is tipped forward to allow one of the BB's to roll into the valve at the end of the barrel. The airpistol is then pointed at the target and the bulb is squeezed gently and out pops the pellet. There is a small rubber washer with an undersized hole to hold back the pellet until there has been a build up in air pressure to overcome the restriction. On the rear plastic screw-out plug there is a thick, effective rubber air seal.

The serial number is not visible. The rubber bulb in the butt has "MILBRO — CUB" caste on each side. Set in the base of the butt is a circular aluminium disc with the following stamped around its edge: "BRITISH MADE UNDER LICENCE", in the centre: "BRITISH PATENT APP. No. 21954 - 5 46. R. BOULET, PARIS, WORLD PATENTEE".

The airpistol was sold in a cardboard box with a rearsight, plain wire push rod for stuck BB's, and a box of 2 mm. BB's that also appears to contain spare washers for the breech restriction. The BB's were labelled "SPARE CHARGES". The rearsight was a taper fit into the rear plastic plug and was calibrated from 5 to 20 yards, yards being a British measurement of length. The sight just pushed into the taper recess. Advertised as firing 500 shots automatically and without reloading, as well as being "practically harmless".

Dr. J. S. E. Gilbart informs me that the actual measured size of the Milbro "Cub" shot is 2·41 mm. or 0·095" which is the same size as our No. 7 shot used for shotgun shooting. The Daisy "Targeteer" used 3 mm. diameter BB's, which is 0·118". Although both used Mini BB's, they are not interchangeable.

The above patent was accepted on the 22nd December, 1948, and entered by Rene Boulet, 11 Avenue Bugeaud, Paris, France. The design was also used for propelling small ball bearings from many articles of everyday use, such as cigarette holders, smoking pipes, etc. For further details of the patent, see *"Guns Review",* October, 1980. A review of the above airpistol appears in *"Guns Review",* March, 1981. According to a French Catalogue of 1949 the Cub was also sold in carbine form with a detachable wire shoulder stock and a very long screw-in barrel. This would certainly increase the aiming properties. It was also sold in either the blued anodised finish or polished bright alloy.

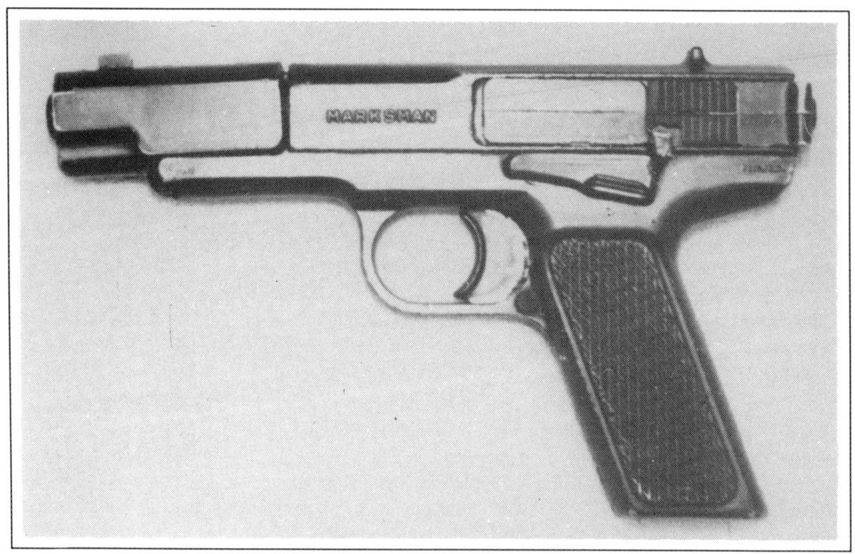

First model Marksman.

First model Marksman, single shot, in partial cocked position.

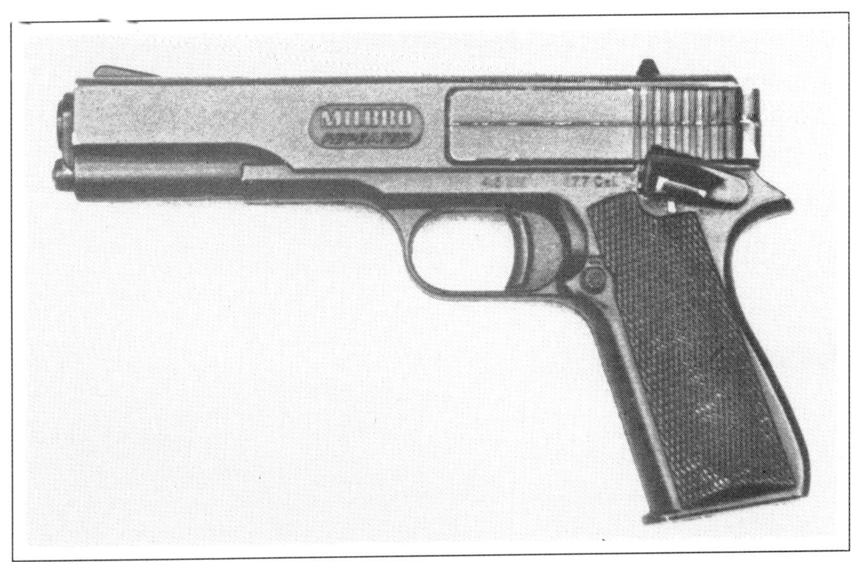

Milbro "G10".

Milbro G10 in cocked position.

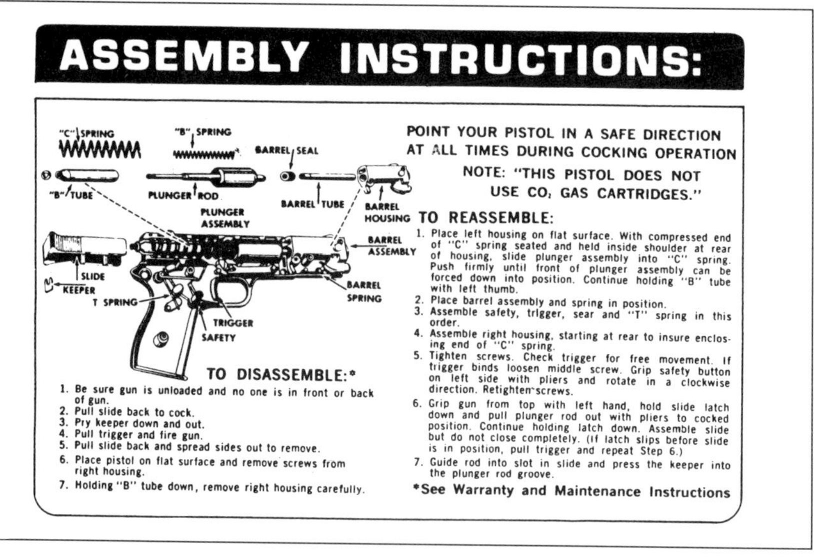

ASSEMBLY INSTRUCTIONS:

POINT YOUR PISTOL IN A SAFE DIRECTION AT ALL TIMES DURING COCKING OPERATION

NOTE: "THIS PISTOL DOES NOT USE CO_2 GAS CARTRIDGES."

TO DISASSEMBLE:*

1. Be sure gun is unloaded and no one is in front or back of gun.
2. Pull slide back to cock.
3. Pry keeper down and out.
4. Pull trigger and fire gun.
5. Pull slide back and spread sides out to remove.
6. Place pistol on flat surface and remove screws from right housing.
7. Holding "B" tube down, remove right housing carefully.

TO REASSEMBLE:

1. Place left housing on flat surface. With compressed end of "C" spring seated and held inside shoulder at rear of housing, slide plunger assembly into "C" spring. Push firmly until front of plunger assembly can be forced down into position. Continue holding "B" tube with left thumb.
2. Place barrel assembly and spring in position.
3. Assemble safety, trigger, sear and "T" spring in this order.
4. Assemble right housing, starting at rear to insure enclosing end of "C" spring.
5. Tighten screws. Check trigger for free movement. If trigger binds loosen middle screw. Grip safety button on left side with pliers and rotate in a clockwise direction. Retighten screws.
6. Grip gun from top with left hand, hold slide latch down and pull plunger rod out with pliers to cocked position. Continue holding latch down. Assemble slide but do not close completely. (If latch slips before slide is in position, pull trigger and repeat Step 6.)
7. Guide rod into slot in slide and press the keeper into the plunger rod groove.

*See Warranty and Maintenance Instructions

Parts diagram for the Milbro G10.

Model: **G10**

Maker: Not known, but made in Torrance, California, U.S.A. Imported by Milbro Sports Ltd., P.O. Box 24, Motherwell, Scotland.

Date: Introduced in 1952.

Valuation: £22n. £5 - £15.

Details: A good "fun" gun. Fires darts, pellets and repeats on around twenty BB's. Interesting action and well illustrated on leaflet enclosed with airgun. Muzzle velocity rather low, but can be an advantage for junior use or even fun firing in the lounge!!!. 8½ inches in length. Fixed sights and has trigger safety catch. Featured in 1966 *"Gun Digest"* as "Marksman". Advertised as 20 shot repeater and weighing 24 oz. The above repeats on BB's only.

Have seen what could be an earlier version of the above with "DIANA REPEATER" cast into the L.H.S. of the action and "PAT. PENDING" followed by "MADE IN LOS ANGELES 25, CALF. U.S.A." cast on the R.H.S. First introduced with the "MARKSMAN" trade name. Advertised in 1958 with a straight hand butt rather than the later type with a moulded grip towards the rear. Was also available with a chrome finish, but for only a short period. Have seen others with "UMA-F" cast into the action on the R.H.S. The "F" appears in the pentagon so would assume that they were destined for the European Market.

Further to the above address cast with the airpistol, I have now found the complete address: Marksman Products Division, Morton H. Harris Inc., 2101 Barrington Avenue, Los Angeles, California, U.S.A.

A change in ownership occurred during 1969, could be the move to Milbro, in which case those marked with "Marksman" were pre-1969 and those marked with "Milbro" could be post-1969, but where does "Diana" fit?

Appears to have been called the "Harris Marksman" in its early days. Mentioned in Smith's *Gas, Air & Spring Guns of the World"*. Seen advertised during 1966 as the Diana Replica ·45 Automatic. This was modelled from the U.S. Government 191A1-45 automatic. There is also a shoulder and hip holster available for the above.

During the middle 1970's they advertised presentation models with either an antique gold finish or antique silver finish. These being available as well as the standard black finish. The presentation models were only available in the States. The first model marksman should be very rare as it was a single shot model and fired either pellets, darts or BB's.

The grip was straight, similar to the straight gripped Webley pre-war Mark airpistol. The small barrel tipped down for loading, but differed from the present model in that the whole front part tipped down and BB's were loaded singly for firing.

The original manufacturer and distributer was Morton H. Harris,236½ S. Roberts Boulevard, Beverley Hills, California, U.S.A. A move obviously took place to the above address in Los Angeles. The piston and action remained almost unaltered and the only major change was when the action was improved for repeater use with BB's. On the first model, darts and pellets were loaded straight into the barrel, whilst BB's were pressed into a "retainer hole" on the air transfer port side.

This retainer hole was a thick black washer that formed the air seal. To open the barrel for loading the action is cocked as normal then the foresight is pushed forward, this releases the barrel. Although it looks like a safety slide in the photograph, it is in fact false. L.H.S. of body lettered "MARKSMAN" and "PATS. PEND." whilst the R.H.S. marked "MORTON H. HARRIS LOS ANGELES CALIF." followed by "MADE IN U.A.S." The "A" is printed under the other letters because a screw head is in the way. This first model must be very rare.

The Milbro G10 may have a serial number stamped on the L.H.S. of the action just under "MILBRO REPEATER" it would appear that this was for export models only.

Morton H. Harris appeared to move around a bit as during 1955 his address was advertised as 2050 Westgate Avenue, Los Angeles 25, California.

During the middle 1970's, some were issued with serial numbers, one seen was 32018, which was stamped just under the Milbro logo cast on the L.H.S. of the action.

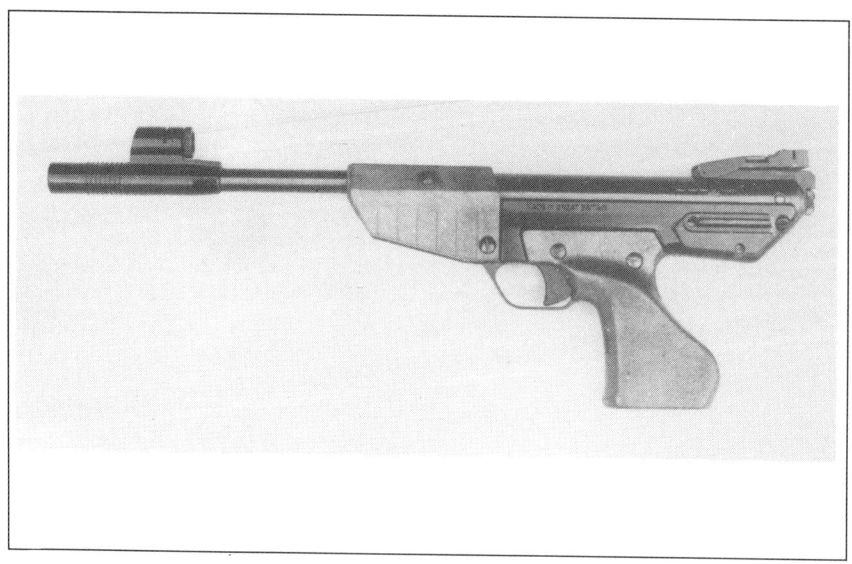

Cougar airpistol.

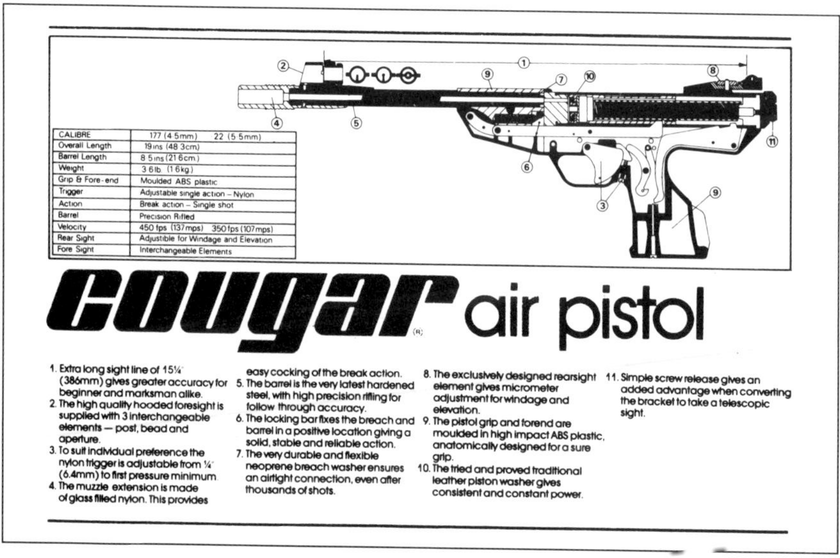

CALIBRE	177 (4·5mm) 22 (5·5mm)
Overall Length	19 ins (48·3cm)
Barrel Length	8·5 ins (21·6cm.)
Weight	3·6 lb. (1·6kg.)
Grip & Fore-end	Moulded ABS plastic
Trigger	Adjustable single action – Nylon
Action	Break action – Single shot
Barrel	Precision Rifled
Velocity	450 fps (137mps) 350 fps (107mps)
Rear Sight	Adjustible for Windage and Elevation
Fore Sight	Interchangeable Elements

cougar® air pistol

1. Extra long sight line of 15¼" (386mm) gives greater accuracy for beginner and marksman alike.
2. The high quality hooded foresight is supplied with 3 interchangeable elements — post, bead and aperture.
3. To suit individual preference the nylon trigger is adjustable from ¼" (6.4mm) to first pressure minimum.
4. The muzzle extension is made of glass filled nylon. This provides easy cocking of the break action.
5. The barrel is the very latest hardened steel, with high precision rifling for follow through accuracy.
6. The locking bar fixes the breach and barrel in a positive location giving a solid, stable and reliable action.
7. The very durable and flexible neoprene breach washer ensures an airtight connection, even after thousands of shots.
8. The exclusively designed rearsight element gives micrometer adjustment for windage and elevation.
9. The pistol grip and forend are moulded in high impact ABS plastic, anatomically designed for a sure grip.
10. The tried and proved traditional leather piston washer gives consistent and constant power.
11. Simple screw release gives an added advantage when converting the bracket to take a telescopic sight.

Specifications for Cougar airpistol.

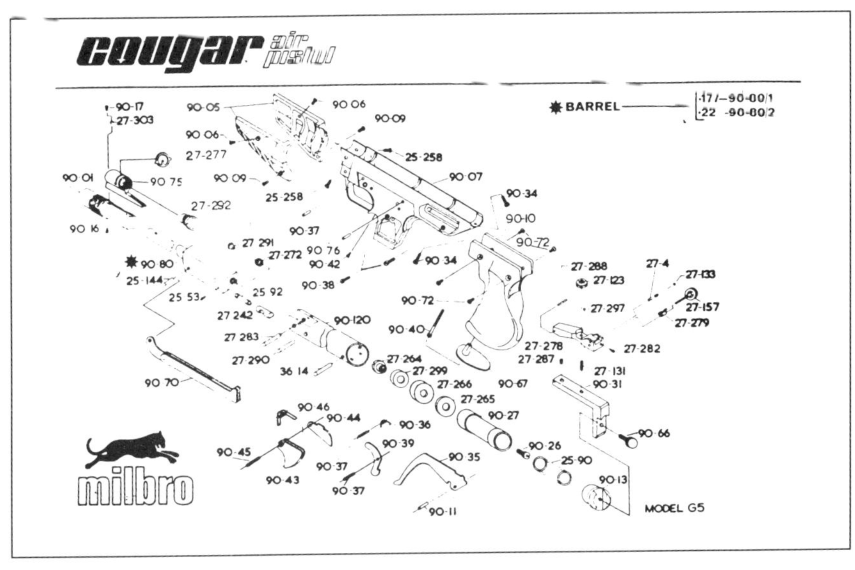

spare parts list.

✱ Not Illustrated

PART NO.	DESCRIPTION	PART NO.	DESCRIPTION	PART NO.	DESCRIPTION
25-53	Screw	27-290	Lock Bar	90-34	Screw
25-90	Main Spring	27-291	Shim	90-35	Cocking Arm
25-92	Spring	27-292	Element Nut	90-36	Spring
25-144	Pivot Pin	✱27-293	Aperture Element	90-37	Pivot Pin
25-258	Screw	27-297	Ball	90-38	Screw
27-4	Spring	✱27-298	Bead Element	90-39	Sear
27-123	Adjusting Wheel	27-299	Block Washer	90-40	Butt Screw
27-131	Elev. Stud	✱27-302	Allen Key	90-41	Adjusting Screw
27-133	Ball	27-303	Spring Washer	90-42	Screw
27-157	Traverse Spindle	36-14	Trigger Pin	90-43	Trigger
27-242	Lock Pin	90-01	Barrel Extension	90-44	Cam
27-264	Piston Nut	90-05	Pr. Cheek Pieces	90-45	Pivot Pin
27-265	Fibre Washer	90-06	Screw	90-46	Spring
27-266	Cup Washer	90-07	Pr. Body Castings	✱90-47	Scope Mount
27-272	Breech Washer	90-09	Screw	90-66	Screw
27-277	Post Element	90-10	Butt Complete	90-67	Butt Plate
27-278	Sight Body	90-11	Pivot Pin	✱90-69	Shoulder Extension
27-279	Sight Blade	90-13	End Cap	90-70	C/Lever Assy.
27-282	Screw	90-16	Screw	✱90-71	Clamp Assy.
27-283	Pivot Pin	90-17	Screw	90-72	Screw
27-287	Spring	90-26	Piston Screw	90-75	Front Sight
27-288	Pivot Pin	90-27	Piston Sleeve	90-80	Barrel (Assy)
		90-31	Sight Platform	90-120	Cylinder (Assy)
				90-76	Pin

Cougar airpistol spare parts list.

Model: **COUGAR**

Maker: **Millard Bros.,**
Lanarkshire, Scotland.
Founded in 1887 and ceased trading 1982.

Date: Introduced late 1978.

Valuation: £40 - £70.

Details: Heavy, well made airpistol Using blued metal, cast metal and heavy duty plastic components. Very similar to the B.S.A. Scorpion. Barrel has extension piece fitted with a tunnel foresight with removable sight blade. Trigger cannot be fired when action is cocked. Heavy duty cast rearsight adjustable for both windage and elevation. The rearsight can be removed for a telescopic sight ramp.

The blued metal air chamber rests on a cast metal trigger action. A shoulder stock fits into the rear of the action. The butt and barrel pivot side plates are made from heavy duty wood-simulated plastic. The L.H.S. of the air chamber is stamped "COUGAR" and has been golded in. Cast in the trigger action on the L.H.S. appears "MADE IN GREAT BRITAIN".

The above is sold complete with spare foresight blades, telescopic sight ramp, shoulder stock, oil and pellets. Advertised weight 4 lbs. The "Original" air rifle foresights fit the above. The above has a piston fitted with a leather washer. Serial number not visible. Length 18½ inches, with a 7⅞ inch rifled barrel. For stripping instructions for the above see *"Guns Review",* November, 1978. Also *"Airgun World",* November, 1978.

It is recommended that the two plastic fore grips are not over tightened otherwise they may split. Advertised muzzle velocities: ·177 - 450 f.p.s. and ·22 - 350 f.p.s.

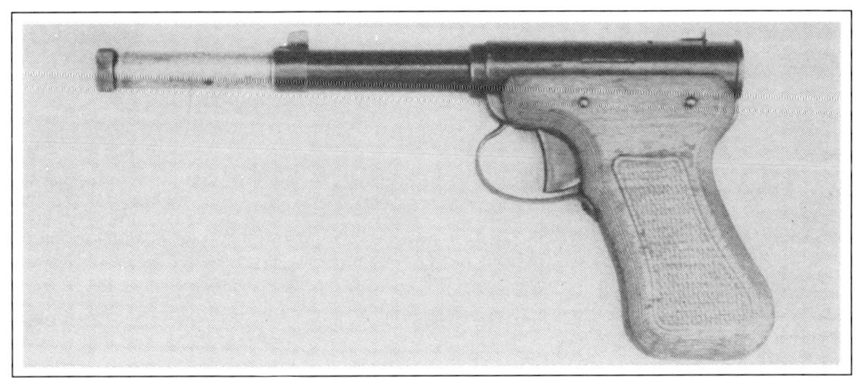

Original Model 2.

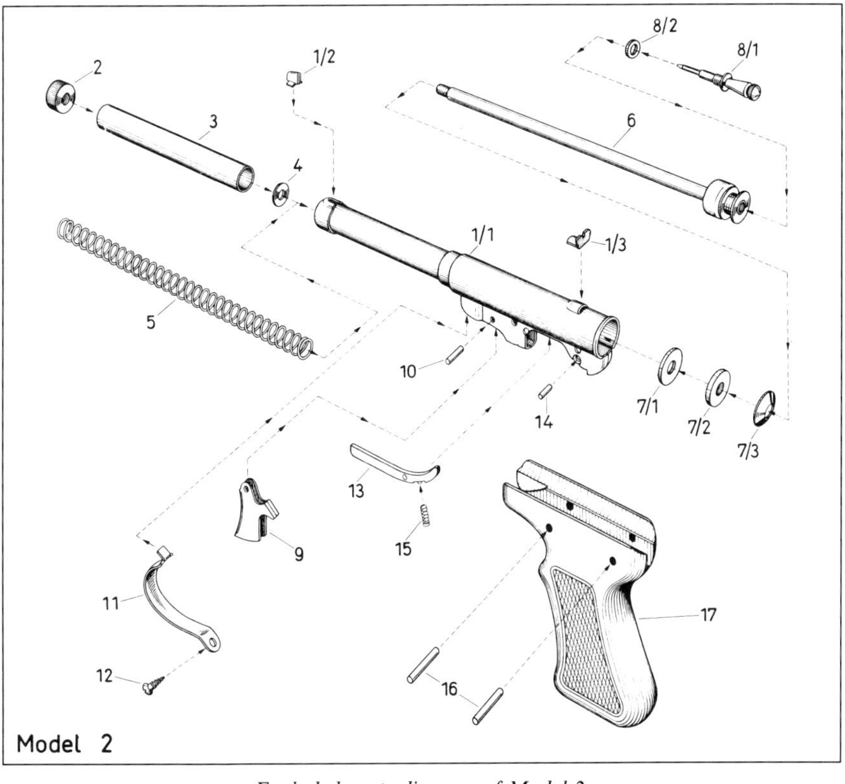

Model 2

Exploded parts diagram of Model 2.

Model: **2.** Gat style airpistol

Maker: **Mayer & Grammelspacher,**
Rastatt, Germany.

Date: From January, 1955 to late 1970's.

Valuation: £5 - £20.

Details: All metal barrel and air chamber with a wooden butt. Normal push-in barrel cocking action and removable screw at rear for loading pellet. Calibre ·177. Have yet to meet a ·22 Gat. Top of air chamber stamped "ORIGINAL" and "MOD 2", with "MADE IN GERMANY" on the L.H.S. just above the butt. The butt is of a light wood with ribbing in a layered pattern around the edge similar to the Webley Senior. The side panels have a pressed chequered pattern. Butt held to the action by two metal pins. Smoothbore barrel with simple non-adjustable sights.

The above appears to be the first air pistol that Mayer & Grammelspacher produced after the War. The pre-war models did not have the updated butt with the ribbing and chequering. Advertised weight 11½ oz., length uncocked 9⅝ inches. See British Diana Model 2 gat for similarity of design.

During the middle of the 1970's, it was advertised in America as the Hyscore Model 814 with a "Hyscore" trade medallion stuck on the butt. It was also sold as the "German Black Falcon" with a falcon trademark stamped on each side of the wooden butt. Could this have been sold under the Falke flag??

The Webley Junior mainspring should fit the above.

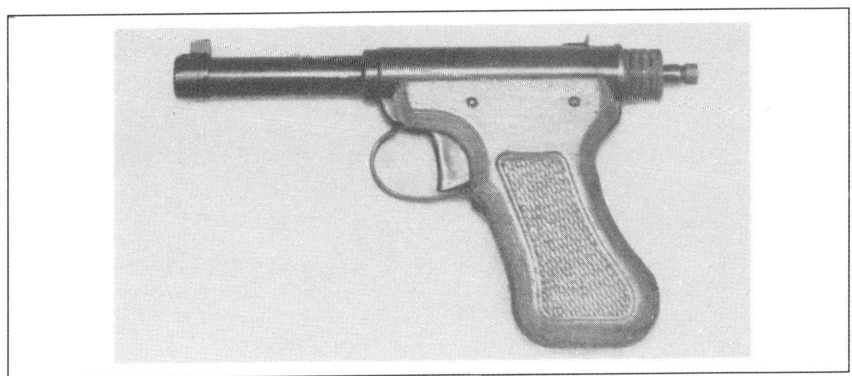

The "Backward" Gat in uncocked position.

Action now cocked and pellet pusher removed. Note its extreme length.

Model: An Australian Gat???

Maker: From the style of the stock "Original":
Mayer & Grammelspacher,
Rastatt, Germany.

Date: From the style of butt and similarity to the "Original" Model 2 gat airpistol, late 1950's to early 1960's.

Valuation: £5 - £25, or even more if you were prepared to pay it.

Details: A gat airpistol in reverse! Every gat seen so far has a push-in barrel, but this one has a pull-out barrel. The stock is identical with that of the Original Model 2. All metal surfaces are blued and the L.H.S. of the air chamber is stamped "MADE IN GERMANY". Fixed sights. The barrel is flush with the end of the outer tube when unfired. To cock the action, the rear knurled portion is gripped and pulled out. After about 2 inches the action is cocked. The rear barrel plus is unscrewed and a pellet introduced and the plug replaced and screwed home. The plug has a pusher rod almost 3¼ inches long which is certainly unusual, the usual length is about one inch. All in all, a very unusual production gat airpistol.

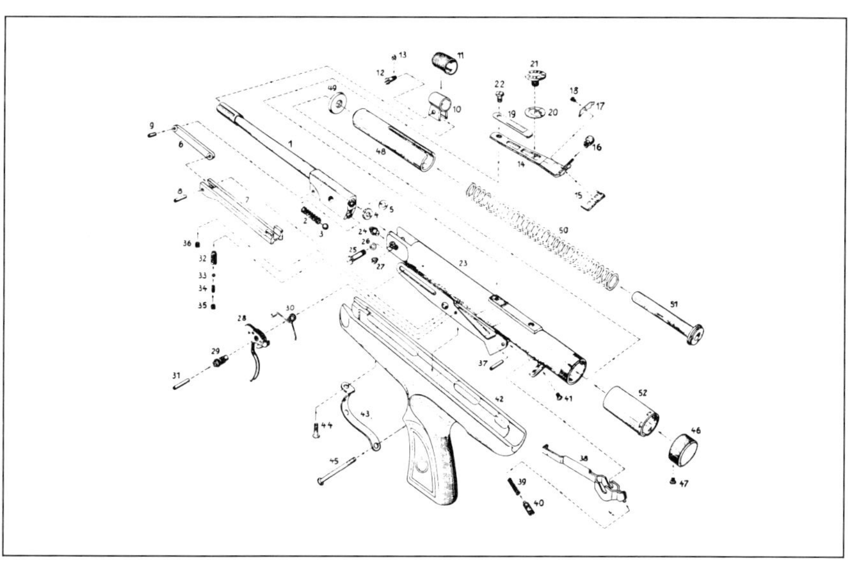

Spare Parts for Air Pistol No. 5

No.	
1	Barrel with locking spring, locking ball washer and compensation disc
2	Locking spring
3	Locking ball
4	Breech washer
5	Compensation disc for No. 4
6	Front cocking lever
7	Rear cocking lever
8	Rear lever pin
9	Front lever pin
10–13	Foresight complete
10	Foresight
11	Rubber foresight cover
12	Foresight screw
13	Locking spring washer for 12
14–22	Rearsight complete
14	Rearsight blade
15	Notch plate
16	Windage nut
17	Windage index spring
18	Notch plate locking screw
19	Notch plate spring
20	Elevating index spring
21	Elevating screw
22	Rearsight screw
23	Compression tube with locking plug
24	Locking plug
25	Barrel axis screw
26	Compensation disc for No. 25
27	Set screw for 25
28	Trigger
29	Trigger pin tube
30	Trigger spring
31	Trigger pin
32–36	Tube for double pull trigger complete
32	Tube for double pull trigger
33	Ball for double pull trigger
34	Spring for double pull trigger
35	Screw for double pull trigger
36	Set screw for 35
37	Hook pin
38	Hook
39	Hook spring
40	Hook screw
41	Set screw for 40
42	Stock
43	Trigger guard
44	Front trigger guard screw
45	Rear trigger guard screw
46	End piece
47	End piece set screw
48	Piston complete
49	Piston washer
50	Main spring
51	Main spring guide
52	Main spring bearing

Spare Parts for Airpistol No. 5

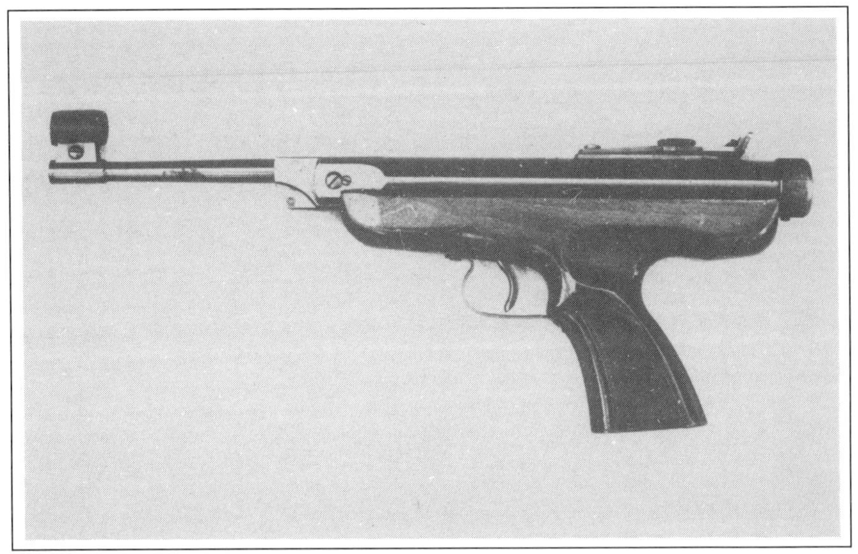

Original Model 5.

Model: **MODEL 5**

Maker: "Original"
Mayer & Grammelspacher,
Rastatt, Germany.

Date: From August 1958 to 1960 with the wooden butt.

Valuation: £30 - £60. Could become scarce as only manufactured for about 3 - 4 years.

Details: The successor to the pre-war Target Model 5 air pistol. Wooden butt with pressed micro chequering and dimple effect with deep grooving on grip, similar to the Webley Senior. Double pull trigger with adjustment through the hole in the trigger guard. Ball bearing barrel latch. 16 inches along barrel line. Hooded foresight. Top of air chamber stamped "ORIGINAL" and "MOD.5" behind the rear sight. Also has "MADE IN GERMANY" on the L.H.S. of the chamber. Serial number not visible. See other Model 5 for trigger adjustment. Although advertised as being available in ·177 only the above is ·22. Advertised weight 2 lb. 13 ozs. The above appeared in the U.S.A. as the "GECADO". These are sometimes advertised as rare items, but they are only the American counterpart of the "Original". It would be like advertising "Original" airguns in the States as rare items. Available in either ·177 or ·22 rifled barrels.

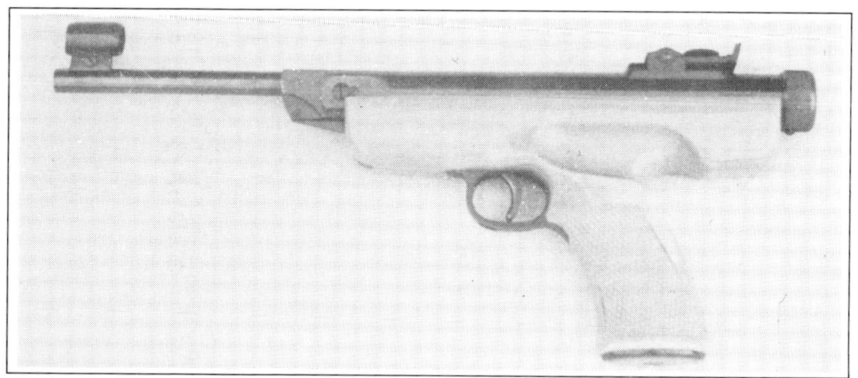

Original Model 5 with grey butt.

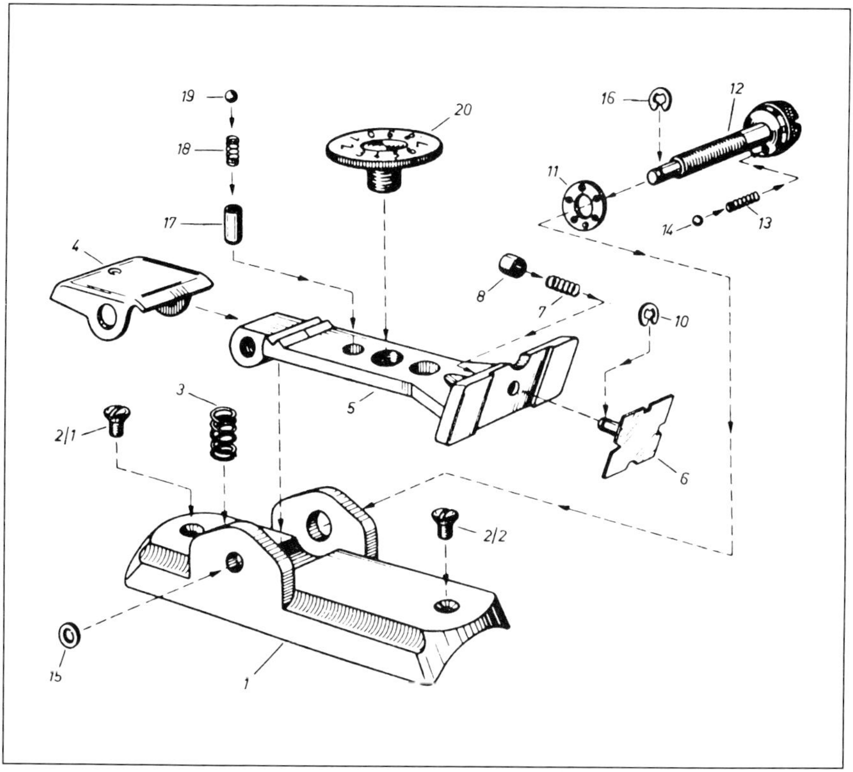

Plastic Micrometer Rearsight for Models 5 and 6 (and Models 25, 25D, 27, 35, 50 former type)

Model: **5**

Maker: "Original" by
Mayer & Grammelspacher,
Rastatt, Western Germany.

Date: With the light grey stock would assume from around the 1960's to the early 1970's.

Valuation: £30 - £60.

Details: The follow-on from the Model 5 with wooden butt. Serial number not visible. Just under 16 inches along the barrel line. Tunnel foresight and plastic rearsight adjustable for windage and elevation. Rearsight has spring loaded revolving blade with four types of grooves. Top of air chamber stamped "ORIGINAL" with "MOD 5" at rear of air chamber. Light grey coloured stock with black plastic trigger guard and base butt plate to pistol grip. Serial number not visible nor is the assumed date stamp on the air chamber. The above is also lacking in the "F" pentagon denoting lower muzzle energy for Europe. Advertised weight 3 lb. 1 oz.

Advertised in the U.S.A. as the Hyscore Model 815T during the middle 1970's. The "Original" Model 5 may also be found with "Diana" on the air chamber accompanied by the Huntress trade label. What is assumed to be a date stamp often appears at the far end of the chamber on the L.H.S. and just above the end of the plastic grip. For example "04 67" would be April, 1969, this appeared on a grey plastic gripped Diana Model 5.

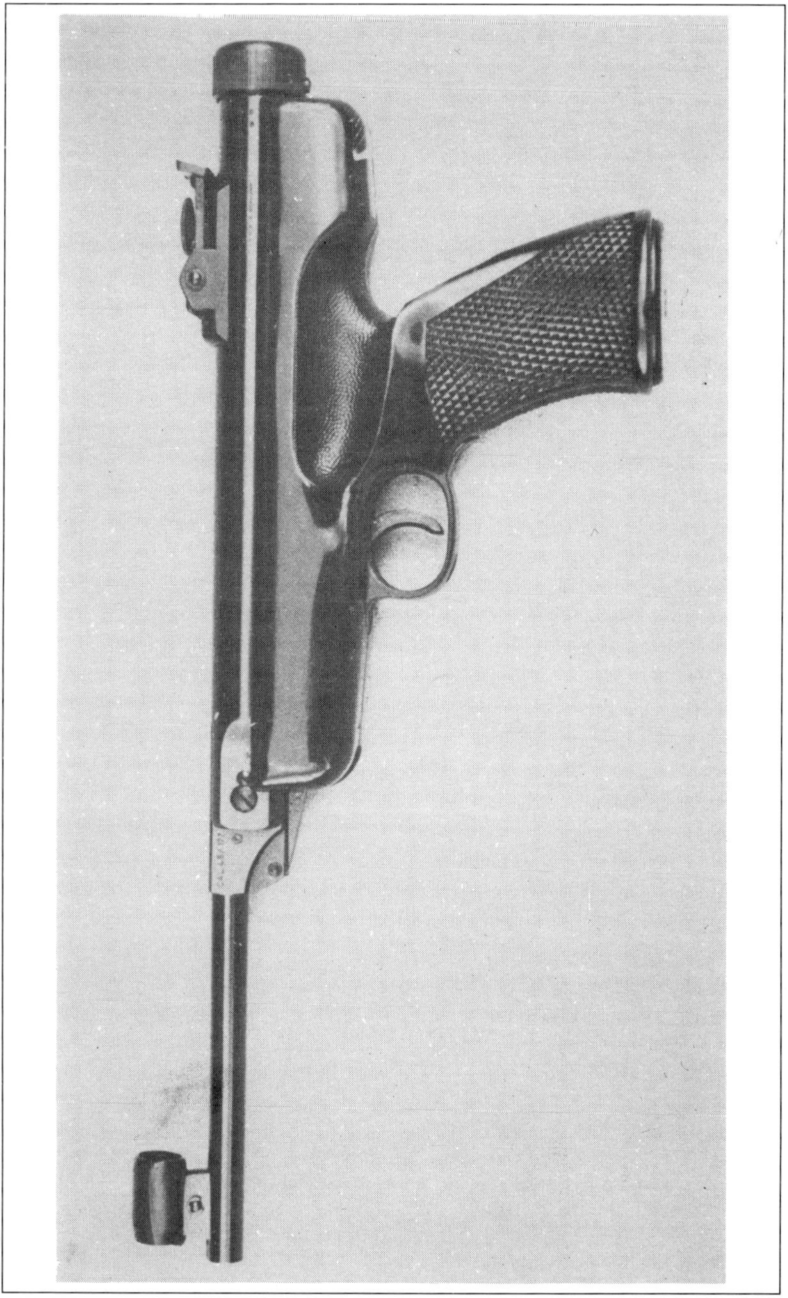

Original Model 5.

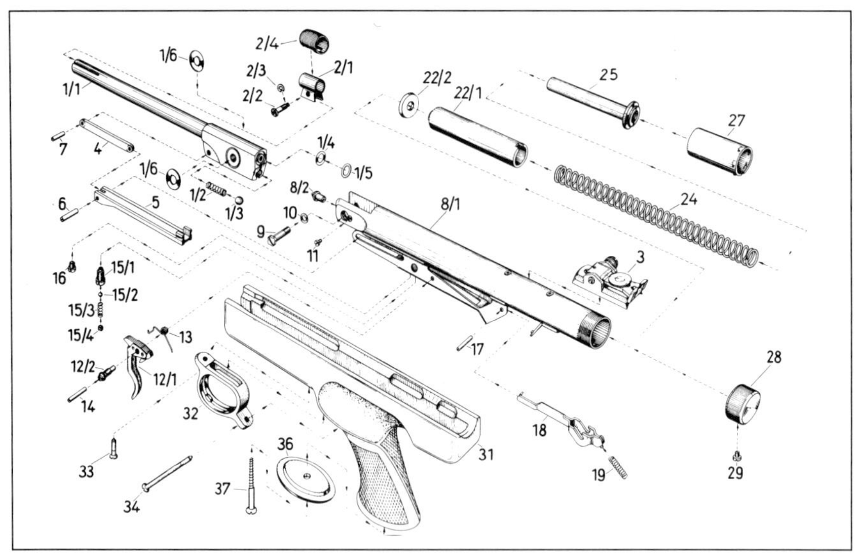

Exploded diagram of the Model 5.

Model: **MODEL 5**

Maker: "Original"
Mayer & Grammelspacher,
Germany.

Date: Early 1970's to 1978. Late 1978, an improved model was introduced called the "5M".

Valuation: £30 - £60.

Details: Sold with either ·22 or ·177 barrels. Moulded plastic stock for right hand use. Rather long in the sight plane, 16 inches long so would recommend two handed use. Has tunnel foresight and plastic rear sight. Stamped "ORIGINAL" on top of air chamber, "MOD 5" at back of rear sight. Calibre is stamped on side of barrel. On the above example is also stamped an "F" in a pentagon, this is to show that it is under the legal limit of muzzle energy for Germany and their limits are lower than ours. Very well made. German Dianas are sold under the trade name "GECADO" in the U.S.A.

Production began in 1957 with a wooden stock. In 1960 this became a grey coloured plastic moulded stock. At a later date the stock was moulded in brown. Sold in the U.S.A. by Winchester as their Model 353. For the German and European market the name Diana is retained along with the Diana huntress trademark. So after the War, Mayer & Grammelspacher manufactured airguns under about three different trade names: Original, Diana and Gecado. This might also include Geco?

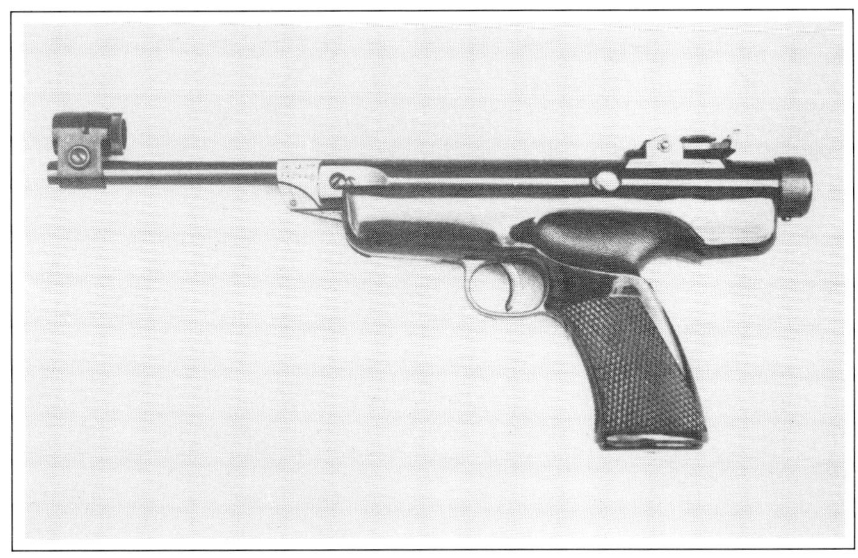

Original Model 6.

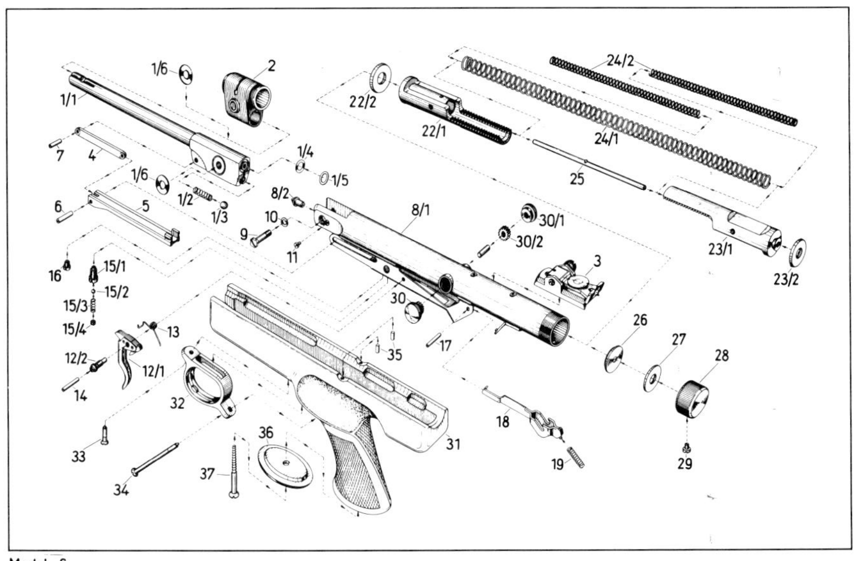

Exploded diagram of Model 6.

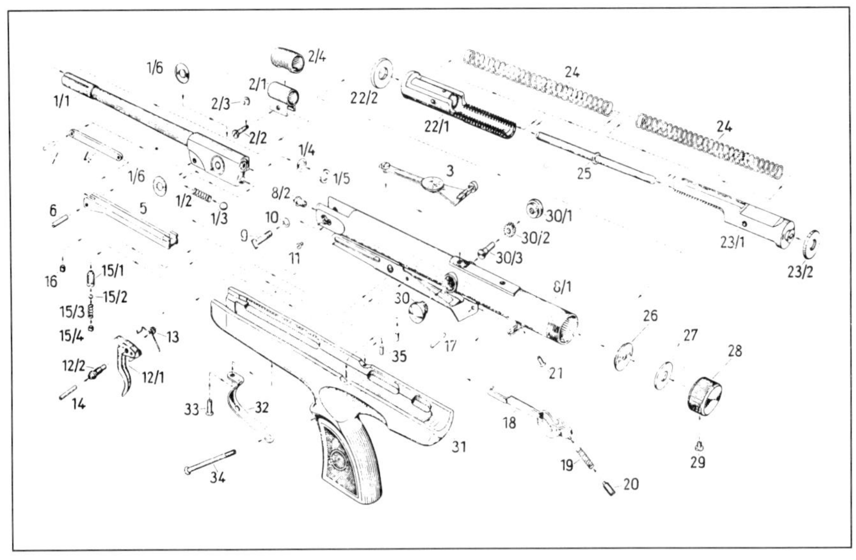

Exploded diagram for Model 6 (1962).

Spare Parts for Air Pistol No. 6 (1962)

No	
1–3	Barrel rifled calibre .177 or .22 with locking spring, locking ball, breech washer, and second washer
1/1	Barrel
1/2	Locking spring
1/3	Locking ball
1/4	Second breech washer (if necessary)
1/5	Breech washer
1/6	Hinge ring
2	Foresight complete, parts 2/1–2/4
2/1	Foresight
2/2	Foresight screw
2/3	Foresight set clip
2/4	Rubber foresight cover
3	Rearsight complete (parts as per list for leaf-spring micrometer rearsight)
4	Front cocking lever
5	Rear cocking lever
6	Rear lever pin
7	Front lever pin
8	Compression tube with locking cone
8/1	Compression tube
8/2	Locking cone
9	Barrel axis screw
10	Washer for axis screw (if necessary)
11	Set screw for axis screw
12	Trigger with trigger tube
12/1	Trigger
12/2	Trigger tube
13	Trigger spring
14	Trigger pin
15	Tube for double pull trigger complete, parts 15/1–15/4

No.	
15/1	Tube for double pull trigger
15/2	Ball for double pull trigger
15/3	Spring for double pull trigger
15/4	Screw for double pull trigger
16	Set screw for tube for double pull trigger
17	Hook pin
18	Hook
19	Hook spring
20	Hook screw
21	Set screw for hook screw
22	Air piston with washer
22/1	Air piston
22/2	Air piston washer
23	Dummy piston with washer
23/1	Dummy piston
23/2	Dummy piston washer
24	Main spring
25	Main spring guide
26	Compensation disc
27	End piece check ring
28	End piece
29	Set screw for end piece
30	Control wheel complete, part 30/1–30/3
30/1	Axis screw
30/2	Control wheel
30/3	Wheel axis
31	Stock
32	Trigger guard
33	Front trigger guard screw
34	Rear trigger guard screw
35	Axis screw protector

Spare Parts for airpistol No. 6 (1962).

Model: **MODEL 6**

Maker: "Original"
Mayer & Grammelspacher,
West Germany.

Date: Introduced around the very early 1960's. November 1978 advertised two new models based on the above action, Models 6G and 6M. They have a new styled body action and simulated wood target grips.

Valuation: £40 - £80.

Details: Advertised as the world's first air pistol without recoil or rebound and is a pleasure to use and fire, although would recommend two-handed use. 16 inches long. Works on the principle of two pistons, one compresses the air whilst the other acts as a dummy weight and travels in the opposite direction when fired. Plastic stock moulded for right handed use. Top of air cylinder stamped "ORIGINAL", "MOD6" at back of rear sight, "MADE IN GERMANY" "DEUTSCHE BUNDESPATENTE AUSLANDPATENTE" also on the air chamber. There also appear "03 77" but cannot say what this means, could be date of manufacture.

Breech of barrel stamped with calibre, serial number and the "F" pentagon denoting level of German muzzle energy. Tunnel foresight has removable rear plug for changeable sight elements. For the price it is very good value. The trigger can be adjusted by holding airpistol upside down and inserting screwdriver through the hole in the trigger guard. The screw in front is the set screw and must be loosened first. Then the double pull adjusting screw can be rotated — clockwise for greater pull and anti-clockwise for lesser pull. The double pull can be eliminated if the screw is turned to the left until no resistance can be felt by the trigger. If turned too far to the right then the trigger is locked. After adjustment, the set screw must be retightened. It is recommended that the airpistol air cylinder must never be oiled.

German Dianas are sold under the trade name "GECADO" in the U.S.A. For details of stripping the Model 6, see *"Guns Review"*, June, 1974 and July, 1974. Advertised as the Hyscore Model 816M in the U.S.A. during the middle 1970's and being fitted with the grey coloured stock. The reader was urged to use the HY-SCORE No. 215 wadcutter pellets. Distributed by Winchester in the U.S.A. as their Model 363. The Hyscore Model 816 appeared in the States during 1966 fitted with the grey coloured stock. For each click of the rearsight adjusters, the point of impact is altered by ²⁄₁₀ of an inch at 25 feet. The velocity measured 15 feet from the muzzle was 426 f.p.s., which according to the American reviewer was a "high velocity for an airpistol". It is doubtful if the above sold in any great numbers as it couldn't be used in N.R.A. (National Rifle Association) competitions because its sight radius exceeded the 10 inch maximum and the trigger pull at its heaviest setting was below the NRA required minimum of 2 lb. When the Model 6 (L.P.6) appeared in the early 1960's it was fitted with a wooden grip similar to that fitted to the first Model 5.

Original Model 10.

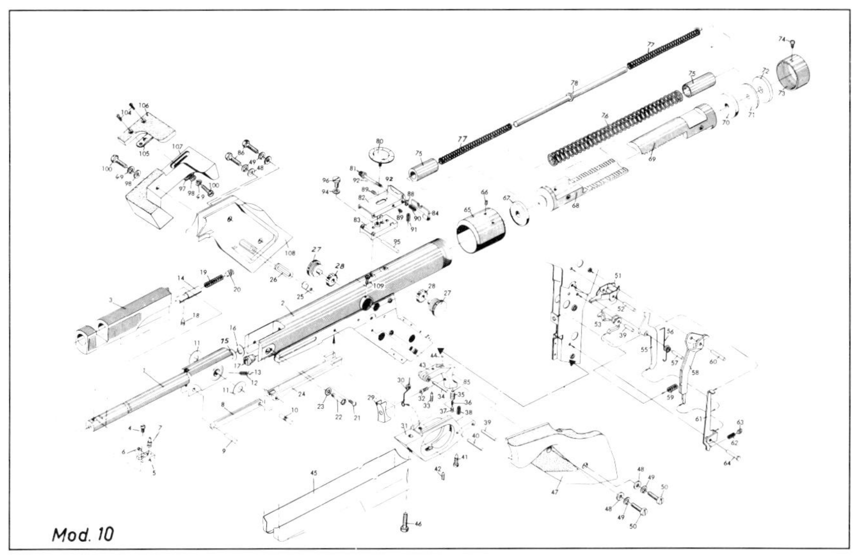

Exploded diagram for Model 10 airpistol.

Model: **MODEL 10**

Maker: **Mayer & Grammelspacher,**
Rastatt, Baden, Germany.

Date: 1975 to present day.

Valuation: £130n - £150n, £90 - £130.

Details: The above is the improved model as from January, 1977. These improvements on the previous model are a detachable extra barrel weight of 80 g., the eccentric sleeve replaced by a cylindrical tube which can be removed, and a rearsight that can be set in three positions thus giving a sighting line of 315,335 or 355 mm. A very well made target airpistol. Sold in fitted case with screwdrivers, test target, pellets, spare rearsight blade and case key. Metal parts to pistol have a pleasing black matt crackle finish. Serial numbers and calibre stamped on L.H.S. of barrel breech. The barrel sleeve is pushed forward and rotated through 180° so as to form a protective cocking aid, it is returned to original position for firing. It is recommended never to introduce mineral oil into the air chamber. For a review, see *"Guns Review",* May, 1975. Advertised weight 42½ oz. Length along barrel line 16 inches. Also available without fitted case, but sold in a carton.

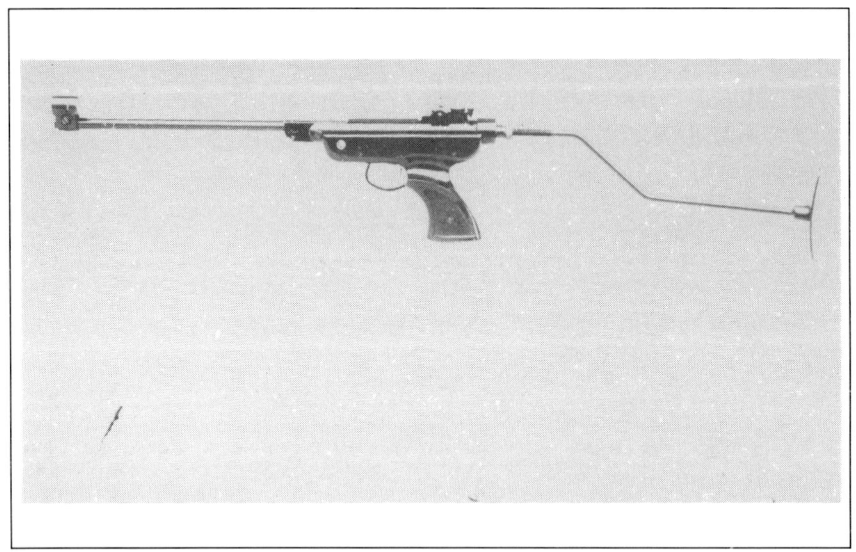

Panther Carbine De Luxe.

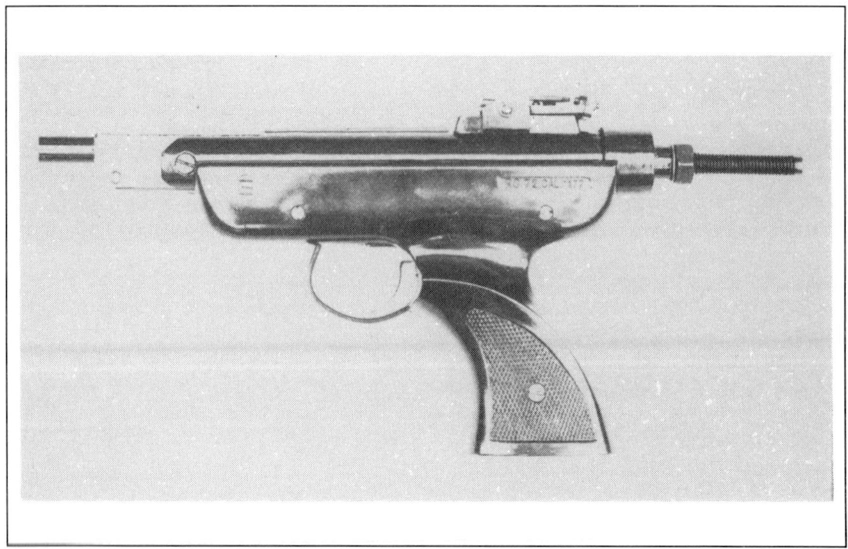

Close-up of Panther De Luxe Carbine action.

Model: **PANTHER DE LUXE in Carbine form, RO72,** also referred to as the **PANTHER ARTILLERY.** Also called the **RO77 ARTILLERY CARBINE.** Panther De Luxe was also called the **IGI DOMINO 203,** quite confusing, isn't it?

Maker: **Gun Toys,** Italy. Imported by Sussex Armoury until their closure during 1982.

Date: The RO72 appeared in 1973 as a short barreled airpistol and sold as the De Luxe version of the RO71. The Artillery version appeared in 1977.

Valuation: £10 - £30.

Details: Long barreled airpistol with detachable screw-in shoulder stock. Sold in ·177 only, but shorter barrel in ·22 was available. 34 inches long with a 13⅜ inch barrel and a 14 inch shoulder stock. Barrel has clamp mounted foresight with interchangeable sight elements and serial number stamped on side of breech. The ·177 barrel is rifled. Short air chamber, must be the most overworked airgun on the market, with rearsight similar to that fitted to German Original airguns. This has a rotating rearsight blade with four types of sights. The rearsight can be removed and a metal scope ramp fitted in its place. Usually fitted with a black plastic grip, but box lid illustration shows a light brown one.

Stock marked with the Guntoy trademark and "RO 72 CAL. ·177" and on the other side "MADE IN ITALY". Trigger adjustment through hole at rear of trigger guard. Advertised weight 7 lbs. There was also a Panther Mark II Carbine with a one piece shoulder stock and pistol grip offered from 1980. It would appear from catalogue illustrations that the rearsight was moved to the breech end of the barrel in the very early 1980's. This Mark II model had a beechwood stock. Advertised muzzle velocity was 300 f.p.s. Left handed grips were available. Millard (Milbro) Brothers of Scotland also sold the short barrel model as the G11 with a different style of shoulder stock. This was composed of two struts instead of just the single wire strut from Sussex Armoury.

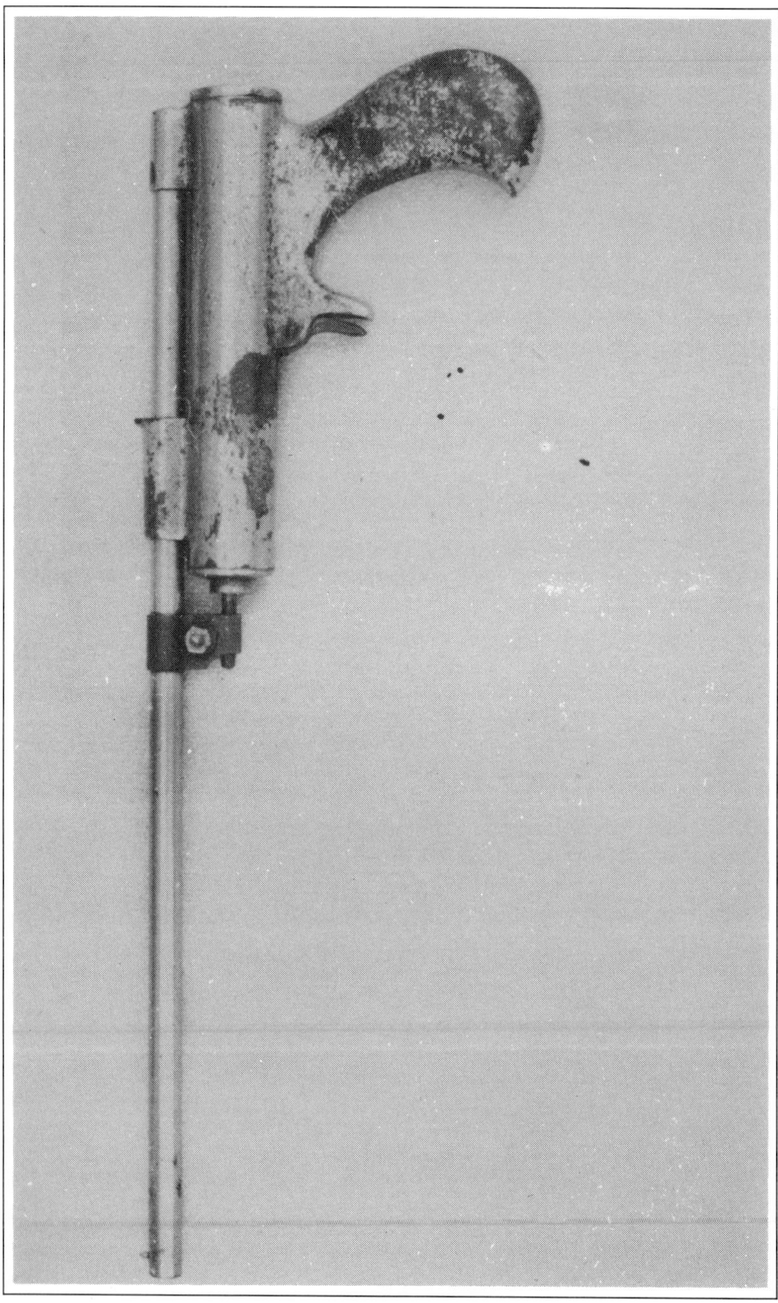

Pope's "Rifle Air Pistol".

Model: **"RIFLE AIR PISTOL"**

Maker: **Pope Bros.,**
45 High Street, Boston, Mass., U.S.A.

Date: Around 1875.

Valuation: £50 - £150. So few appear on the market that it is difficult to assess the above. It helps to compare its rarity with other airguns, i.e. Webley Mk. II Service air rifle.

Details: All metal with nickel plating overall. Serial number not visible. Trigger and barrel clamp only parts not plated. Butt drilled for simple wire stock, hence name "Rifle Air Pistol". 11 inches along barrel and 12 inches from tip of barrel to base of butt. Thin flat section main spring. Trigger has small adjuster screw in front. Stamped on air chamber plug at rear of action "POPE BROS., U.S.A.", then around the plug "CANADA MAR. 23 '75, BELGIUM OCT. 21/74. PATD. JUNE 6, DEC. 5, 71. NOV. 17 '74. ENGLAND JULY 1, FRANCE, OCT. 20". The barrel is pulled forward to cock the action and load the pellet, then pushed back and pressed hard into the breech to affect an air seal. Care should be taken that the barrel clamp does not slip over the lower cocking arm that is connected to the piston, as did happen during testing. Contrary to what is stated in Smith's, see page 34, the action can be fired with the action cocked and open for loading. For details of the original box and accessories, see *"Guns Review"*, November, 1978.

It has been suggested that the Pope airpistol was in fact made by Quackenbush under licence for the Pope Bros. See *"Airguns"* by Eldon G., Wolff, pages 73 & 74. The above style was improved upon and patented by Bedford & Walker in 1876. The improved air pistol is often referred to as the "EUREKA". For details of various patents of Quackenbush, Pope, Bedford & Walker, see *"Guns Review"*, September, 1977. The above was available in two models, blacked finish or nickel plated. A black, velvet lined, walnut case could also be purchased.

Each one was supplied with the wire skeleton shoulder stock. Rear and fore sights are simple raised projections with no adjustment. ·22 pellets can be used if they are first pushed into the barrel a small way to "size" them to the correct width. The above design was patented by Quackenbush in 1874 and assigned to Pope. The Patent number being 156890. This was Quackenbush's first patent.

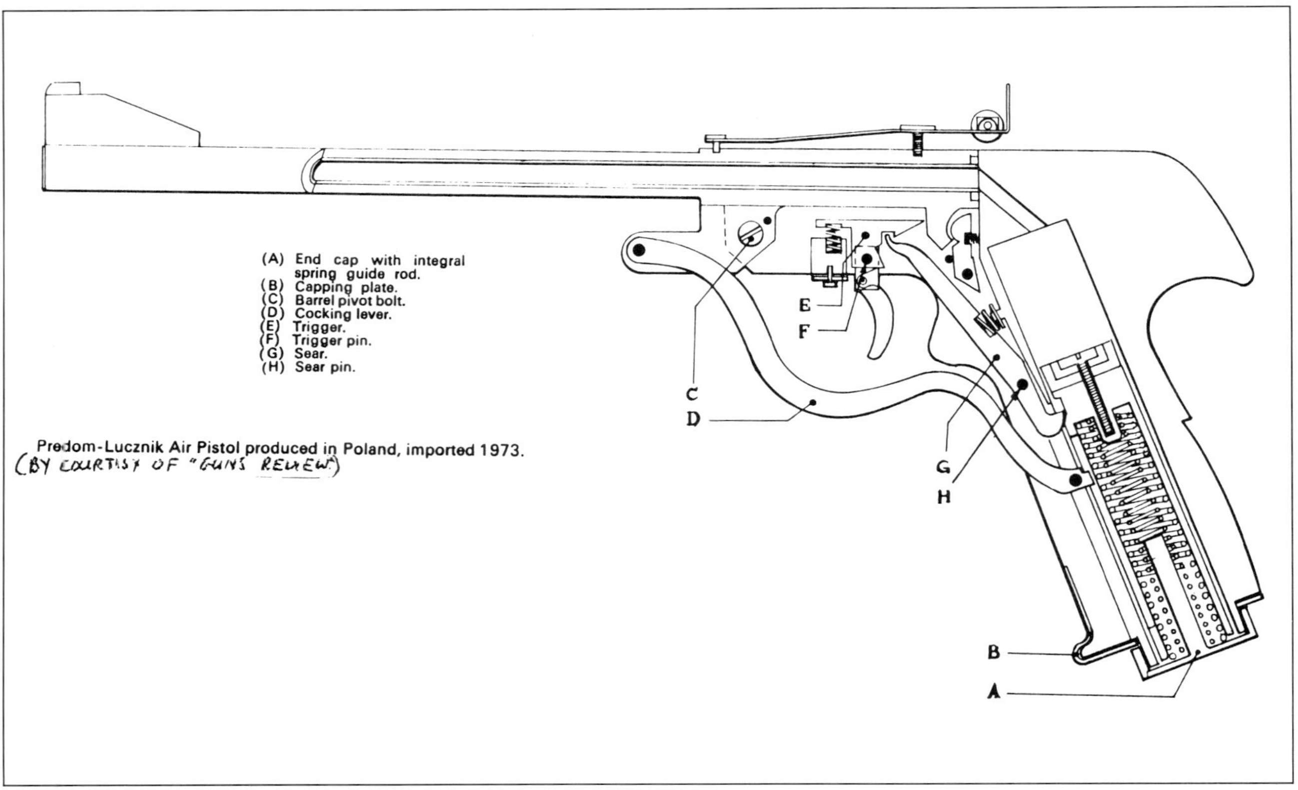

Predom-Lucznik Airpistol produced in Poland, imported 1973. (By courtesy of "Guns Review").

Predom-Lucznik Airpistol.

Model: **PREDOM AIRPISTOL**
also known as the **Model 170.**

Maker: **Predom Lucznik,**
Poland.

Date: Middle 1970's to present day.

Valuation: £40 - £80.

Details: Very similar to Walther LP53. All black finish with black grips. Appears to have year stamp on side of barrel and serial number. Various markings appear stamped on the barrel, body and cocking lever that also acts as the trigger guard. Cast in the L.H.S. of the body is "PREDOM-LUCZNIK" followed by "Wz 1970 and KAL. 4·5 mm". The internal design appears to follow that of the Lincoln airpistol. Such is the pace of progress. A very well made target airpistol. Advertised weight 38 ozs. Approximate muzzle velocity being 350 f.p.s. For a review, see *"Guns Review",* March, 1975.

The rifling does not go right to the end of the barrel, but stops about an inch or so from the muzzle. This could be for some sort of cocking aid, as it is with the Walther LP53. Serial numbers seen begin with P and Z, and G. Was advertised on the continent as being available with a 4 x 15 telescopic sight that was mounted on top of the barrel in place of the rearsight. Available in ·177 only.

'Record' airpistol with cocking aid in place.

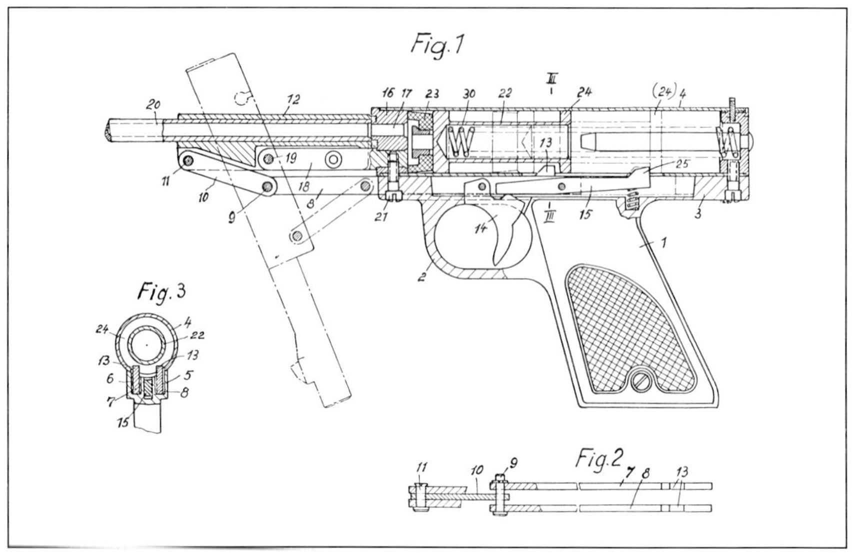

Patent drawing for the "Record" airpistol, dated 21/9/67.

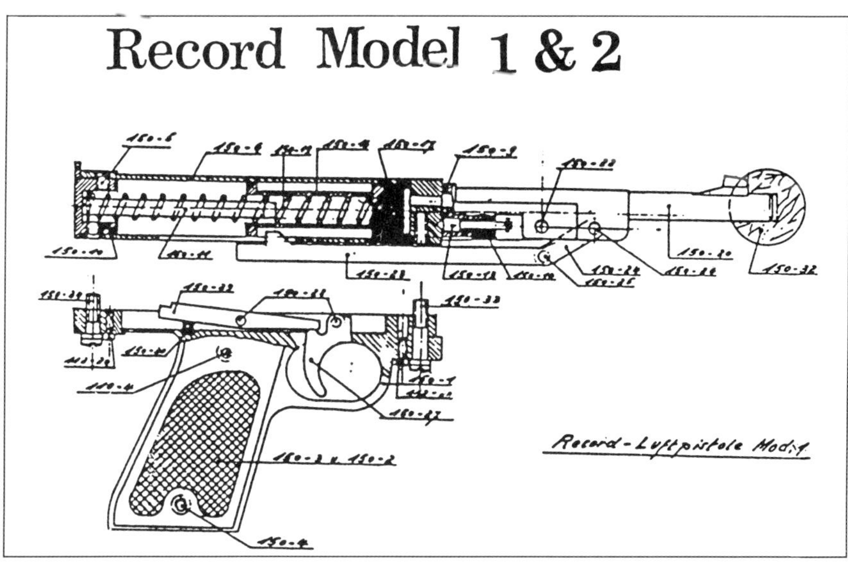

Record Model 1.

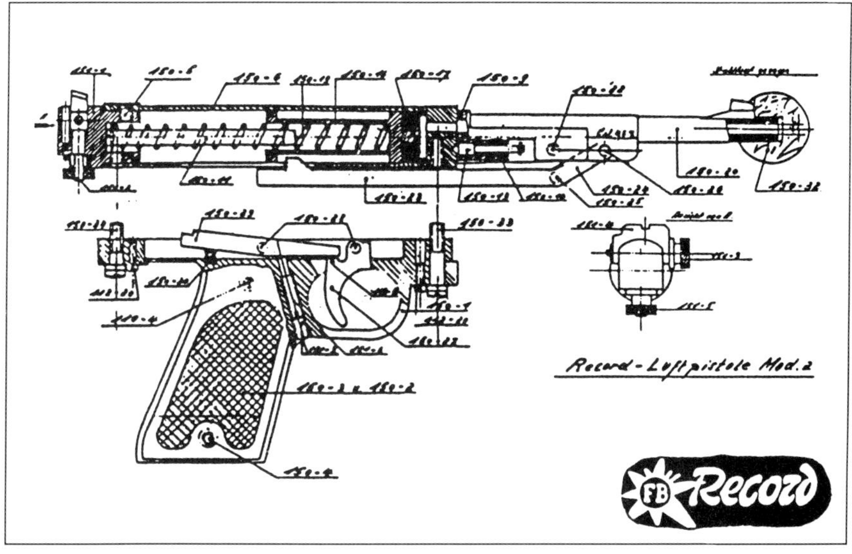

Record Model 2.

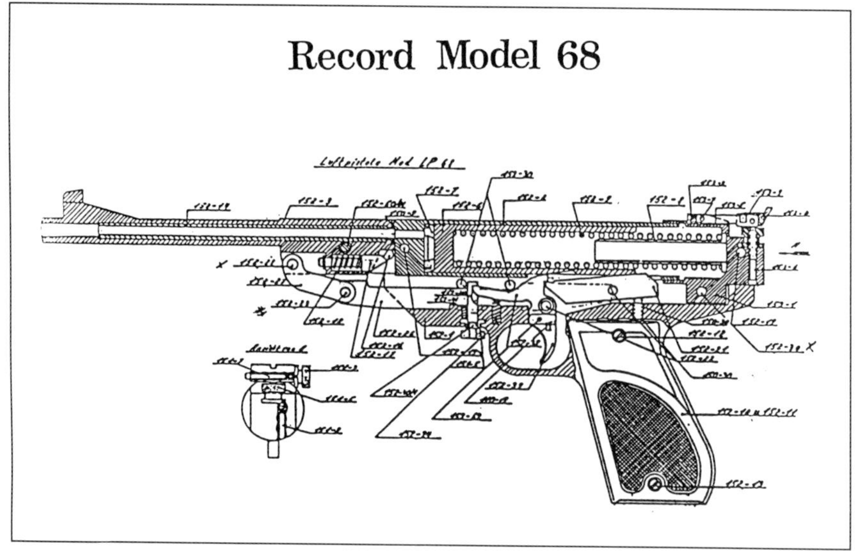

Record Model 68.

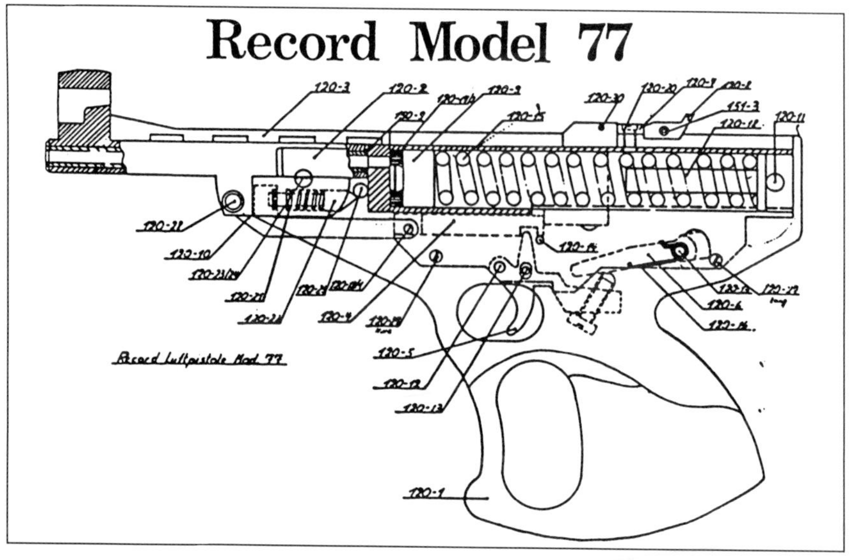

Record Model 77.

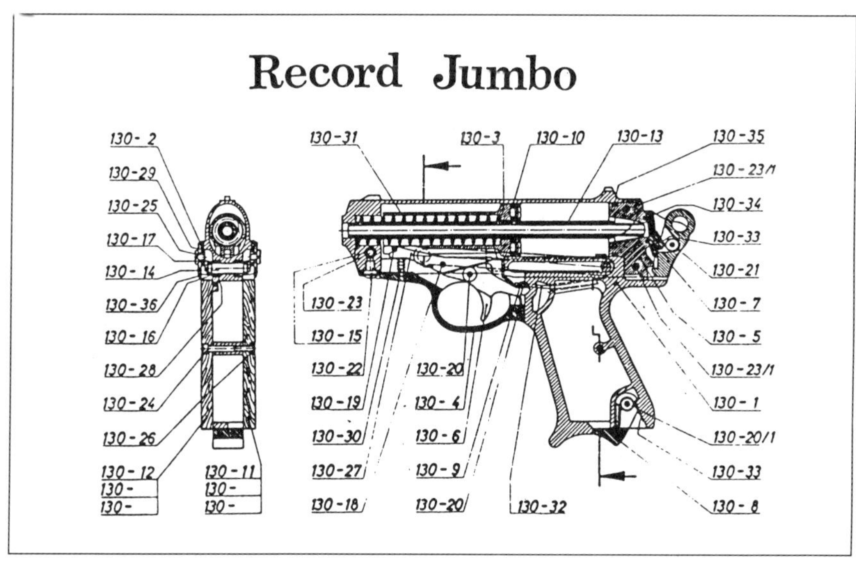

Record Jumbo.

Model: **"RECORD".** Appears to be **Model 1.** Other models available are **Model 2** and a larger version **Model 68** and **Model 77.**

Maker: See *Details* below. Imported and distributed by: John Rothery (Wholesale) Ltd., 22 Stamshaw Road, Portsmouth, Hants., PO2 8LR.

Date: Design patented during 1967, so actual manufacture must have been after this date.

Valuation: Most models from £10 - £30.

Details: Very similar in design to the Em-ge LP3, but smaller and cheaply made. Almost made entirely from alloy castings. Brown plastic grips. Sights appear to be non-adjustable. 10¾ inches long with a 5 inch smoothbore barrel. Cast into the frame on the L.H.S. just above the trigger is "FB" in a star followed by "RECORD". On the R.H.S. of the frame is stamped "FOREIGN". Supplied with a wooden cocking aid similar to that supplied with the Walther LP53, this fits over the end of the barrel and placed in palm of hand for cocking. Serial number not visible.

Address for the above maker as follows: Fritz Barthelmes KG D-7920 Heidenheim Oggenhausen Vereinigt Filzfabriken AG D 7928 Glengen. Apologies for the lack of commas, but the above is printed as it appears on the instruction leaflet. Above address also associated with the initials "VFG". Available in ·177 smoothbore only. Have been supplied with another address for the above: Fritz Barthelmes Sportwaffenfabrik, 7921 Oggenhausen, Kr. Heidenheim a.d., Breuz Heidenheim Strasse 10, West Germany.

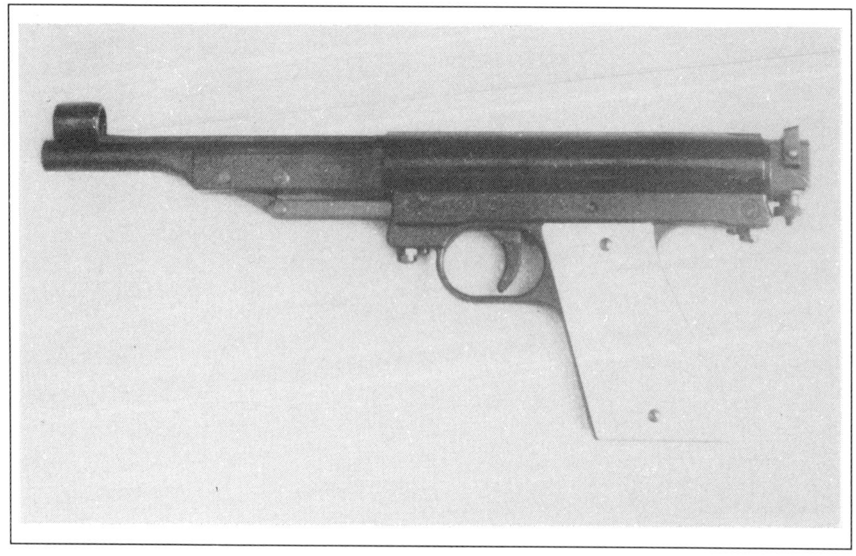

Rekord Target Model 2.

Model: **2**

Maker: **Fritz Barthelmes Sportswaffenfabrik,**
7921 Oggenhausen, Kr. Heidenheim,
a.d., Breuz Heidenheim Strasse 10, West Germany.

Date: Late 1970's.

Valuation: £5 - £15. £5a.

Details: Appears to be the target model of the Model 1. See previous pages. All metal construction with white plastic grips. 5⅛ inch rifled ·177 barrel with tunnel foresight cast with barrel. Very similar in design to the Em-Ge airpistols. 10¾ inches long, with the rearsight, this is increased to 11½ inches. The rearsight is all metal and fully adjustable. L.H.S. of barrel marked "Cal 4·5" and same side of air chamber marked "FB Record" and on other side "MADE IN WEST GERMANY". Serial number not visible. White grips moulded for right hand use. Other models from the Barthelmes stable include the LP68, LP77 and in 1982 the introduction of something called the "JUMBO"!!

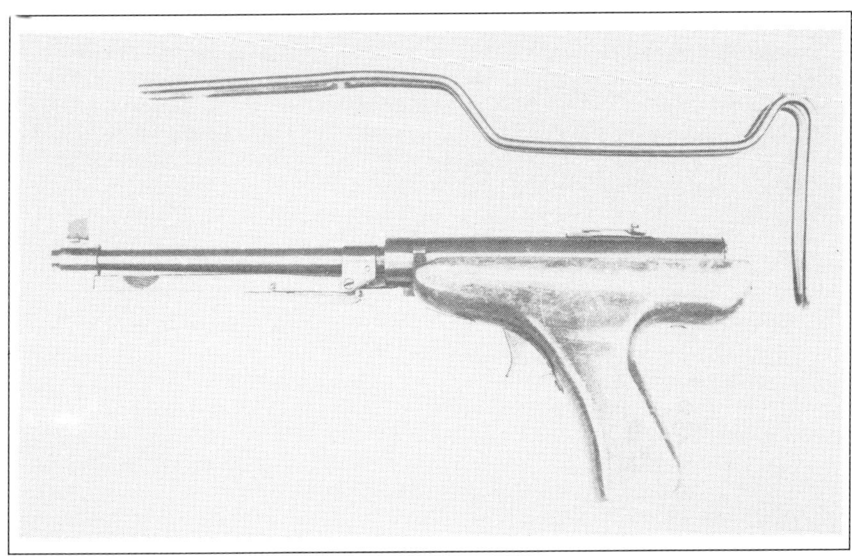

The Relum Pistol-Carbine (The Hurricane).

Model: **RELUM PISTOL-CARBINE. The Hurricane Airpistol.**

Maker: Actual maker not known, but Relum originates from Hungary.

Date: Available in small numbers from about 1957 to 1963. Usually sold through mail order catalogues.

Valuation: £20 - £50.

Details: A neat, well made airpistol. Similar design to the later A.S.I. Center target airpistol. Sold at nearly the same price as the Relum break action air rifle. All metal construction with deep blued finish. Underlever cocking lever held in place by spring loaded ball bearing, as is the slide out loading gate. Dovetail mounted foresight and spot-welded rearsight which is adjustable for elevation only. Side of barrel is stamped "FOREIGN", no other marks appear on the airpistol. Action can be released when cocked and loading gate can be operated whether action is cocked or not. Example examined was in ·22.

Well made shoulder stock plugs into the rear of the wooden stock by way of two drilled holes. This allows a very steady hold when firing the "Pistol-Carbine". The barrel is rifled. Advertised weight 3 lb. 14½ inches long and 24 inches with the shoulder stock. It was advertised as having a range of 25 yards. The rifling has 6 lands and grooves instead of the more usual twelve. Available in either ·22 or ·177 calibre. The air chamber contains a double mainspring as is the general practice with Relum airguns.

The length of shoulder stock varies the overall length of the airgun when fitted, advertised length was 24 inches, whilst length of one featured in *"Guns Review"*, May, 1975 was 25½ inches, and finally the above specimen reached 27 inches! (Is this a record?). Some stocks were not drilled for the wire section shoulder stock. Should you ever wish to remove the stock, first unscrew the sear adjuster screw, which is behind the grip. If the adjuster screw is present, then undo the main bolt which runs through the actual grip. Remove the butt holding the airpistol upside down because the sear spring rests on the butt and is prone to fall out if the action is separated in the upright position. The sear at the rear of the action can be pulled out, but take care when replacing that it faces in the correct direction as it can easily be replaced facing the wrong way. Replace stock and action in reverse: main stock bolt, then the adjuster screw, then adjust for trigger and sear engagement.

The barrel can be removed by first removing the action from the stock and then either cocking the action and leaving the cocking lever down, or removing the cocking lever pivot screw and moving cocking slide to one side to reveal a small grub screw on the underside of the air chamber. Loosen this and the barrel can be unscrewed by turning as if to tighten, as the thread is reverse, i.e. clockwise, will loosen, whilst anti-clockwise will tighten. The setting of the barrel is quite critical as it can mean the difference between the loading tap not fitting at all, so try turning the barrel a fraction of a turn in its final position and testing with the loading tap for best fit before grinding the loading gate thinner. Some sears cannot be removed with the sear in place as it goes through it into the body, so remove sear first before the rear chamber plug.

A boxed example seen, had the name "Hurricane" on the lid.

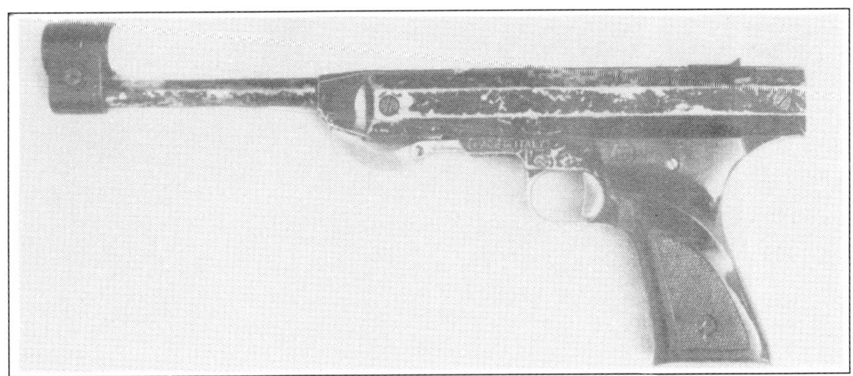

The Standard RO71, or Panther.

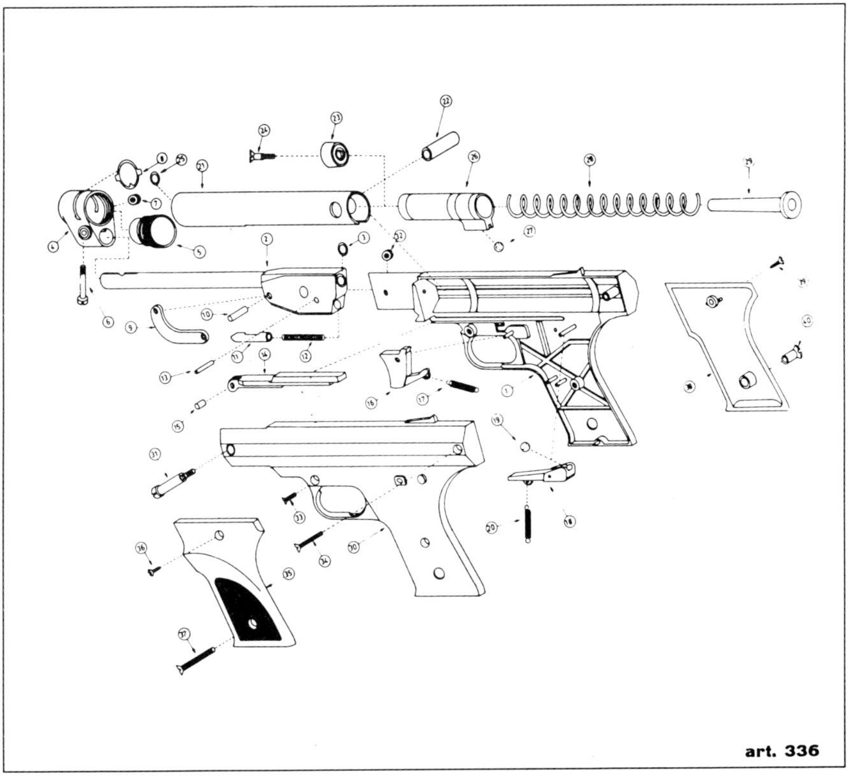

art. 336

Exploded diagram of the RO71.

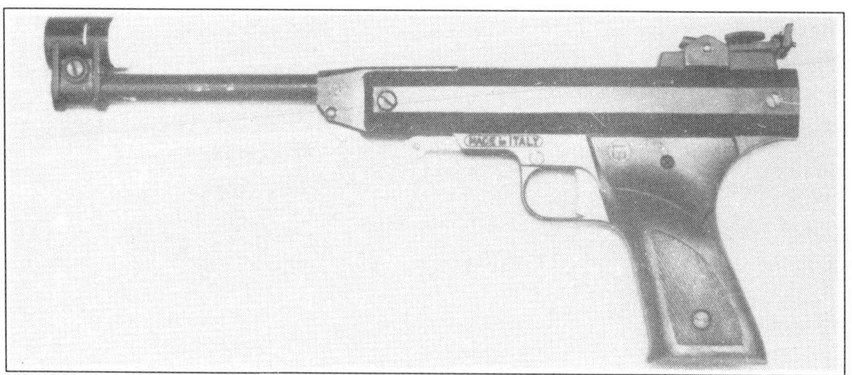

Panther De Luxe with fully adjustable sights.

Model: **RO71,** also called **Panther Standard.** Another importer refers to the Standard as the **Igi 202** and De Luxe as the **Igi 203.**

Maker: **Guntoys** of Italy. Imported by Sussex Armoury, 34 North Street, Hailsham, Sussex.

Date: Introduced into Britain in 1973.

Valuation: £18n - £20n, £5 - £25.

Details: The Italians seem to import well-made airguns at very reasonable prices and one of these is the RO71. The Standard model was issued with a strange combination of sights, a foresight with interchangeable elements and a rearsight that would only do justice to a Gat airpistol. 13¼ inches long with a 7¼ inch rifled ·177 barrel. Serial number stamped on L.H.S. of breech. Extensive use of alloy in the construction with brown plastic grips and black/white plastic foresight. Advertised weight 2 lb. 1 oz. It would appear that they are available in ·177 only. The trigger is fitted with an anti-bear device, once action is cocked it must be fired.

There is also a De Luxe Model slightly longer and fitted with a fully adjustable rearsight. Cast on the L.H.S. of the action "MADE IN ITALY" whilst on the other side "RO17 CAL. 4·5-177". Double linked cocking lever. The De Luxe Model Panther is called RO72. During the very late 1970's the Standard was sold with the fully adjustable rearsight as fitted to the De Luxe Model, but still with the plainer style of stock. A ·22 version was finally introduced during 1980. Advertised M.V. of the Standard 220 f.p.s. Also appears to have been up-dated with a scope ramp. The trigger on the Standard is non-adjustable whilst it is adjustable on the De Luxe. Although fitted with right hand grips, left hand grips are available for a small extra charge. See *"Airgun World",* July, 1980 for a small review. Muzzle velocities appear to vary — one reviewer gives the above 325 f.p.s. The scope ramp is a small strip of black plastic that screws in place of the rearsight.

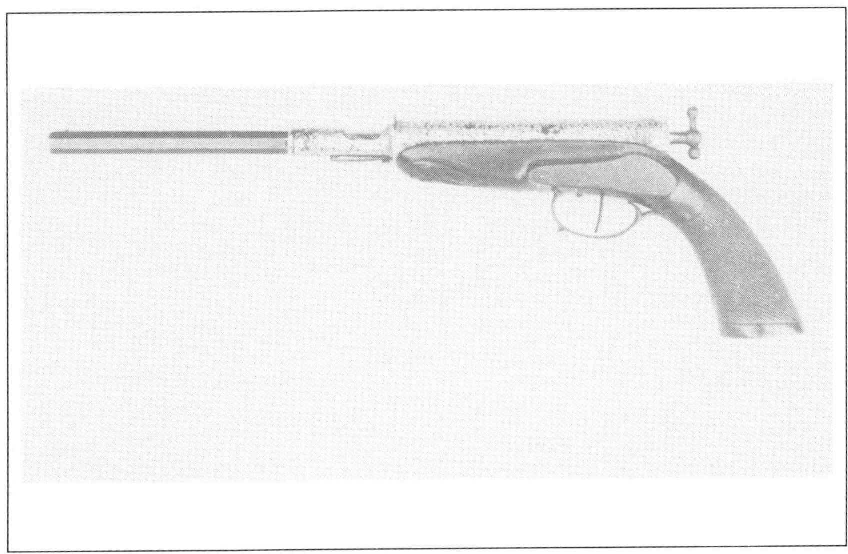

The I. J. Siptonon Gallery Airpistol.

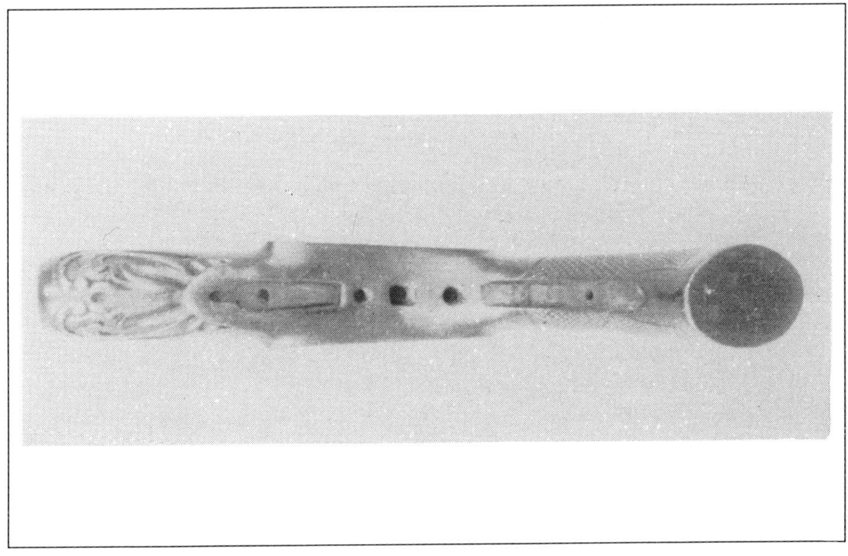

Underside of stock, illustrating the ornate carving and inletting.

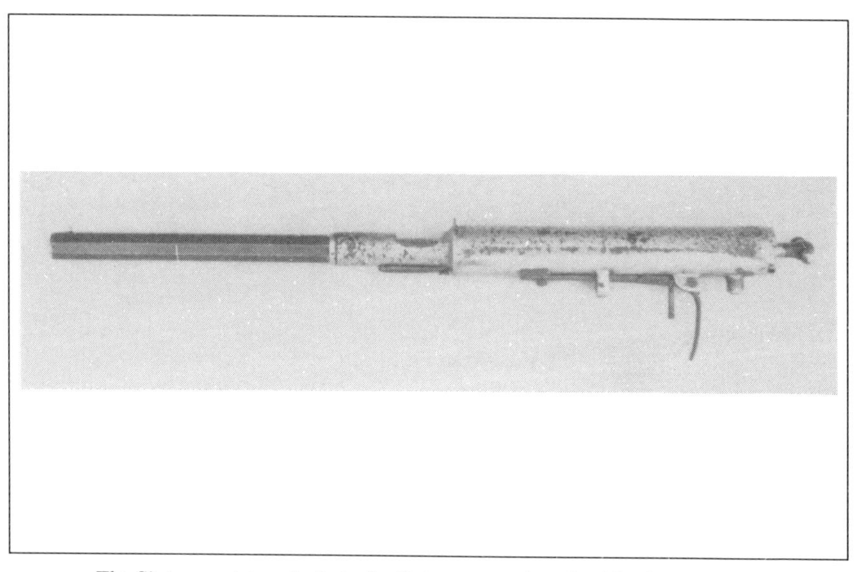

The Siptonon stripped of stock. Note extreme length of both trigger and adjuster screw to clear thickness of stock

Model: **GALLERY SALOON AIRPISTOL**

Maker: **I. J. Siptonon**

Date: Could be late 1800's to early 1900's.

Valuation: £100 - £300.

Details: A gallery saloon target airpistol built on the lines of a duelling pistol. It follows the European type of finish in having the barrel blued and the rest of the action nickel plated, although the tip of the barrel still bears traces of nickel plating. To operate, the plunger at the rear of the air chamber is pulled out until the sear engages, and is then pushed in, the barrel is held in place by a key-way and is first rotated slightly anti-clockwise looking from the top of the airpistol and is pulled forward to reveal the breech of the barrel for loading the pellet.

The calibre is ·22 smoothbore. Barrel is 8¼ inches long (21 cms) and has 17 stamped on one of the octagonal flats. The pellets load in the same way as for the Quackenbush Model 1 push-in barrel air rifle, only in this case, after the pellet has been placed into the barrel breech it is pushed back and rotated clockwise to lock the barrel and bring the foresight into the upright position. The chamber and barrel support are nickel plated and has "XVII" cut into the underside as well as the trigger mechanism. The simple rearsight is machined from part of the chamber. The trigger and sear adjustment screw are very long so that they can protrude through the rather thick wooden stock. The thin metal strip for the barrel keyway is stamped 17 and is blued. The simple all metal cup piston washer and centre push/pull rod are also stamped 17. The efficiency of such an arrangement must have been very low as air can freely escape from both the outside and inside of the washer. Again, the piston reminds me very much of that fitted to the Quackenbush Number 1 air rifle. The end chamber plug is also stamped 17 and has a simple spring that folds over on itself and presses against the cocking rod. This could be for keeping the rod held in the out position so that when the action is fired the end of the rod rests against the piston and affects some sort of air seal. This means that the cocking rod would be protruding from the end plug until the trigger is pulled: on flying forward, there is a danger that it would catch the back of your hand, but such are the joys of target shooting.

The face of the rear chamber is marked "I. J. SIPTONON – BREVETE – 460". This number might be the patent number as there is already "17" and "XVII" (which is 17 now that one has worked it out!) stamped and marked all over the place. There is a small hole drilled on the rim of the rear plug and this may be for a ring spanner for tightening down the plug. The little pull handle with the dumb-bell cross piece screws onto the end of the cocking rod. As a point of interest NEVER fire the above with the cocking handle out, but push it into the rest position, as there is a danger that it will fly off if the action is fired with it sticking out.

The one piece wooden stock has been hand chequered and scroll engraved at the front on the underside. It is a very lightweight and coloured wood that has been darkly stained. It is stamped "XVII" and has been skilfully worked upon to inlet the pistol action. Notice that the grip is right back and gives the appearance of a duelling pistol. The action is held in place to the stock by two screws, the rear screw is under the rear tang of the trigger guard, whilst the front screw also acts as the trigger guard screw.

Two things are slightly unusual about the above, firstly the breech is too small for loading the old fashioned target darts and the calibre is ·22, very early airguns rarely had this calibre and I wonder just how old the above really is?

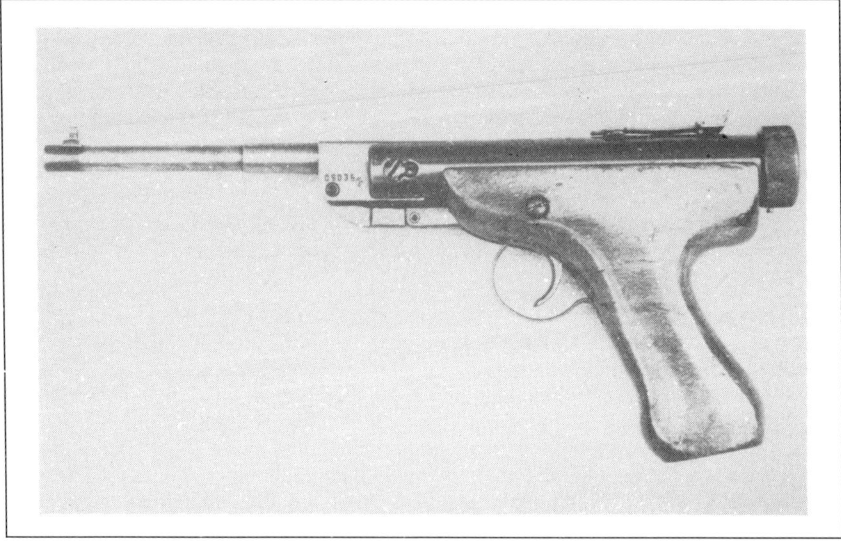

Slavia ZVP.

Model: **"ZVP" SLAVIA**

Maker: **Presne Strojirenstvi,**
Brod, Czechoslovakia.
Imported by Edgar Bros., Vale Road, Woolton, Liverpool 25.

Date: Not known, but above model looks prior to Slavia Tex 086, so would assume 1950 - 1970.

Valuation: £5 - £20. £9a.

Details: Serial number of above 09035, measures just under 13½ inches long. Break barrel action, rifled. Looks like the earlier model to the present Tex 086. Have seen an air rifle bearing the name "Slavia" with "Relem" so could be that airguns called Slavia, Tex, and Relem are made by the same company. Serial number stamped on side of barrel breech along with an unusual circular stamp. On top of air chamber is stamped "SLAVIA ZVP MADE IN CZECHOSLOVAKIA" plus a circular trademark. Wooden stock. Available in ·177 only. Advertised weight 3 lbs. Apparently each airpistol was packed with a test card. When removing the stock you must first unscrew the trigger guard screw as the other end of the guard is pinned into the action. When the guard screw has been removed, the guard can be turned away from the stock as it is free to rotate around the action pin.

The Sportsman Junior.

Model: **SPORTSMAN JUNIOR**

Maker: **Baron Mfg. Co.,** U.S.A.

Date: Late 1940 to early 1950. Seen advertisement dated 1948.

Valuation: £20 - £40.

Details: A single shot pull-out plunger operated airpistol. Die-cast metal construction with a 2½ inch brass screw-in barrel, smoothbore and ·177 calibre. Appears to be made in two major parts, lower half comprising of grip and trigger mechanism, upper half made of a tube of similar diecast metal containing the air chamber and plunger along with the barrel etc. Two screws hold this lot together. Very simple in operation. The rear plunger knob is pulled back until a notch has been exposed in the rod and this is pulled down onto the lip of the rear chamber plug. This simple sear arrangement then waits for the trigger to be pulled. On pulling the trigger, the plunger rod is gently eased upward and out of engagement and away it goes.

The pellets could be loaded by two methods, by unscrewing the brass barrel and inserting into the breech end or by muzzle loading. Cast in the L.H.S. of the action is "SPORTSMAN JR.", whilst on the other side "BARON MFG., CO., PATENT PENDING, MADE IN U.S.A." Sights are fixed and cast with the airpistol. The advert of 1948 described it as the "3 in 1 Airpistol" as it could fire BB's, darts, and pellets. Also it was modelled from a "famous target pistol"??? The barrel and air chamber, according to the advert, were made from steel. 8 inches long and 4 inches deep with a weight of 15 oz. There was also a holster for the Sportsman Junior. There was no mention of a Senior model.

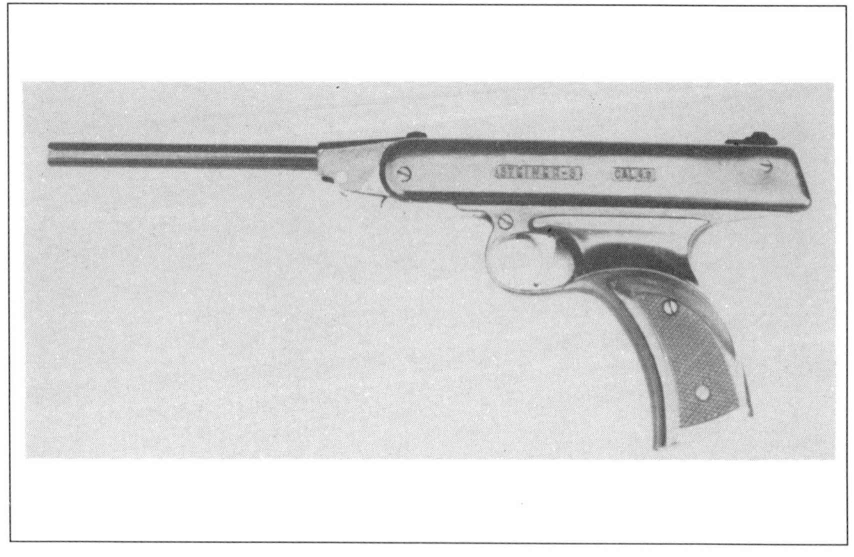

The Steiner – S Airpistol.

Model: **STEINER – S**

Maker: **B.B.M.,**
Italy.

Date: Middle 1970's to very early 1980's.

Valuation: £10 - £30.

Details: A basic die cast construction airpistol, although well put together using nuts and bolts. 14 inches long with a 7¼ inch, ·177 rifled barrel. Fixed sights and the foresight is situated near the barrel breech, which is most unusual. The air chamber sits in between the two halves of the outer chamber casing. Brown grips cast for right handed use although they are easily used with the left hand. Cast in L.H.S. of body "STEINER – S" and "CAL. 4·5", whilst on the other side is "B.B.M. MADE IN ITALY". Trigger is not adjustable and there is no anti-bear trap device on the trigger mechanism. Action is blacked except for the trigger and cocking lever as they are bare cast alloy.

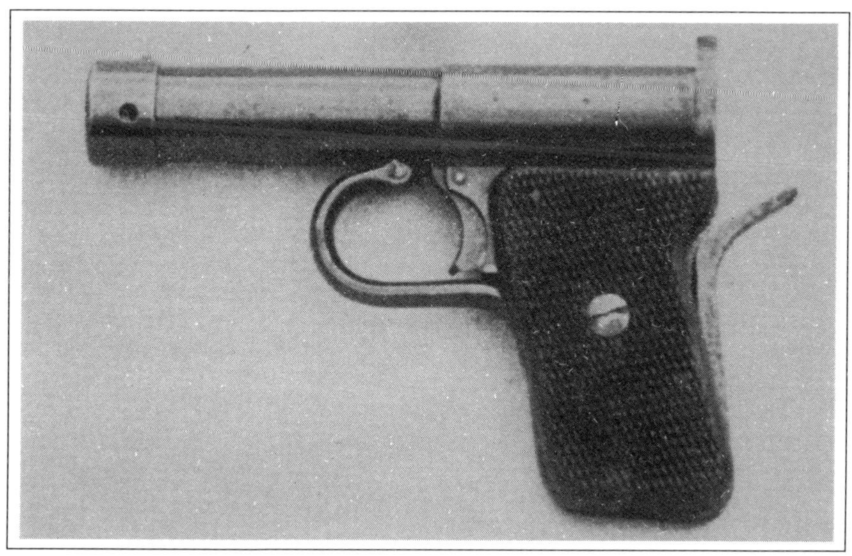

Tell II Airpistol.

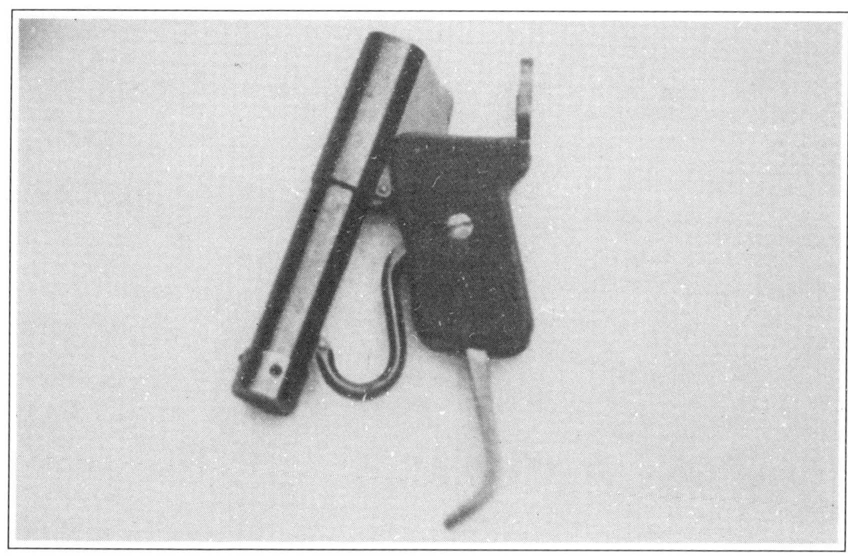

Tell II in cocked position.

Model: **TELL II**

Maker: It has been suggested that "TELL" was a trade name for: **J. P. Sauer & Son,** Suhl, Germany, and earlier that of: **Oscar Will** of Zella St., Blasii, Germany.

Date: Around 1927 - 1936.

Valuation: £30 - £80.

Details: A "dainty" design. Small, but very well made. Barrel is 5¼ inches long. All metal with wooden chequered grips. Same cocking action as Acvoke. On top of air cylinder is "D.R.G.M. W TELL II W D.R.P." and has "Made in Germany" stamped on load lever. The front cylinder end cap is a bayonet fit and can be removed by pushing the cap in and rotating in a clockwise direction, or the body of the airgun in an anti-clockwise direction.

Seen advertised in 1927 as the "New "Tell" Air Pistol", price 15/-, in a neat box. Advertised weight 14 oz., with fluted walnut grips, although all examples seen have chequered grips. I have seen some with "MADE IN GERMANY" stamped on the cocking strap that falls down from the grip, and have also seen quite a few with letters stamped on the back strap cocking lever. "H.C.B." and "M.A.C." being two examples.

By 1933 there appears to have been four variations of the Tell II:

i) Nickel plated, wooden grips and smoothbore.
ii) Nickel plated, wooden grips and rifled.
iii) Nickel plated, red, blue or yellow varnished wooden grips and smoothbore.
iv) Nickel plated, red, blue or yellow varnished wooden grips and rifled.

All the above were sold in cardboard boxes with 100 slugs. I have never seen any of the above, only the common blued version. The monogram stamped on either side of "TELL" on top of the barrel is made up of the letters W, W, and V which stand for "Venuswaffenwerk" the name of the factory of Oscar (Oskar) Will at Zella St. Blasii, founded in 1844 and sold to Wilhelm Foss just after W.W.1. The address is also given as Zella Mehlis, this being the same place as previous because during 1919 St. Blasii became Mehlis.

Have one authenticated account of a Tell II being found during a search of a captured German submarine during W.W.2. It being found in a drawer in the captain's room.

Tell III.

Tell III in cocked position. Note how rear chamber block is drawn towards the piston. See "Air Rifles" 3rd Ed., Daisy Model C, for similarity of design.

Model: **3**

Maker: **Wilhelm Foss, Venuswaffenwerk,** Zella Mehlis, Thuringia, Germany.

Date: 1936/37 to around 1939.

Valuation: £200 - £400.

Details: A very rare and much sought after airpistol. The period of manufacture was very short and the actual number in circulation must have been very small. Measures 10 inches long (25.5 cms) along the barrel/chamber and from tip of barrel to base of butt 11 inches (28 cms). Barrel is 5⅛ inches (13 cms) and was in ·177 rifled in the above example. Dovetail mounted foresight and side of the barrel stamped "Kal. 4½ mm, Cal. ·177", the barrel pivots very much like the Haenel Model 26/28, but the cocking link is on top of the chamber and as the barrel is pulled down the top cocking rod is drawn forwards, pulling the rear chamber block towards the piston and thus cocking the action.

So in this type of action, the piston does not move as the action is being cocked. At the end of the barrel's travel, the sear engages and when the barrel is pulled up, the piston, spring under tension, and the rear chamber block are pushed back until the barrel has locked into the firing position. This system is identical to the Daisy Model C air rifle, see *"Air Rifles" Third Edition.* The top of the cocking arm is stamped "TELL MOD 3" with a standing man (William Tell) holding a break action air rifle which is partly open, what looks like a sex symbol between his legs is in actual fact an apple with an arrow through it, and not a heart as was first thought! Stamped on the side of the air chamber is "VENUS – WAFFENWERK, ZELLA – MEHLIS" and in smaller letters "MADE IN GERMANY".

The grip is solid bakelite with brown/black flow patterns, chequered with stippled top portion. Both sides have a brass medallion with "TELL" set in a red background. The rearsight is in two parts and can be adjusted for both windage and elevation. The serial number, in this case 59, is stamped under the rearsight blade: The action is blued overall. Weight 2 lbs. 4 ozs. (1 kilogram). The box is very similar to that for the Dollar Mark II and I would safely say that it came from the same manufacturer. It is a deep purple/blue with gold embossed lettering and picture. The box measures 10¾ x 6⅛ x 1⅛ inches. Inside the lid is a rather gaudy coloured label with instructions printed in German, English and French as follows:-

> ***Opening and Cocking:*** *The right hand clasps the pistol at the pistol grip, whilst with the left hand the barrel is being folded in such a way that the end of the barrel lies against the palm of the hand. By means of co-operation of both hands the barrel is being pressed downwards until the noticeable entrance of the valve into the trigger rest. (Whatever this means!)*
>
> ***Loading and Closing:*** *The opened pistol leaves the barrel free for the introduction of the pellet (Diabolo). After insertion swing barrel back into its initial position, and the pistol is ready for firing.*
>
> ***Trigger Regulation:*** *The Tell 3 has adjustable trigger slack, by means of a set screw located near the rearsight. The turn of this screw — with a screwdriver — to the right brings the trigger into a "sensitive" position, whilst a turn to the left makes the trigger pull harder.*
>
> ***Care of Pistol:*** *Insert from time to time a few drops of best gun oil into the guide slits of the cocking lever, whilst the pistol is open, as well as into the two turning links on the barrel. After that, fire the pistol several times without pellet, and clean the barrel with the brush accompanying the pistol.*
>
> This last piece of advice should not be heeded to.

The box base is divided into compartments for the airpistol, cleaning brush and a small sample tin of "Luftgewehr Diabolokugein". As can be seen the pellet tin bears the "Venus – Waffenwerk" logo of V.W.W. as seen on the Tell 2 airpistol as well as the William Tell standing figure.

The patent for the design for the Tell 3 is number 483899, provisional number being 19606/37. Its application took place on the 15th July, 1937 and was accepted on the 27th April, 1938. The box states that the patent had been applied for so I would assume the initial date of manufacture to be around 1936/7 and as the War started in 1939, this caused the cessation of production.

The patentee was Wilhelm Foss, Venuswaffenwerk, Zella-Mehlis, Thuringia, Germany, and his British agent was Cruikshank and Fairweather of 86 St. Vincent Street, Glasgow C2, and a London address – 65/66 Chancery Lane, WC2. The patent dealt with the cocking links being above the air chamber, thus not having to accommodate the links underneath and leading to a more streamlined shape. The barrel being in line with the air chamber was also felt to aid accuracy and ease of shooting. From the Patent drawing it would appear that there are two types of trigger design, one having sear adjustment through a hole in the top of the chamber and through the cocking link whilst the other had no adjustment at all. The above example, serial number 59 would appear to be the former.

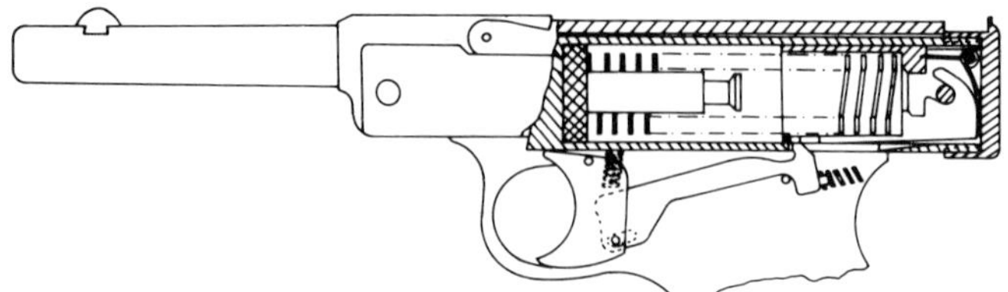

Fig. 1

It is assumed that the above is the first pattern as it has no trigger adjustment and the barrel is the wrong shape for the example serial number 59. The diagram shows that action at rest and just after having been fired. Note that the sear slides and has an oval trigger pin hole to give the sensation of being a double pull trigger. Note also that there is no hole at the top of the air chamber or cocking link for any form of sear adjustment.

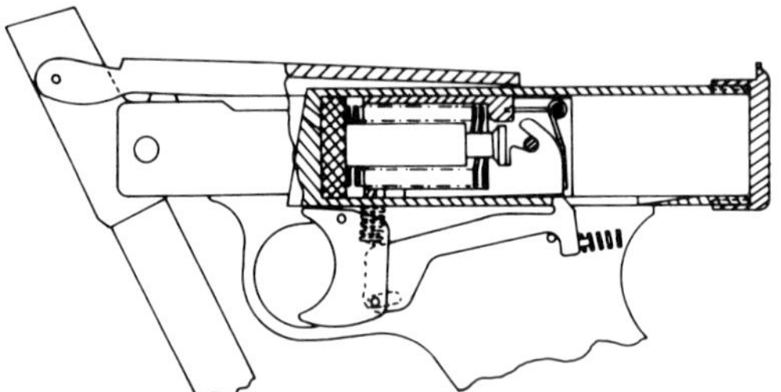

Fig. 2

The second illustration shows the action with the barrel fully down and the cocking link has drawn the rear inner chamber block towards the piston, thus compressing the mainspring. The sear engages with the piston rod and thus the action is now cocked. It is hard to see how this action can work because in order for the sear to engage it must be pushed down so that the piston rod can ride over the sear and as it pivots, the front portion must surely come in contact with the mainspring and stop any further downward motion of the sear.

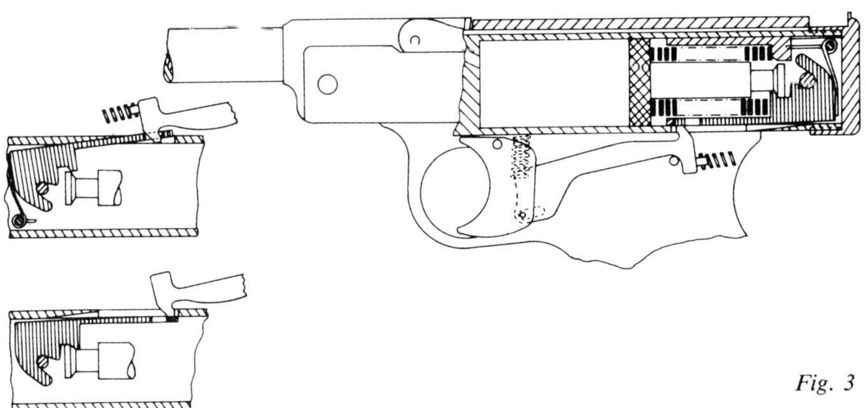

Fig. 3

Now we have the action cocked and ready to go. On pulling the trigger the sear is pushed rearwards until the tip of the sear reaches a slot in the rear chamber block, this allowed the block to tip downwards and release the piston rod and away goes the piston. From the diagrams I still don't think it ever worked.

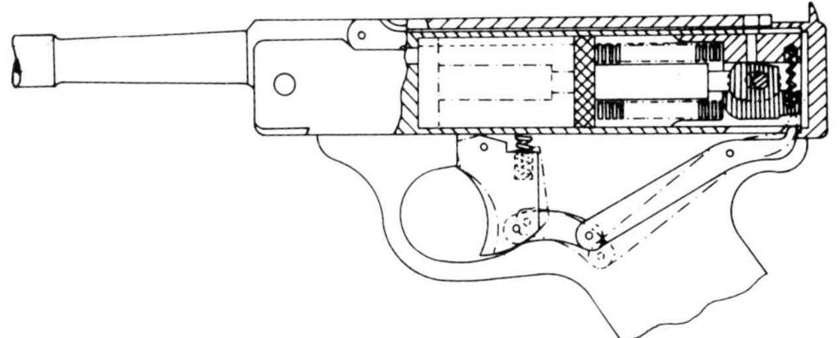

Fig. 4

The second pattern of trigger action would appear to have been used because it works, and is the type used on serial number 59. You can see that there is room below the sear for it to rise and fall as the piston rod tumbler sear rides over it. Note the large bearing surfaces of the sear arrangement, so much so that it is hard to see how it could wear out. *(Diagrams by courtesy of "Guns Review").*

All in all, a very rare and interesting airpistol.

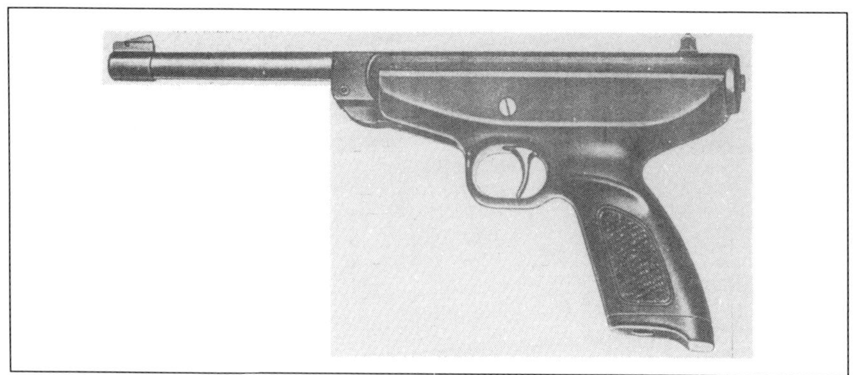

The Tex 086.

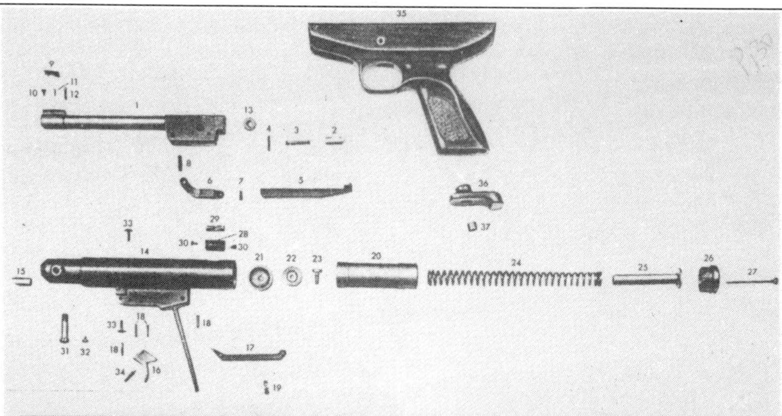

Serial No.	Number of pcs.	Designation
1	1	barrel
2	1	front breech pivot
3	1	breech pivot spring
4	1	breech pivot pin
5	1	cocking lever
6	1	joint
7	1	cocking lever pin
8	1	joint pin
9	1	front-sight
10	1	barrel sealing
11	1	front-sight screw
12	1	front-sight pin
13	1	front-sight spring
14	1	casing
15	1	rear breech pivot
16	1	trigger
17	1	trigger lever
18	4	pin of the cartridge magazine
19	1	trigger spring

Serial No.	Number of pcs.	Designation
20	1	piston
21	1	sealing ring
22	1	insert
23	1	piston screw
24	1	piston spring
25	1	piston spring guide
26	1	casing nut
27	1	screw-driver
28	1	sight body
29	1	back-sight lamella
30	2	back-sight screw
31	1	breech screw
32	1	safety screw
33	2	cartridge magazine screw
34	1	trigger screw
35	1	pistol grip
36	1	foot of the pistol grip
37	1	pistol grip nut

Exploded Diagram and Parts List for the Tex 086.

Model: **TEX 086**

Maker: Produced by **Zbrojovka Brno (Armament Works),** Uhersky Brod, Czechoslovakia.
Appears to be linked with the name "Slavia", and have seen Relum airguns bearing both Slavia and relum trade names. Imported by Edgar Bros. Exported from Czechoslovakia by Omnipol, Praha.

Date: From around 1970 to early 1980's, although precise dates are not known.

Valuation: £20 - £40.

Details: Appears to follow on from the Slavia ZVP. Very well made. All metal with black moulded grip for either hand. 13½ inches long. Rifled barrel. Foresight adjustable for elevation, whilst rearsight for windage. Serial number stamped on L.H.S. of barrel breech, for above 111102. Stamped on top of air chamber "TEX – 086" and on the L.H.S. of chamber "MADE IN CZECHOSLOVAKIA". Moulded grips have trademark on both sides with chequering. A small screwdriver can be removed by unscrewing the knurled head protruding from the end of the air chamber. This is used for trigger adjustment and for the sights. A very neat idea. For review of the above see "Guns Review", July, 1976. Advertised weight 2¾ lbs. Available in ·177 only.

The original instruction manual describes the barrel as being "tipping barrel, rifled bore, and for shooting small bullets diabolo or shot corns No. II are used." The sights are best described as follows, straight from the manual: "the possibility of adjusting direct the correction for line of a new backsight and the altitude correction by means of a special adjustable foresight." It goes on to say that each airpistol is tested with seven pellets fired from 25 feet into a 1 inch circle, five or more bulls within the circle pass. The advertised length of the TEX 086 is 13½ inches, whilst the barrel is 7¼ inches. Its muzzle velocity is given as 312 f.p.s.

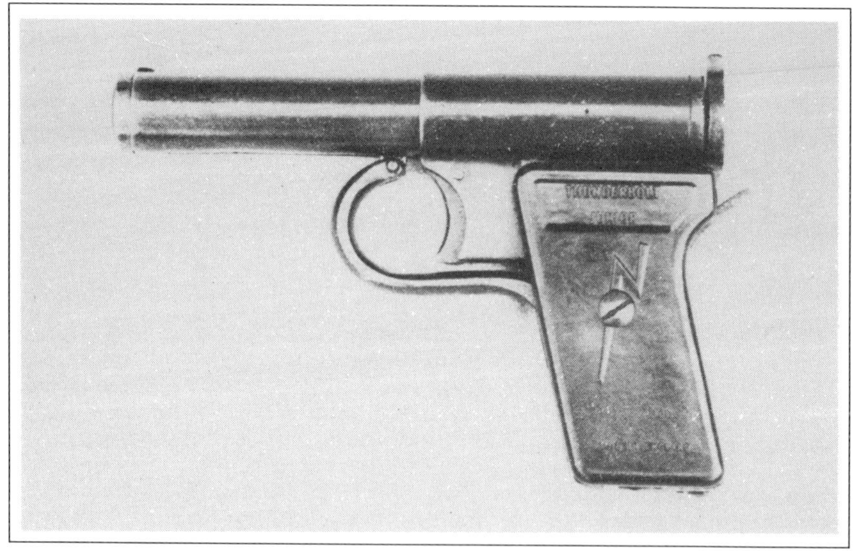

Thunderbolt Junior.

Model: **THUNDERBOLT JUNIOR**

Maker: **Produsit Ltd.,**
78 Lombard Street, Birmingham 12.
About 8,000 were manufactured and were advertised as the "Big Chief" airpistol.

Date: Would assume from 1947 to very late 1940's. Very few examples of this airpistol appear to have survived.

Valuation: £50 - £150.

Details: Same basic design as the Tell II and the Acvoke but is about half way between in size. Brown mottled grips with "THUNDERBOLT JUNIOR" at the top and "MADE IN ENGLAND" at the base. There also appears a streak of lightning on each grip. The more you examine the above the more striking is its similarity to the Tell II airpistol. The front of the air chamber screws out in the normal fashion. Stamped at the back of the barrel cover plate appears "PROV. PAT. 13749". No serial number is visible. Measures 6½ inches along barrel line and 7½ inches from barrel to base of butt. A patent prior to the above is featured in *"Guns Review"*, September, 1980. See *"Guns Review"*, November, 1980 for details of the patent for the above.

The first model Titan Airpistol.
The barrel is fitted with bolt and is rotated and drawn forward to load.
Only one is known to exist. (Acknowledgements to "Guns Review".)

The Titan Airpistol, Third Model. (Acknowledgements to "Shooting Times".)

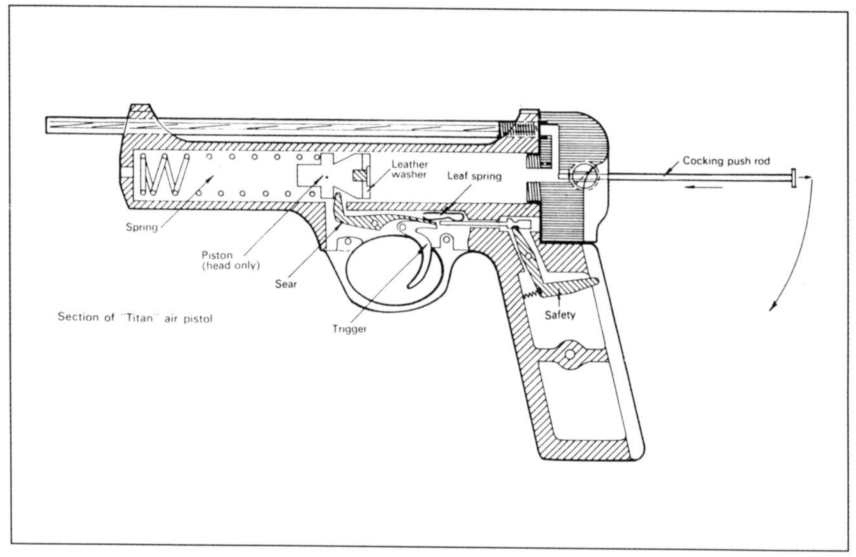

Cross-section of the Titan Airpistol (assumed Third Model). (Acknowledgements to "Guns Review".)

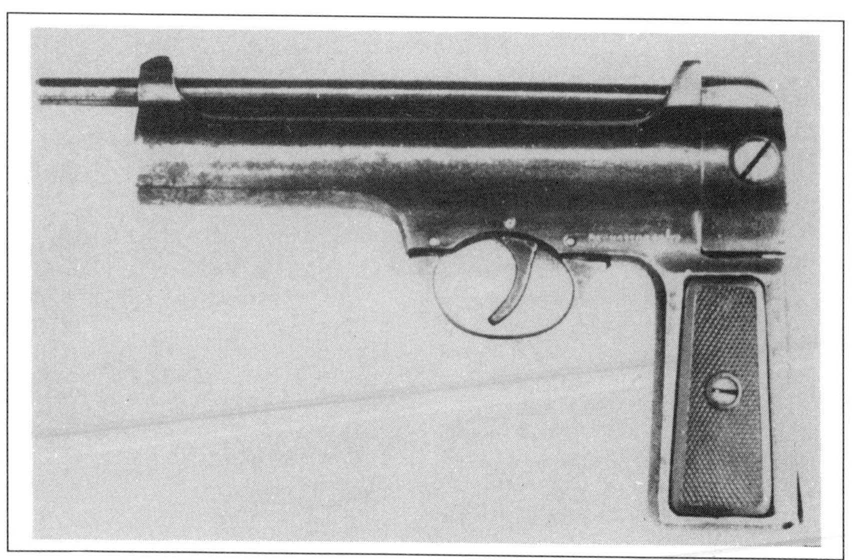

The Titan Airpistol.

The Titan Airpistol (Fourth Model)
(Acknowledgements to "Guns Review".)

Model: **TITAN AIRPISTOL**

Maker: Could be **Frank Clarke** of 6 Whittall Street, Birmingham, who patented the above design.

Date: The very late 1910's to middle 1920's.

Valuation: A rare airpistol. £50 to over £100. £44a.

Details: A very plain, robust airpistol with very few parts to go wrong. All metal with a blued finish. Black vulcanite-like grips with fine chequering, these are countersunk into the cast frame of the airpistol and held in place by a single screw. Fitted with a 7 inch ·177 smoothbore barrel that overhung the action in a similar fashion to the Westley Richards "Highest Possible". Stamped on the side of the action near the trigger guard "PAT. no. 110999/17". This referred to the first patent taken out by Frank Clarke in 1917, but the design was quite different. See *"Guns Review"*, July, 1979. The Patent covered the sliding barrel over the air chamber and action cocked by means of a rod plunger through the rear of the action. The rod being able to rotate and be turned in a downwards position for firing. Only one example is known to exist of this first design.

The improved patent was made in 1922 in conjunction with J. E. S. Lockwood, 3 New Street, Birmingham. This covered the example shown with minor differences, i.e., early airpistols appear to not have the safety device actuated by the cocking rod. The Titan was produced with the Junior airgunner in mind.

Serial number of above is 30 and appears stamped on the lower inside face of the rotating rear plug and can only be seen when in the loading position. This model does not have the safety device.

Tongue in cheek, there would appear to be four variations of the Titan: –

First Model: Manufactured about 1917-1918 when the first patent was made. Barrel is fitted with a turn over bolt and slides forward for loading. It is stamped "PATENT No. 847/17" which is the provisional patent number of Patent 110999/17. The airpistol is also marked "MADE IN ENGLAND". The barrel is supported by two standing brackets and grossly overhangs the end of the air chamber. See *"Guns Review"*, November, 1976.

Second Model: From about 1919 to 1921. As featured by model serial number 30. Barrel overhangs action by 1⅛ inches and does not have a safety device.

Third Model: 1921 to about 1924. The common rare model with safety device. Body stamped "THE TITAN AIRPISTOL" and has wider grips with a "T" monogram in the grip.

Fourth Model: Middle 1920's. May have a flared grip, i.e. fans out towards the bottom. The barrel extends far beyond the end of the action. Barrel measures 9¼ inches long and is still smoothbore. The foresight is attached to the barrel and not to the barrel support as with the second and third models. See *"Guns Review"*, 1976. Air chamber can be stripped from the front, whereas on the above the mainspring can only be removed from the rear.

The muzzle velocities of the various models appear to lie between 250 and 350 f.p.s. To load, the rear plunger rod is raised up so as to be in line with the barrel, it is then pressed right in until the action cocks, there may be minor clicking noises — this is the sear riding along the mainspring.

When action is cocked, withdraw rod and rotate the rear chamber plug anti-clockwise, the end of the barrel is now visible and the pellet is inserted, rear plug and returned to upright position and cocking rod is returned to recess running down the rear of the grip. The Titan is now ready to be fired. The barrel is screw mounted into the rear support. To remove the mainspring the rear air chamber plug can be unscrewed when the cocking rod is in the horizontal position. Some confusion may exist over who actually manufactured the Titan because according to a 1925 Catalogue of Gavin Clyde Bell of Glasgow — HE MADE IT!! See *"Shooting Times"*, May 17th-23rd, 1979.

The Voere Airpistol.

Model: **A VOERE AIRPISTOL**

Maker: **Voere,**
Austria.

Date: Would assume 1950's/1960's.

Valuation: £20 - £40.

Details: What this airpistol and the Westley Richards "Highest Possible" have in common is that they are both very ugly. I would love to know where the person who designed the above is now, and what he has designed since. It is based on the German Diana Model 15 action with a much shortened barrel. 13¼ inches (34 cms) along the barrel/chamber and from tip of barrel to base of butt 13¾ inches (35 cms). Barrel is 5¼ inches long (13 cms) and in ·177 with very soft rifling. The two fixed sights sit on top of the barrel and are only 3¾ inches apart! The top of the air chamber at the rear is stamped with the triangular trademark of Voere with a pine tree logo. Both sides of the massive wooden grips are pressed with chequering and the Voere trade name. Trigger adjustment is by way of grub screw with coarse thread in the wooden butt at the rear of the grip. All in all, one hell-of an airpistol!

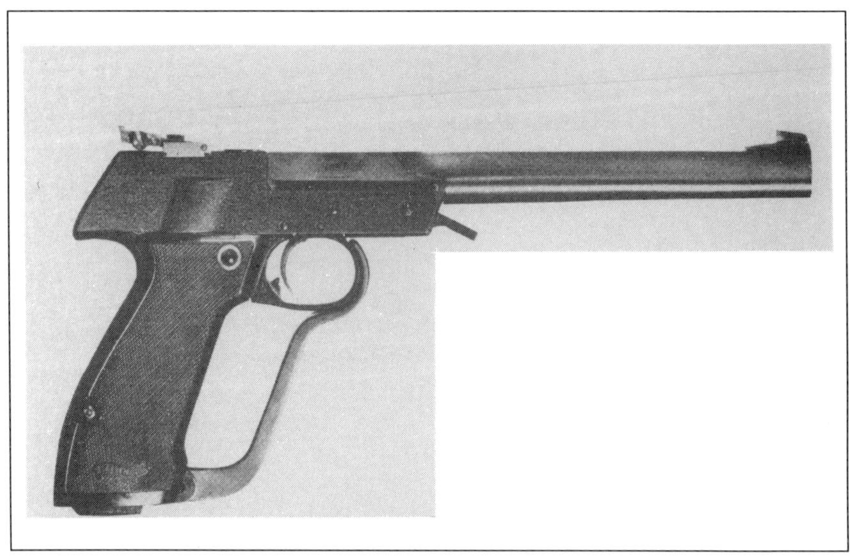

The Walther LP2

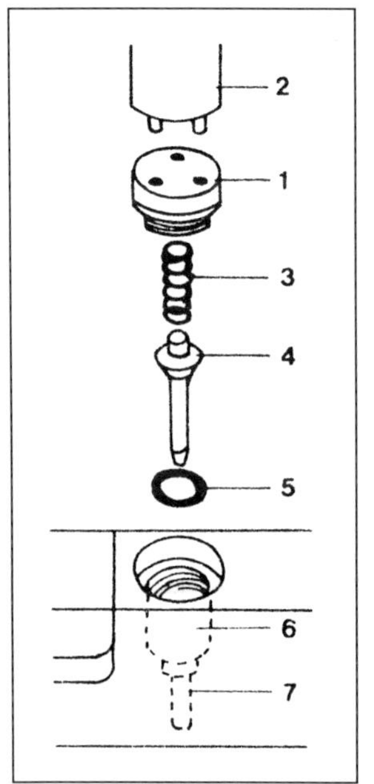

*Fig. 1:
The LP2 valve mechanism.*

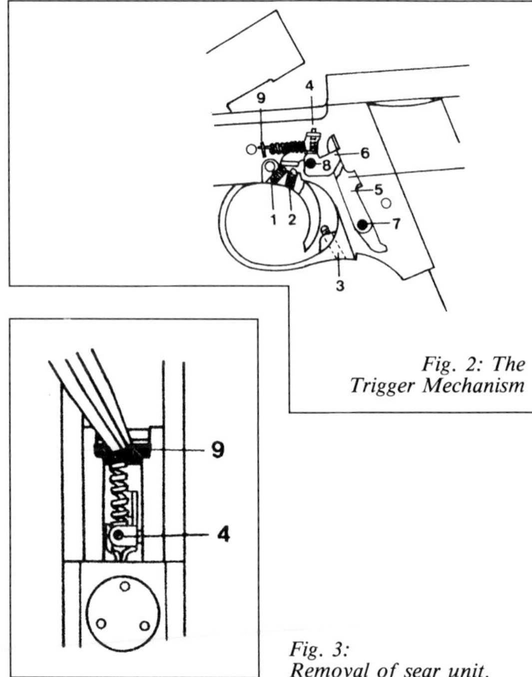

Fig. 2: The Trigger Mechanism

*Fig. 3:
Removal of sear unit.*

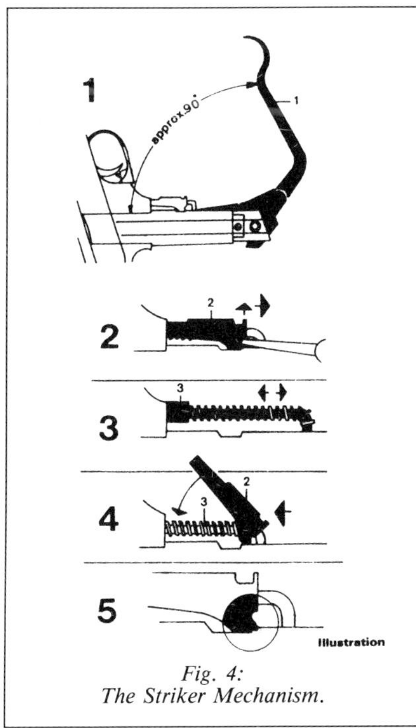

Fig. 4:
The Striker Mechanism.

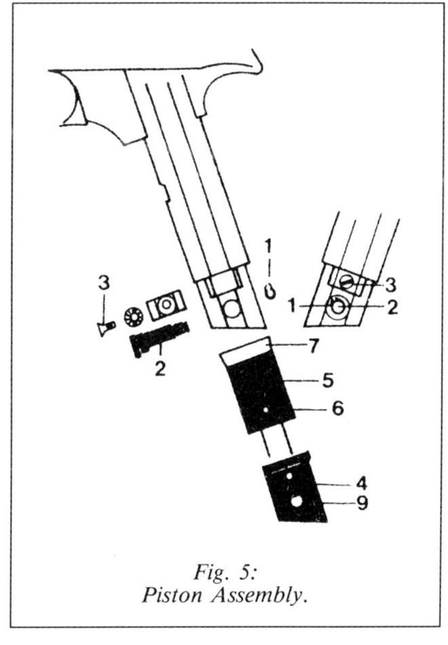

Fig. 5:
Piston Assembly.

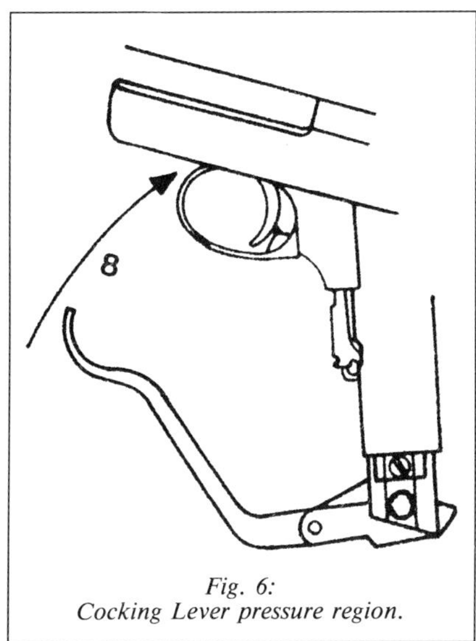

Fig. 6:
Cocking Lever pressure region.

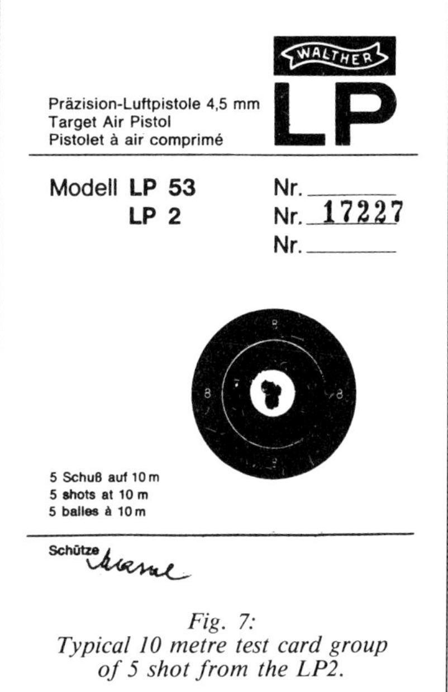

WALTHER
LP
Präzision-Luftpistole 4,5 mm
Target Air Pistol
Pistolet à air comprimé
Modell LP 53 Nr.
LP 2 Nr. 17227
Nr.
5 Schuß auf 10 m
5 shots at 10 m
5 balles à 10 m
Schütze

Fig. 7:
Typical 10 metre test card group of 5 shot from the LP2.

Model: **LP2**

Model: **Carl Walther,**
79 Ulm/Donau, West Germany.

Date: From around 1965 to 1973 when the LP3 was introduced.

Valuation: £100 - £200.

Details: A high grade single pump stroke pneumatic recoiless airpistol. The type of airpistol that is supplied with a test card of five shots at 10 metres and shows one slightly jagged hole. Quite a heavy airpistol weighing 46 ozs., 1.3 kilograms. Smooth blacked barrel with a crackle finish to the action, black plastic grips. On example seen, 17227, the L.H.S. of the barrel was stamped "WALTHER LP Mod. 2. – Carl Walther Ulm/Do.", and on the other side the serial number, "MADE IN GERMANY" and the F-in pentagram. Basically you cock first, then load to fire because the air is sucked into the chamber from the barrel and if a pellet is placed into the barrel first it might restrict the air flow.

A wooden match grip was available as an extra as was a fitted de luxe carrying case, although these are rarely seen.

The cocking action works in both directions, on the downward path the cocking lever closes the air valve, cocks the spring loaded hammer and pulls the piston down to the bottom of its stroke. The upward stroke compresses the air for firing. The trigger is fully adjustable and is described elsewhere. At 10 metres, bench rest, it should produce ⅜ inch groups. The 9½ inch barrel is ·177 rifled with 12 grooves, right hand twist with one complete turn every 16½ inches. The average muzzle velocity was given as 390 f.p.s. A review appears in *"Guns Review"*, January, 1970.

A nice idea with this design is that you can release the trigger by the cocking lever and return it to rest, there is no anti-bear trap device which saves having to fire the airpistol when cocked unnecessarily.

The stripping and maintenance of the LP2 is quite simple for such an expensive airpistol. When delving into the innards, remember that dust and grit is the downfall of these airpistols and any stripping must be done in clinical conditions. For lubricating the piston washer use a heavy duty high pressure silicon grease, such as AVIA Avilub or BP PR9136 or the equivalent.

I am indebted to my friend Dennis Commins for the following details and further information can be gained from *"Guns Review"*, June, 1975. Should the seal fail to hold air, and you can hear it hissing out into the barrel on the upward stroke of the pumping lever, then you may need to strip and clean the valve under the three holed cap on top of the action, just in front of the rearsight. See Figures 1 and 2. First, obtain or make the special three pronged tool for unscrewing the top cap. To make the tool, first place a piece of paper over the top cap (**1**) and either press hard on it or rub with a soft pencil to mark the location of the three holes. Now place this template on the end of a round bar with a squared off face and mark the position of each of the three holes with a centre punch. Use a drill size so that 3/32 inch round rod can be fixed into each hole and ground down so that 1/10 inch is standing proud. Finally drill a hole for a tommy bar at the other end. Clutching your tool, you can now advance towards the cowering Walther.

Pull down the cocking/pumping lever and leave in its most downward position, remember that the action is now cocked and on no account touch the trigger. With your special tool unscrew the locking cap **(1)**, and remove with its washer. Now take out the spring **(3)** and valve **(4)**, finally prise out the seal **(5)**. Clean all parts thoroughly and the valve housing **(6/7)** and make sure that the valve **(4)** can slide up and down under its weight in the air port **(7)**. When reassembling, smear the seal **(5)** with silicon grease and push home with a piece of doweling, replace valve and spring, slightly smear the washer of the cap and screw down **(1)**. Now, keeping the fingers crossed, close the cocking lever, load pellet and fire.

The next problem can occur if you can cock and action, but it will not fire; refer to Figures 3, 4, and 5. The first thing to try is the trigger stop screw **(3)**, this might be screwed in too far and blocking the trigger. Unscrew gradually until the trigger does release the action. If this doesn't work, then the trigger might be misadjusted. To reset the trigger mechanism, unscrew the two trigger screws **(1 & 2)** until they project about 1 mm. Now unscrew the trigger stop screw **(3)** until the trigger can be pulled back to touch the trigger guard. Making sure that the barrel is not occupied with a pellet, cock the action and screw the trigger adjusting screw **(1)** in until its head is flush with the trigger face. Now screw in screw **(2)** by quarter turn stages trying the trigger after each quarter turn until the sear is released and the airpistol fires the pellet. Finally make finer adjustments to screw **(2)** until the correct sear let-off is reached for your usage. The length of the first stage of trigger travel can now be made by turning both screws **(1)** and **(2)** equal amounts in the same direction, i.e. anti-clockwise to lengthen the first stage pull and clockwise to shorten. Screw **(3)** is now screwed inwards until the correct travel is reached where the trigger lets off the action without any slack after travel. The trigger pull is set at the factory for 500 grams, but adjustment can be made by opening the barrel and turning screw **(4)** anti-clockwise to decrease the pull and clockwise to increase the trigger pull.

General wear of the trigger action is very unlikely, but should removal be necessary, first remove the barrel and grips, then drive out pin **(7)** and allow the hammer catch to fall down, with a little help if needed. Now look at plate **(9)** and make a note of which hole the spring is fastened, then drive out pin **(8)** and grasp plate **(9)** and with a pair of fine nosed pliers, lift out the sear unit complete. Clean all parts, replace those that look a bit dodgy, and reassemble in the reverse order.

Pellet shavings from proud pellets dropping into the action can also cause problems. The only cure is to strip the trigger action and clean out the lead pollution and in future use a pellet pusher to size the pellets part way into the barrel.

Another reason for the action to cock and yet not fire is for the striker and its associated parts to have failed. To dismantle the striker, first make sure the action is uncocked and then remove the grips. Draw down the cocking lever so that it is about 90° to the grip, (see illustration). With a thin screwdriver, lever up the part **(2)** until both sides are out of the notch, pull downwards and remove. Pull the striker unit downwards and out, now clean and replace what looks broken or worn. To reassemble, first smear the sides of the striker with thin grease, hold the trigger in the pulled to fire position and insert the striker unit **(3)** and push home into its rightful position. Now take the stop **(2)** and holding as shown in Figure ?, at an angle of 45°, push it over the rod against the spring **(3)** and then turn flat and push it up into the striker recess, at the same time pushing downwards on the other end until it clicks into the notch and is correctly seated. Now close the cocking lever and re-cock and fire action dry to test. Sounds complicated, but it is really common sense and logical when the above is done without losing one's cool.

Apparently, if your LP2 has wooden grips, by overtightening the top screw, this can jam the striker and prevent the trigger action from functioning freely — with wooden grips, I would check that first.

Should the cocking lever become stiff to operate, then check the valve as in the first section, if not, then go on to the next section which is the piston/washer might need replacing or lubricating. First remove the striker mechanism as explained earlier, then, referring to Figure ?, remove circlip **(1)** and drive out bolt **(2)**, undo and remove **(3)** making sure that you do not loose the washer. Push off the retained plate and the bearing plate **(4)** will now drop down and out. Turn the pistol over and repeat on the other side. Now draw out the piston. Clean all parts and the air chamber and with the top valve removed, clean and if possible blow through to clean thoroughly and remove any traces of foreign bodies.

Regrease as specified before and to reassemble, first refit the piston **(5)** with washer **(7)** and pin **(6)**. Carefully introduce it into the air chamber, taking care not to damage edges of washer against cylinder sides. Grease the washer and push home into the air chamber. Reassemble the striker mechanism as in section two, but only insert the bearing plate **(4)** on one side and fit the retained piece and screw **(3)** but do not tighten down fully. Do the same to the other side. Now insert the eccentric bolt **(2)** and leave its head protruding so that its head can be turned with an 8 mm. spanner. Turn the bolt **(2)** left/right whilst closing the cocking lever until a point is reached when the cocking lever has a firm, but manageable counter pressure for the last 60° of its travel, see the first illustration. Now drive home the eccentric bolt making sure that its head is fully in the recess and refit the circlip **(1)**. Now pull down the cocking lever fully and refit the main valve as in the first section and then test the action. Basically the LP2 is quite a simple airgun.

A simpler type of valve key can be made by first sticking a price label to the top of the valve cap and gently rubbing with a soft pencil to outline the three pin holes. Remove and re-stick to a piece of flat steel, centre-punch the three depressions and drill with a 3/32 inch drill, prefereably with a drill stand so they are at least accurate and perpendicular to the flat metal face. Now insert three pins and then introduce it to the valve cap and give a sharp tap to unscrew.

The LP2 started life as patents DBP 1,164,279, June, 1961, for the cocking lever; and DBP 1,428,627, December, 1963, for the valve opening striker. It became available during July, 1965 and production ceased late 1971 in favour of the LP3, but LP2's were still being sold well into the middle 1970's. Only around 20,000 were produced and started from number 00001. The LP2 is now quite a rare airpistol and well worth acquiring should one come your way.

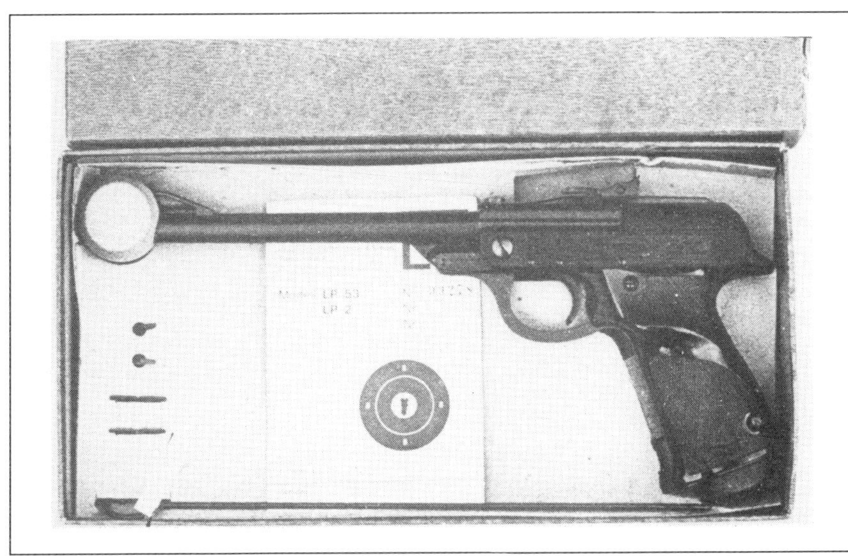

Walther LP53 in original box with accessories.

Walther LP53 in cocked position.

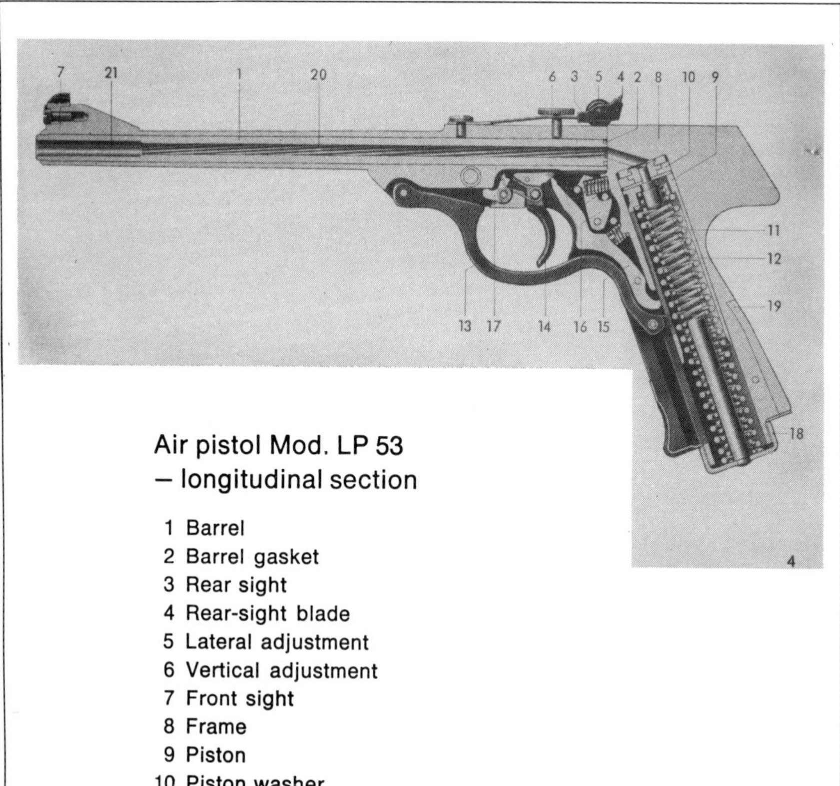

Air pistol Mod. LP 53
– longitudinal section

1 Barrel
2 Barrel gasket
3 Rear sight
4 Rear-sight blade
5 Lateral adjustment
6 Vertical adjustment
7 Front sight
8 Frame
9 Piston
10 Piston washer
11 Outer spring
12 Inner spring
13 Cocking lever
14 Trigger
15 Trigger bar
16 Locking pawl
17 Trigger safety pawl
18 Cylinder cap
19 Grip plate
20 Rifling
21 Widening of bore for muzzle

5

Airpistol Model LP73 — longitudinal section.

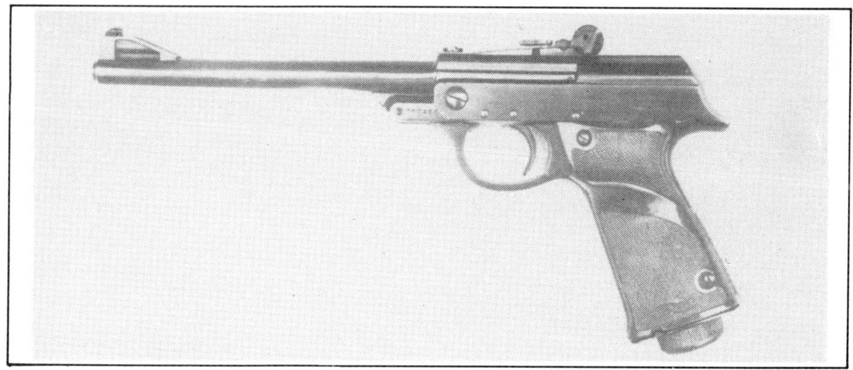

Early Model LP53 fitted with brown grips, curved rear to action, and blacked finish to body instead of crackled finish.

Model: **LP53**

Maker: **Carl Walther, Sportwaffenfabrik,** 79, Ulm-Donau, Germany.

Date: 1953 to 1976.

Valuation: £75 - £150.

Details: Measures 13 inches from barrel to butt with a 9¼ inch barrel. Barrel and trigger guard blued whilst the action has a crackled finish. Serial number stamped on L.H.S. of barrel, near the pivot pin, serial number of above 099278. Black moulded grips for right hand use bear the Walther name. Smooth area on L.H.S. of frame above the grip has "WALTHER – LP Mod53 – Cal. 4·5 – Walther's patent". This can be stamped with either "MADE IN GERMANY" or "MADE IN WEST GERMANY". On the R.H.S. of the barrel is stamped the "F" in the pentagon for Germany muzzle energy limit. Sold in brown cardboard box with compartments for wooden cocking aid for end of barrel, two sapre foresight blades, two rear sight blades, and a barrel cleaning rod. Included in the box should be a manual and a test card for five shots from 10 metres. Barrel weights can also be obtained. A de luxe padded case for the LP53, with or without barrel weights could also be ordered. Advertised weight 40.6 ozs. The LP53 was designed after the Walther Olympic pistol. Advertised accuracy was 1 inch circle at 20 to 25 feet, and at that distance, each click of the adjuster screws on the rear sight will move the point of impact ⅛ of an inch. Only about 8 inches of the barrel is rifled as the final inch has been widened to accept another type of cocking aid other than that supplied. The mainspring and air chamber is in the butt.

The butt contains two mainsprings, one inside the other, as does the Relum Tornado air rifle. Early models had brown grips and lacked the black crackled finish to the action body. During the middle 1960's the muzzle weights were available and around the 1970 mark the rear of the airpistol was redesigned to give a slant back to the top of the grip rather than the earlier concave shape. Apparently the LP53 was used in early advertisements for the James Bond films. The LP53 was the second airgun to be produced by Walther. Apparently, when the first were produced, about 850 were called the LP52 when production first began during 1952, but after minor changes in design during 1953, production really got underway and from that date it became the LP53. These first 850 LP52's must surely be desirable collector's items. The LP52 may have been fitted with chequered walnut grips. production of the LP53 began with serial number 1000, or 1001 and ceased with number 124500 in 1976.

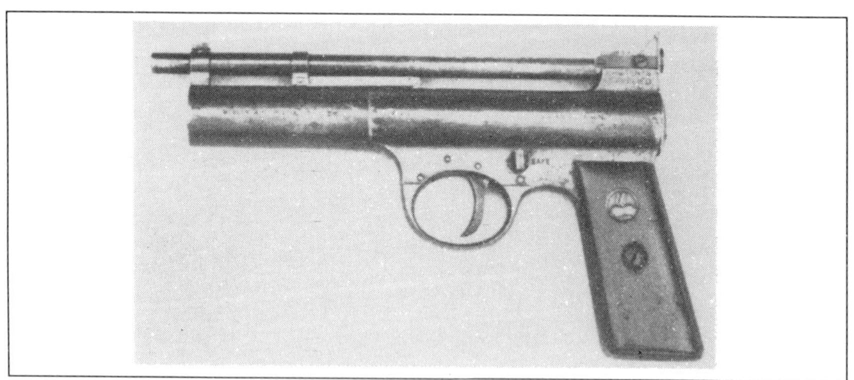

Webley Mark I (second model).

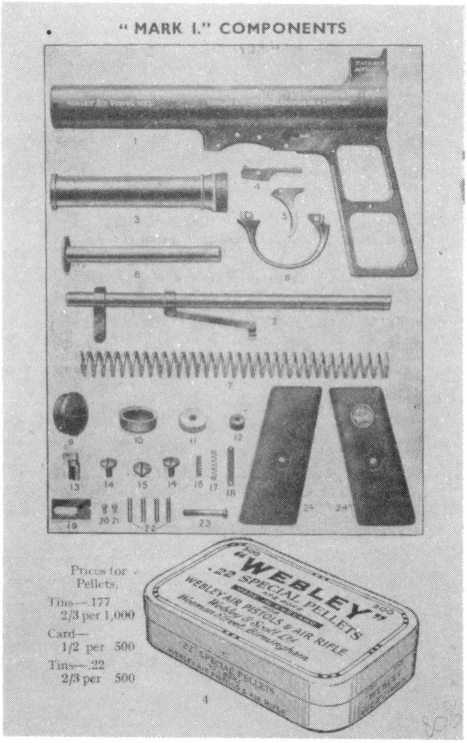

"MARK I." COMPONENTS
"WEBLEY"
.22 SPECIAL PELLETS
WEBLEY AIR PISTOLS & AIR RIFLE
Prices for Pellets.
Tins—.177
2/3 per 1,000
Card—
1/2 per 500
Tins—.22
2/3 per 500

Webley "Mark I" Parts Diagram (first model).

The first model Webley Mark I airpistol with one spring clip barrel catch.

Model: **MARK I (Second Model)**

Maker: **Webley & Scott Ltd.,**
89-91 Weaman Street,
Birmingham, England.
Address at time of manufacture.

Date: With spring clips for barrel latch, 1924.

Valuation: £75 - £200.

Details: The first model had only one clip for holding the barrel in place, and this was on the R.H.S. of the transfer port housing. Very soon after the introduction, and within the same year a second clip was added. Towards the end of 1924 the idea of spring clips was dropped and the sliding catch introduced. The second model was sold in either ·22 or ·177 and I have seen the odd rare smoothbore barrel. The action stripped from the rear only and was fitted with a spring guide that had to be fed into the air chamber before the mainspring. L.H.S. of air chamber stamped "WEBLEY AIR PISTOL MARK I" followed by "WEBLEY & SCOTT LTD, BIRMINGHAM & LONDON" and on the side of the transfer port "PATENTS APPLIED FOR". The serial number is stamped in the usual place, just above the L.H. grip. There is no trigger adjustment. See later model for its introduction.

The patent for the above design, number 219872 of 1923 was finally accepted in August, 1924, so the Mark I may even have begun production in 1923. The rearsight is mainly adjustable for elevation only, but is a little sloppy to either left or right. These early Mark I's were fitted with walnut grips. A review of the Mark I appeared in *"Country Life"* dated October 18th, 1924, and even then the airpistol performed well. The following is a quote of velocities obtained and pellet speeds measured 5 yards from the muzzle, about 4.5 metres:

·177 pellet weighing 8 grains
a) 361 f.p.s.
b) 374 f.p.s.
c) 366 f.p.s.
average velocity being 367 f.p.s.

·22 pellet weighing 15 grains
a) 274 f.p.s.
b) 273 f.p.s.
c) 271 f.p.s.
average velocity being 273 f.p.s.

Many purists of pellet testing will discount the above but they do give some idea of the Mark I's performance. The London address at the time of manufacture was 55 Victoria Street, Westminster, London S.W.1. Each airpistol was sold with a spare piston and breech washer, and sample packet of pellets. A one clip Mark I has been seen, serial number 118, whilst twin clip models with serial numbers 241, 472 and 578 have been noted.

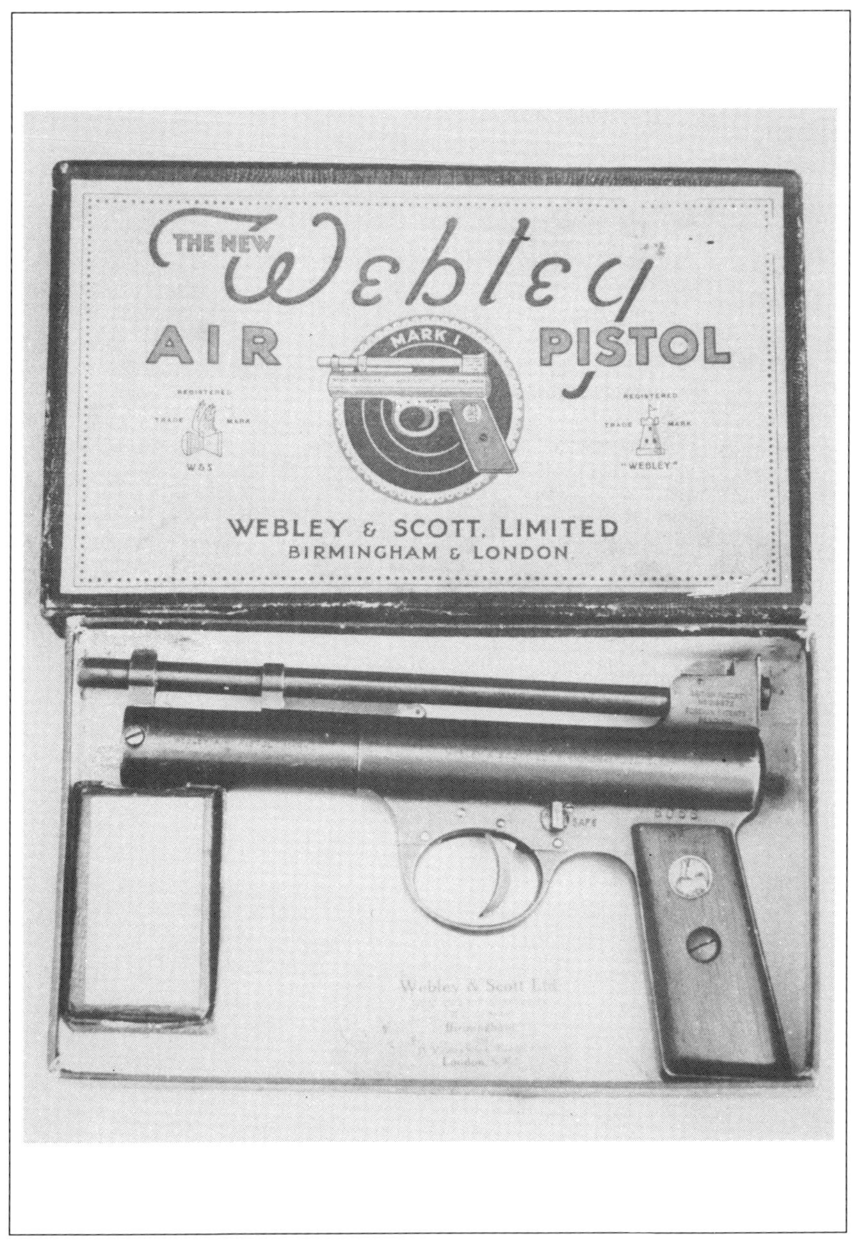

Webley Mark I.

Model: **MARK I**

Maker: **Webley & Scott Ltd.,**
Weaman Street,
Birmingham, and
55 Victoria Street,
Westminster,
London S.W.1.
Addresses at time of manufacture.

Date: Above variation from late 1924 to end of 1925.

Valuation: £50 - £150, boxed examples even more.

Details: ·22 rifled barrel. Air chamber strips from rear only. Rearsight is adjustable for elevation only. L.H.S. of air port housing stamped "BRITISH PATENT 219872 FOREIGN PATENTS PENDING" and same side of air chamber stamped "WEBLEY AIR PISTOL MARK I WEBLEY & SCOTT LTD., BIRMINGHAM & LONDON". The serial number is stamped just above the L.H. grip. There is no provision for trigger adjustment. Nothing appears stamped behind the trigger guard.

The barrel pivot screw is one piece on these early Mark I's, and a convenient replacement is the pivot screw from the Junior airpistol. Serial numbers seen for the above variation run from 2428 up to 9643, although the range will be beyond these figures. The early models had "PATENTS APPLIED FOR" stamped on the side of the frame, near the barrel housing.

Pre-war Webley Mark I airpistol.

Webley Mark I with etched patents.

Model:	**MARK I**
Maker:	**Webley & Scott Ltd.**
Date:	1925 - 1926.
Valuation:	£50 - £100.

Details: Serial number of the airpistol in the upper illustration on page 185 is 13114. Fitted with a smoothbore barrel. The number is also stamped on the back of the barrel support arm, but this does not match. Trigger adjustment, but no locking screw for the adjuster screw. Walnut grips with brass medallion. Action strips from rear only. Stamped on safety pin side: "WEBLEY AIR PISTOL MARK I" and "WEBLEY & SCOTT LTD. BIRMINGHAM & LONDON", whilst on the other side is just "BRITISH PATENT 219872". See *"Airgun World",* March 1979.

On Webley Mark I, serial number 17158, the patents and numbers are etched on the R.H.S. of the air chamber. It could be that on the airpistol shown on the previous page, upper illustration, (serial number 13114), the etched patents have long since disappeared. I have seen similar etching on a Webley Mark I air rifle. See *"Air Rifles" Second Edition.* The patents etched are as follows:

PATENTS GRANTED

GREAT BRITAIN No. 219872	JAPAN PATENT No. 9186/24
BELGIUM BREVET No. 316878	SWITZERLAND AND PATENT No. + 112976
FRANCE BREVETE No. 578498 S.G.D.G.	
SPAIN PATENT No. 89433	AUSTRALIA PATENTED 21-12-23
ITALY BREVETTATO No. 229158	U.S.A. PATENTED U.S.A. 7-7-25
GERMANY D.R.P. No. 414833	CANADA PATENT 1925

The airpistol in the lower illustration on page 185 has the same body stampings as 13114, and non-locking trigger adjustment screw. The last three digits of the serial number are stamped on the forward lug of the trigger guard. These can only be seen when the guard has been removed.

Only three Webley Mark I's have been seen with etched patents and these had serial numbers, 12786, 13114 and 17158. When replacing the rear chamber plug, take care that your fingers do NOT slide around the edge when you screw home by hand. The outer edge can be razor sharp and to slide about on this edge WILL cut your thumb or finger. *(Author's comment — OUCH!!!).*

To find examples with etched patents that are readable is quite rare, they appear to lie between serial numbers 12245 and 177777, although others outside these numbers will exist.

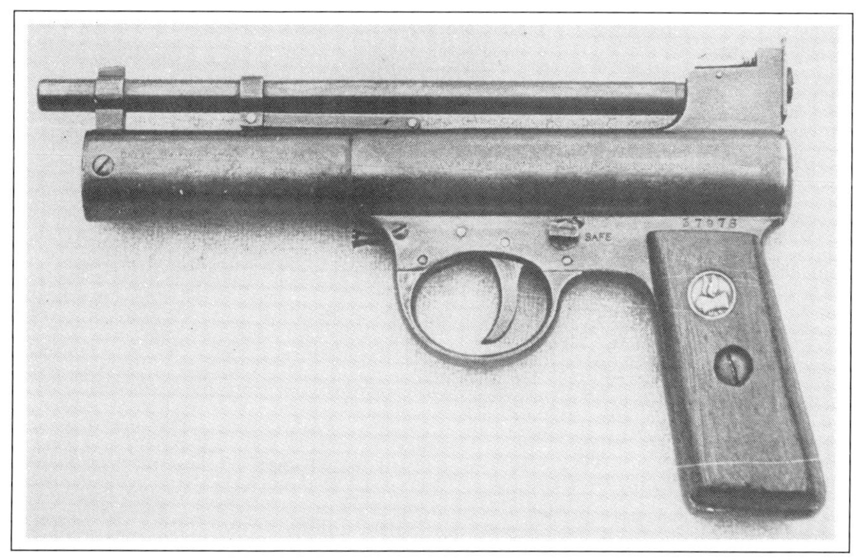

Pre-war Webley Mark I.

Webley Mark I stamped with patents, but has no trigger adjustment locking screw.

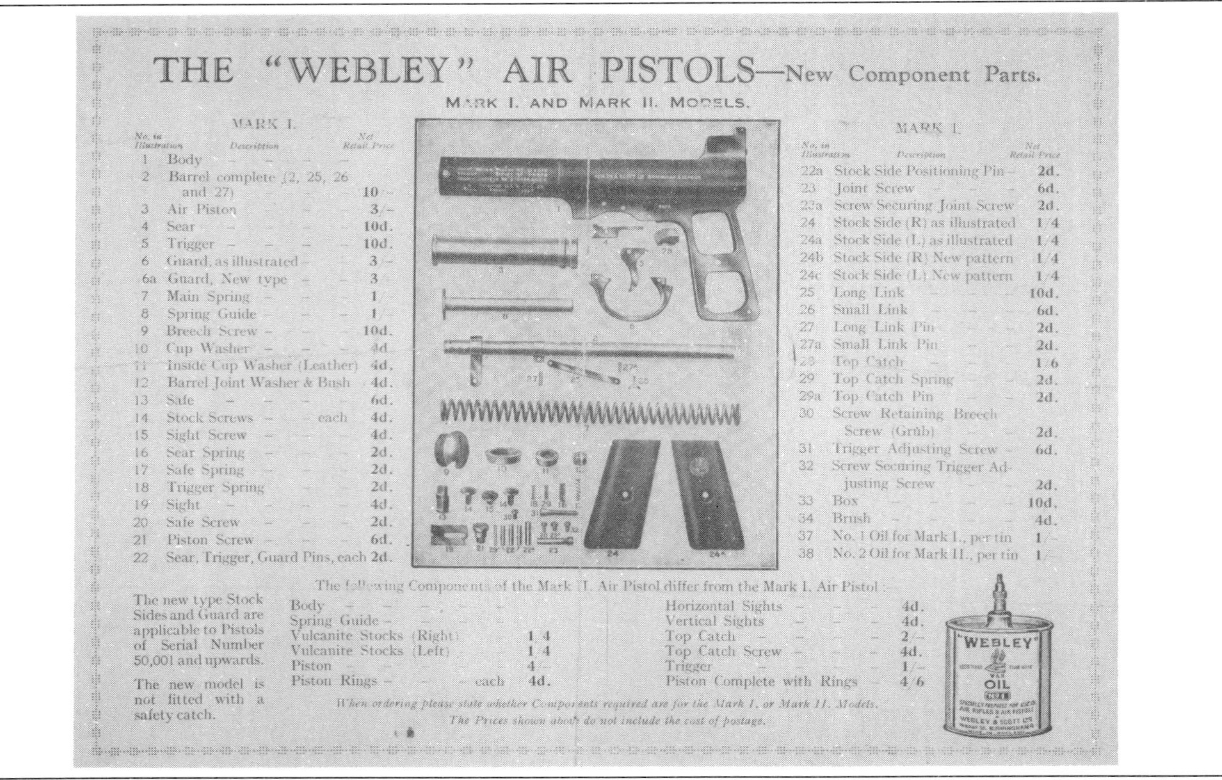

THE "WEBLEY" AIR PISTOLS—New Component Parts.

MARK I. AND MARK II. MODELS.

MARK I.

No. in Illustration	Description	Net Retail Price
1	Body	
2	Barrel complete (2, 25, 26 and 27)	10/-
3	Air Piston	3/-
4	Sear	10d.
5	Trigger	10d.
6	Guard, as illustrated	3/-
6a	Guard, New type	3/-
7	Main Spring	1/-
8	Spring Guide	1/-
9	Breech Screw	10d.
10	Cup Washer	4d.
11	Inside Cup Washer (Leather)	4d.
12	Barrel Joint Washer & Bush	4d.
13	Safe	6d.
14	Stock Screws — each	4d.
15	Sight Screw	4d.
16	Sear Spring	2d.
17	Safe Spring	2d.
18	Trigger Spring	2d.
19	Sight	4d.
20	Safe Screw	2d.
21	Piston Screw	6d.
22	Sear, Trigger, Guard Pins, each	2d.

MARK I.

No. in Illustration	Description	Net Retail Price
22a	Stock Side Positioning Pin	2d.
23	Joint Screw	6d.
23a	Screw Securing Joint Screw	2d.
24	Stock Side (R) as illustrated	1/4
24a	Stock Side (L) as illustrated	1/4
24b	Stock Side (R) New pattern	1/4
24c	Stock Side (L) New pattern	1/4
25	Long Link	10d.
26	Small Link	6d.
27	Long Link Pin	2d.
27a	Small Link Pin	2d.
28	Top Catch	1/6
29	Top Catch Spring	2d.
29a	Top Catch Pin	2d.
30	Screw Retaining Breech Screw (Grub)	2d.
31	Trigger Adjusting Screw	6d.
32	Screw Securing Trigger Adjusting Screw	2d.
33	Box	10d.
34	Brush	4d.
37	No. 1 Oil for Mark I., per tin	1/-
38	No. 2 Oil for Mark II., per tin	1/-

The following Components of the Mark II. Air Pistol differ from the Mark I. Air Pistol:—

Body		Horizontal Sights	4d.
Spring Guide		Vertical Sights	4d.
Vulcanite Stocks (Right)	1/4	Top Catch	2/-
Vulcanite Stocks (Left)	1/4	Top Catch Screw	4d.
Piston	4/-	Trigger	1/-
Piston Rings — each	4d.	Piston Complete with Rings	4/6

The new type Stock Sides and Guard are applicable to Pistols of Serial Number 50,001 and upwards.

The new model is not fitted with a safety catch.

When ordering please state whether Components required are for the Mark I. or Mark II. Models.
The Prices shown above do not include the cost of postage.

The "Webley" Air Pistols — New Component Parts.

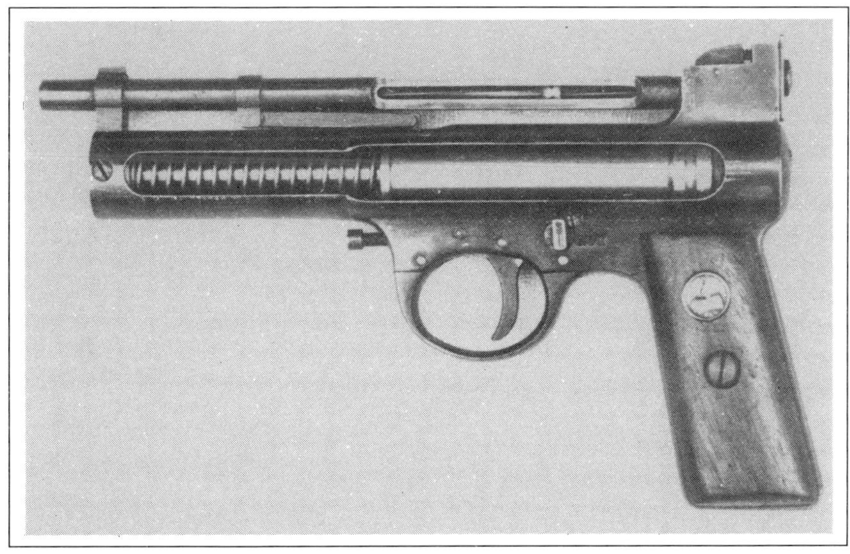

Exhibition model Webley Mark I No. 20170.

Model: **MARK I**

Maker: **Webley & Scott Ltd.,**
Birmingham, England.

Date: 1925 - 1938.

Valuation: £50 - £100.

Details: All metal with Walnut grips, with Webley brass medallion set in one of them. Has a safety catch on the same side as the brass medallion. The 7 inch barrel is rifled. Serial number of the above is 37978. Strips from the front, as on post-war airpistols. Serial number is stamped just above the grip. On the same side is stamped: "WEBLEY & SCOTT LTD., BIRMINGHAM & LONDON" whilst on the other side of the chamber is "WEBLEY AIR PISTOL MARK I", "MADE IN ENGLAND". Towards the end of the chamber, at the barrel pivot pin, is stamped a host of patents, as follows:

GREAT BRITAIN Patent No. 219872
BELGIUM Brevet 316878
FRANCE Brevete 578498 S.G.D.G.
U.S.A. Patented U.S.A. 7-7-25
Canada Patent 1925
JAPAN Patent No. 9186/24
Switzerland Patent No. + 112976
Australia Patented 21-12-23
Spain Patent No. 89433
Italy Brevettato 229158.
Germany D.R.P. 414833

Advertised in 1935 with an accuracy test of ten consecutive shots in a 1 inch circle at ten yards. On airpistol number 39877, the address on the L.H.S. of the air chamber is given as "BIRMINGHAM" only. See *"Airgun World",* March, 1979.

Towards the end of the manufacture of the straight grip Mark I the body stampings were changed as follows: L.H.S. of air chamber stamped "WEBLEY AIRPISTOL MARK I" whilst on R.H.S. "WEBLEY & SCOTT LTD BIRMINGHAM" and further along towards the barrel pivot only three patents were mentioned: Great Britain, U.S.A., and Canada; could this have been because we were entering World War Two? These body stampings are identical to the straight grip pre-war Mark I. From a record of serial numbers seen, the range of the above common model ran from 20828 to 48687, although other collectors will see Mark I's outside this range.

A gradual range of variations occurred as follows: "JJ" inspection initials stamped behind the trigger guard seen from 19802 to 25426 inclusive. "A.W." appears on 27581 up to 30835. Nothing appears on 39317. From 39912 onwards, up to 48687 letters J, M, T and S are used in order of appearance. "BIRMINGHAM & LONDON" address became "Birmingham" only sometime between numbers 30835 and 39317. Originally the air chamber stripped from the rear only, but by number 39317 either end of the air chamber could be removed. The body stampings remained unaltered until, between 46323 and 47947, they were changed to the set that appeared on the pre-war slant grip Mark I, that is, only bearing three patents.

The Mark I was also sold in the U.S.A. by the Stoeger Mail Order and some of these may find their way back home. They vary in body stampings from the usual Mark I as follows, one example, serial number 34955, has been seen with "BRITISH PATENT 219872" stamped on the front part of the action, followed by "WEBLEY & SCOTT LTD, BIRMINGHAM & LONDON" on the rear part of the action. On the R.H.S. appears "A. F. STOEGER INC., NEW YORK, SOLE U.S. AGENTS" and beneath this "WEBLEY AIR PISTOL MARK I, MADE IN ENGLAND" at the front end "U.S.A. PATD, JULY 7, 1925". For the Webley collector this variation is a must. Another variation is a very early Mark and is the transitional model from the etched patents to that with stamped patents. It combines the lettering of the previous model with that of the above Mark I. The serial number of the example seen was 18417, and on the L.H.S. of the chamber is stamped the world patents, but with "WEBLEY AIR PISTOL MARK I" between the French and Spanish patent. On the same side is stamped "WEBLEY & SCOTT LTD., BIRMINGHAM & LONDON" whilst on the other side appears "MADE IN ENGLAND" followed by the full set of other World Patents.

The air chamber strips from the rear only and the trigger adjustment screw has no locking grub screw. The inspection letters "J.J." are stamped just behind the trigger guard. This represents quite a rare variation of the Webley Mark I airpistol as the last etched patents model is 17158 and the first model with stamped patents had a serial number of 19802.

Pre-war, slant grip, Webley Mark I.

Box lid for above.

Model: **MARK I (Pre-war)**

Maker: **Webley & Scott**

Date: Production of slant grip Mark I, 1935-1939.

Valuation: Boxed pre-war Webley airpistols are quite rare and if the airpistol is in very good condition, then they offer good investment opportunities. For the above, suggest £100 - £150. Without box £50 - £100.

Details: Serial number 62634 with 634 appearing on the front of the frame. Serial number stamped on the L.H.S. of the frame just above the trigger. The grips are black with no "Webley" name at the top part. Stamped on the L.H.S. of the air chamber is "OIL HERE — WEBLEY MARK I — MADE IN ENGLAND", on the other side of the chamber appears "WEBLEY & SCOTT LTD., BIRMINGHAM" and at the barrel pivot end:

"GREAT BRITAIN PATENT No. 219872"
"U.S.A. PATENTED U.S.A. 7-7-25"
"CANADA PATENT 1925".

The above has a ·177 barrel that has no serrations for gripping the barrel, as do post-war Mark I's. The label on the lid of the box is blue. See *"Guns Review"*, June, 1978.

A pre-war Mark I, number 57603, has "WEBLEY AIR PISTOL MARK I" stamped on the L.H.S. of the air chamber in smaller letters.

In 1939, the above was advertised with the fact that each Mark I was tested for grouping at ten yards — "the test being ten consecutive shots in a one inch circle." It was also stated to have had walnut grips, but I have only seen black vulcanite. Serial numbers for the pre-war slant grip Mark I started from 50,001. This model was first called the "Mark II". Each airpistol was supplied in a box containing barrel brush, sample of pellets, and a barrel joint washer. Webley oil "No. 1" was also recommended. The highest serial number seen for the pre-war slant grip Mark I is 65057.

First models had now warning stamped on the rear air chamber plug and these were held in place by a small grub screw. By number 60270, the chamber plug was stamped "NOT TO BE REMOVED", but was still held in place by a grub screw, by 63217, the plug was finally pegged so that removal was now well-nigh impossible. Inspection letters used were L, A, O, H, in order of appearance. These appeared usually on the side of the action near trigger adjustment locking screw.

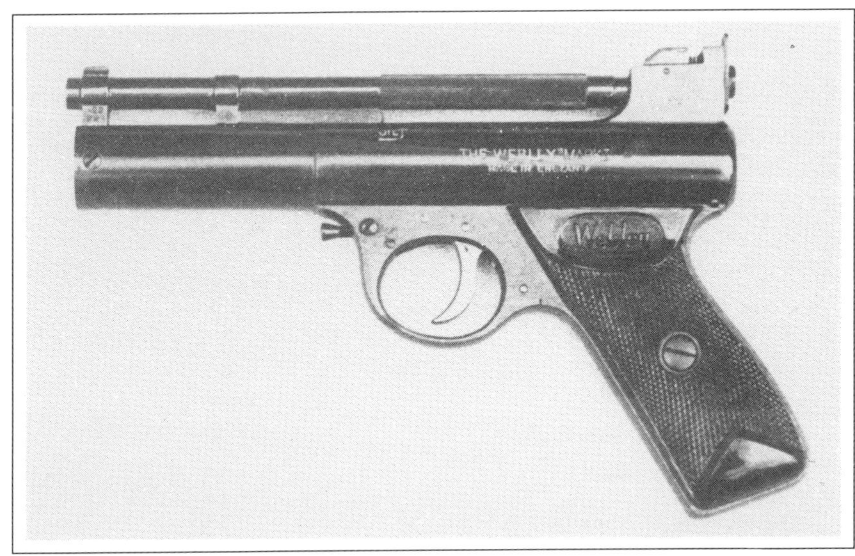

Webley Mark I.

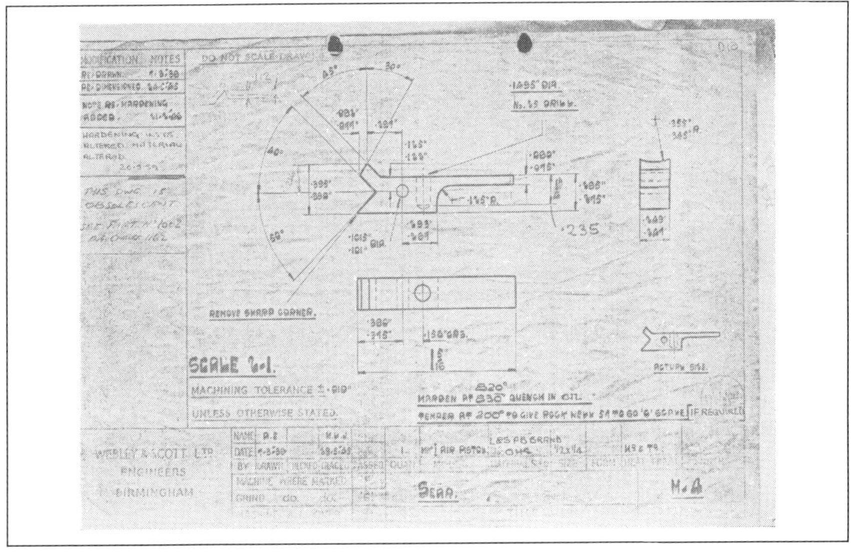

Diagram of Mark I sear.

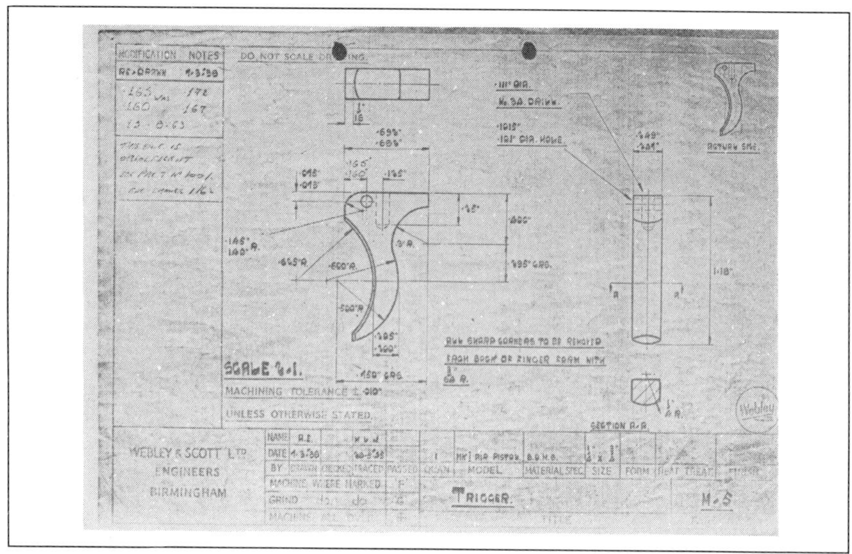

Diagram of Mark I trigger.

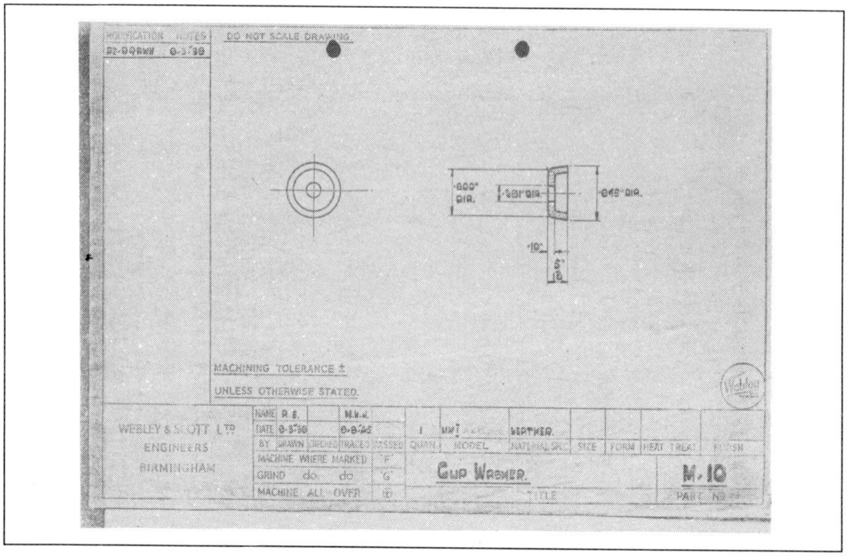

Diagram of Mark I cup washer.

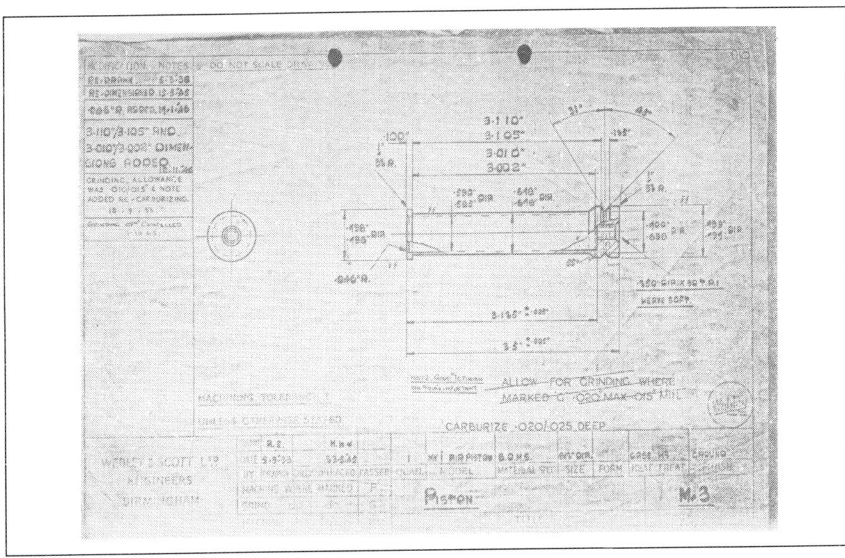

Diagram of Mark I piston.

Model: **"MARK I"**

Maker: **Webley & Scott**

Date: Production from 1946 to 1964.

Valuation: £50 - £100.

Details: Postwar slant grip model. Black grips. Single lever cocking action, so can be harder to cock. Trigger adjustment. Four pin trigger action. Address stamped on side of air chamber is "Birmingham" so made after the move of the factory. Barrel support arm stamped "·22 Mark I". Interchangeable barrels are available ·22/·177. L.H.S. of air chamber stamped "THE WEBLEY "MARK I" MADE IN ENGLAND" whilst on R.H.S. "WEBLEY & SCOTT LTD., BIRMINGHAM 4" and further along twards the barrel pivot "WEBLEY PATENTS".

Produced the same time as the "Senior". They were both discontinued in 1964, and when the "Premier" appeared, it merged the "Mark I" trigger adjustment and the "Senior" double barrel cocking lever. Advertised in 1960 as having the following muzzle velocities: Range 20 feet, ·22 — 314; ·177 — 350. Velocities in feet per second. Advertisement also stated that all Webley airpistols are capable of grouping within 1 inch from a fixed rest at thirty feet. Advertised as weighing 30 ozs., overall length 8½ inches and having a 6½ inch barrel with machine cut rifling. Each airpistol was supplied in a cardboard box with "Webley Special Pellets" and a spare washer. For an extra cost of 5/- they could be supplied nickel plated.

It would appear that the cocking long link, part number J9 is interchangeable with the long cocking link, part number M25, from the Mark I airpistol and vice versa. Mark I's stamped "BIRMINGHAM 4" were made from 1946 to 1958, when a move of factory occurred, and from 1958 to 1964, the airpistols were stamped "BIRMINGHAM".

After the War, Webleys appear to have dropped the practice of stamping serial numbers on their airguns, so it would appear that the numbers found are only batch numbers, i.e., just a way of keeping a certain number of airguns together as they passed through the factory, or being "jobbed" around the Birmingham gun making centre. The following details are for Mark I's made in the 1946 - 1964 period.

Batch numbers seen, run from 67 to 2350. Inspection marks used are M, &, Z, B, ". ", J, although many have been seen without any marks. Usually these inspection stamps are found behind the trigger guard. Some were produced with no warning about removal on the rear air chamber plug. Under the left hand grip is often stamped numbers that do not tally with the batch number. On the Mark I these do not appear to be date stamps, although on the "Premier" for some time a date was stamped. It is also interesting to note that rear air chamber plugs without warnings of non-removal were also fitted to the Senior.

The mark I airpistol barrels are particularly soft and bend very easily, especially the ·22 barrel, that has a thinner wall thickness. It is advisable not to try and fit a stronger mainspring than that specified, and NEVER fire the airpistol with the barrel in the upright cocked position — either one of these actions will bend the barrel.

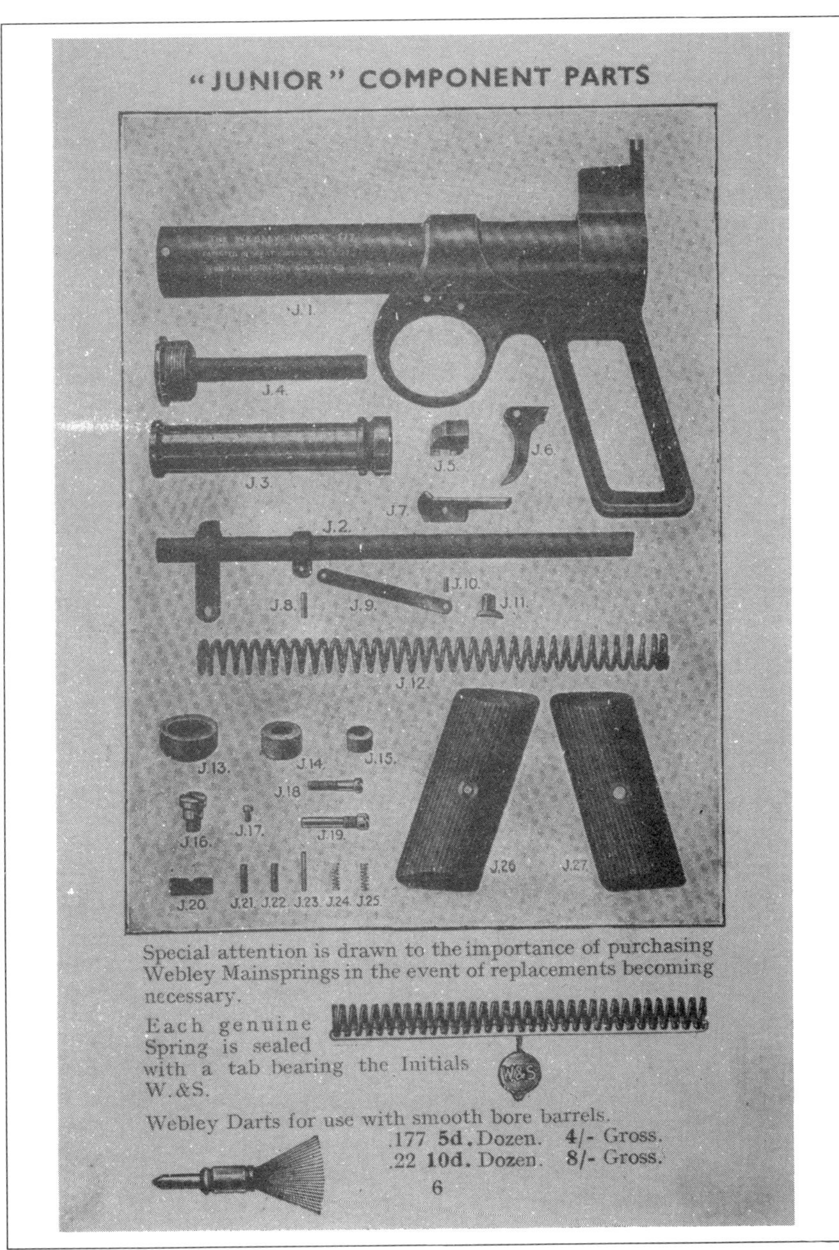

Pre-war Webley Junior (first model)

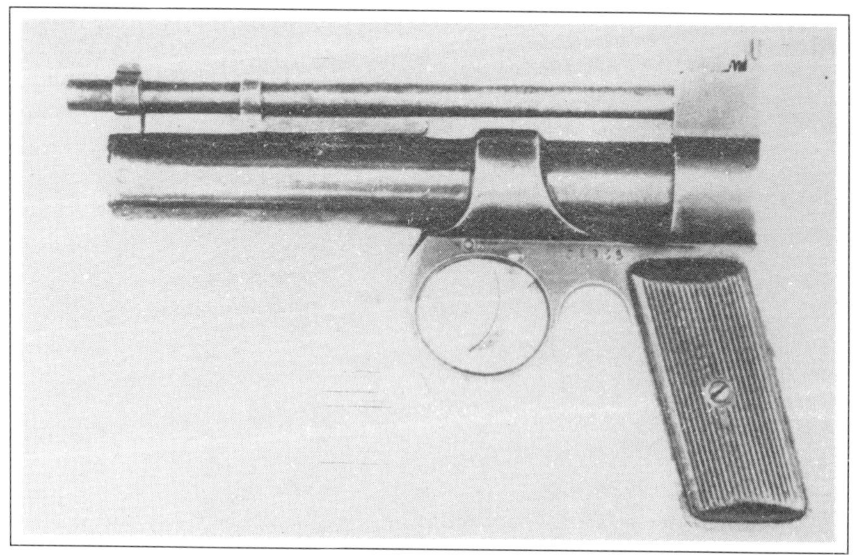

First model pre-war Junior.

Model: **JUNIOR**

Maker: **Webley & Scott Ltd.,**
Birmingham, England.

Date: First model appeared around 1930, and later changed to the more common variety, with blued metal grips, during 1931.

Valuation: £40 - £100.

Details: This must be the rarest variation of the Webley Junior. Three major differences from the next model, i.e., adjustable rearsight, ribbed wooden grips, and may or may not have lettering stamped on the air chamber. On the example seen, J1955, there was no lettering at all on the air chamber, but on an earlier version, J121, see *"Guns Review"*, June, 1978, had the full range of patents stamped on the air chamber. By serial number J1233, these had disappeared. It would also appear that the adjustable rearsight came and went in a very short period of production. This ranged from about number J1233 to somewhere between J4000 and J7530. From the spares diagram, it will be seen that the adjustable rearsight appears on a frame stamped with the same lettering that is on most of the pre-war Juniors. Even this was not constant as pistol number J1794 is stamped, but number J1955 is plain. Some earlier Juniors will also be seen with tinplate grips but still have the adjustable rearsight, for example J3882.

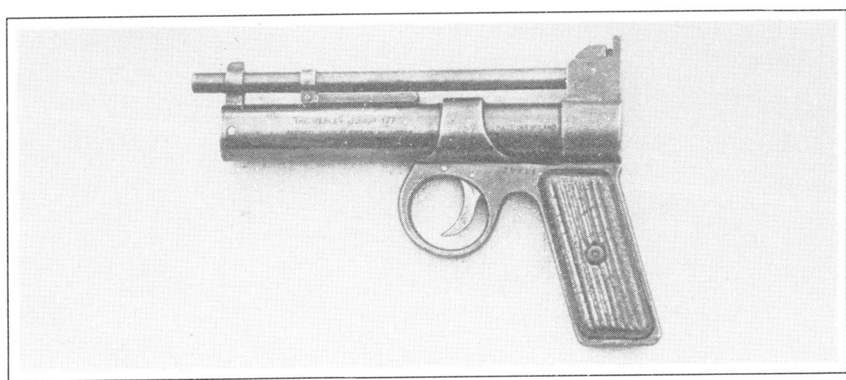

Pre-war Junior.

Pre-war "Junior" with trigger adjustment similar to Mark I airpistol (non original).

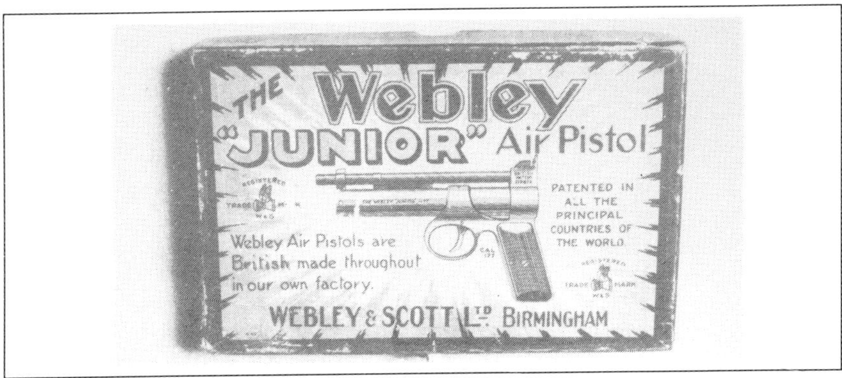

Box lid for pre-war "Junior".

Model: **"JUNIOR" pre-war.**

Maker: **Webley & Scott**

Date: 1930 - 1939.

Valuation: £20 - £80.

Details: All metal with tin grips. Smoothbore barrel, 6½ inches long. Non-adjustable rear sight. Serial number of above J9911. All pre-war "Juniors" have a "J" prefix to the serial number. Airpistol measures 9 inches from tip of barrel to base of butt. Stamped on L.H.S. of chamber "THE WEBLEY "JUNIOR" ·177 – PATENTED IN GREAT BRITAIN No. 219872 AND ALL PRINCIPAL COUNTRIES", also "MADE IN ENGLAND". On the L.H.S. is stamped "WEBLEY & SCOTT LTD. BIRMINGHAM". For further reading see *"Guns Review",* August and September 1975 and June 1978.

1939 advert showed Webley Junior with wooden grips, these had finer grooves in the same direction as the tinplate grips usually seen on pre-war Juniors. An article appears in *"Guns Review",* September, 1979, regarding the pre-war Webley Junior with the trigger adjustment screw. On no account insert spaces into the piston in order to aid compression of the main spring. This only causes either the spring guide to foul the inside head of the piston or the main spring to bound, in each case the action will not cock.

Towards the end of the production of the pre-war Junior the lettering was altered on the air chamber to "WEBLEY JUNIOR ·177 WEBLEY & SCOTT BIRMINGHAM MADE IN ENGLAND". No other lettering appeared. The first models to appear after the War added "4" to the Birmingham address. These last pre-war models may have also been fitted with the short nosed barrel. This change of lettering appeared between airpistols numbered J21551 and J25065.

One would assume that the first serial number was J1 and the highest number seen J29854. The first models were fitted with wooden grips and I have seen two of this type, J1718 and J1794. They were also available with a simple rearsight, see parts diagram. Earliest model with tin grips seen is J3671. Inspection letters seen have either been stamped behind the trigger guard on the L.H.S. of the frame, these include "S", "I", "A", "H", and "C", in order of appearance.

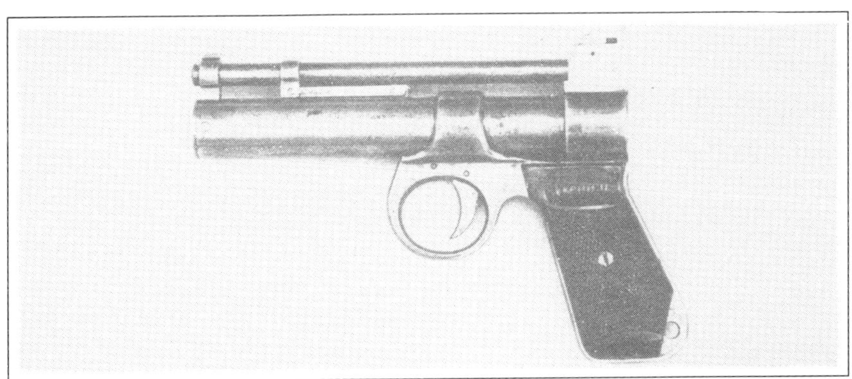

Webley "Junior" post-war.

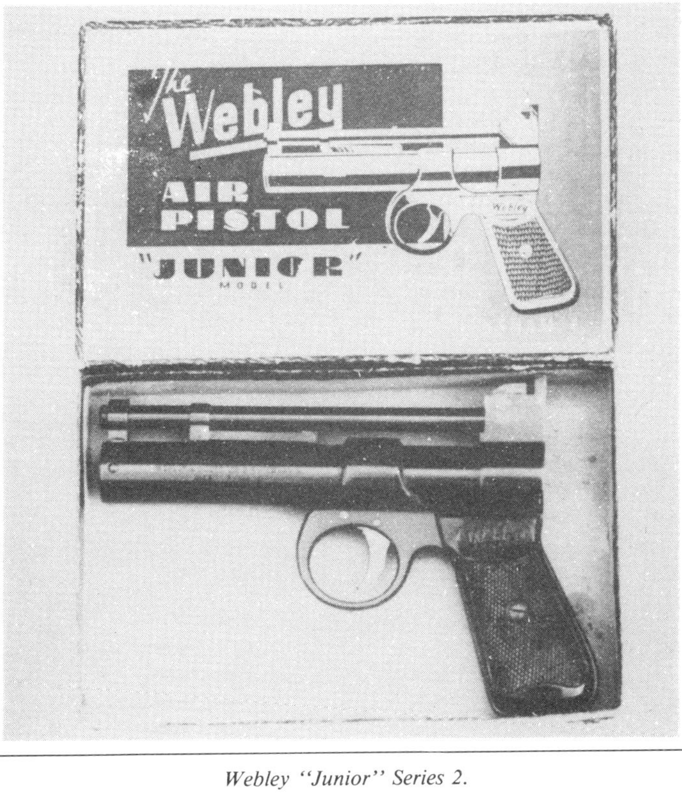

Webley "Junior" Series 2.

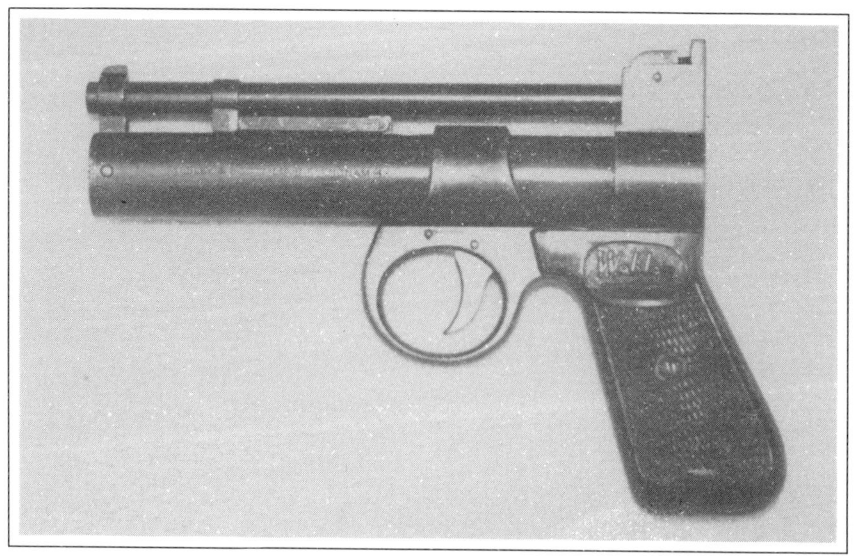

1946 to 1950 Webley Junior with forward extensions to the grips.

Model: **"JUNIOR" Post-war.**

Maker: **Webley & Scott.**

Date: Production 1946 - 1977. Above example 1946 - 1950.

Valuation: £20 - £70.

Details: Above has a non-adjustable rearsight, the adjustable rearsight was added in the 1950's. The batch number appears on the front of the air chamber, near the barrel pivot pin. Although a batch number does appear under the left hand grip, the above is 4019, whilst 019 appears stamped at the front. The only stamping that appears on the above is on the L.H.S. "THE WEBLEY "JUNIOR" ·177, WEBLEY & SCOTT LTD. BIRMINGHAM 4, MADE IN ENGLAND". Overall length is 7¾ inches with a 6⅛ inch smoothbore barrel. Advertised weight 24 ozs. Referred to as the "Webley Junior Air Pistol (Series 2)" when it first appeared in 1946.

Batch numbers seen for the above model run from 290 up to 5120. Inspection marks used, in order of appearance, are "J", "F", "Y", the "F" being very common. When it first appeared after the War it was called the "Series 2" Webley Junior. In the late 1940's the design of the grips was altered for a short period of production. The chequering became more coarse and the top portion was extended along the frame towards the trigger. This variation appeared by batch number 955 and continued right through to the next model. All barrels fitted were smoothbore, unless replaced by a Junior Mark 2 barrel.

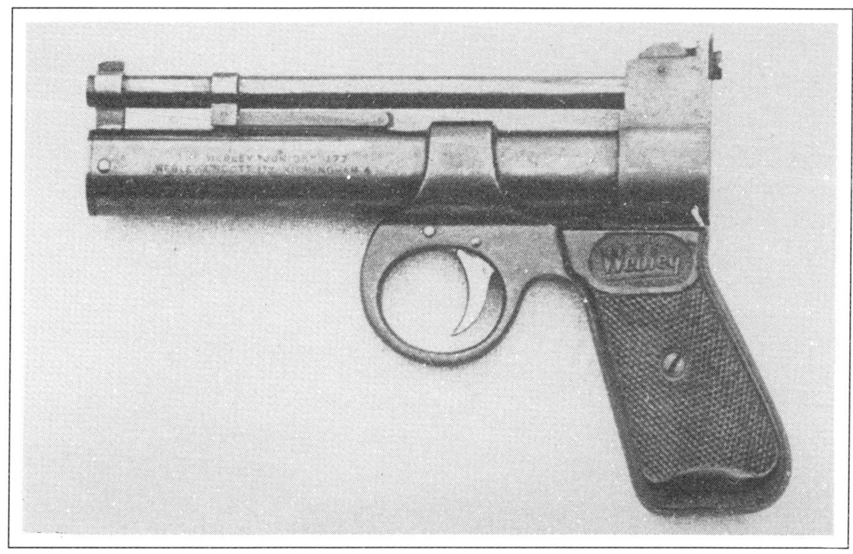

Post-war "Junior", approx. 1950-1958.

Model:	**"JUNIOR"**
Maker:	**Webley & Scott**
Date:	Production 1946 - 1977, above model 1950 - 1958.
Valuation:	£20 - £70.

Details: In the 1950's, an adjustable rear sight was added. This is a simple blade sight without the two way adjustment as found on the more expensive models of Webley airpistols. The two way adjustable sight came at a later date. The only stamping that appears on the above is on the L.H.S. of the air chamber: "THE WEBLEY "JUNIOR" ·177 WEBLEY & SCOTT LTD BIRMINGHAM 4 MADE IN ENGLAND". The batch number appears at the front flat near the barrel pivot, also under the L.H. grip. Serial number of the above is 1779. Advertised as weighing 24 ozs., overall length 7¾ inches with 6⅛ inch smoothbore barrel.

Up until 1958, they could be ordered nickel plated at an extra cost of 5/-. Batch numbers seen for the 1950 to 1958 variation appear to run from 118 to 2325 and use inspection marks, P, V, F, and J marks usually stamped behind the trigger guard.

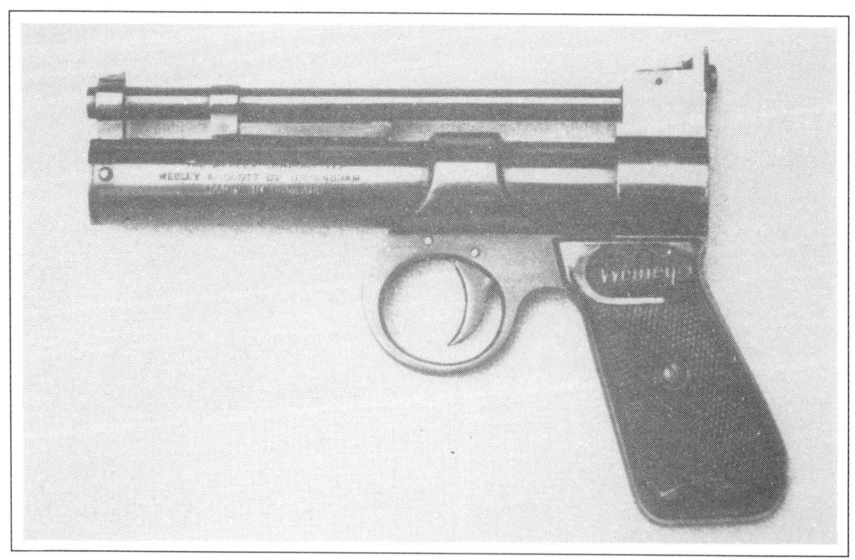

Post-war "Junior", 1958 - 1973.

*Chrome plated Webley Junior, 1958 - 1973. The grips and rear sight blade are not original. See **"Guns Review"**, September, 1979 for article on above.*

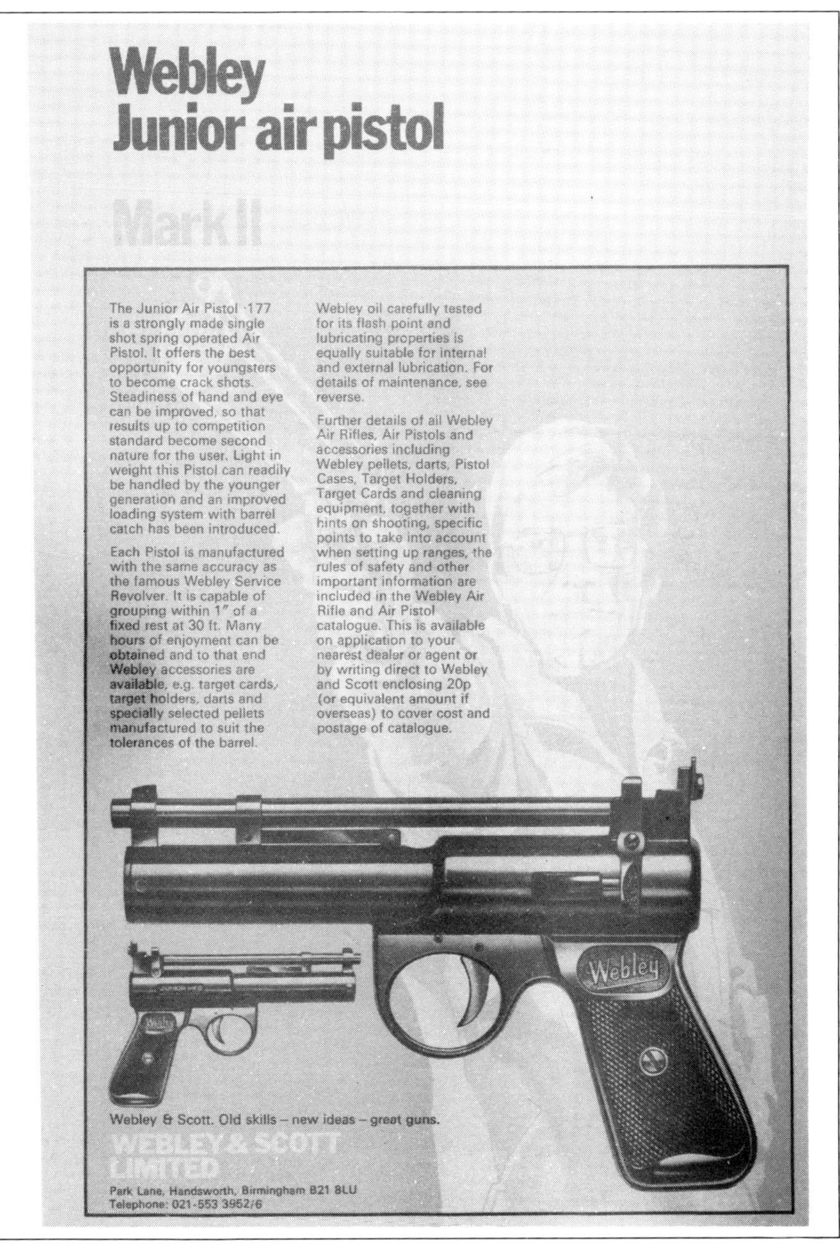

Webley
Junior air pistol
Mark II
The Junior Air Pistol ·177 is a strongly made single shot spring operated Air Pistol. It offers the best opportunity for youngsters to become crack shots. Steadiness of hand and eye can be improved, so that results up to competition standard become second nature for the user. Light in weight this Pistol can readily be handled by the younger generation and an improved loading system with barrel catch has been introduced.
Each Pistol is manufactured with the same accuracy as the famous Webley Service Revolver. It is capable of grouping within 1" of a fixed rest at 30 ft. Many hours of enjoyment can be obtained and to that end Webley accessories are available, e.g. target cards, target holders, darts and specially selected pellets manufactured to suit the tolerances of the barrel.
Webley oil carefully tested for its flash point and lubricating properties is equally suitable for internal and external lubrication. For details of maintenance, see reverse.
Further details of all Webley Air Rifles, Air Pistols and accessories including Webley pellets, darts, Pistol Cases, Target Holders, Target Cards and cleaning equipment, together with hints on shooting, specific points to take into account when setting up ranges, the rules of safety and other important information are included in the Webley Air Rifle and Air Pistol catalogue. This is available on application to your nearest dealer or agent or by writing direct to Webley and Scott enclosing 20p (or equivalent amount if overseas) to cover cost and postage of catalogue.
Webley
Webley & Scott. Old skills – new ideas – great guns.
WEBLEY & SCOTT LIMITED
Park Lane, Handsworth, Birmingham B21 8LU
Telephone: 021-553 3952/6

Front of Webley Junior Mark II brochure.

Instructions for the use and maintenance of the Webley Junior Mark II Air Pistol

To cock and load the Pistol

Hold the grip of the Pistol in the right hand and with the right thumb depress the chequered pad of the barrel stirrup to release the barrel, as illustrated. Lift the barrel clear of the stirrup with the left hand, then turn the hand over so that the back of the hand is towards the body, grip the barrel firmly and rotate until the sear is heard and felt to engage.

N.B. *Never* allow the barrel to spring back before the sear is engaged *nor* pull the trigger until the barrel is returned to its firing position.

Insert a pellet into the breech end of the barrel until flush with the end. Close the barrel and squeeze down until the stirrup clicks into engagement and is seen to overlap the end of the barrel.

Caution

Never fire the Pistol unless the stirrup is properly engaged or without a pellet in barrel, otherwise damage may occur.

Always remove an unused pellet before putting the Pistol away.

Lubrication

From time to time apply a few spots of Webley oil or cleaner to:

Stirrup fulcrum pin.
Return plunger housing.
Trigger and sear fulcrum pins.
Barrel pivot pin.
Link pivot.
Link swivel.
Piston skirt via slot in body.
Piston seal via barrel joint washer.

For optimum accuracy and power, it is desirable to use Webley special pellets – do not be put off with a substitute.

Specification

Calibre	·177 (4·5)
Weight	$23\frac{1}{4}$ oz (660 gms)
Length overall	8 in (203·2 mm)
Length of barrel	$6\frac{1}{8}$ in (155·5 mm)
Smooth bore	
Rear sight adjustable laterally	
Velocity	290 f.p.s. (88·5 m.p.s.)

Instructions for replacement of component parts

This Air Pistol is dismantled from the MUZZLE end.

When found necessary to change any internal component, first see that the Pistol is fired, i.e. not cocked. Remove axis screw from front end, pull barrel back – towards breech end – when the link on top of air chamber can be withdrawn. With the aid of the lug at the muzzle end of the barrel unscrew the cap at the front of the Pistol, remove spring guide and main spring, press trigger back and the piston may then be withdrawn. When reassembling, see that the screwed cap at the front end of the body is screwed in so as to allow the axis pin hole to come in line with the two holes in the body. Should the pistol, after long service, lose velocity or penetration, it may be due to lack of lubrication of the piston, weakening of the spring or the wearing of the barrel joint washer. Both the spring and joint washer can be easily replaced.

A complete Repair Service is available for all Webley products.

PART LIST FOR Mk II JUNIOR AIR PISTOL

PART No.	DESCRIPTION OF PART	No. OFF
J2	BARREL ASSEMBLY	1
J3	PISTON	1
J6	TRIGGER	1
J7	SEAR	1
J8	LONG LINK PIN	1
J9	LONG LINK	1
J10	SMALL LINK PIN	1
J11	SMALL LINK	1
J12	MAINSPRING	1
J13	CUP WASHER	1
J14	INSIDE WASHER	1
J16	PISTON WASHER SCREW	1
J18A	STOCK SCREW	2
J19	JOINT SCREW	1
J20	REAR SIGHT	1
J21	SEAR AND TRIGGER PIN	2
J24	SEAR SPRING	1
J26A	STOCK SIDE R.H.	1
J27A	STOCK SIDE L.H.	1
J29	SIGHT SCREW	1
J29A	SIGHT SCREW WASHER	1
S32	BARREL CATCH SPRING	1
S33	BARREL CATCH SPRING PLUNGER	1
J1011	SPRING GUIDE NOT SOLD AS A SEPARATE COMPONENT	1
1367	BARREL JOINT WASHER	1
1440	BARREL CATCH	1
1479	BODY WITH SPRING GUIDE J1011	1
1491	BARREL CATCH JOINT SCREW	1
1571	PASSAGE SCREW	1

Webley Junior Mark II Parts List and details.

Webley Junior Mk. II.

Model: **"JUNIOR MK. II"**

Maker: **Webley & Scott**

Date: Production 1973 - 1977, of Mark II model.

Valuation: £20 - £70. Boxed, as high as £90.

Details: Alloy frame model with transfer stick-on name label. Label reads "WEBLEY & SCOTT LTD — JUNIOR MK. II — MADE IN ENGLAND". Batch number stamped at front of airpistol. Number of above 196. Rifled barrel, although I have seen one with smoothbore, but this may have been a replacement from an earlier model Junior. A powerful airpistol for its size. Two pin trigger action. Adjustable rear sight. Advertised accuracy as being able to group pellets within a one inch circle at thirty feet from a fixed rest. Advertised weight 23¼ ozs. Batch numbers seen for the Junior Mk. II run from 70 to 994. Inspection marks usually behind the trigger guard and I have seen 1, 7, L, and D. The batch number is also stamped under the left hand grip. Most of the barrels by now are rifled, although smoothbore have been seen.

Webley Mk. II (target model) No. 37411.

Model: **MARK II (Target Model)**

Maker: **Webley & Scott Ltd.**

Date: 1925 - 1930. The serial numbers were included in the series for the Mark I airpistol and were numbered concurrently so actual number of Mk. II's manufactured is not known.

Valuation: £75 - £150

Details: All metal with 7 inch barrel. Fully adjustable rear sight, similar to the later post-war airpistols. Safety catch on L.H.S. of frame. Very deep dark brown chequered grips with "W&S" set on the upper edge. Trigger adjustment but with no locking screw. Serial number of above 24232 appears above the left hand grip and the last three digits appear at the front near the barrel pivot pin. Initials "JJ" are stamped on the underside of the frame near the trigger guard. L.H.S. of air chamber stamped "WEBLEY & SCOTT LTD BIRMINGHAM & LONDON" with the following patents:

"GREAT BRITAIN PATENT No. 219872
BELGIUM BREVET No. 316878
FRANCE BREVETTE No. 578498 S.G.D.G.
U.S.A. PATENTED U.S.A. 7-7-25
CANADA PATENT 1925"

Whilst on the other side appears "WEBLEY AIR PISTOL MARK II (TARGET MODEL)" followed by "MADE IN ENGLAND" then the following patent marks:

"JAPAN PATENT No. 9186/24
SWITZERLAND PATENT No. +112976
AUSTRALIA PATENTED 21 - 12 - 23
SPAIN PATENT No. 89433
ITALY BREVETTATO No. 229158
GERMANY D.R.P. No. 414833

Air pistol strips from the front only. There is no rear air chamber plug. The piston should have two phosphor-bronze piston rings. The Mk. II model was finally replaced by the Senior around 1930. The above has a two piece barrel pivot screw. For further details see *"Guns Review",* June, 1978, also *"Airgun World",* March, 1979.

Earlier examples differ slightly in that the L.H.S. of the action is stamped "WEBLEY AIR PISTOL MARK II (TARGET MODEL) followed by "WEBLEY & SCOTT Ltd., BIRMINGHAM & LONDON", whilst on the other side of the action only one patent is mentioned, "BRITISH PATENT 219872". The trigger adjuster screw has no locking screw as on later models. One such example seen with serial number 14154 was scratched with the name "E. Egan, Storm, 1925".

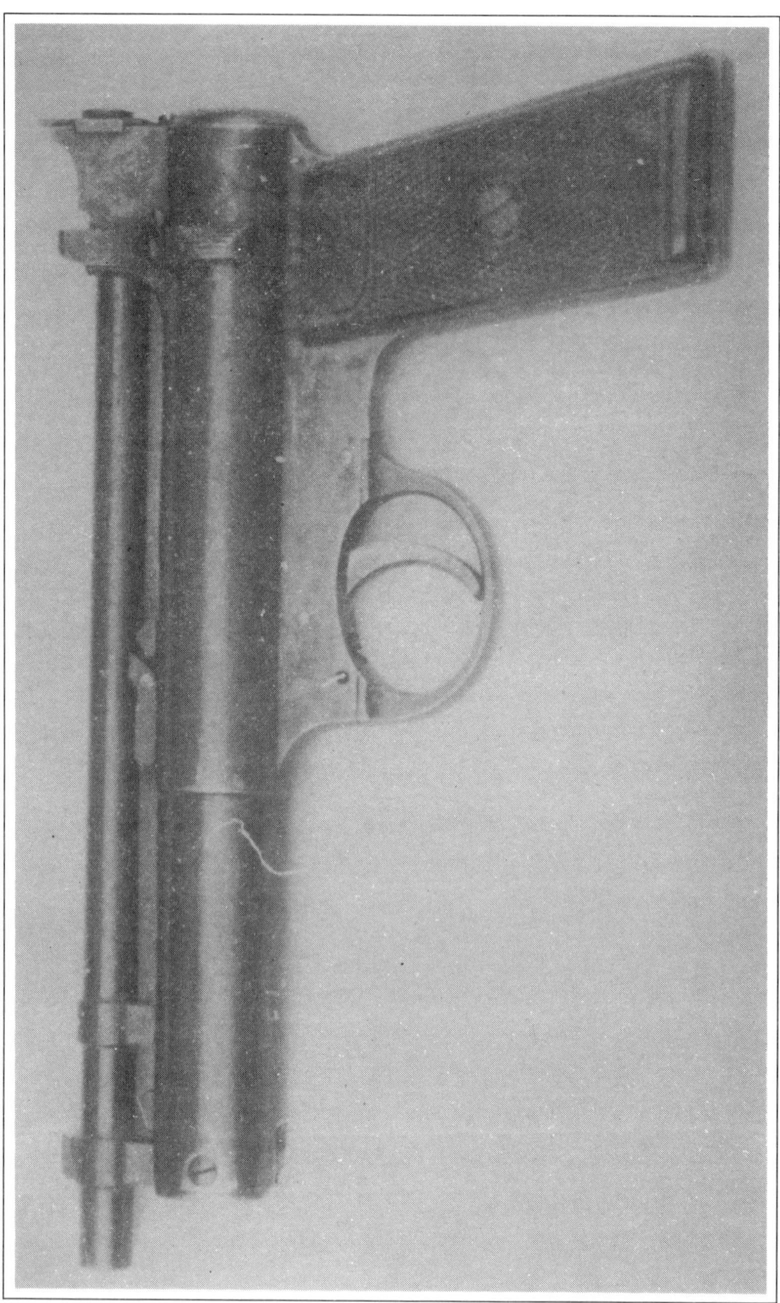

Pre-war straight grip Webley Senior.

"SENIOR" COMPONENT PARTS

"Webley" No. 1 Oil for use on Piston Washers of MK1 and Junior Pistols, Price **1/-**

"Webley" No. 2 Oil for use on Piston Rings of Senior Pistol, Price **1/-**

New type Components referred to at S7a, S23a, and S24a apply to Pistols of Serial No. 7,000 and upwards.

2

Straight Grip "Senior" Parts List.

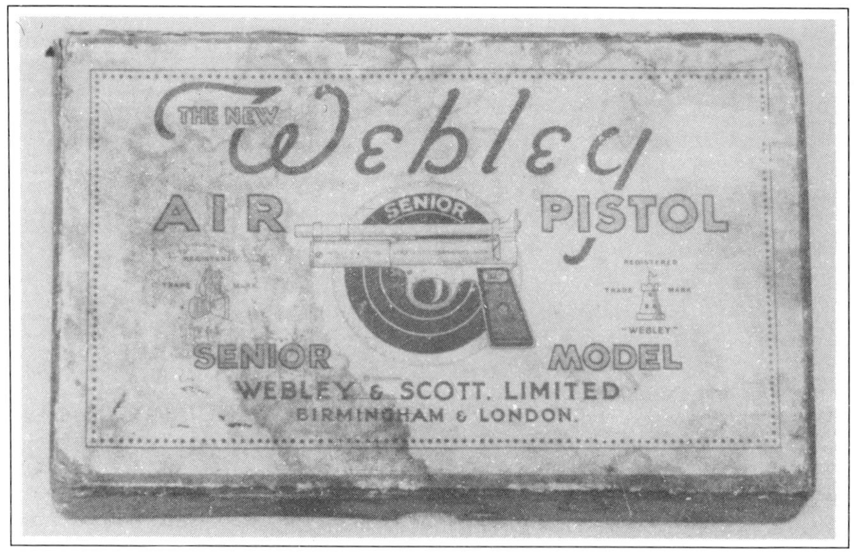

Box lid for pre-war straight grip Webley Senior.

Model: **SENIOR FIRST MODEL with straight grips**

Maker: **Webley & Scott Ltd.,**
Weaman Street, Birmingham.
(Address at time of manufacture).

Date: 1930 to 1935

Valuation: £75 - £150

Details: The improved model to take the place of the Mk. II Target airpistol. Advertised weight 33 ozs. Straight grips with "W & S" cast at top. No trigger adjustment. L.H.S. of body stamped "THE WEBLEY SENIOR MADE IN ENGLAND" followed by the patents granted:

GREAT BRITAIN PATENT No. 219872
BELGIUM BREVET No. 316878
FRANCE BREVETE No. 578498 S.G.D.G.
U.S.A. PATENTED U.S.A. 7-7-25
CANADA PATENTED 1925

The serial number is stamped above the L.H. grip and always has the prefix letter "S". The R.H.S. of the body is stamped "WEBLEY & SCOTT LTD., BIRMINGHAM" followed by the following patents:

JAPAN PATENT No. 9186/24
SWITZERLAND PATENT No. + 112976
AUSTRALIA PATENTED 21-12-23

SPAIN PATENT No. 89433
ITALY BREVETTATO No. 229158
GERMANY D.R.P. No. 414833

The last three digits of the serial number appear stamped on the front air chamber plug. Rifled barrel is seven inches long and overhangs at the end. Rearsight fully adjustable for windage and elevation. The double linked cocking lever bears the patent number 326703. The piston was fitted with a phosphor-bronze ring. The patent 219872 was completed in 1924 and covered the use of the barrel mounted above the air chamber and used to cock the action. For further details of this patent, see *"Guns Review",* December, 1979.

The patent 326703 dated 1930 dealt with the double linked cocking lever as an aid in adding extra leverage to the barrel and making cocking easier to achieve. See *"Guns Review",* March, 1980. The above was available nickel plated for an extra charge of 5/-. It was also available in smoothbore and I have seen one such barrel that extended beyond the barrel pivot for about half an inch. Lowest number seen is S2426 to highest seen, S5602.

It would appear that the serial numbers for the straight grip Senior run from 1 to 7,000 only as at this number parts S7 (trigger guard), S23 and S24 (grips) underwent a change and became the slant grip model.

From the lid illustration shown on page 214, you will notice that the Senior shown has a trigger system with adjustment as is fitted to the Mark I and Mark II Target Models. The same system was also first fitted to the Senior and it was only after the first thousand or so that the more usual Senior vertical sear system was fitted. On serial number S1191, all the body stampings were the same as for the rest of the straight grip Seniors, but the trigger action was of the adjustable type. This variety is extremely rare. The straight grip with the Mark I trigger action was advertised right up to 1935 and cost 45/- as opposed to the Mark I, which cost 30/-, whilst the humble junior came third at 20/-.

The first models of the straight grip Senior were fitted with the Mark I trigger action and these are very rare. Only a very small number were produced before the more reliable Senior action came into being with the vertical sliding sear arrangement.

Webley pre-war slant grip Senior.

Model: **SENIOR**

Maker: **Webley & Scott Ltd.,**
Birmingham, England.

Date: From 1935 to the outbreak of W.W.2.

Valuation: £50 - £100

Details: The "Slant Grip Senior". Serial number S15864 stamped just above the trigger. The above also has "P" stamped on the L.H.S. near the serial number. ·22 rifled barrel with no serrations for gripping. Cocking lever double jointed with the following stamping: "PATENT No. 326703". Stamped on L.H.S. of body "OIL HERE" with arrow between the two words, also appears "THE WEBLEY "SENIOR" — MADE IN ENGLAND". Rear air chamber plug stamped "NOT TO BE REMOVED" and has been pegged. R.H.S. of body stamped "WEBLEY & SCOTT LTD. BIRMINGHAM" and the following patent details:

"GREAT BRITAIN PATENT No. 219872"
"U.S.A. PATENTED 7-7-25"
"CANADA PATENT 1925"

Last three digits of serial number stamped on front chamber plug. The above model was introduced to take the place of the straight gripped Senior. All pre-war Seniors had a "S" prefix letter to their serial numbers. The grips are brown, chequered, but without the "WEBLEY" name. Advertised weight 33 ozs. It was recommended to use Webley Oil No. 2, as the Senior was fitted with "special metal rings". The straight model was advertised in 1935 and I have seen the above model advertised in 1939, so I would assume the introduction to lie between the two dates. Advertised velocities: ·177 - 416 f.p.s., ·22 - 330 f.p.s. Period of production was very short, so it could become a desirable collectors item.

In the January, 1939 *Webley Handbook,* the Senior was offered with the alternative finish of either nickel or chrome. They also advertised a canvas carrying case for airpistols. Serial numbers for the slant grip pre-war Senior start from 7,000, the highest number seen being S17578. The slant gripped Senior is more common than the straight gripped model. Early models had the rear air chamber plug held in place by a grub screw, but between numbers S13798 and S15691, it became pegged.

Small letters were stamped on the L.H.S. of the frame, these being S, P, J and C, in order of appearance. On nearly all seen, there is a "J" inside a triangle stamped under the L.H. grip, except on the highest number seen, and this bears an "R" inside a triangle. Early models also could be stripped from both ends of the air chamber until the end plug was pegged.

Webley Senior airpistol.

Webley Senior box lid.

Later style of box lid for Webley "Senior".
This lid top was also used for the Premier when it first appeared.

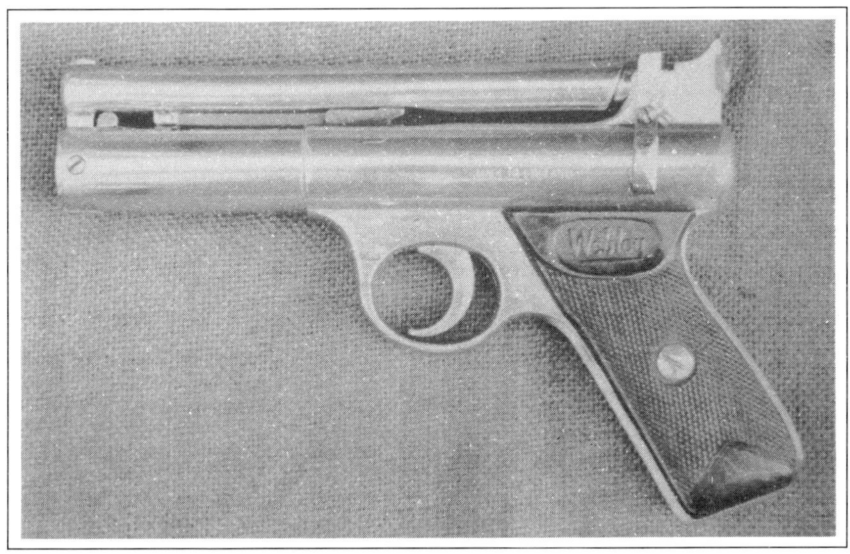

Nickel plated Webley "Senior", number 2202.

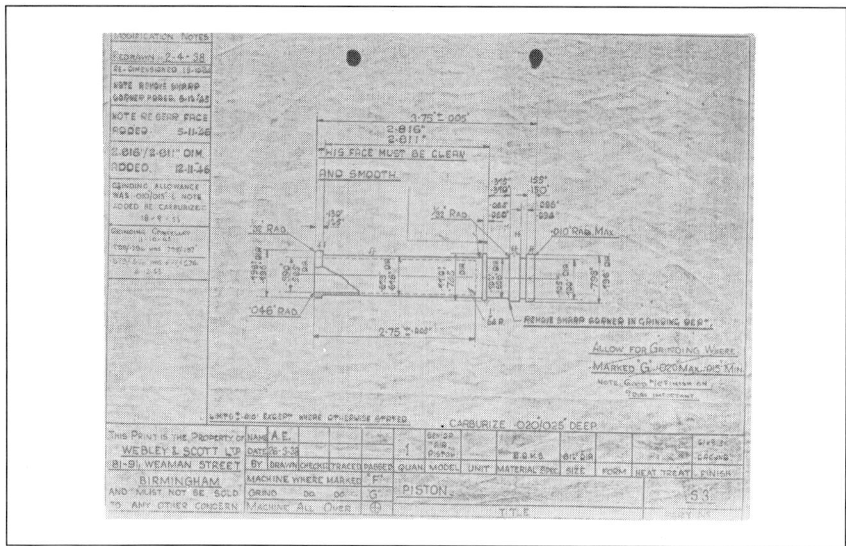

Diagram of "Senior" piston.

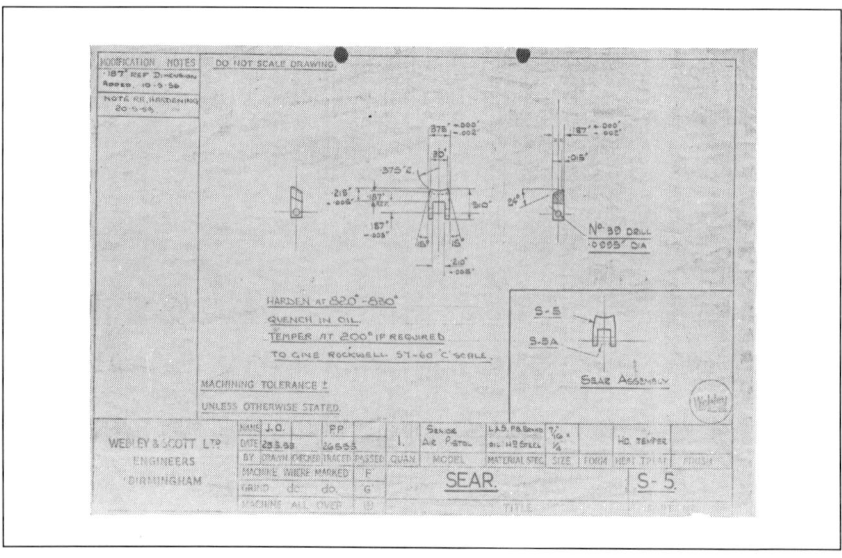

Diagram of "Senior" sear.

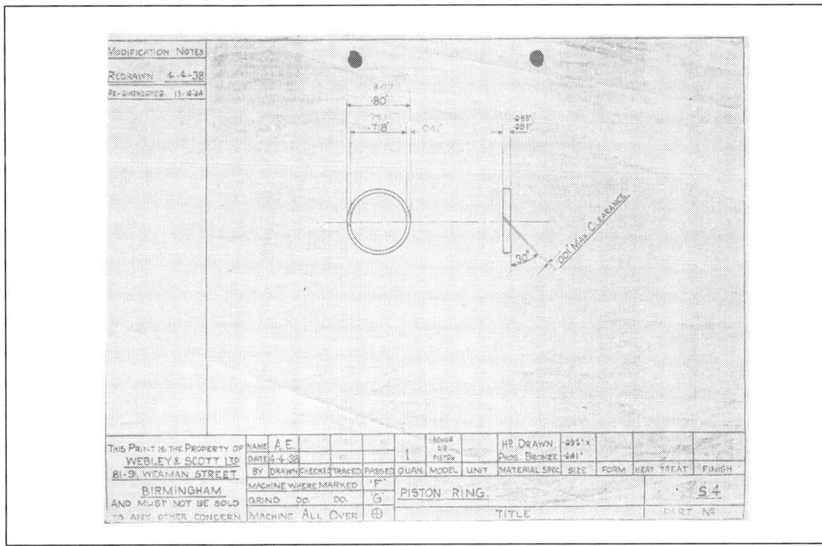

Diagram of "Senior" piston ring.

Model: **"SENIOR"**

Maker: **Webley & Scott Ltd.**

Date: 1946 to 1964

Valuation: £40 - £90

Details: All metal with double linkage for easier barrel cocking. Gives 40% extra leverage than Mark I. Brown grips. On the side of the air cylinder is marked "THE WEBLEY "SENIOR" MADE IN ENGLAND", and on the other side "WEBLEY & SCOTT LTD. BIRMINGHAM 4". Air pistols marked "Birmingham 4" were made between 1946 and 1958, whilst those with just "Birmingham" were made after. This was due to a move of place of manufacture. Marked "WEBLEY PATENTS" at barrel end of air cylinder and has a batch number stamped at the front of the airpistol.

1960's catalogue gave the following muzzle velocities in feet per second: ·177 - 360, and for ·22 - 330, these for 20 ft. range. Advertised as weighing 33 ozs., overall length 8½ inches and having a 6½ inch barrel with machine cut rifling. Piston was fitted with metal ring similar to car piston as opposed to leather washer as fitted to "Junior" and Mark I airpistols. The Senior also had a strengthened barrel. Webley's sold two types of lubricating oil for their airguns: Type 1 for leather washers, and Type 2 for the Senior with its piston ring. Up until 1958, they were offered with a nickel plated finish for an extra 5/-. The later style box lid was used for the Premier, just the name of the airpistol was changed, this of course showed a "three pin Premier" on the box lid.

Senior sears are very robust and should last the life of the airpistol, but occasionally it happens that the sear appears to fail and the action will not cock. Fear not, for it may not be the sear at fault. When the barrel has been over-exerted in cocking the action, the links and pins will work loose and stretch so that the full length of travel for the cocking slider cannot be made as the front of the barrel support arm will rest against the lower front of the support groove in the front of the air chamber

This can be corrected by the following method. First place the pin support brackets in a vice, complete with cocking arms, and close vice so that this tightens up the linkages, next place the cocking arm in a vice and gently hammer one end so that there is a slight concave dish in its length as you look at it when fitted in place. In other words, its two ends go up as the centre goes down. This method works. The only alternative is to replace all the cocking linkage and pins. If the above is done carefully it will not be noticeable, unless you have read the above and can spot this tightening on the next Senior you buy! Early Seniors had no warning about removal on the rear air chamber plug. For Seniors made from 1946 to 1958, the lowest batch number seen is 127, going up to 2329, and inspection marks stamped behind the trigger guard being D, a dot, B, F and R — the D being very common. Occasionally other numbers appear under the L.H. grip, but they do not appear to be a date stamp.

Batch numbers for 1958 to 1964 appear to run from 265 to the highest seen, 1592. Inspection marks seen are D, R, and F — again D being very common. Maybe D worked harder! One Senior seen had SA132 stamped on the side of the frame. What does "SA" stand for? The author has been told "State Armoury", South Africa, Saudi Arabia, and any other combination of SA. Other numbers beside the batch number appear under the L.H. grip. The batch number is also stamped on the barrel catch and will of course match that stamped on the front chamber plug. A very interesting substitute for the mounting pins on the trigger guard of one Senior seen were matches.

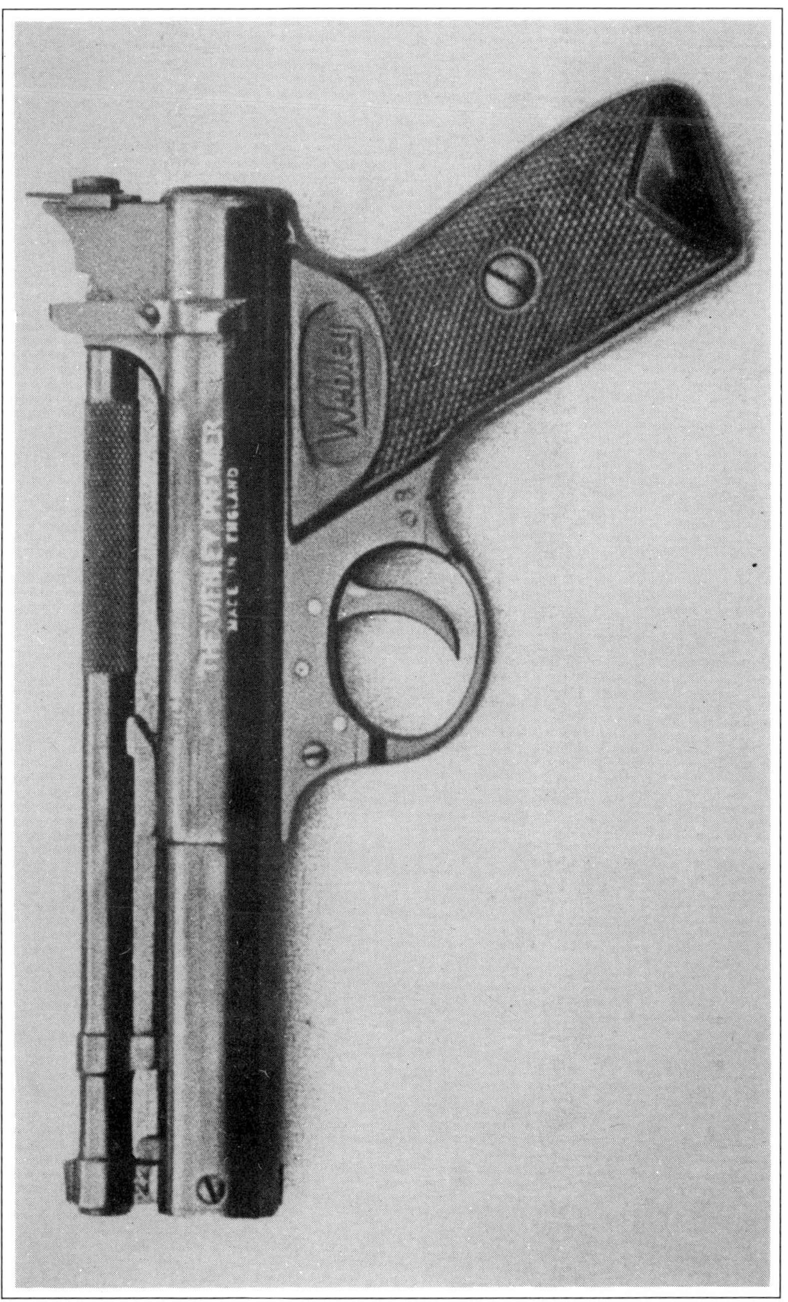

"B" series Premier

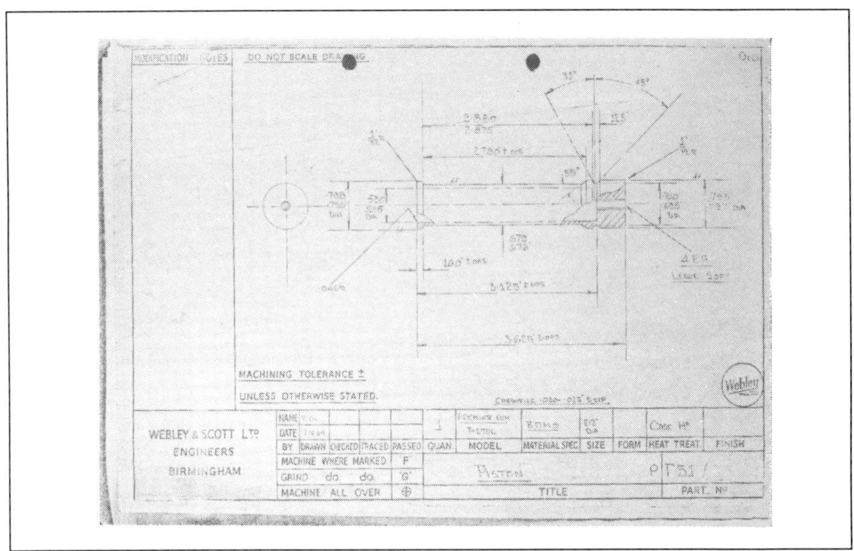

Diagram of the Premier's piston.

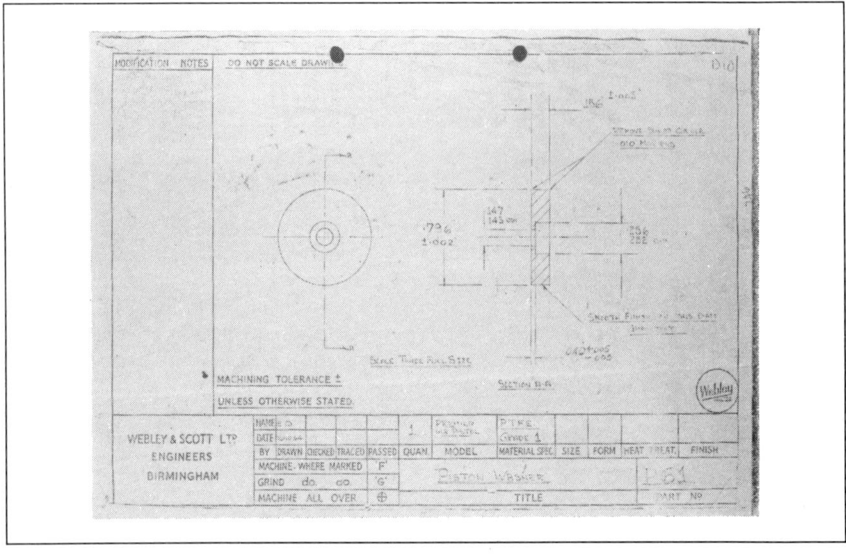

Diagram of the Premier's piston washer.

Model:	**PREMIER "B" SERIES**
Maker:	**Webley & Scott**
Date:	Production began in 1964 and ended in 1977 (I assume the date of the model shown on page 223 to be between 1966 and 1970.
Valuation:	£50 - £90

Details: The first series of Webley Premiers had four pin trigger actions. A fifth pin was added when series "D" was introduced, this fifth pin acted as a trigger stop. Brown grips, all metal and blued. Batch number stamped on front of air chamber near barrel pivot. The Premier merged the Mk. I trigger adjustment and the Senior double barrel cocking linkage, stirrup barrel catch, and a fully adjustable rear sight. Air chamber has "THE WEBLEY PREMIER — MADE IN ENGLAND" stamped on the side. The R.H.S. of the air chamber is stamped "WEBLEY & SCOTT LTD — BIRMINGHAM".

As from January 1965, a code letter was stamped on the L.H.S. of the body as above and indentified minor differences in production as follows:

Prior to, and including "A" were the first model.

Code "B" had two variations of piston washer combinations, first variation had a distance piece P57 whilst the second variation had a washer P58 and a chamfer on the front face.

Code "C" had the variations as for "B" plus parts numbered sear, P1002; trigger, P1001; trigger adjustment screw P56/2; piston P60; and piston washer P61.

Code "D" saw the introduction of the fifth pin and so ended the production of the "Four-pin trigger action Premiers". The "D" series had the variations of the previous series, plus trigger stop pin M22; barrel joint washer P1023 (this change eliminating the need for toll M36), also a new mainspring P1032, that could be used in the Senior and Mk. I airpistols, as well as previous models of the Premier.

Further to the above, the first "A" series Premier was fitted with a leather washer assembly, piston part number P51 fitted with outer washer M10, inner washer M11 and centre screw M21 — interesting to note that these are Mark I airpistol parts. Tool M36 was a round bar with a projection in the front for tapping in the leather breech washers. With the introduction of rubber breech washers with more elasticity, it was found that tool M36 was no longer necessary. Four pin Premiers are quite rare, and I have only seen five examples with batch numbers from 126 to 2262. Inspection letters seen being R, and F. Other numbers appear stamped under the L.H. grip, but these appear to bear no relationship to either batch number nor date of manufacture:

Batch No.	*No. under grip*	
126	4	5
707	9	5
2262	1	6

"D" series Webley Premier.

D series Premier with extended barrel.

Webley Premier "E" series.

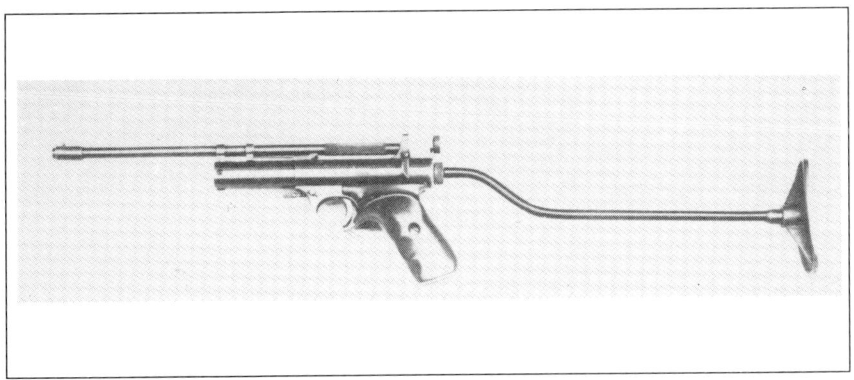

Customised Webley Premier, No. 571.

Model: **"PREMIER" Series "D" and "E", and even "F", which either appears all metal blued, or lacquered.**

Maker: **Webley & Scott**

Date: 1964 - 1977.

Valuation: £50 - £90.

Details: The model on page 226 is all metal with brown grips. "D" prefix stamped on trigger frame. Early model, so assume around 1966/67. Trigger adjustment and double linkage to cocking lever. Interchangeable barrels ·22/·177. Five pin trigger action. Stamped on side "THE WEBLEY PREMIER" "MADE IN ENGLAND" and on the other side of air chamber "WEBLEY & SCOTT LTD. BIRMINGHAM". Calibre of barrel is stamped on the barrel mount where it pivots at the front. Have also seen Webley Premiers with "E" stamped on the trigger action and would assume that this denotes the "E" Series. The identification stampings appear to be the same. "E" series were also fitted with brown grips.

Although the lacquered Premier started with the "E" Series, I have seen a blued Premier stamped "F" on the action and behind the trigger guard, this was also date stamped under the grip "1 73". Could be some over-lap in production.

D SERIES: Batch numbers seen from 1218 to 3978, with the following numbers stamped under the left hand grip:

Batch No.	*No. under grip*	
1218	5	7
1781	5	8
3978	12	7

E SERIES: Batch numbers seen from 40 to 1164. In this series I have not seen any inspection stamps behind the trigger guard. Batch and grip numbers seen:

Batch No.	*No. under grip*	
40	7	0
972	3	72 (could be date stamp)
1010	10	9
1164	10	9

F SERIES: Blued finish only. Lacquer finish is dealt elsewhere. I have only seen two of this type, both had "L" inspection stamp behind the trigger guard. Numbers seen as follows:

Batch No.	*No. under grip*	
337	8	72
446	10	72 These could be the start of date stamping, month followed by year.

The funny thing about these batch numbers is that up to date, I have never found an obvious duplicate airpistol bearing the same batch number as one would expect.

Smoothbore barrels for the Premier will have an "S" stamped on the front face of the barrel support arm and is plainly visible when viewing the airpistol from the front.

Should you find an airpistol that does not cock, no matter what, and you've checked all the obvious causes, try looking at the front chamber fulcrum over which the long cocking link rides — if this is heavily grooved, then the action will not cock as the cocking slider cannot travel any further back. The only remedy is to either rebuild up the fulcrum with weld, or melt out the braise and refit another, or find a secondhand chamber and swop the barrel and action.

COMPONENT PARTS OF MARK I, SENIOR AND PREMIER WEBLEY AIR PISTOLS

Description	No. in Illustration Premier	Senior	Mark I
Barrel Complete	S2-S26-S27 S28-1006-S37	S2-S25-S26 S27-1006-S37	M2-M25-M26 M27a-1006
Barrel	S2	S2	M2
Small Link	S26	S26	M26
Intermediate Link	S27	S27	Not required
Long Link	P55	S25	M25
Long Link Pin	1006	1006	1006
Small Link Pin	1006	1006	M27a
Barrel Link Spring	S37	S37	Not required
Barrel Joint Washer	1023	1023	1023
Barrel Joint Screw	S21	S21	S21
Screw Securing Joint Screw	S22	S22	S22
Rear Sight (Vertical)	S17	S17	M19
Rear Sight (Horizontal)	S18	S18	Not required
Sight Screw	S15	S15	S15
Sight Screw Washer	S15a	S15a	S15a
Barrel Catch	1005	1005	Not required
Barrel Catch Spring	S32	S32	Not required
Barrel Catch Spring Plunger	S33	S33	Not required
Barrel Catch Joint Screw	S34	S34	Not required
Barrel Catch Stop Screw	Not required	S35	Not required
Top Catch	Not required	Not required	M28
Top Catch Spring	Not required	Not required	M29
Top Catch Pin	Not required	Not required	M29a
Sear	1002	S5	1002
Sear Peg	Not required	S5a	Not required
Sear Spring	M16	Not required	M16
Trigger	1001	S6	1001
Trigger Spring	M18	S16	M18
Trigger Adjusting Screw	P56	Not required	P56
Screw Securing Trigger Adjusting Screw	M32	Not required	M32
Sear Trigger and Guard Pin	M22	M22	M22
Trigger Guard	S7	S7	S7
Mainspring	M.7	S8	M7
Spring Guide	S9	S9	M8
Stock Side Left	S24a	S24a	M24c
Stock Side Right	S23a	S23a	M24b
Stock Screw	S14	S14	S14
Stock Pin	S20	S20	S20
Piston *See Note* 2 (P60 illus.)	P51	S3	M3
Piston Inside Washer	P61	Not required	M11
Piston Outer Washer	Not required	Not required	M10
Piston Screw	P59	Not required	M21
Piston Ring	Not required	S4	Not required

Note 1 S26-S27-1006. Due to change in pattern, when ordering these components for pre-war senior air pistols it is necessary to purchase as an assembly.

Note 2 **Code Letter Identification.**
As from January 1965 the code letter should be quoted on all orders for "Premier" air pistol parts. The code letter is stamped on the pistol body (left hand side to the rear of the trigger guard).

For Pistols marked Code Letter 'A'
AS LIST ABOVE

For Pistols marked Code Letter 'B' refer to Parts List.
Some early production models incorporated two variations of piston washer combinations identified as follows:

1. Piston P51B, Screw P59, Washer P61 and Distance Piece P57. Identified by distance piece.
2. Piston P51B, Screw P59, Washer P58 identified by chamfer on front face.

For Pistols marked Code Letter 'C'
Changes as for code letter 'B' plus Sear P1002, Trigger P1001, Trigger Adj. Screw P56/2, Piston P60, Piston Washer P61.

Special attention is drawn to the importance of purchasing Webley Mainsprings in the event of replacements becoming necessary.

Apply to your nearest Dealer for Prices and Supplies of Webley Pellets, Darts and the new Webley Shooting Gallery.

For Pistols marked Code Letter 'D'
Changes as for code letters 'B' & 'C' plus Trigger Stop Pin M22. The number of Pins M22 in this code is now five.
Joint Washer P1023, Eliminating Tool M36, New Mainspring P1032.
Standard for all Premier, Senior and Mark 1 Air Pistols.

Note 3 Retail Prices may be obtained on application to your nearest Webley Stockist and all spares should be ordered through him.

Note 4 All Webley Air Pistols should be dismantled from the MUZZLE end. On no account attempt to remove the BREECH SCREW.

USE WEBLEY OIL, WEBLEY PELLETS AND ACCESSORIES FOR BEST RESULTS.

WEBLEY & SCOTT LTD.
(Incorporating W. W. GREENER Ltd.)
PARK LANE · HANDSWORTH · BIRMINGHAM B21 8LU
A Complete repair service is available for all Webley products

C48/69 **PASTE ON CARD AND KEEP FOR REFERENCE**

Component Parts of Mark I, Senior and Premier Webley airpistols.

Webley "Premier" — all metal — lacquered finish.

Model: **PREMIER "E" Series, with lacquered finish.**

Maker: **Webley & Scott**

Date: Production 1964 - 1977. Assume the above model to be around 1973 - 1974.

Valuation: £50 - £90

Details: Five pin trigger action, all metal, but has a black lacquer finish on frame, barrel is still blued. This airpistol has the same trade stamps as previous models of the Premier. The batch number is stamped in front, near the barrel pivot. The lacquer finish could be the start of trying to cut production costs. The above has a small "F" stamped on the underside of the trigger guard where it joins the body of the airpistol.

I have seen most of the above with black grips although one or two have been seen with brown grips. Towards the end of this series the body stampings on the R.H.S. were dropped and only "THE WEBLEY PREMIER MADE IN ENGLAND" appeared stamped on the L.H.S. Lacquer finish "E" Series batch numbers seen from 2 up to 940. Inspection marks behind trigger guard, O, F, D AND H although F is very common. Some have been seen with nothing stamped behind the guard. There now appears to be a date stamp under the L.H. grip and I have seen the following:

Batch No.	*Date Stamp*	*Batch No.*	*Date Stamp*
2	8 73	269	11 73
9	1 74	521	6 73
38	Nothing under grip.	525	9 73
44	10 73	539	9 73
122	6 73	778	12 0 (odd one out)
134	11 73	890	3 73
186	5 73	940	9 9 (another odd number)
193	1 74		

From the above, all the lacquered Series E Premiers were produced in 1973 and very early 1974.

Webley 'Premier'.

Model: **PREMIER. Series "E", lacquered.**

Maker: **Webley & Scott Ltd.,**
Birmingham.

Date: Premiers made between 1964 and 1977. The above model appeared prior to the introduction of the alloy Premier Mk. II so assume around 1974 - 1975.

Valuation: £40 - £80

Details: All metal frame, but has a factory black lacquer finish. Black plastic grips. On the R.H.S. of the air chamber is a recess which contains a black and silver name label bearing the following: "WEBLEY & SCOTT LTD. — WEBLEY PREMIER — MADE IN ENGLAND". Batch number stamped at front near the barrel pivot pin, also under the LH grip. Also has the letter "E" stamped into the frame. Could this be the "E" series? Still has the five pin trigger action but the two trigger guard pins have been lacquered over and it appears that the trigger and sear are added after the lacquering. The batch number is also stamped on the large fixing lug of the trigger guard. This lug enters the body in front of the trigger. Batch numbers seen run from 14 to 966 with the following inspection marks behind the trigger guard, 2, o, F, 3, date stamps appear under the L.H. grip as follows:

Batch No.	*Grip Stamp*		*Batch No.*	*Grip Stamp*	
14	7	75	852	6	75
41	5	75	891	2	75
674	9	74	966	6	75
730	3	74			

All the above have the Series letter "E" stamped on the side of the frame.

Webley Premier Mark II

When you're serious about shooting, this is the air pistol to choose.

The Webley Premier II is the finest standard weapon of its kind on the market. It is certainly unrivalled value for money. The Premier II is powerful—you can be certain of a clean kill against vermin. It upholds the Webley tradition for accuracy* and for robust construction. Yet this is no cumbersome heavyweight. The Premier II weighs a mere 31 oz. and expertly balanced, is a positive pleasure to handle.

You have the choice of ·177 calibre for target shooting or ·22 calibre for field work. Both feature an adjustable rearsight and trigger pull, a rifled barrel for added accuracy—plus an improved barrel catch for positive lock.

Worthy companion of the famous Webley service revolvers, the Webley Premier II is the perfect all-rounder for all those who relish friendly competition.

Webley supplement your enjoyment with a full range of shooting accessories. For example, target cards and holders, darts, specially manufactured pellets to match barrel tolerances, Webley gun oil and handsome Webley-Custom pistol cases.

SPECIFICATION

Calibre	·177 (4·5) or ·22 (5·5)
Weight	31 oz. (4·27 kg)
Length Overall	8[illegible]″ (21·1 cm)
Length of Barrel	6[illegible]″ (16·7 cm)
Velocity ·177	350 fps (107 M/sec)
·22	310 fps (94·5 M/sec)

Webley & Scott. Old skills—new ideas—great guns

WEBLEY & SCOTT LIMITED

Park Lane, Handsworth, Birmingham B21 8LU
Telephone: 021-553 3952/6

Front of information leaflet for Webley Premier Mark II

Side by Side and Over and Under Shotguns
Revolvers
Single Barrel Shotguns
Air Rifles and Air Pistols
Seat Sticks
Sports Starting Pistols

Target Launchers
Decoys
Blanks, Pellets and Cartridges
Gun, Rifle, Pistol Cases and Covers
Telescopic Sights
Cleaning Equipment

WEBLEY & SCOTT LIMITED
Park Lane, Handsworth
Birmingham B21 8LU
Telephone: 021-553 3952

Shoot with safety

Instructions for the use and maintenance of the Webley Premier Mark II Air Pistol

To cock and load the Pistol

Hold the butt of the Pistol in the right hand, press the barrel catch lever forward with the right thumb to release the barrel, then grasp the barrel in the left hand near the breech (with the back of the hand towards Pistol body – see illustration) and pull barrel away from Pistol rotating it as far as it will go until it becomes parallel with the body, the sear will then engage and is indicated by a slight click. Care must be taken to retain a firm hold of the barrel, do not touch the trigger until the sear is fully engaged otherwise the barrel will fly back and possibly cause damage or injury. Insert a pellet into the breech end of the barrel so that it is flush with the mouth of the barrel then close the barrel and squeeze down until the barrel catch clicks into engagement and is seen to overlap the end of the barrel.

Caution

Never fire the Pistol unless the barrel catch is properly engaged or without a pellet in the barrel otherwise damage may occur to the mechanism. Always remove an unused pellet before putting the Pistol away.

Adjustable Backsight

If elevation or direction does not suit range or user it can be adjusted vertically or laterally. Move the sights the way you desire the shot to go by loosening and retightening the sight screw.

Trigger Adjustment

To adjust trigger pull weight, unscrew the keeper screw on left hand side of trigger guard. Adjust the adjusting screw at the front of the trigger guard to the trigger pull weight required. Tighten keeper screw.

Caution

Before firing ensure keeper screw has been tightened, great care must be taken in adjusting below 4 lbs pull off weight if instantaneous discharge is to be avoided.

Lubrication

From time to time apply a few spots of Webley oil or cleaner to:
Barrel catch screw.
Barrel catch spring plunger.
Sear and trigger pins.
Barrel joint screw.
Link fulcrum.
Link pins and swivels.
Piston, via body slot.
For optimum accuracy and power, it is desirable to use Webley special pellets – do not be put off with a substitute.

Specification

Calibre	·177 (4·5) or ·22 (5·5)
Weight	31 oz. (4·27 kg)
Length overall	8 5/16 in (21·1 cm)
Length of barrel	6 19/32 in (16·7 cm)
Velocity ·177	380 fps (107 M/sec)
·22	310 fps (94·5 M/sec)

Instructions for replacement of component parts

The Air Pistol is dismantled from the MUZZLE end.

When found necessary to change any internal components, see that the Pistol is fired, i.e. not cocked. Remove screw securing joint screw from left hand side of body, then remove barrel joint screw from right hand side. Remove barrel from spring guide slot and pull backwards towards breech and when the link on top of air chamber can be withdrawn. With the aid of the lug at muzzle end of the barrel unscrew the spring guide from front of Pistol and remove mainspring. With the trigger pressed back the Piston may now be withdrawn. To renew the piston washer, lever off old washer with a small screwdriver. Spring new washer (small diameter hole first) over the flanged boss on piston front, ensuring that it is securely located behind the flange before re-assembling piston into body. The trigger must again be held back. When re-assembling ensure that the spring guide is screwed in so as to allow the barrel joint screw hole to come into line with the two holes in the body. Should the Pistol, after long service, lose velocity or penetration, it may be due to lack of lubrication of the piston, weakening of the mainspring or wearing of piston washer and joint washer. Both spring and joint washer can be easily replaced.

Interchangeable barrels

The Pistol can be supplied with barrel ·177 or ·22 or with both. To exchange barrels first see that the Pistol is "fired", remove screw securing, and barrel joint screws from front end, pull barrel back – towards breech end when the link on top of air chamber can be withdrawn, the barrel assembly removed and the new barrel fitted.

A complete Repair Service is available for all Webley products.

PART LIST FOR PREMIER Mk II AIR PISTOL

PART No.	DESCRIPTION OF PART	No. OFF
C/9	LINK FULCRUM NOT SOLD AS SEPARATE COMPONENT	1
C/10	SPRING GUIDE NOT SOLD AS SEPARATE COMPONENT	1
C/11	BODY AND SPRING GUIDE ASSEMBLY	1
C/12	PASSAGE SCREW	1
C/16	SEAR	1
C/17	SEAR SPRING	1
C/18	SEAR TRIGGER AND STOP PIN	3
C/19	TRIGGER	1
C/20	TRIGGER SPRING	1
C/21	TRIGGER ADJUSTING SCREW	1
C/22	SCREW SECURING TRIG. ADJ. SCREW	1
C/26	PISTON WASHER	1
C/27	PISTON	1
C/28	MAINSPRING	1
C/32	SMALL LINK	1
C/33	INTERMEDIATE LINK	1
C/34	LINK PIN	3
C/35	BARREL LINK SPRING	1
C/36	LONG LINK	1
C/37	BARREL ·177 CALIBRE SOLD ONLY AS ASSEMBLY	1
C/38	BARREL ·22 CALIBRE SOLD ONLY AS ASSEMBLY	1
C/39	BARREL ASSY. ·177 COMPRISING OF PARTS Nos. 32, 33, 34, 35, 36 & 37	1
C/40	BARREL ASSY. ·22 COMPRISING OF PARTS Nos. 32, 33, 34, 35, 36 & 38	1
C/41	BARREL JOINT SCREW	1
C/42	SCREW SECURING JOINT SCREW	1
C/46	BARREL CATCH SPRING	1
C/47	BARREL CATCH SPRING PLUNGER	1
C/48	BARREL CATCH	1
C/49	BARREL CATCH SCREW	1
C/50	BARREL JOINT WASHER	1
C/54	HORIZONTAL SIGHT	1
C/55	VERTICAL SIGHT	1
C/56	SIGHT WASHER	1
C/57	SIGHT SCREW	1
C/61	STOCK PEG	1
C/62	STOCKSIDE, LEFT HAND	1
C/63	STOCKSIDE, RIGHT HAND	1
C/64	STOCK SCREW	2
C/65	NAME PLATE	1

Reverse of Webley Premier Mark II information leaflet.

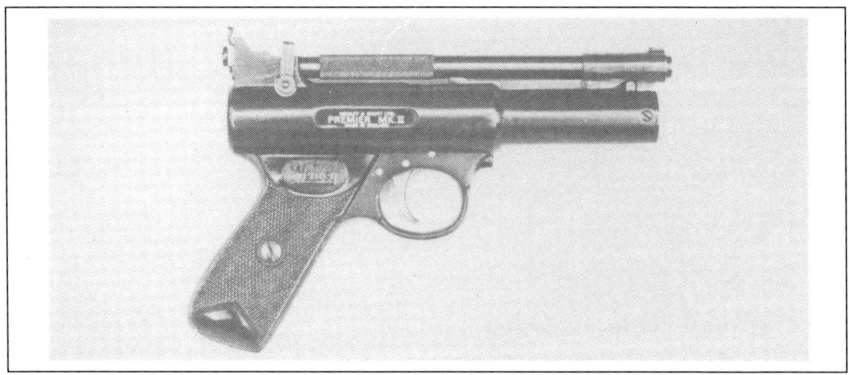

Webley Premier Mark II.

Model: **"PREMIER MK. II"**

Maker: **Webley & Scott**

Date: Production 1964 - 1977, assume above to be around 1975 - 1977.

Valuation: £40 - £80

Details: The last of the Premiers. Alloy air chamber set around a metal liner. Three pin trigger action, adjustable trigger. The chain of Premier variants show a gradual progression towards trying to produce a very good airpistol against continuing mounting production costs, from all metal machine work to semi-automatic casting, etc. This has produced a light, yet sturdy model that should give years of use, as in the case of all Webleys of years past. Set in a recess is a plastic stick-on label "WEBLEY & SCOTT LTD. — PREMIER MK. II — MADE IN ENGLAND". This being on the side of the air chamber. A batch number is stamped at the front of the airpistol near the barrel pivot.

Advertised in 1976 as being able to give a one inch group at 30 feet. Advertised weight 37 ozs. When sold in the U.S.A. by Beeman's Precision Airguns, they were offered with the option of walnut grips.

Sold in lift up box with outer slip on card sleeve. Contents included a small brown envelope of pellets, guarantee card, a Webley 6 yard airpistol target card, a fact sheet dealing with performance and parts diagram as well as safety etc. Advertised weight 31 oz. When removing pins from the trigger action it is advisable to remove them from right to left as the airpistol is pointing away from you and replace pins from left to right. So when removing pins, have airpistol pointing to the right and when replacing pins, turn airpistol over so that it now points to the left. The first models of the Mk. II appear to have been fitted with a barrel as shown in the parts diagram, but at a later date the barrel was fitted with a cast shroud to the front that formed the foresight and pivot for the cocking linkage.

The date stamp was not used on the Premier Mk. II and only the batch number appears under the grip. Batch numbers seen run from 20 up to 966. Inspection marks used include 2, 1, 3, L, O, and D.

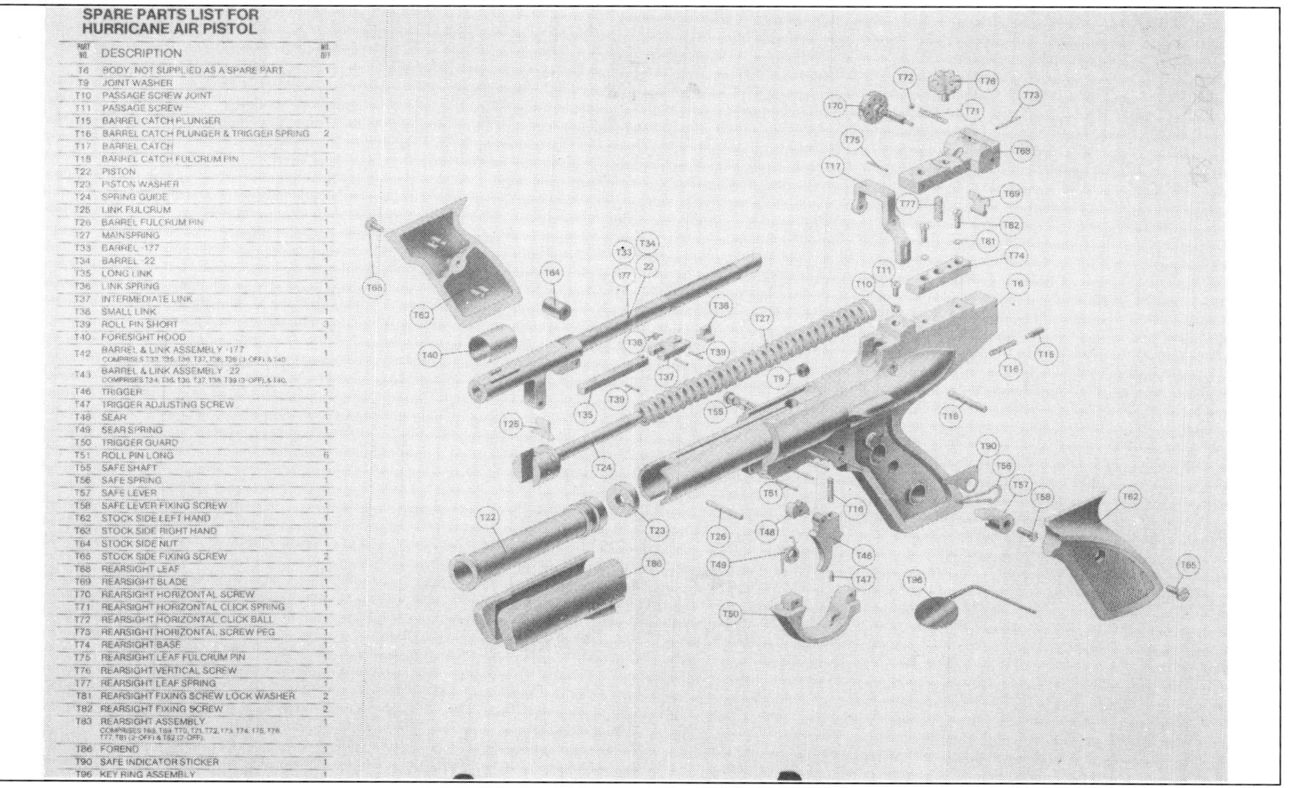

SPARE PARTS LIST FOR
HURRICANE AIR PISTOL

PART NO.	DESCRIPTION	NO. OFF
T6	BODY NOT SUPPLIED AS A SPARE PART	1
T9	JOINT WASHER	1
T10	PASSAGE SCREW JOINT	1
T11	PASSAGE SCREW	1
T15	BARREL CATCH PLUNGER	1
T16	BARREL CATCH PLUNGER & TRIGGER SPRING	2
T17	BARREL CATCH	1
T18	BARREL CATCH FULCRUM PIN	1
T22	PISTON	1
T23	PISTON WASHER	1
T24	SPRING GUIDE	1
T25	LINK FULCRUM	1
T26	BARREL FULCRUM PIN	1
T27	MAINSPRING	1
T33	BARREL ·177	1
T34	BARREL ·22	1
T35	LONG LINK	1
T36	LINK SPRING	1
T37	INTERMEDIATE LINK	1
T38	SMALL LINK	1
T39	ROLL PIN SHORT	3
T40	FORESIGHT HOOD	1
T42	BARREL & LINK ASSEMBLY ·177 COMPRISES T33, T35, T36, T37, T38, T39 (3-OFF) & T40	1
T43	BARREL & LINK ASSEMBLY ·22 COMPRISES T34, T35, T36, T37, T38, T39 (3-OFF) & T40.	1
T46	TRIGGER	1
T47	TRIGGER ADJUSTING SCREW	1
T48	SEAR	1
T49	SEAR SPRING	1
T50	TRIGGER GUARD	1
T51	ROLL PIN LONG	6
T55	SAFE SHAFT	1
T56	SAFE SPRING	1
T57	SAFE LEVER	1
T58	SAFE LEVER FIXING SCREW	1
T62	STOCK SIDE LEFT HAND	1
T63	STOCK SIDE RIGHT HAND	1
T64	STOCK SIDE NUT	1
T65	STOCK SIDE FIXING SCREW	2
T68	REARSIGHT LEAF	1
T69	REARSIGHT BLADE	1
T70	REARSIGHT HORIZONTAL SCREW	1
T71	REARSIGHT HORIZONTAL CLICK SPRING	1
T72	REARSIGHT HORIZONTAL CLICK BALL	1
T73	REARSIGHT HORIZONTAL SCREW PEG	1
T74	REARSIGHT BASE	1
T75	REARSIGHT LEAF FULCRUM PIN	1
T76	REARSIGHT VERTICAL SCREW	1
T77	REARSIGHT LEAF SPRING	1
T81	REARSIGHT FIXING SCREW LOCK WASHER	2
T82	REARSIGHT FIXING SCREW	2
T83	REARSIGHT ASSEMBLY COMPRISES T68, T69, T70, T71, T72, T73, T74, T75, T76, T77, T81 (2-OFF) & T82 (2-OFF).	1
T86	FOREND	1
T90	SAFE INDICATOR STICKER	1
T96	KEY RING ASSEMBLY	1

Spare parts list for Hurricane airpistol.

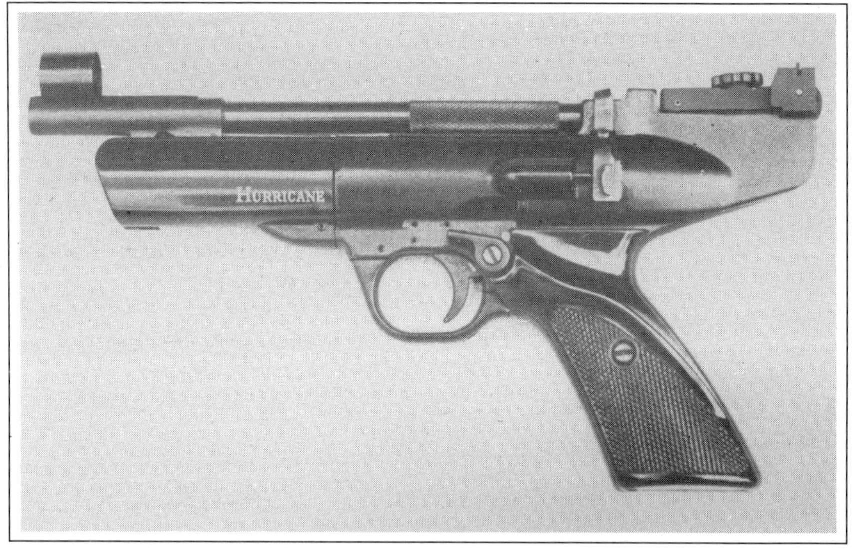

Webley Hurricane

Model: **HURRICANE**

Maker: **Webley & Scott,**
Frankley Industrial Park, Birmingham.

Date: Current model, production began 1977.

Valuation: £30 - £70.

Details: Took over from the Webley Premier Mk. II. Sold in a well planned presentation box. Has a compartment for fitting the airpistol, plus its telescopic sight without removal. Extensive use of plastics and alloys have produced a light, handy airpistol, yet is just as durable as its predecessor. Non-automatic safety catch. Hooded foresight and fully adjustable rear sight. Rear sight is removable for telescopic sight and fitting ramp. Advertised muzzle velocities 420 — ·177 and 330 — ·22.

Under the right hand grip is a number cast with the frame of the airpistol. Cast number of above 2066B. See *"Airgun World",* October, 1978. Advertised weight 2 lb 6 ozs. Have seen a ·177 barreled Hurricane with "2066 A" cast under R.H. grip. Details of stripping the Hurricane are shown in *"Airgun World",* January, 1983.

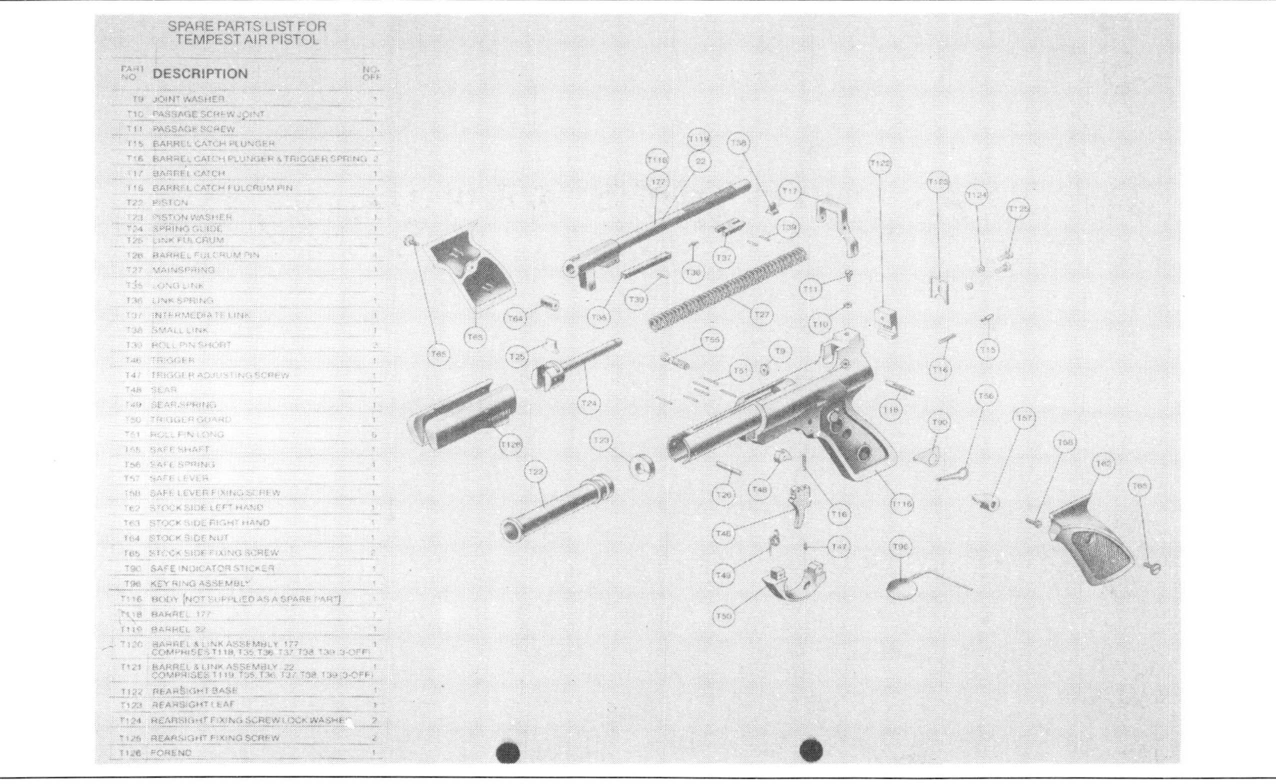

SPARE PARTS LIST FOR
TEMPEST AIR PISTOL

PART NO	DESCRIPTION	NO. OFF
T9	JOINT WASHER	1
T10	PASSAGE SCREW JOINT	1
T11	PASSAGE SCREW	1
T15	BARREL CATCH PLUNGER	1
T16	BARREL CATCH PLUNGER & TRIGGER SPRING	2
T17	BARREL CATCH	1
T18	BARREL CATCH FULCRUM PIN	1
T22	PISTON	1
T23	PISTON WASHER	1
T24	SPRING GUIDE	1
T25	LINK FULCRUM	1
T26	BARREL FULCRUM PIN	1
T27	MAINSPRING	1
T35	LONG LINK	1
T36	LINK SPRING	1
T37	INTERMEDIATE LINK	1
T38	SMALL LINK	1
T39	ROLL PIN SHORT	3
T46	TRIGGER	1
T47	TRIGGER ADJUSTING SCREW	1
T48	SEAR	1
T49	SEAR SPRING	1
T50	TRIGGER GUARD	1
T51	ROLL PIN LONG	5
T55	SAFE SHAFT	1
T56	SAFE SPRING	1
T57	SAFE LEVER	1
T58	SAFE LEVER FIXING SCREW	1
T62	STOCK SIDE LEFT HAND	1
T63	STOCK SIDE RIGHT HAND	1
T64	STOCK SIDE NUT	1
T65	STOCK SIDE FIXING SCREW	2
T90	SAFE INDICATOR STICKER	1
T96	KEY RING ASSEMBLY	1
T116	BODY [NOT SUPPLIED AS A SPARE PART]	1
T118	BARREL .177	1
T119	BARREL .22	1
T120	BARREL & LINK ASSEMBLY .177 COMPRISES T118, T35, T36, T37, T38, T39 (3-OFF)	1
T121	BARREL & LINK ASSEMBLY .22 COMPRISES T119, T35, T36, T37, T38, T39 (3-OFF)	1
T122	REARSIGHT BASE	1
T123	REARSIGHT LEAF	1
T124	REARSIGHT FIXING SCREW LOCK WASHER	2
T125	REARSIGHT FIXING SCREW	2
T126	FOREND	1

Spare parts list for Tempest airpistol.

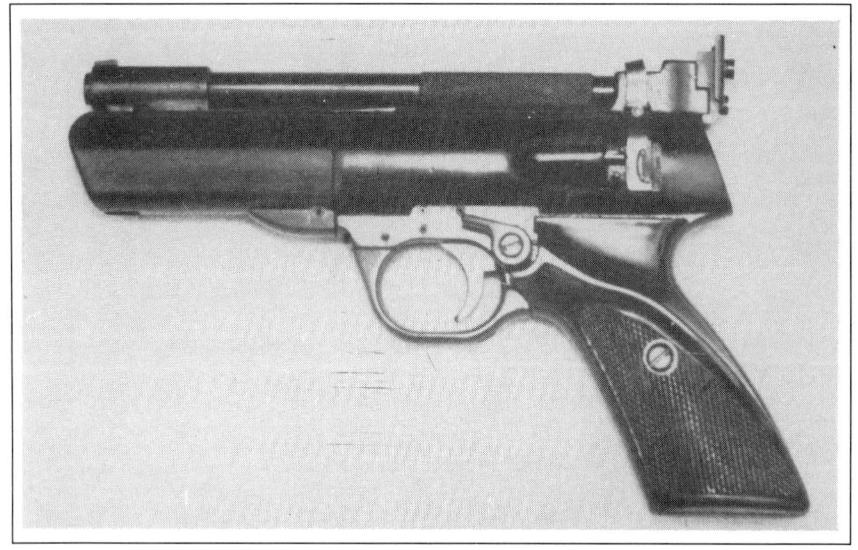

Webley "Tempest".

Model: **"TEMPEST"**

Maker: **Webley & Scott Ltd.,**
Park Lane, Handsworth, Birmingham B21 8LU,
and, from 1983:
Frankley Industrial Park, Birmingham.

Date: Introduced 1979.

Valuation: £30 - £70.

Details: The pocket version of the Hurricane. Light well made airpistol. Shortened barrel and rearsight assembly. Same air chamber and grips as the Hurricane. Rearsight adjustable for windage and elevation. Cast under the R.H.S. grip "2066A" and stamped "R". Grips moulded for right hand use only. Trigger adjustment by way of small hole through underside of trigger guard. Adjustment being carried out by Allen screw provided. Forward plastic shroud marked "Tempest" on either side and "WEBLEY & SCOTT LTD. BIRMINGHAM ENGLAND" on the underside. Top of barrel shroud stamped with the calibre.

For a review, see *"Airgun World",* May, 1979. Available in either ·22 or ·177 calibre. Advertised weight 32 oz. and muzzle velocities for ·22 330 f.p.s. and 420 f.p.s. for ·177. During the very early 1980's Beeman's Precision Airguns of America were selling some Tempest airpistols with serial numbers. If purchased between September 1st and December 15th, 1980, you could claim back $7.50 rebate — WOW!! Some of these could find their way back into Britain still bearing serial numbers ready to confuse future Webley collectors. A review of the Tempest appears in *"Sporting Air Rifle",* November, 1985.

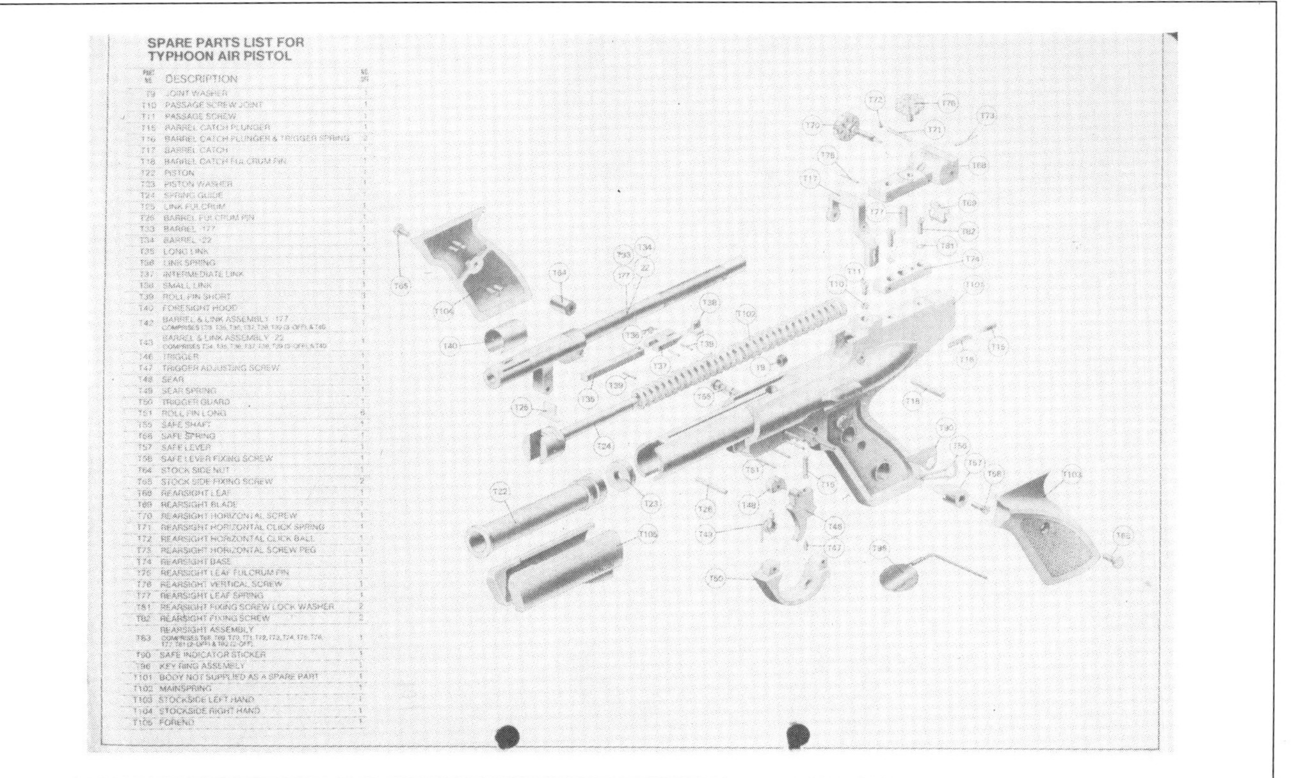

SPARE PARTS LIST FOR TYPHOON AIR PISTOL

PART NO.	DESCRIPTION	NO. OFF
T9	JOINT WASHER	1
T10	PASSAGE SCREW JOINT	1
T11	PASSAGE SCREW	1
T15	BARREL CATCH PLUNGER	1
T16	BARREL CATCH PLUNGER & TRIGGER SPRING	2
T17	BARREL CATCH	1
T18	BARREL CATCH FULCRUM PIN	1
T22	PISTON	1
T23	PISTON WASHER	1
T24	SPRING GUIDE	1
T25	LINK FULCRUM	1
T26	BARREL FULCRUM PIN	1
T33	BARREL ·177	1
T34	BARREL ·22	1
T35	LONG LINK	1
T36	LINK SPRING	1
T37	INTERMEDIATE LINK	1
T38	SMALL LINK	1
T39	ROLL PIN SHORT	3
T40	FORESIGHT HOOD	1
T42	BARREL & LINK ASSEMBLY ·177 COMPRISES T33, T35, T36, T37, T38, T39 (3 OFF) & T40	1
T43	BARREL & LINK ASSEMBLY ·22 COMPRISES T34, T35, T36, T37, T38, T39 (3 OFF) & T40	1
T46	TRIGGER	1
T47	TRIGGER ADJUSTING SCREW	1
T48	SEAR	1
T49	SEAR SPRING	1
T50	TRIGGER GUARD	1
T51	ROLL PIN LONG	6
T55	SAFE SHAFT	1
T56	SAFE SPRING	1
T57	SAFE LEVER	1
T58	SAFE LEVER FIXING SCREW	1
T64	STOCK SIDE NUT	1
T65	STOCK SIDE FIXING SCREW	2
T68	REARSIGHT LEAF	1
T69	REARSIGHT BLADE	1
T70	REARSIGHT HORIZONTAL SCREW	1
T71	REARSIGHT HORIZONTAL CLICK SPRING	1
T72	REARSIGHT HORIZONTAL CLICK BALL	1
T73	REARSIGHT HORIZONTAL SCREW PEG	1
T74	REARSIGHT BASE	1
T75	REARSIGHT LEAF FULCRUM PIN	1
T76	REARSIGHT VERTICAL SCREW	1
T77	REARSIGHT LEAF SPRING	1
T81	REARSIGHT FIXING SCREW LOCK WASHER	2
T82	REARSIGHT FIXING SCREW	2
T83	REARSIGHT ASSEMBLY COMPRISES T68, T69, T70, T71, T72, T73, T74, T75, T76, T77, T81 (2 OFF) & T82 (2 OFF)	1
T90	SAFE INDICATOR STICKER	1
T96	KEY RING ASSEMBLY	1
T101	BODY NOT SUPPLIED AS A SPARE PART	1
T102	MAINSPRING	1
T103	STOCKSIDE LEFT HAND	1
T104	STOCKSIDE RIGHT HAND	1
T105	FOREND	1

Spare parts list for Typhoon airpistol.

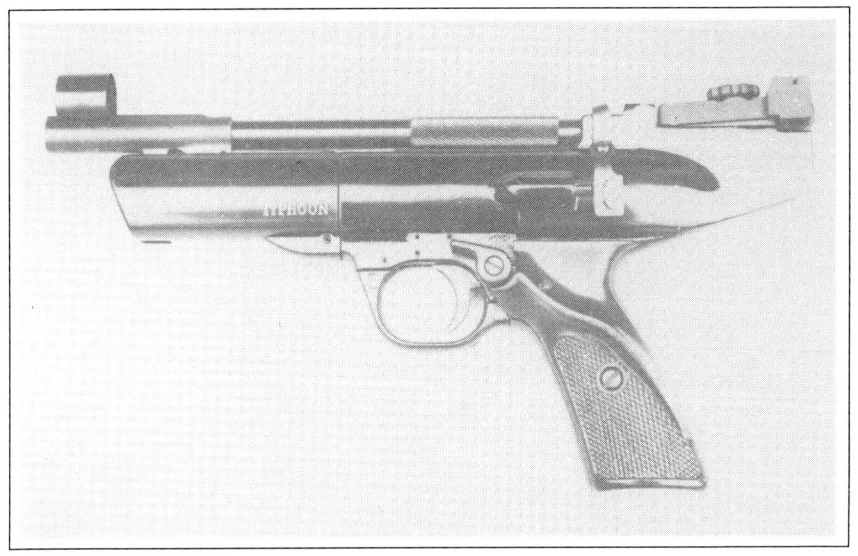

Webley "Typhoon".

Model: **"TYPHOON"**

Maker: **Webley & Scott Ltd.,**
Birmingham, England.

Date: Introduced 1977 as a replacement for the Junior Mk. II. Production ceased during 1982.

Valuation: £40 - £70.

Details: The "junior" version of the Hurricane. Basically the same size in everything except the grip. Diecast body with black plastic fore-end. This has to be removed in order to change the barrel. Rearsight can be removed and a telescopic sight ramp screwed in its place for mounting the scope. Butt fitted with brown grips as opposed to the Hurricane fitted with black. Many parts will interchange with the above from the Hurricane. Fitted with 8 inch rifled barrel. Trigger action adjusted through hole in guard and needs Allen key for doing it. Action fitted with manual safety catch. Piston is fitted with the, now common, PTFE self lubricating, self adjusting, self cushioning, self everything piston washer. The washer has a split across one side to facilitate removal and fitting so it is not to be assumed broken when first seen. Barrels available in either ·22 or ·177. Advertised muzzle velocities are 360 f.p.s. for ·177 and 280 f.p.s. for ·22. Advertised weight 37½ oz., or 2 lb. 5½ oz.

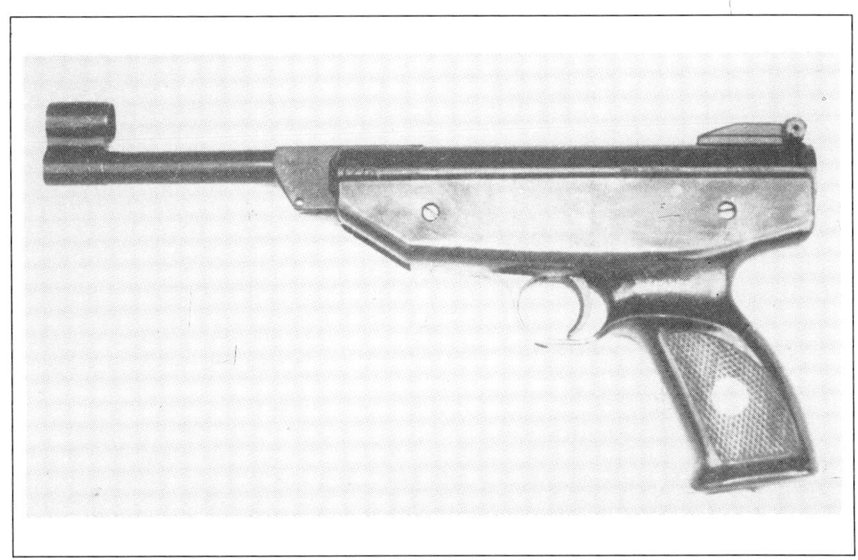

Weihrauch HW70.

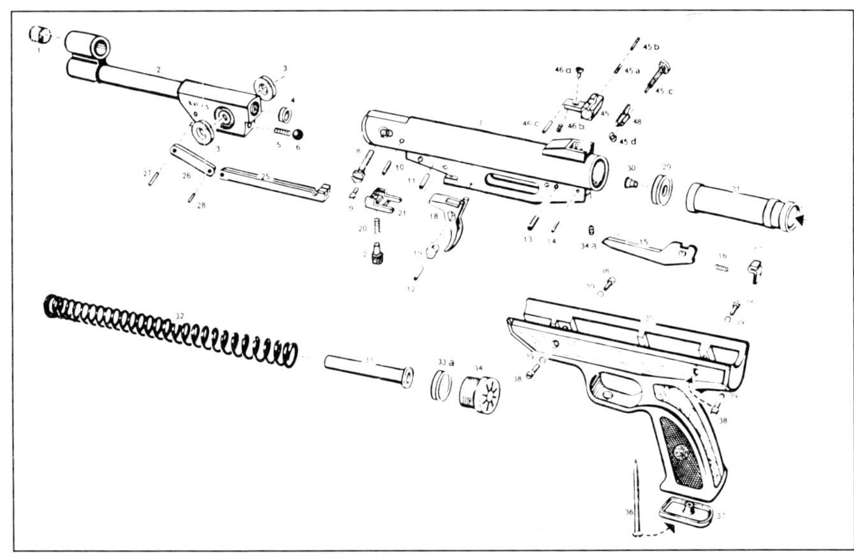

Parts diagram for the Weihrauch Model HW70.

Model: **HW 70**

Maker: **H. Weihrauch,**
West Germany
Imported by Milbro, Millard Bros., P.O. Box 24, Motherwell, Lanarkshire, Scotland ML1 4UP, until the early 1980's, then by the Hull Cartridge Company.

Date: Current model.

Valuation: £30 - £60

Details: Surprisingly low recoil, so has been popular with target shooters. Grip set well back under the rear sight so this may help counteract the recoil. Plastic grip moulded for either hand. Pistol measures 13¾ inches long. Deep, hard blueing on barrel and air chamber. Tunnel foresight. Stamps on barrel and air chamber are "whited" in with paint. Side of air chamber stamped "MADE IN GERMANY" plus serial number, the other side is stamped "H. WEIHRAUCH, SPORTWAFFENFABRIK MELLRICHSTALT". Side of barrel breech is stamped "KAL. 4·5" plus the "F" in the pentagon denoting the German limit of muzzle energy, which is lower than ours. The other side of the barrel breech has "HW 70". During the middle of 1977, the Hull Cartridge Co. Ltd. advertised a "Hofmann HW70" airpistol as being made for them by Weihrauch, Germany. Price then was £32.51, and available in ·177 only. Advertised muzzle velocity 356 f.p.s., and weight 2 lbs. 5 oz.

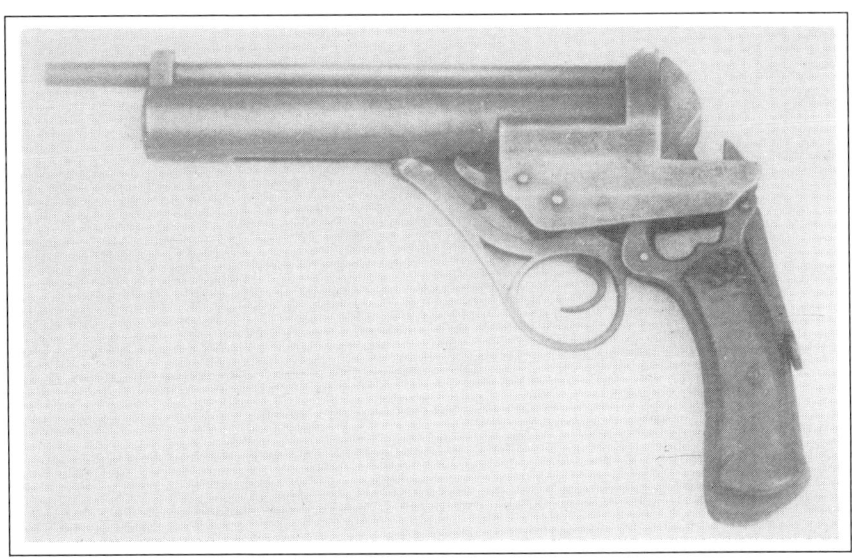

First model Westley Richards "Highest Possible". Note plain horn grips, open heart shaped frame, and dovetail for simple rearsight blade that is missing.

Westley Richards "Highest Possible".

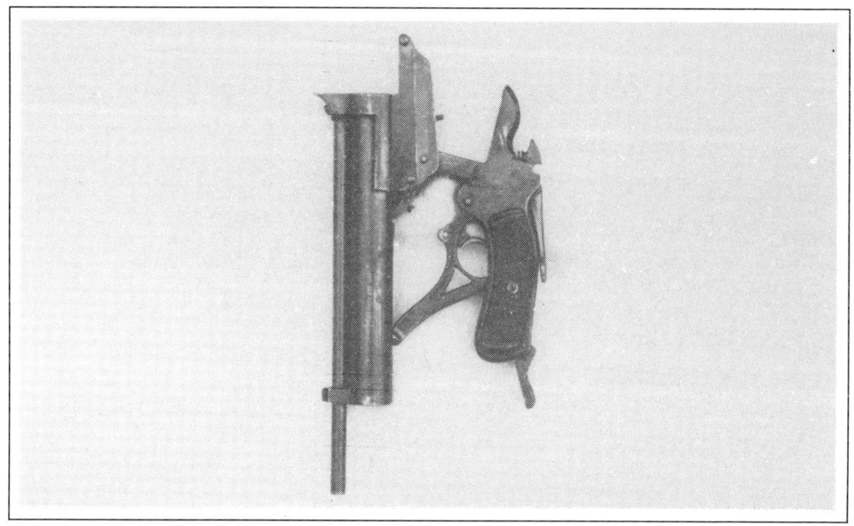

Westley Richards "Highest Possible" in cocked position.

Model: **"HIGHEST POSSIBLE"**

Maker: **Westley Richards & Co.,** London, or by **Edwin Anson,** 14 Steelhouse Lane, Birmingham

Date: From around 1907 to about 1921, when an up-rated design with the barrel running through the piston was introduced. See *"Shooting Times",* June 22 - 28, 1978.

Valuation: £150 - £450.

Details: Engraved on the L.H.S. of the air chamber "WESTLEY RICHARDS — HIGHEST POSSIBLE — AIR PISTOL". On the frame near the sear is stamped the serial number, 1052, which also appears on various other parts. On the L.H.S. of the frame is engraved "WESTLEY RICHARDS & CO^{m} LONDON W" and near the action latch appears "PATENT 24837 1907" for further details of this, see patent *"Guns Review",* January, 1979. Black chequered vulcanite grips. 9¾ inch rifled barrel. Rear sight appears to be adjustable for elevation only. Length from tip of barrel to base of butt is 13¼ inches. The above design was patented by E. Anson, a relative of W. Anson, of the well known partnership Anson and Deeley. There is some doubt as to who actually produced the above, as was the case with the first models of the Lincoln air rifle. Even the first Britannia's were produced in Germany under Cox's Patent. Apparently models of the "Highest Possible" exist without the name of Westley Richards, could it be that E. Anson made them for Westley Richards, or even the other way around. Another point of interest is that Deeley was manager of Westley Richards, although who "tooled-up" for the production of the above is not quite clear. The "Highest Possible" was also available nickel plated. Highest serial number seen is 1052. Inside of grips are usually scratched with the serial number or part of it and the rifling appears to be anti-clockwise.

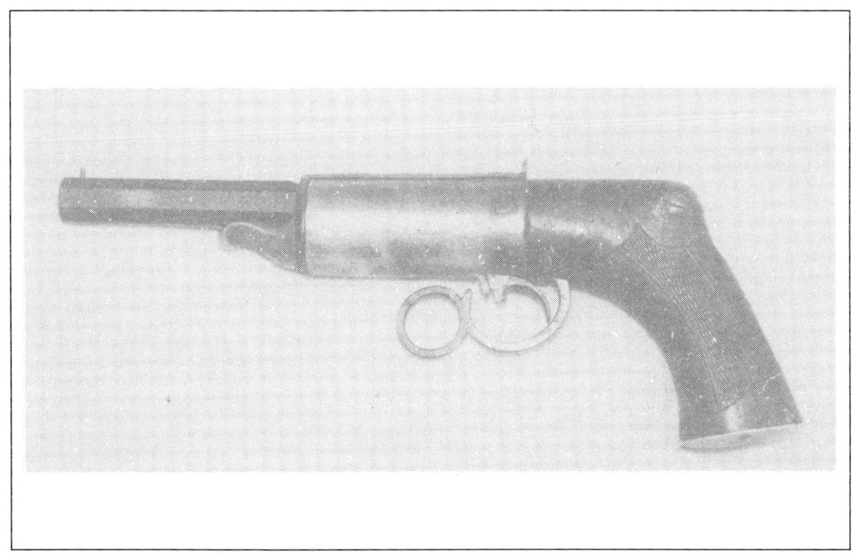

A. F. Wirsing Gallery airpistol.

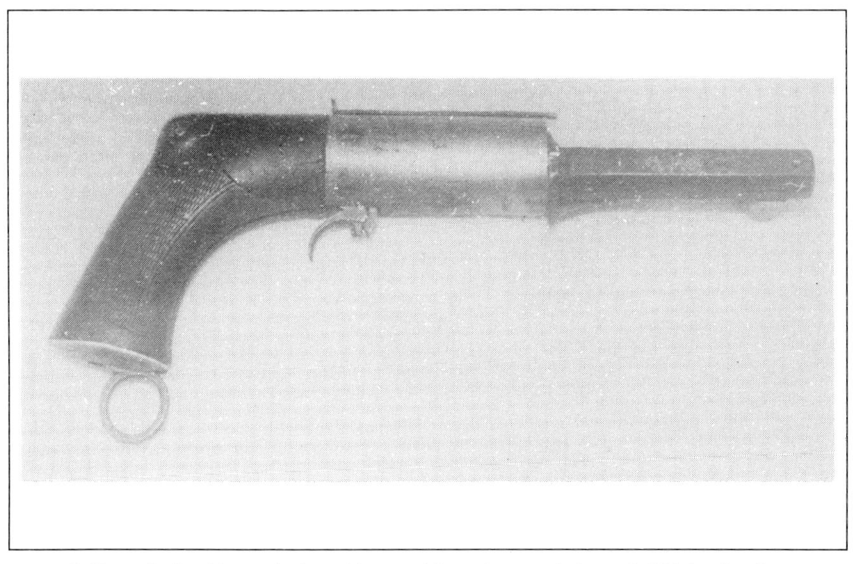

Gallery airpistol in cocked position and barrel rotated through 90° for loading.

Model: **ST. LOUIS TYPE GALLERY AIRPISTOL**

Maker: **A. F. Wirsing,**
Cincinnati, Ohio, U.S.A.

Date: Early to late 1800's.

Valuation: It is difficult to put a value on an airgun that rearely appears on the market, ultra-rare airguns are now fetching prices around £500 in auctions and it could be assumed that the above might fetch anything from £200 to £500.

Details: An unusual gallery target airpistol. Measures 14½ inches long with a 4¾ inch smoothbore barrel whose bore is slightly larger than ·25. Wooden butt is one piece with white metal butt cap. The stock appears to fix straight into the brass air chamber and is held in place by five wood screws. The pivot for the cocking lever is at the top of the butt. Hand chequered. The butt is almost cut into two pieces to accommodate the cocking lever. There are two slots in the back of the grip for fitting a shoulder stock. The cocking lever and sear are the exact copy of the Blickensdeorfer & Schilling gallery air rifle (*"Air Rifles",* second edition by Hiller). Brass air chamber measures 4 inches in length and 1¾ inches in diameter. A long strip of thin metal is screwed on top of the air chamber. This acts as both rearsight and latch for the barrel. The rearsight has an adjusting screw for elevation only. The barrel rotates a quarter of a turn to the right in order to load. A small brass fore-end is screwed to the underside of the barrel.

The serial number is not visible. Engraved on top of the barrel flat is "A. F. WIRSING & CO." A tall brass pillar foresight with an arrow engraved on top of the barrel in line with the aim of the sights. The above design appears to be of the St. Louis type, but with secondary New York City characteristics. See *"Airguns"* by Eldon G. Wolff for further details. The above maker is listed as "Wirsing & Schemann" by Eldon G. Wolff, so the above airpistol was made either before Wirsing teamed up with Schemann or after a separation took place. Weight 2 lb. 10 oz.

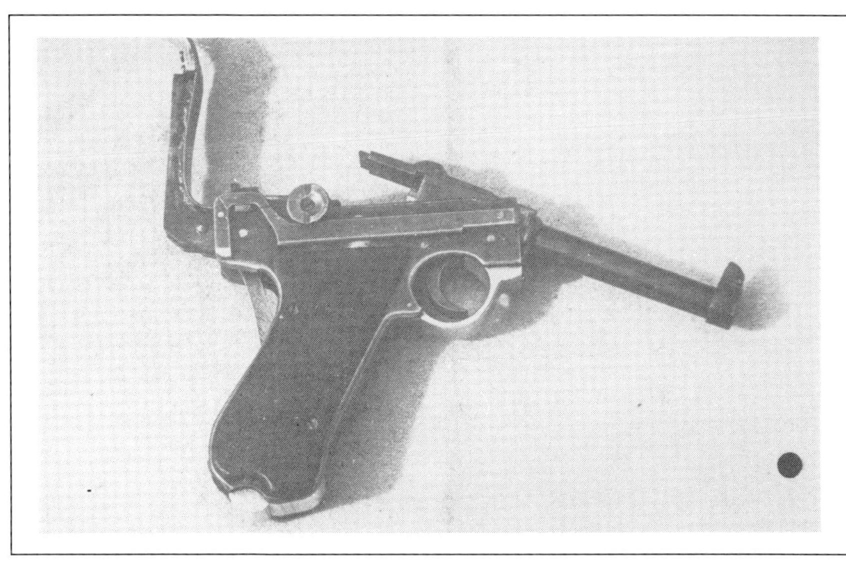

R.H.S. showing barrel broken for loading of pellet. Butt strap raised and cocking arm lowered to engage with piston. Pistol is cocked by snapping down the butt strap smartly. Trigger pull is smooth and well regulated, although it does not appear to be adjustable.

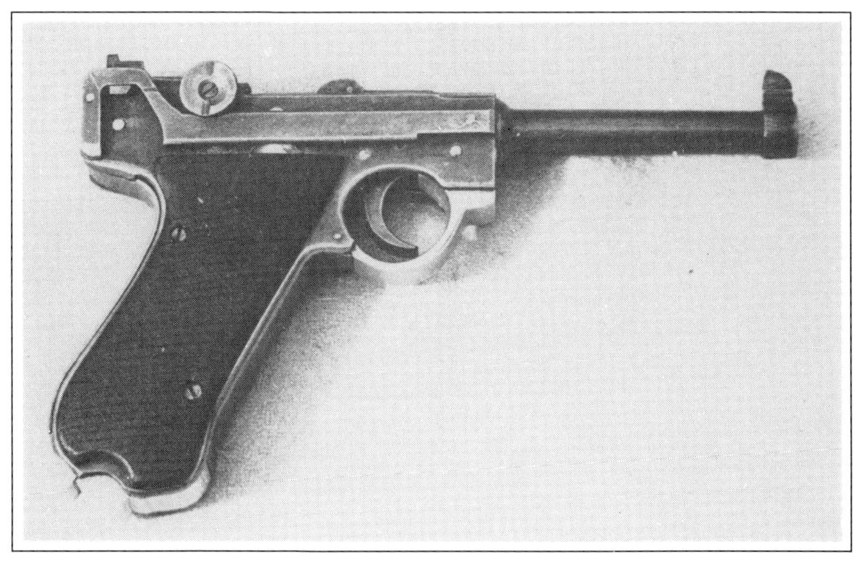

R.H.S. view.

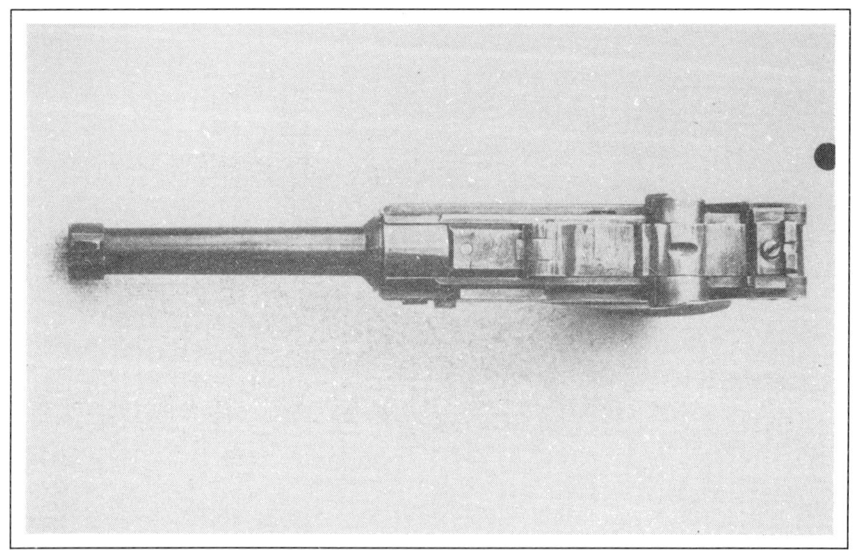

Top view.

"Luger" style airpistol.

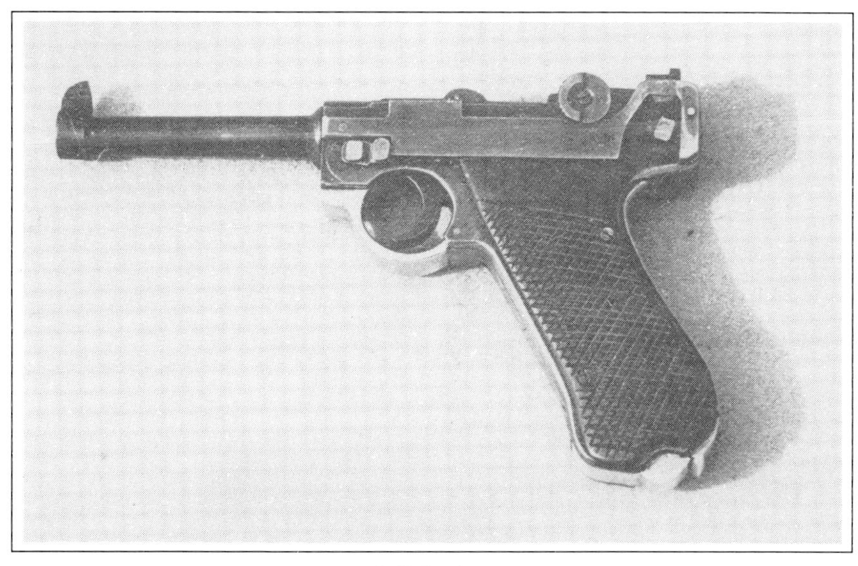

L.H.S. view.

Model: **Not known, but obviously a copy of a German Luger.**

Maker: Not known, but would assume German.

Date: Not known, but would assume sometime between 1939 and 1945.

Valuation: Not known, but would assume due to rarity value to be around £50 - £100.

Details: The above specimen has no markings whatsoever. All metal except for the trigger guard and base of butt, which are alloy. Most parts have file marks as though they have not been finished off properly. Has some characteristics of Haenel airpistols, i.e. barrel breaking to load pellet and separate cocking action. Air cylinder in butt similar design to Walther LP53. Weighs 1.35 kgs., or 3 lbs. Even the chequering of the grips do not match. Appears to be a "one-off". Measures 9 inches along barrel to rear sight.

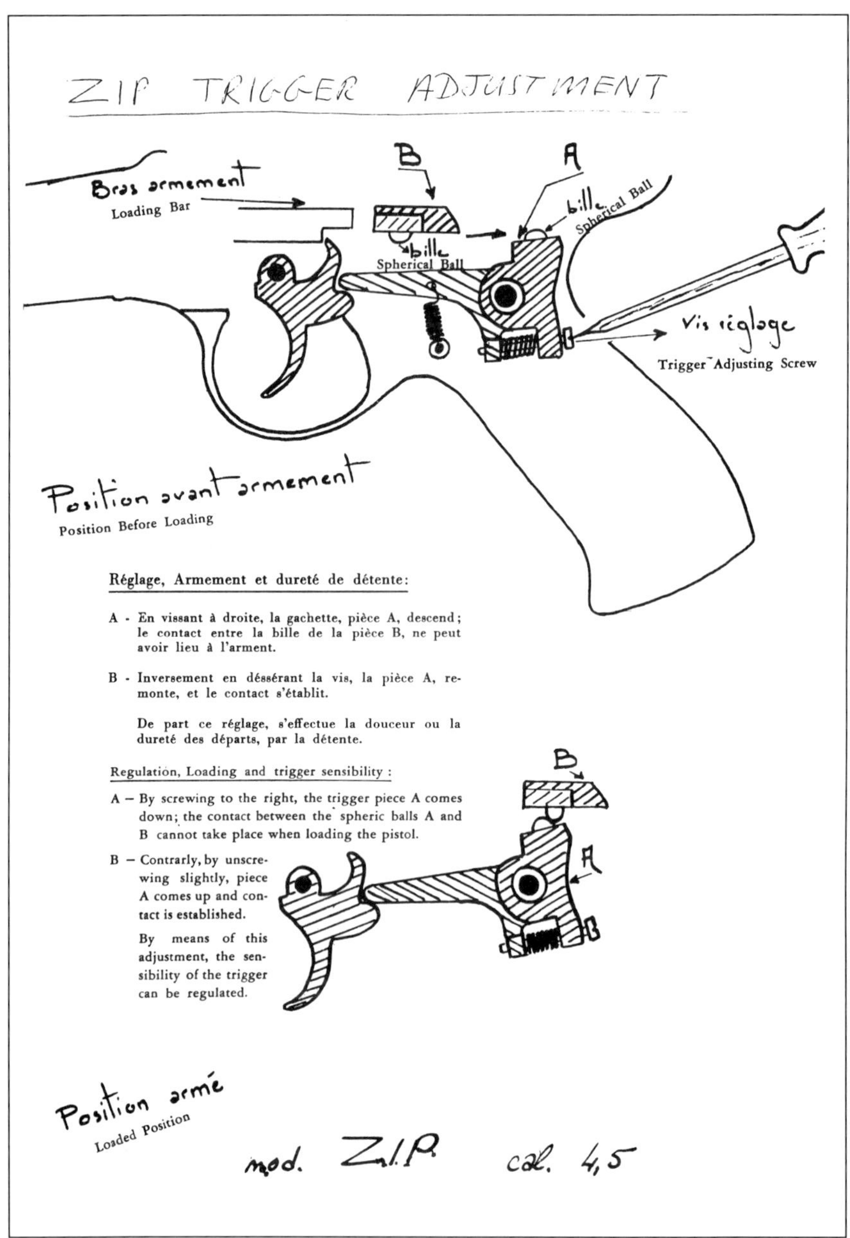

ZIP TRIGGER ADJUSTMENT
B
A
Bras armement
Loading Bar
bille
Spherical Ball
bille
Spherical Ball
Vis réglage
Trigger Adjusting Screw
Position avant armement
Position Before Loading
Réglage, Armement et dureté de détente:
A - En vissant à droite, la gachette, pièce A, descend; le contact entre la bille de la pièce B, ne peut avoir lieu à l'arment.
B - Inversement en déssérant la vis, la pièce A, remonte, et le contact s'établit.
De part ce réglage, s'effectue la douceur ou la dureté des départs, par la détente.
Regulation, Loading and trigger sensibility :
A – By screwing to the right, the trigger piece A comes down; the contact between the spheric balls A and B cannot take place when loading the pistol.
B – Contrarly, by unscrewing slightly, piece A comes up and contact is established.
By means of this adjustment, the sensibility of the trigger can be regulated.
B
A
Position armé
Loaded Position
mod. Z.I.P. cal. 4,5

Zip trigger adjustment.

Zip airpistol.

Model: **ZIP**

Maker: **Mondial** of Italy.

Date: Introduced sometime in 1976. See *"Guns Review",* July, 1976.

Valuation: Featured in the *"Guns Review", Airgun Guide,* April, 1976, and price quoted around £10, so today's value could be around £15 - £20. Secondhand value £10 - £20.

Details: Made almost entirely from alloy castings, yet is a well made airpistol. Held together by nuts and bolts, fully adjustable rear sight with hooded fore-sight. Long sight plane of 12½ inches. Total length 13½ inches. Twin cocking levers and interrupting sear on trigger when barrel is cocked. All the refinements of a more expensive airpistol. Brown plastic grips cast for right-handed use. Barrel has a steel rifled insert with alloy exteria. Cast with the frame on the L.H.S. appears "CAL m/m 4·5", the word "OIL" and on the air chamber "MONDIAL" set in a diamond with three "olympic" circle trademark followed by the name "ZIP". Near the barrel pivot crew appears the serial number, this being for the above E10924 and appears under the black paint finish. On the R.H.S. of the frame is cast "MADE IN ITALY". Trigger adjustment by way of a screw through the back of the grip.

Oil Cans

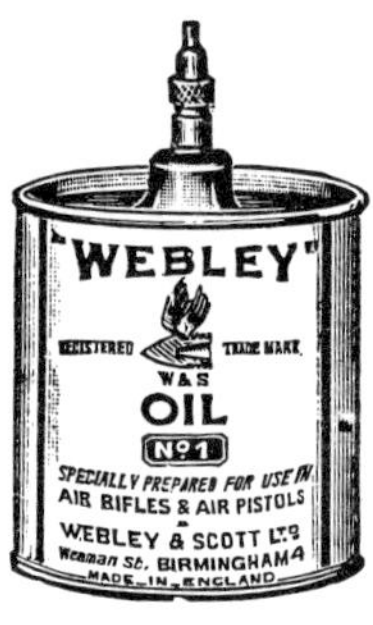

No. 1 OIL.
For use in Webley Air Pistol Mark I and Junior Model, and other Air Pistols and Rifles where piston is fitted with leather washers.

No. 2 OIL.
For use in Webley Air Rifles and Senior Air Pistols where Piston is fitted with piston ring.

"WEBLEY" OIL CAN

Available in two grades, see above. This style of tin with screw top tip, and sold from around 1924 to 1939.

Pellets

"BEATALL" PELLETS

Appeared during the middle 1930's and continued after W.W.2. From the appearance of the above tin lid, would assume to be pre-war, dating from around 1933/95 to 1939 and maybe for a short period after, but more often found in paper packets after the war. Manufactured by Lanes Bros.

Sold in "boxes" of 500 (·177) and 1000 (·177), and in 500 only for ·22. Lid colours were cream background with deep blue front ring with red background to the two semicircular name panels, with a red ring to outer and inner edge to the deep blue front panel.

B.S.A. "PYLARM" PELLETS

"Pylarm pellets appeared during the late 1930's and were intended as a cheaper pellet than the Standard B.S.A. pellet that was available in rectangular boxes at the same time and earlier. Sold in ·177 and ·22, with lid labels as shown, the only difference being in the pellet size. Sold in tins of 500 and 1000 in ·177 and in 500's for ·22. Average weight of 10 ·177 pellets was found to be 7.31 grains.

After the Second World War, the standard pellet name was dropped in favour of the "Pylarm" brand name. They were manufactured by Eley Bros. Lid label is red centre bar and outer rim with yellow upper and lower segments. Text is in black.

"BULL DOG" AIR RIFLE PELLETS

Pre-war pellets, but still referred to as slugs on other parts of the box. These were found with a German Tell air rifle. Although the packets boasted "perfect fit ensuring great force" the actual variation in size ranged from dropping straight through the barrel to sitting on top of the bore like some obese lead pellet. I also like the purely sexist reference to "all Boy's airguns", this being the same philosophy that is held in the Sahara desert in which a woman's hand must never be allowed to touch the udder of a camel otherwise it will turn the milk sour and the camel sterile! Bull Dog brand pellets were manufactured by Lane Brothers, 45a New Church St., Bermondsey, London SE, address at time of manufacture. Would date the above as 1910 to 1920's.

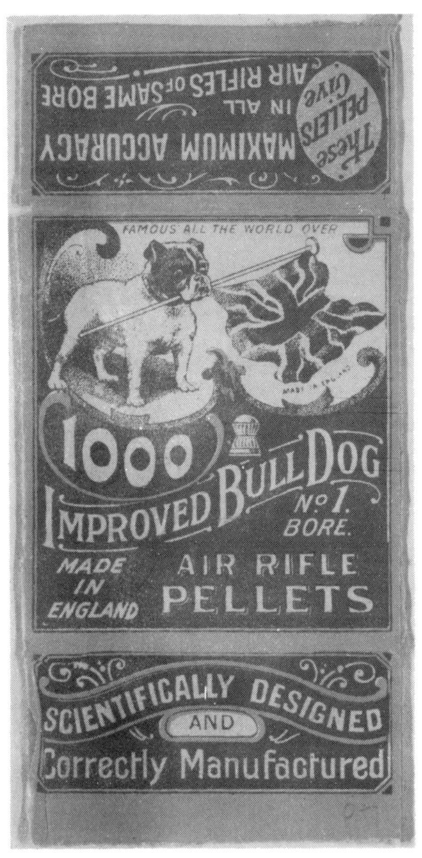

"IMPROVED" BULL DOG PELLETS

To date, one of the most colourful and artistic box labels seen. Printed with four colours, red, white, blue and mustard.

Bull Dog pellets first appeared in the middle 1920's and were even around after W.W.2., although in different designed boxes.

The above appear to have been produced up to 1939.

With the same standard label, they were available in the following sizes: ·177 in 500's and 1000's, and in 500's only for ·22 and ·25. Boxes of 1000 ·177 pellets measure 2¾ x 2⅜ x 1⅛ inches.

JOHN BULL WAISTED PELLETS

I associate these with cycle shops — as a child I used to buy John Bull cycle tyres and accessories so there may be some connection. Packets of 100 seen by the obvious firm of SLUGS Ltd., Sidcup, Kent, England. I would assume these to be available in the 1950's to early 1970's.

CAC WAISTED AIR RIFLE PELLETS

Pale green plastic box with hinged lid. Same design as Hyscore and advertised during the middle 1970's. Lid label shows a target shooter complete with ear protectors, firing at a target, rather faint in the photograph, but the bulls eye can just be seen. These were originally from New Zealand and were available during the 1980's.

CHAMPION SPECIAL 20 PELLETS

Average weight 10.54 grains, available in small numbers throughout the 1970's and 1980's, although not readily available. Pellet on lid bore no resemblance to contents, usual round head with waist, ribbed and thick rear skirt. Lid with black printing and faded yellow background. This style of lid label also appeared for ·22 (450) and for ·25 (350).

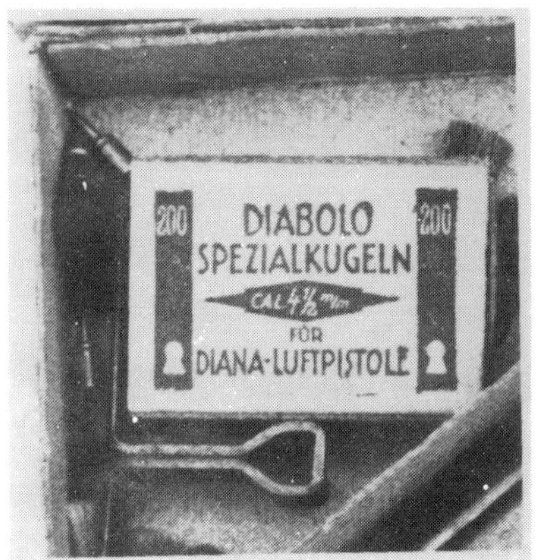

DIANA DIABOLO PELLETS

These were found in a boxed pre-war German Diana tinplate airpistol, assumed Model 1. The first airpistol produced by Diana and cocked by a key that was placed on the nipple protruding from the end of the butt.

The sample box of waisted pellets was brown in colour and made from a very coarse cardboard. The box opened in the same manner as a box of matches. I would assume that the above dates from the middle 1920's to the middle 1930's and was a sample packet.

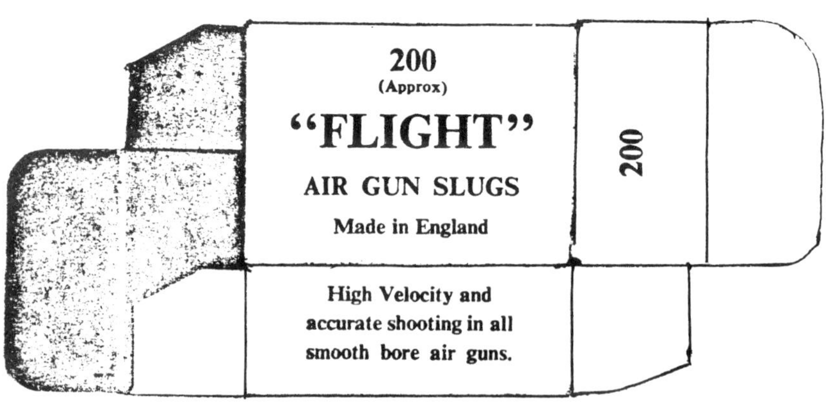

"FLIGHT" AIR GUN SLUGS

Black printing on white card boxes. Found in 200s' but no doubt other packets were available. Measures 2¾ x 1¼ x ¾ inches. Would assume these to date from the 1950's and 1960's. Note the good old "66" and "99" speech commas so rarely seen these days, also the awareness that these cup slugs were better in smoothbore airguns. Apart from the front, one side and one flap, there is no other printing on the boxes.

PELLET TEST PACK

White enamelled tin with black plastic insert with nine compartments, each containing a sample selection of ·177 pellets. A plan of contents was fixed to the inside of the lid as follows:

WASP	WEBLEY	H&N POINTED
MARKSMAN	MILBRO CALEDONIAN	H&N MATCH
BULLDOG	ELEY MATCH	(Label missing as this compartment was blank)

I would assume the above to date from the 1960's to 1970's.

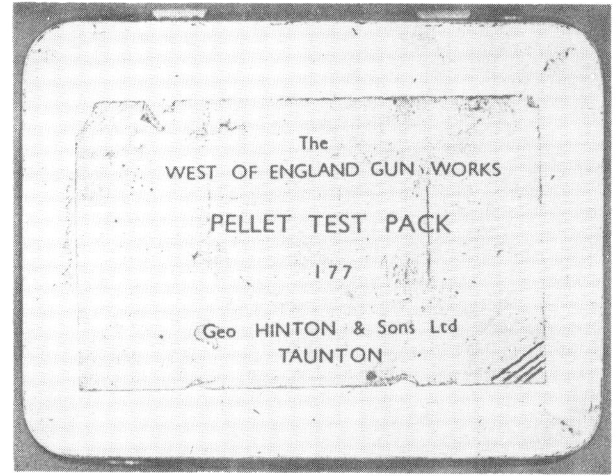

HUSTLER AIRGUN PELLETS

Round cardboard container of approximately 250 ·22 pellets, although the label refers to ·177. Blue background label with purple pellets, three in number. The first, as seen in the photograph bears the name and size of pellet, the second pellet shape has "Enjoy hours of straight shooting with with Hustler 177 Air Gun Pellets. Precision made from the Highest Quality materials", the other pellet shape contains "Made in N.Z. by Sexton Engineering Ltd., Totara Ave., New Lynn, Auckland, N.Z." In the blue portion is the number of pellets, but in this case there is a white/black stick-on label on the lid with the following "Approx 250 ·22 Calibre".

KING AIRGUN SLUGS

Deep green packet with blue printing. Measures 1⅜ x 1¼ x ⅝ inches. The slug is of the domed head and hollow base with flat sides with four raised ribs. Usually referred to as "hollow slugs". Earliest advert seen for King slugs is during the middle 1920's and they were sold in ·177 and ·25 only. The ·177's were offered in boxes of 100, 200, 500 and 1000, whilst the ·25 slugs were sold in 500's only. By the 1930's the ·25 size appears to have been discontinued. By 1939, they would appear to have been renamed the "Queen" hollow slugs.

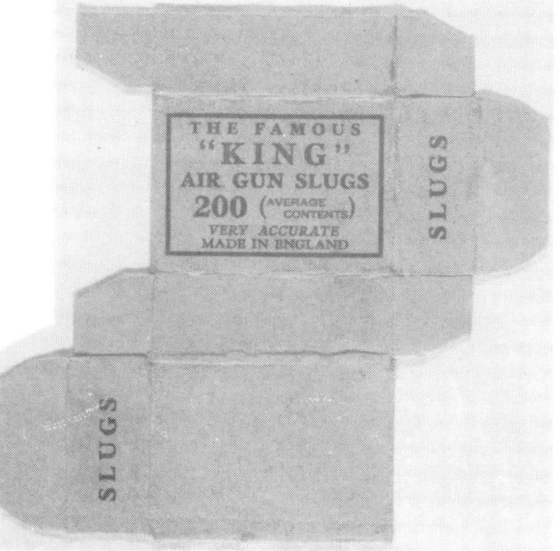

KING AIRGUN SLUGS

Bright deep yellow with blue printing. Packets of 200 measure 1⅞ x 1¼ x ⅝ inches. I would assume same time period as above for packets of 100. The average weight of the "King" hollow slug is ·36 grams or 5·55 grains. They were manufactured by Lanes Ltd.

LANE'S CAT SLUGS

Black and white label on packets of 100 cup-shaped slugs. Intended for smoothbore airguns. Sold in boxes of 100 and 200 for ·177 only.

Appeared in the late 1930's and again just after 1945. During the middle 1950's they were also sold in packets of 500. Before 1939 they were sold in round tins with the same design on the lid.

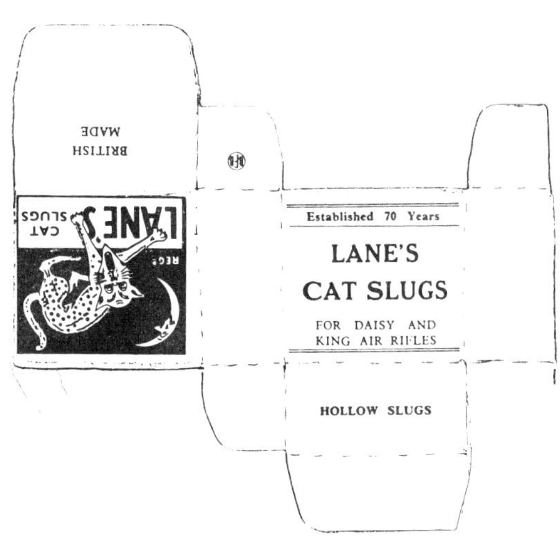

LANE'S CAT SLUGS

Coarse cardboard outer measuring 1¾ x 1¼ x ⅝ inches. Average contents 200 simple cup slugs. Assumed age middle to late 1930's with a brief appearance after 1944. Average weight of the slugs is 6·95 grains. The design of the cat logo is from a different die to that which printed the later style of 100 packet.

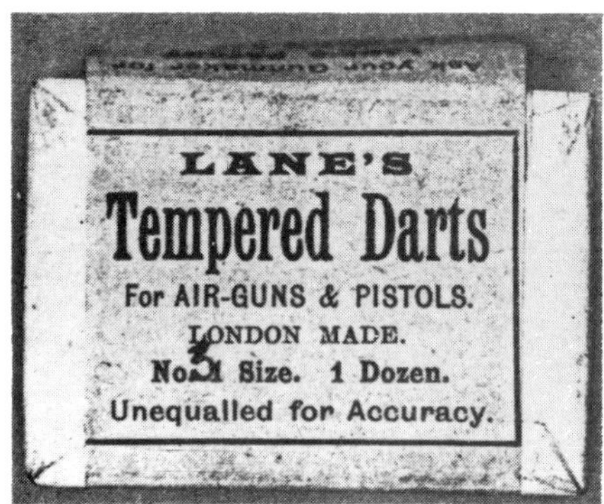

Front

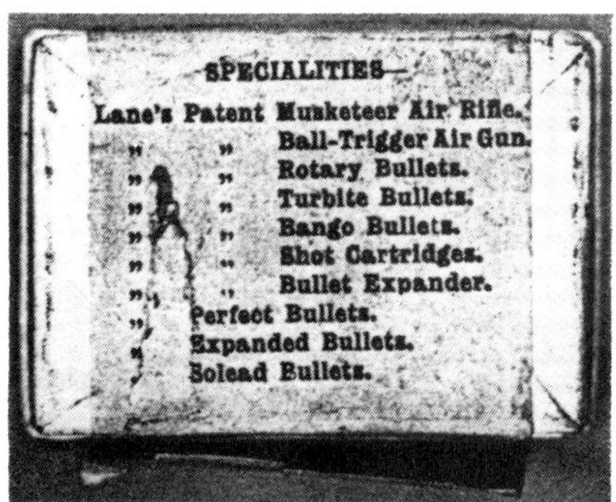

Back

LANE'S TEMPERED DARTS ·25

White cardboard box with yellow wrap around label. Above illustrations show front and back printing with "Ask your Gunmaker for LANE'S PATENT "BANGO" BULLETS" on one side and on the other "Ask your Gunmaker for LANE'S PATENT MUSKETEER AIR RIFLE Price 35/-". Box measures 2 x 1½ x ⅝ inches. Average weight of each dart being 31·9 grains. Interesting to note that airgun ammunition was referred to as "bullets" and not as pellets. As the packet mentions the Musketeer it is safe to assume that these date from the same period, from around 1903 onwards. Before 1903 they were sold in lift-up-lid wallets as shown. These for the Lane's Ball Trigger Air Rifle (Gem style). It would appear that these darts were available in all three calibres. The address at the time of manufacture being 45a, New Church Street, Bermondsey, London SE. As regarding calibres, I'm not sure if ·22 darts were available from this firm during this early period. For the early style of box see the illustration of a page from a 1902 catalogue (see page 263).

April 15, 1902. THE SPORTING GOODS REVIEW. 71

LANE'S AIR GUN AMMUNITION

Lane's Patent "ROTARY" Bullets

Lane's "PERFECT" Bullets

Lane's "EXPANDED" Bullets

Lane's "MIDGET" Bullets

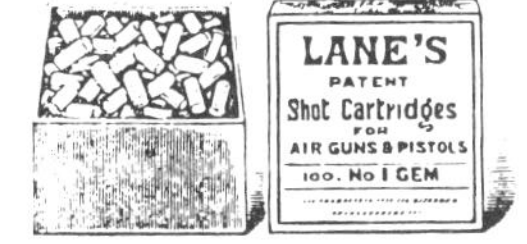

Lane's Patent Shot Cartridges

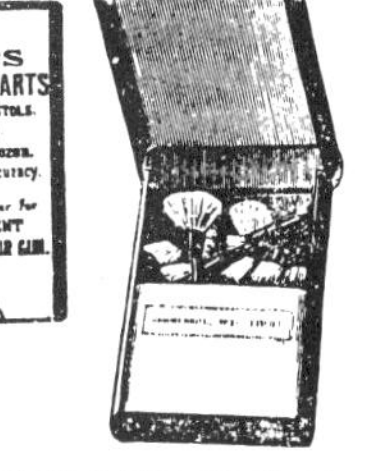

Lane's "TEMPERED" Darts

Lane's "B. B." PELLETS

ARE THE BEST

Write for Price List and Samples.

ADDRESS:

LANE BROTHERS,

45a, New Church Street, Bermondsey, London, S.E.

Telegrams: "Smokeless, London." WHOLESALE ONLY.

Selection of Lane's Airgun ammunition for 1902.

LANE'S "TRIUMPH" PELLETS

The "Triumph" brand, also may have been referred to as the "Demon" Match Slugs, appeared during the late 1920's, as the patent numbers on the tin lid are both dated from 1928, numbers being 308943/28 and 160/28. During the 1930's they were sold in boxes of 500 ·177 for 10d, 1000 ·177 for 1s./6d. and in ·22 (500) for 1s./3d. The tin above is the latter in ·22. Pale green colour with black lettering. A very popular pellet in its day and "used by most of the air rifle clubs in the Birmingham area". Average weight of pellets as found in the tin was 17·2 grains. These seem to have ceased appearing after W.W.2. Details of the patent 308943/28 may be found in *"Guns Review",* October, 1976. The tin was originally sealed with red canvas tape.

SPARE CHARGES FOR THE MILBRO CUB

I have rarely seen the word "charges" used in place of the more usual term for round shot. These charges for the Milbro Cub date from the late 1940's to early 1950's. The small buff coloured box with a red and yellow label opened and closed like a match box. Box measures 2¼ x 1½ x ¾ inches. The wording on the lid can quite clearly be read from the photograph, whilst on the underside is printed "NOMINAL QUANTITY 2000". There was also pencilled prices of 3/6, which equates to 17½p in foreign English money. From the box seen, the contents would appear to be two packets of "special gauge shot" and there may have been spare washers for the rear breech of the Cub. This "special gauge shot" is 2·41 mm, or 0·095 inches, which is equivalent to number 7 shotgun pellet size.

MILBRO SLUGS

Cup shaped slugs for smoothbore airguns. Seen in packs of 500, although they may have also been sold in packs of 100 and 250. Black printing on white card. Very plain and printed on one side only, so would assume these were the first to appear from Milbro. Suggested age being late 1940's to very early 1950's. Note that King and Daisy trade names appear first and King being a pre 1939 manufacturer, so it was assumed by Milbro that there would be plenty of King air rifles still about.

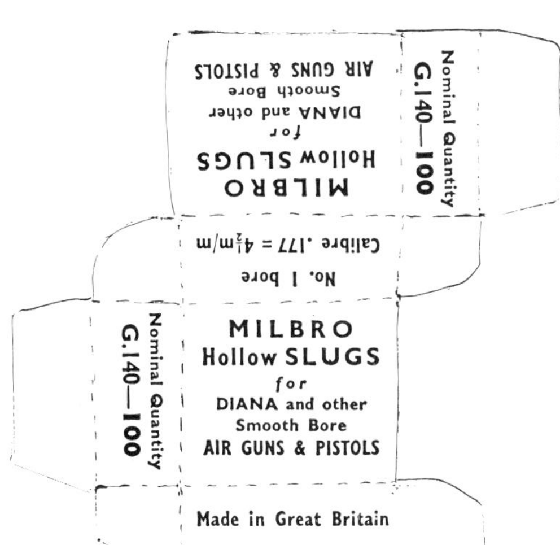

MILBRO HOLLOW SLUGS

Cup slugs for smoothbore airguns. Sold in packets of 100, 200 and 500. Labels have black writing on white background. Sold during the 1950's and 1960's and can still be found loitering at the back of many a shop pellet shelf. Available in ·177 only. Boxes of 200 were coded G.142.

MILBRO JET LIGHTWEIGHT WAISTED PELLETS

Sold in boxes in both ·177 and ·22. Mustard colour boxes with black printing and the pellet logo has a white background. Note the use of both Diana and Milbro trade names and the mention of the title Great Britain. They appear to have been sold during the 1960's and early 1970's. Advertisements claimed an extra 25 to 100 f.p.s. increase in velocity over other pellets. Pellet weights were 7·5 g. for ·177 and 14 grains for ·22. The ·177's were sold in boxes of 100, 200 and 500, whilst the ·22's were sold in 200 and 500 boxes only.

MILBRO "CALEDONIAN" PELLETS

As a coincidence, one of their addresses in London was 467, Caledonian Road, London N7. These were supplied for a short while in tins, but will mostly be found in boxes. Red coloured tin and sold in 100's, 200's and 500's for ·177 and in 200's, 250's and 500's in ·22. They were given away with the "Comet Shooting Set". Would assume the time span of the tinned variety to be from late 1950's to middle 1960's. Advertised pellet weight for the ·177 was 8·5 gr., and 14·5 gr. for the ·22.

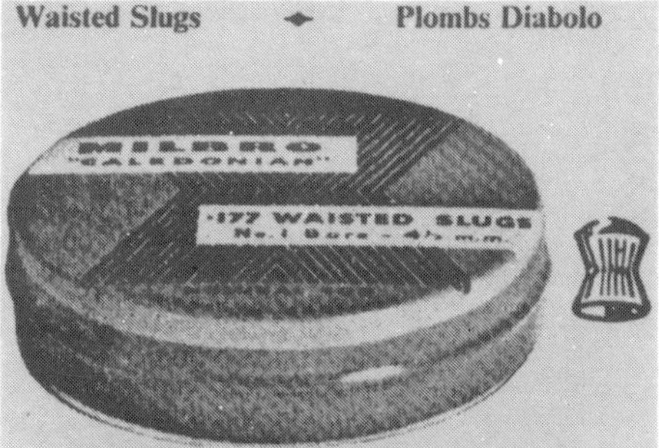

Sample tin of 100 ·177 Milbro "Caledonian" pellets.

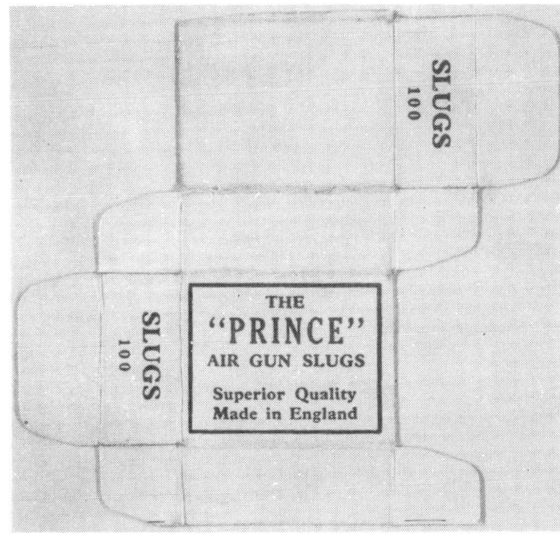

THE "PRINCE" AIR GUN SLUGS

Post-war, and I would assume 1950's to 1960's. The other associated names of "King" and "Queen" are pre-war, 1939. Simple printing, black on white and seen in packets of 100, although it is safe to assume that they were sold in larger quantities. Straight sided slugs with a shallow domed head and hollow inside. "Prince" slugs were manufactured by Lanes Ltd.

"TARGET" AIRGUN SLUGS

Post-war and I would assume 1950's. Packets contained the usual cup shaped slugs with four raised ribs around the circumference of the skirt. I think they were called "Target" slugs because on this slight ribbing. Unusually brightly coloured box, being very deep blue with bright yellow printing. Box measures 1¾ x 1¼ x ⅝ inches.

"TARGET" AIRGUN SLUGS

Packets of 500 measure 2⅛ x 1¾ x ⅞ inches and are amber-yellow with bright red printing. Very colourful and pretty.

RATTER PELLETS

A heavyweight pellet introduced in 1983, specially designed for vermin shooting. Tins contained about 450 pellets.

Manufactured by Lanes Limited, Faraday Way, St. Mary Cray, Orpington, Kent.

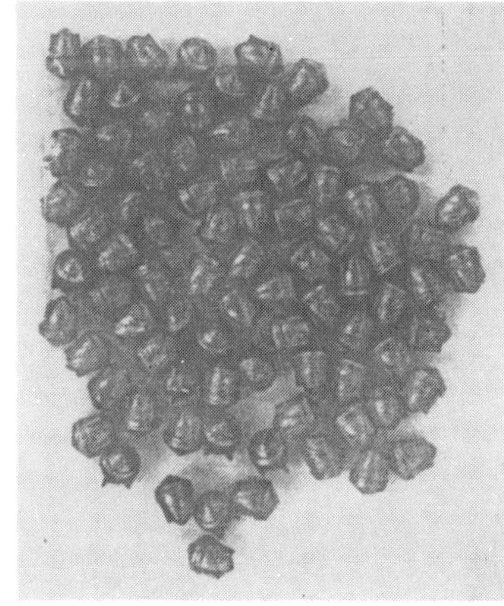

SILVA PELLETS

These originate from Australia and appear to date from the good old days of Dan Dare! Notice the futuristic shape of the projectile, almost as though they should contain little green men! Average weight being 5.24 grains, assumed to be made from a light lead alloy.

Manufactured by Smith & Chesney, Makrickville, New South Wales, Australia. Assume to be 1950's to 1960's date. Found in the original brown paper envelope with red label. It would appear that Australians wouldn't give a XXXX for their pellets either!

"SPITFIRE" ·200 PELLETS

Marketed by Sussex Armoury, Hailsham, Sussex. Dates from around 1980 to 1983 when the firm stopped trading. From the style of tin, I would assume manufacture by Cammel of the Wirral. Label had outer blue border with red inner bull. Average weight of pellets 9·34 grains. Advertised as being made for the Jackal 2020 air rifle.

TARGET AIR-GUN SLUGS

Packet of 100 that turned up in a Webley Junior airpistol box, 1950 to 1958 type, hence slightly confirming my belief that these are post-war. Pale green background with blue printing. Box measures 1½ x 1¼ x ⅝ inches.

VIPER PELLETS

Lid label with yellow and red viper. Dateing from the 1970's. Average weight of ·22 pellet being 12.79 grains. Also available in ·177 and ·25.

WEBLEY SPECIAL PELLETS

Pale green label with black printing. Round tin which is not usual for Webley pellets. I would assume tins of ·22 and ·25 to be a different colour. Running around the edge of the lid: "500 WEBLEY ·177 SPECIAL PELLETS No. 1 BORE FOR AIR PISTOLS & AIR RIFLES", and the flying winged pellet trademark, as seen on the action of the Mark II Service air rifle and on the brass medallion on the grip of the Mark I airpistol. Very safe to assume that the above tin is dated from the middle 1920's.

"WEBLEY" ·22 SPECIAL PELLETS

Orange tin with black printing. It would appear that the standard colour code of Webleys was orange for ·22 and pale green for ·177. Note that they were made for "Webley Airpistols" and ONE "Air Rifle"!! This style of tin appeared in 1924 and right up to the move from Weaman Street to Park Lane, Handsworth, Birmingham 21, in 1958. Clues to tin's age: must be pre-1958 as it has Weaman Street address, could be pre-war, as Birmingham does not have a "4" area code and these appeared after W.W.2., hence I would assume the age of the above tin to be between the middle 1920's, this being after they had stopped making the Mark I air rifle, and up to 1939. The edge of the tin bears the winged pellet trademark. The above tin would appear to be the first design as it appears on a spares list for the spring clip Webley Mark I airpistol. This would tally with the production of the Mark I air rifle, which was about one to two years before the Mark II Service. Hence the above tin is quite rare. The above tin, with identical lettering, is also found coloured green for 1000 ·177 "Special Pellets". One of these tins contained a leaflet with the Birmingham 4 address.

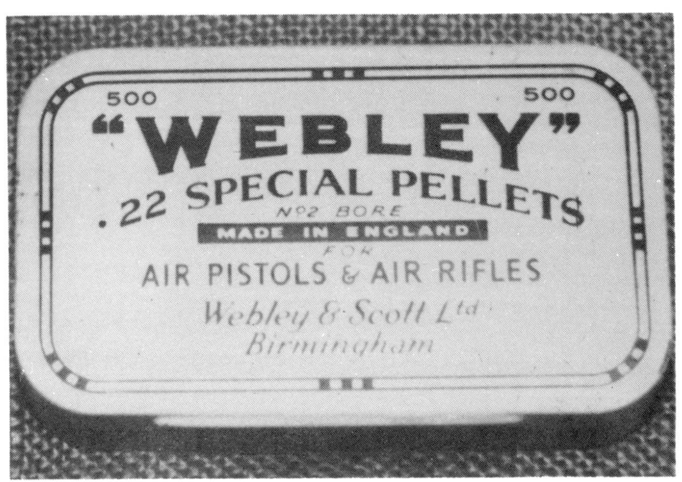

"WEBLEY" ·22 SPECIAL PELLETS

Orange for ·22, with black printing. Note that we now have "Air Rifles" and the address is just Birmingham. From this I would suggest that the above tin dates from 1958 to the middle 1960's, when the circular Webley logo appeared. Many of the above have been seen with over stickers bearing varying messages as to changes in contents, hence orange tins with ·177 labels etc. Average weight of ten pellets was 14·5 grains (·22).

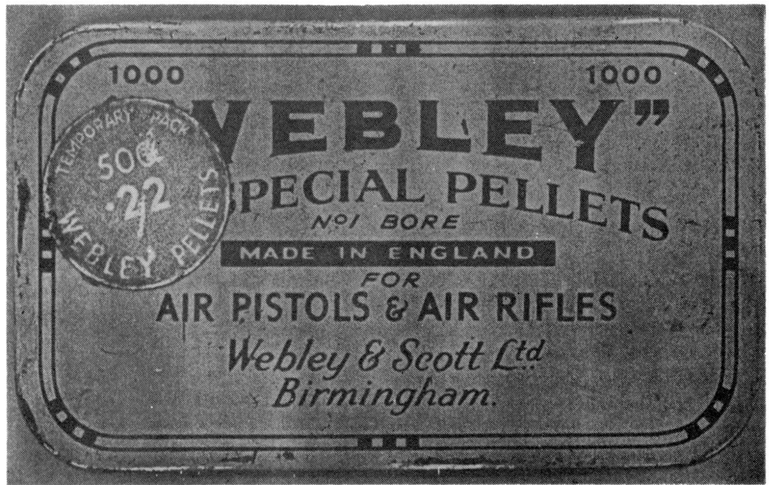

Green tin for 1000 (·177) with over stamp temporary label for 500 (·22).

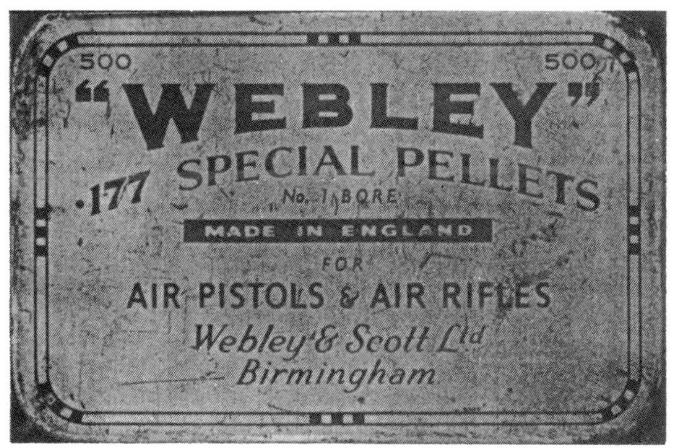

GREEN ·177 (500) TIN OF WEBLEY PELLETS

1958 to middle 1960's period, measures 3 x 2 x ⅝ inches (British units). Labelling same as for ·22, only smaller tin obviously for ·177. Average weight of ten pellets 8·42 grains.

Prices for Pellets:

·177
2/3 per 1,000
1/2 per 500

·22
4/6 per 1,000
2/3 per 500

DARTS

For use with Smooth Bore Barrels.

Price:
5d. per dozen.
4/- per gross.

FOR THE BEST SHOOTING RESULTS it is essential to use "Webley" Special Pellets, which are obtainable in neat boxes from all leading Stores and Gun Dealers. They are made of pure lead and carefully gauged for regularity and dimensions.

PACKETS OF 1000 WEBLEY PELLETS

These first appeared about 1925 and were available right up to 1939. They were packed in cardboard boxes of 1000 in either ·22 or ·177. When they first appeared in the middle 1920's, the wording on the packet lid was as follows:

Interesting to note that in the middle 1920's Webley were only manufacturing two airguns, the Mark I air rifle and the Mark I airpistol, hence the quote "Webley airpistol and rifle pellets". By the middle 1930's, this statement became "WEBLEY AIRPISTOLS AND AIR RIFLE" because now we had the production of the Junior, Mark I, Mark II and Senior airpistols, but still only one air rifle, the Mark II Service air rifle.

"WEBLEY"
·177 Special Pellets
(No. 1 BORE)
WEBLEY AIRPISTOL AND RIFLE PELLETS
WEBLEY & SCOTT LTD.,
WEAMAN STREET
BIRMINGHAM

Quotes & Catalogues

Taken from a 1960's American gun catalogue. Only the Americans with their fine command of English could make such a statement:

"THIS DESIGN IS A MERGER OF TWO PATENTS — EACH OLDER THAN THE OTHER"

A 1983 reviewer of a gun catalogue ended a sentence with the sweeping statement:

"ILLUSTRATED WITH ILLUSTRATIONS"

Taken from a letter regarding possession of arms for self protection, again, American in origin (from the Bible - Luke, Chapter 11, Verse 12):

"WHEN A STRONG MAN ARMED KEEPETH HIS PALACE,
HIS GOODS ARE IN PEACE"

From a small booklet titled "The New Sport", the following quote is the last paragraph at the end of a little story about shooting B.S.A. air rifles in the home and garden:

"AIR RIFLES SEEM TO ME JUST THE THING TO KEEP THE BOYS AT HOME, AND IF YOU'VE ANY DAUGHTERS, THEY'RE JUST THE THING TO BRING THE BOYS TO YOUR HOME".

So watch out any girl who is reading this and your father has just bought you an air rifle!

A G. C. Bell & Sons Catalogue of 1925/26 contained a host of quotes that nowadays makes one's hair curl; even at the top and bottom of each page there was a quote that made one tingle with excitement, such as:

"GO AFTER HIM WITH A GUN"!!!

A picture of a dead rat with all legs pointing skywards, with the message:

"CONVICTED AND SHOT AT DAWN"

In 1926, rats were destroying £70,000,000 of foodstuffs each year, so the youth of yesteryear were summoned with the following message that even the R.S.P.C.A. would be up in arms about:

"NOW BOYS, DON'T LET RATS OVERRUN THE WORLD, AND FOR FIFTY TWO WEEKS EACH YEAR GO AT HIM WITH PISTOL, CATAPULT AND TRAP. EVERY BOY CAN HELP REDUCE THE RAT PLAGUE".

Now for the parents and guardians of these little horrors, hell-bent on destroying it if it moved:

"LORD ROBERTS SAID: "EVERY BRITISHER SHOULD BE TAUGHT HOW TO HANDLE A RIFLE AND SHOOT STRAIGHT" (now comes the advertising!) SO IT RESTS WITH YOU (parent or guardian) TO DO YOUR DUTY TO YOUR YOUNGSTERS. PURCHASE YOUR BOY AN AIRGUN TO START WITH, AND WE CAN CHEERFULLY SAY (now this bit will really hurt!) THAT EVERY DOG, CAT AND RAT THAT IS NOT BURIED WILL GIVE YOUR HOUSE A WIDE BERTH."

Another quote from the catalogue makes your chest swell with pride:

"IN THE LADDER OF PATRIOTISM, EVERY SHOT COUNTS"

Now what does that mean?

Targets

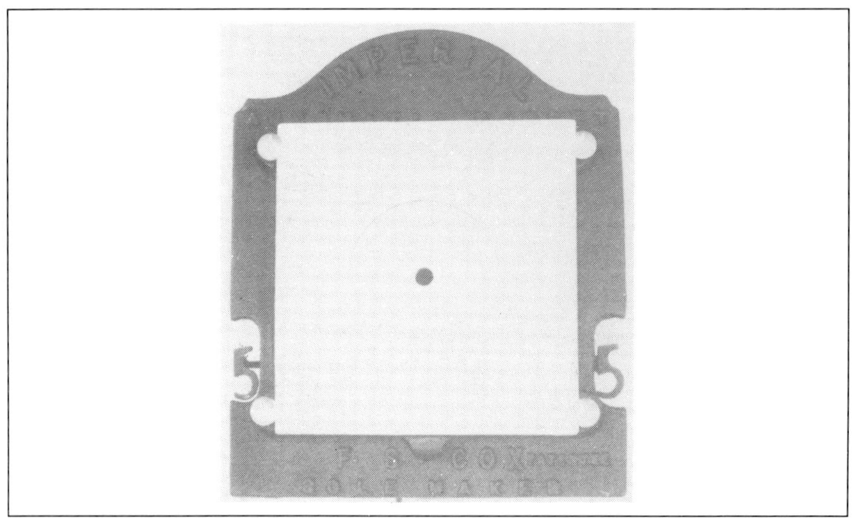

The Imperial Automatic Target

Model: **THE IMPERIAL AUTOMATIC TARGET**

Maker: **Frederick Stanley Cox,** (of Britannia fame)
6 Freer Road, Handsworth, Birmingham, England.

Date: Seen advertised 1932-33, so would assume late 1920's to middle 1930's, or even earlier.

Valuation: £30 - £70.

Details: They don't make targets like this anymore! Cast iron, and made to last lifetimes! Front measures 8 inches by 10, and weighs 14 lbs. Removable quarter inch thick face with three grooves cut around bull's eye. Cast in the front of the frame "IMPERIAL AUTOMATIC TARGET" and underneath the face "F. S. COX PATENTEE SOLE MAKER". Behind the face is a solid cast brass bell with "COX'S AUTOMATIC TARGET BELL" cast around the outer surface, as if there was any doubt as to its origin. Pivoting behind the target face is a projection that when struck falls back and hits another piece of metal that then strikes the bell, at the same time a figure five appears on either side of the target face. A piece of string is tied to the first metal strip and this string can be as long as the target is away from the shooter. To re-cock the action, the string is pulled and the action is ready again. Originally the figure fives were painted red. Cost 30/- (£1.50) in 1933, the same price as a Webley Mark I airpistol and 5/- (25p) dearer than a Warrior airpistol, so the above target was very expensive, not only that, it must have required a very substantial wall fixture in order to keep it in position! All in all, "one hell of a target".

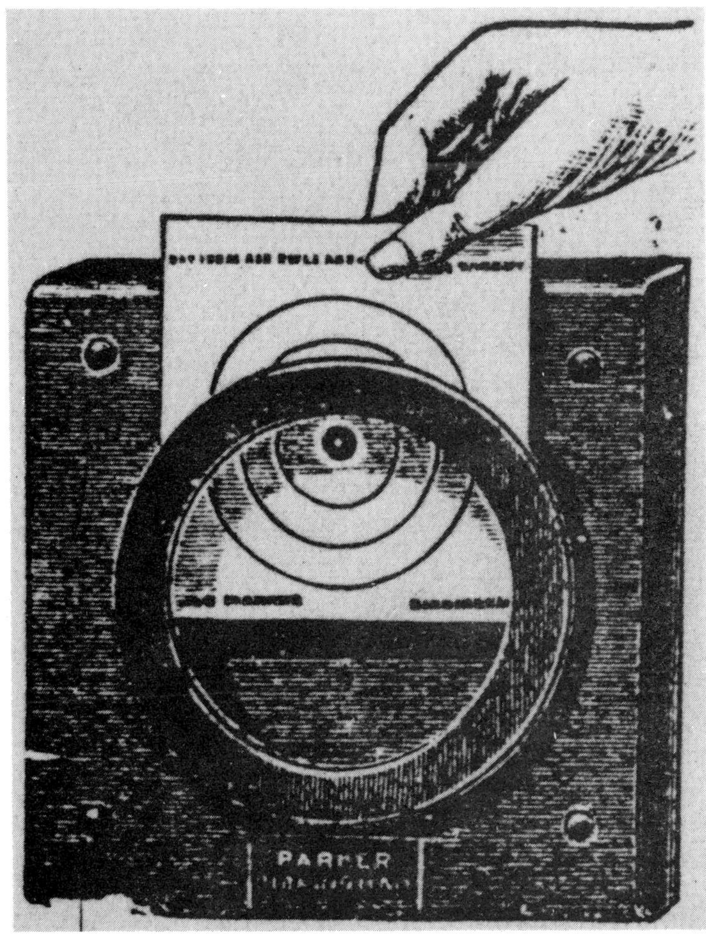

THE PARKER-HALE FOUR INCH TARGET HOLDER AND PELLET TRAP

Although advertised in Parker-Hale catalogues from around the late 1930's to 1955, a very similar pattern was sold as a B.S.A. target and pellet trap in 1939. The similarity is too close and it can be assumed that these were produced and sold to either B.S.A. or Parker Hale with their names on the front just under the circular target card outer frame.

As can be seen, the holder had a cast frame front and a rear that acted as the pellet trade, a simple, yet strong target holder. It was packed in a box measuring 6½ inches (16·5 cm) square. Advertised weight was 2¾ lbs. It was listed as their part number A.R.T.7 and the cards as Number 52's. The B.S.A. price in 1939 was 6/6 (32½p), and in 1947, the price had risen to around 16/- (80p), including Purchase Tax.

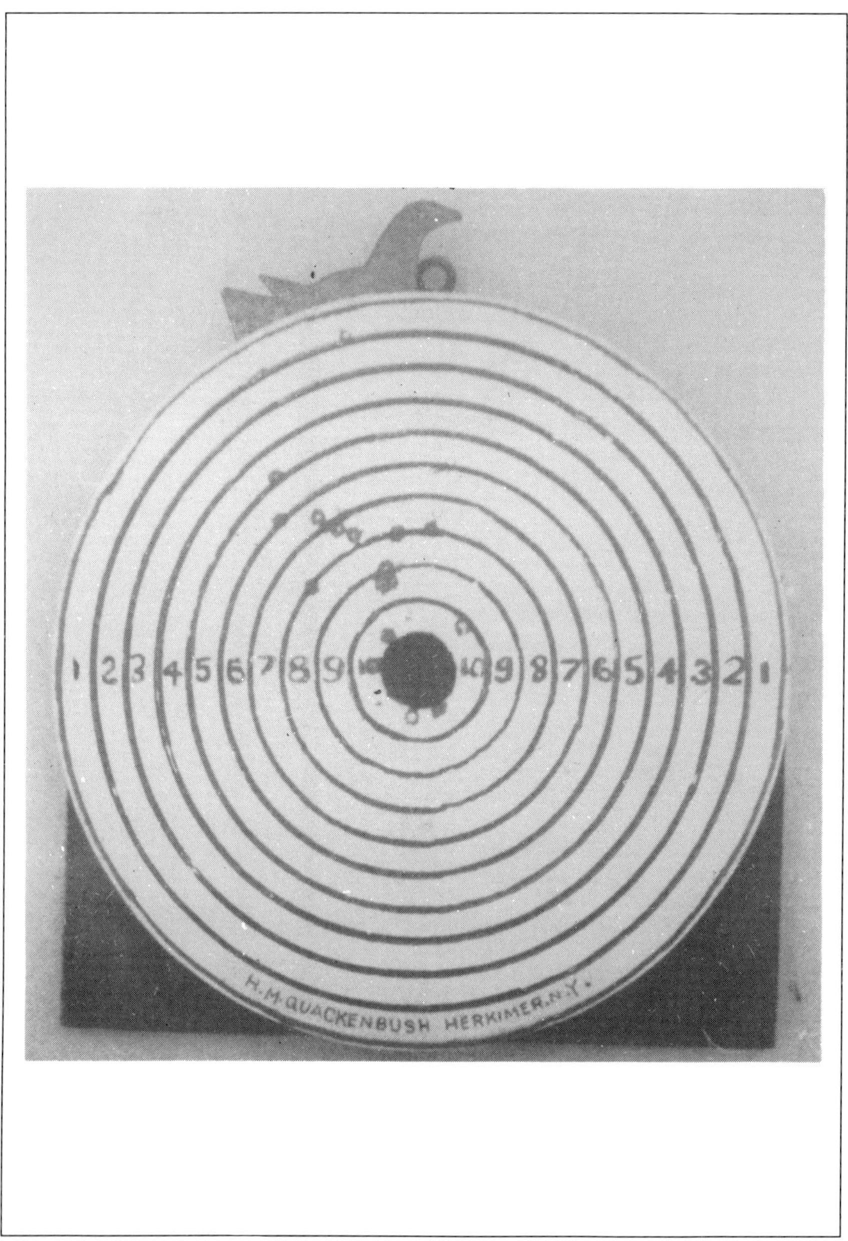

The cast iron Quackenbush Bell Target.

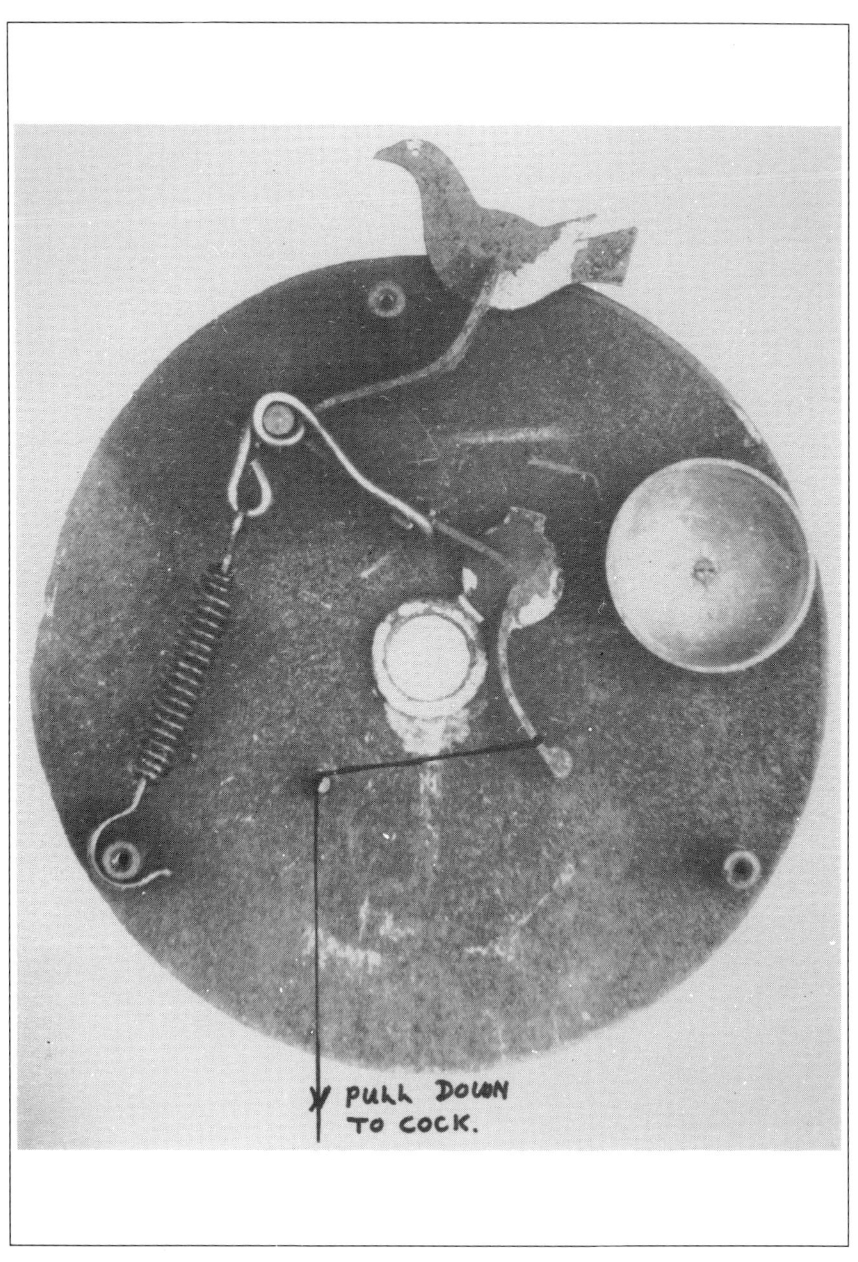

Reverse side of Bell Target in uncocked position.

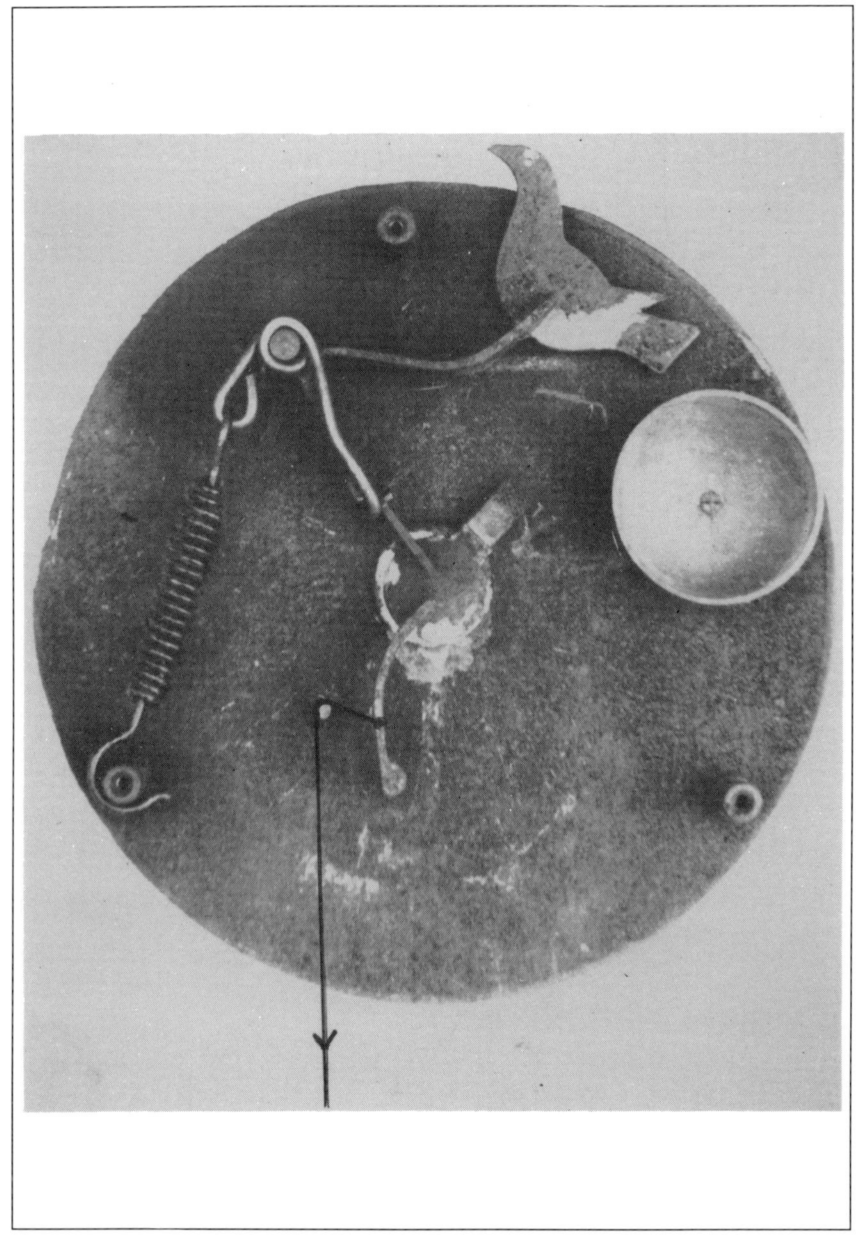

Bell Target in cocked position.

QUACKENBUSH BELL TARGET

Henry Marcus Quackenbush was born in 1847 and passed on during September, 1933. The interest in producing airguns died with him. He started his own airgun business after working for the Remington Arms Co., Ilion, New York. He sited his factory on the banks of the Mohawk River at Herkimer, New York, during 1871. During this period the Quackenbush Bell Target was manufactured.

Heavy cast iron circular target measuring 11¾ inches across with a 1¼ inch central hole for ringing the bell. The target face is split into ten rings, each about ½ an inch apart, and labelled from 1 to 10 for scoring. Normally the target face would be coated with white non-drying paint and after each competitor, the face would be wiped in order to erase the pellet marks, i.e. to "wipe the slate" clean. Cast in the outer ring towards the bottom "H.M. QUACKENBUSH, HERKIMER, N.Y." The whole target is fixed with three screws to a wooden backing plate that has a fixed hook at the top.

In the uncocked state the hen, or chicken, appears visible, poking out of the top of the rim of the target face, but when the bell is cocked, the hen is pulled down out of sight, only to pop up again when the black painted bullseye has been struck. To cock the action the hen is pushed into the target, or a piece of string or wire is fixed as in the photograph and pulled down. When this is pulled down the centre bull is held in place by a lip of metal. As the bull is struck by a pellet the bull is pushed back and past the edge of the lip and springs up thus ringing the bell and exposing the cock! Appears to work well with most airguns of moderate power upwards.

Any old target must be rare. A collector once turned up at an Arms Fair with a cast iron Chinese bell target and was offered from £15 up to £50 for it, but he would not part with it. So can assume that this is about the right value of the above, somewhere between £50 - £70.

TARGET HOLDERS & TARGETS

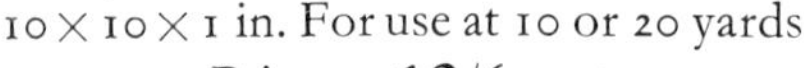

$10 \times 10 \times 1$ in. For use at 10 or 20 yards
Price: **13/6** net.

$6\frac{1}{2} \times 6\frac{1}{2} \times 1$ in. For use at 5 yards.
Price: **8/-** net.

Prices for TARGETS:

Large Size	-	**12/-**	per 1,000
Small Size	-	**8/6**	per 1,000

THE ABOVE TARGET HOLDERS have been specially designed for outdoor or indoor use, and are so arranged that the Pellets, after passing through the cardboard Targets, are trapped and caught.
Special WEBLEY Targets, suitable for the above, are obtainable from all principal Stores, Gun Dealers or Sports Depots.

WEBLEY TARGET HOLDERS

These were seen advertised from 1925 to the late 1930's. The first reference is in the Mark I air rifle handbook, and the last was in the Webley leaflet that also included the slant grip Senior, so one could say the date of availability was up to 1939. Their price did not alter during this period of time, almost 15 years, which is quite an achievement. The circular portion that holds the target card would appear to be cast iron. Note the two sizes, the larger for 10 and 20 yard range, whilst the smaller for 5 yards.

Index

W

X

Y

Z